WITHDRAWN

Dispatches from the
Ebony Tower

Dispatches from the Ebony Tower

Intellectuals Confront the African American Experience

Edited by Manning Marable

Columbia University Press
New York

Columbia University Press
Publishers Since 1893
New York   Chichester, West Sussex
Copyright © 2000 Columbia University Press
All rights reserved

Library of Congress Cataloging-in-Publication Data

Dispatches from the ebony tower : intellectuals confront the African American
experience / edited by Manning Marable.
    p. cm.
  Includes bibliographical references and index.
  ISBN 0-231-11476-1 (cloth)—ISBN 0-231-11477-X (pbk.)
    1. Afro-Americans—Study and teaching (Higher) 2. Blacks—Study and teaching
  (Higher) 3. United States—Race relations—Study and teaching (Higher) 4. United
  States—Ethnic relations—Study and teaching (Higher) I. Marable, Manning, 1950–

E184.7.D57 2000
305.896'073'0711—dc21   99-055525
                                                                                 CIP

Casebound editions of Columbia University Press books are printed on permanent and
durable acid-free paper.

Printed in the United States of America

c 10 9 8 7 6 5 4 3 2 1
p 10 9 8 7 6 5 4 3 2 1

Contents

Preface

The great challenge every editor faces in the construction of a volume of academic essays is bringing together independent and frequently divergent perspectives into a general intellectual conversation about a common issue or theme. There have been literally hundreds of articles published in scholarly journals during the past thirty years on the definition, character, and meaning of black studies. Even a short list of prolific and widely read scholars whose writings have largely defined the field of African American studies—which would certainly include Molefi Asante, Henry Louis Gates Jr., Harold Cruse, Maulana Karenga, Audre Lorde, Cornel West, Angela Y. Davis, bell hooks, and Amiri Baraka—would probably disagree about what black studies is, and what it should become. Scholars involved in gender studies, ethnic studies, queer studies, and other new fields of inquiry are engaged in similar debates, which are also informed at times by larger political questions about the status of minority groups within U.S. society today. My hope here is not to come up with definitive answers or solutions but to generate a set of fruitful and provocative questions about black studies—concerning its past, present, and future—while also encouraging a more constructive conversation among scholars in the field.

Dispatches from the Ebony Tower is the product of more than a quarter-century of my involvement in African American studies. My first real job after graduate school was my appointment in 1974 in the Afro-American Studies Program at Smith College in Massachusetts. Hired to teach African American literature at Smith that same year was Johnnella Butler. Both of us were in our twenties, and saw the growing field of scholarship, as literary critic George Kent put it, as an adventure of blackness in Western culture. My first guest lecture in an African American studies course was in the introductory level course at the University of Massachusetts at Amherst, which was taught by anthropologist Johnnetta Cole. I became acquainted with the work and ideas of a number of black intellectuals who taught African American studies in the area at that time, including John Bracey, Bill Strickland, Michael Thelwell, Paul Carter Harrison, and Sonia Sanchez. My knowledge and involvement in the field expanded yet again when I developed an informal affiliation with the administrative staff and scholars at the Institute of the Black World in Atlanta in 1976. As a young scholar, I was privileged to meet and develop relationships with Vincent Harding, Howard Dodson, and Robert Hill. Through IBW I had the honor of knowing Walter Rodney. And, for all of its limitations, IBW was for me then, and remains now, a standard by which research in African American studies should be judged. In the twenty years since that time, I have taught at the Africana Studies and Research Center at Cornell University, was hired to reestablish Charles S. Johnson's Race Relations Institute at Fisk University, which I briefly directed, created and chaired the Africana and Hispanic Studies Program at Colgate University, from 1983 until 1986, served as professor and chairman of the Black Studies Department at Ohio State University, and, since 1993, founded and directed the Institute for Research in African American Studies at Columbia University. During this period I have spoken at or visited the majority of black studies departments, programs, and research centers that currently exist in the United States. My experiences have provided some insights into what African American studies was first conceived to be and what it has evolved into as a body of intellectual work and academic programs, with all its strengths and contradictions.

When I was appointed at Columbia University, my immediate idea was to reconstitute a project that W. E. B. Du Bois conceived and implemented at Atlanta University a century ago. Du Bois hosted an annual conference, bringing together scholars and researchers to examine and discuss some problem or aspect of the black experience. The Institute for Research in African-American Studies sponsored in 1994 an international conference on the admittedly ambitious theme "Politics and Theory in the Black World." Other conferences followed on themes such as "The Crisis of Black Youth," "Race and Revolution in Cuba," "Race-ing Justice:

Black Americans and the Prison Industrial Complex," and "The Future of African American Studies." Between 1994 and 1998 the institute collected and published many of the papers and presentations generated by these conferences, as well as other solicited papers, in an annual research volume, *Race and Reason*. In 1999 the institute initiated a quarterly journal, *Souls*, whose title was inspired by Du Bois's classic statement on what it means to be black in white America, *The Souls of Black Folk*, first published in 1903. Many of the scholars in the African American studies extended intellectual community with whom I have worked and whose ideas have shaped the field have generously supported and contributed to this new project, including Cornel West, Eric Foner, Angela Y. Davis, Johnnetta Cole, Darlene Clark Hine, Beverly Guy-Sheftall, Herbert Aptheker, Sonia Sanchez, Robin D. G. Kelley, Gerald Horne, George Fredrickson, Michael Eric Dyson, Michelle Wallace, Howard Winant, Melba Joyce Boyd, Nikhil Pal Singh, and Dennis Brutus. I say "intellectual community" deliberately here, because their body of scholarly work is defined not by racialized boundaries but by their pursuit of knowledge about the experiences, aspirations, and struggles of black folk. Debates and disagreements are healthy and necessary within every community and help all of us to improve the quality of our work. You do not have to be black to be an outstanding scholar of African American studies.

An important dimension of this reader is the effort to include perspectives about black studies that reflect the full range of the field as it is presently defined. Three decades ago Martin Kilson was one of the sharp but often sympathetic critics of the newly developing African American programs. His reflections about black studies provide another dimension in thinking about the field. Molefi Asante and Maulana Karenga have been absolutely central to the development of black studies. There are important aspects to the theoretical perspective of Afrocentricity about which I have been critical, and much of my own research and theoretical orientation must be highly problematic to the scholars of Afrocentricity. But both Asante and Karenga have very generously contributed their essays here.

Many volumes that are organized to present essays by different authors on a common topic or theme cannot completely represent a field, and such limitations are certainly present here. The volume also has a critical shortcoming that is reflected throughout African American studies as a whole. For example, more than one half of all black people are women. Black women have been pivotal to every aspect of black history, culture, and society. Yet African American women's voices and experiences are seriously underrepresented in most black studies curricula and programs. Male scholars have been extremely slow to integrate the critical dimensions of gender and sexuality into their work, which has always compromised the intellectual potential and development of African American studies. As long as the works of Anna Julia Cooper, Ida B. Wells-Barnett, Mary Church Terrell, Claudia Jones, Ella Baker, Alice Walker, Toni Morrison, Sonia Sanchez, Barbara Smith, Angela Y. Davis, Leith Mullings, bell hooks, Paula Giddings, Patricia Hill Collins, Hazel Carby, Audre Lorde, Johnnetta Cole, Nell Irvin Painter, Cathy Cohen, Barbara Ransby, and hundreds of other brilliant black women scholars and writers are not fully accepted or acknowledged as being essential to the definition of African American studies, the field will never represent or reflect a meaningful interpretation of the black experience.

The basic organization and framework of the chapters in *Dispatches from the Ebony Tower* was provided by the reflections of St. Clair Drake, noted anthropologist and the chairman of the Program in African and Afro-American Studies at Stanford University. In 1973 Drake wrote about his ideas on "the role of the black scholar," which he attributed to Allison Davis. Davis was

> very insistent that every black scholar should try (1) to make some contribution to general theoretical work in his discipline. . . . So, while rooting oneself in fighting for one's people, one also tried to make a contribution at the highest theoretical level of scholarship; (2) to decide upon some aspect of the social structure in which to become an expert at the empirical level . . . ; and (3) to select a problem that contributed to racial advancement, as we used to call it. Today we call it Black liberation.[1]

All three points are represented in the reader. Part 1, "Theorizing the Black World," presents several empirical and theoretical studies of black societies in the postcolonial, post-civil rights period since the 1960s. It is true that Havana is not Harlem, but both are in different ways connected to the dynamics of globalization, economic marginalization, and political struggles that include race. It is from these different sites of resistance and social development that the new structural challenges confronting black people in the next century may be understood.

"Mapping African American Studies" attempts to do exactly that, providing a spectrum of opinions on the field. The contributing authors have all in various ways addressed the question "What is black studies, either as an intellectual project or a discipline, and what may be its future?" "Afrocentricity and Its Critics" presents very divergent perspectives on the main theoretical paradigm that defines much of the current scholarship in African American studies. Part 4, "Race and Ethnicity in American Life," explores issues of the black experience in a comparative text with other racialized ethnic groups and examines the politics of contemporary race relations in American society. Few African American scholars have been more influential in defining how American society understands black history and thinks about race than John Hope Franklin and Cornel West.

In developing and preparing this volume there have been many individuals whose contributions were absolutely essential to this process. *Race and Reason* and *Souls* were and are largely planned and produced by Columbia University graduate and law students who are employed in the Institute for Research in African-American Studies. Timothy McCarthy, Karen Jackson-Weaver, Kristen Clarke, and Sherell Daniels worked hundreds of hours to edit and produce these publications. Karen Jackson-Weaver also provided invaluable help in the arrangement and organization of the papers, checking periodically with authors on their revisions and editing. Johanna Fernandez, a history doctoral candidate at Columbia, contributed an essay on Harlem that appears here, and she also helped to coordinate the institute's 1997 delegation to Cuba, which inspired my essay in this volume on African Americans and the Cuban revolution. Another Columbia history doctoral candidate, Devin Fergus, was the principal coordinator of the institute's 1996 conference on "The Future of Black Studies," which in turn generated several of the papers here.

The institute's secretarial staff, Theresa Wilcox, Diane Tinsley-Hatcher, and Jennifer Jones, all helped to type and format parts of the manuscript at different stages. Daria Oliver, my executive assistant at the institute, helped to coordinate the academic conferences we have sponsored since 1994 that generated many of the papers in this book. My editor and friend at Columbia University Press, Kate Wittenberg, was very receptive from the beginning of our informal discussions about such a reader on African American studies, back in 1996, and was instrumental in helping me to revise and improve the manuscript in many respects. Susan Pensak carefully read through the entire work, suggesting a number of important editorial changes and revisions that make the book much better than when she first was presented the initial manuscript. My research assistant John McMillian, a doctoral candidate in history, shares my deep interest in the history of black studies and African American thought. His background research and, more important, our conversations about the field and the different ideological debates and personalities within it were critical in the conceptualization and development of this book. Special thanks also goes to my agent and friend, Marie Brown.

It is unlikely that Oliver C. Cox, Horace Mann Bond, Charles S. Johnson, or E. Franklin Frazier thought of themselves as "scholars of black studies." Their social science research was anchored to methodologies in specific disciplines. But each of these intellectuals possessed a broad social vision and commitment to what Allison Davis termed "racial advancement." Leith Mullings is a cultural and medical anthropologist, a feminist theorist and scholarly interpreter of the black experience in the urban U.S. as well as West Africa. Most of her colleagues in anthropology would not immediately associate her with black studies. But through the sharing of our ideas, exploring and debating various theoretical premises and paradigms, I have learned more from her about the significance and larger meaning of black studies than from anyone else. Leith's scholarly work passes every standard of excellence from the perspective of traditional disciplines. But, like St. Clair Drake, Oliver C. Cox, and so many other black scholars in our tradition, Leith is also about the serious business of "racial advancement." And, to me, that's what black studies is all about.

November 1, 1999

Most of the articles that comprise *Dispatches from the Ebony Tower* were originally published, frequently in very different versions, in the journals of the Institute for Research in African-American Studies at Columbia University: *Race and Reason* (Academic Year 1994–1995 to Academic Year 1997–1998) and *Souls: A Critical Journal of Black Politics, Culture and Society*, January 1999 to the present.

Published in *Race and Reason*: Molefi Asante, "Afrocentrism, Race and Reason," vol. 1 (1994–1995), pp. 20–22; Amiri Baraka, "Multinational, Multicultural America vs. White Supremacy," vol. 1 (1994–1995), pp. 23–24; Melba Joyce Boyd, "Afro-centrics, Afro-Elitists, and Afro-Eccentrics: The Polarization of Black Studies Since the Student Struggles of the Sixties," vol. 1 (1994–1995), pp. 25–27; Johnnella Butler, "African American Studies and the 'Warring Ideals': The Color Line Meets the Borderlands," vol. 4 (1997–1998), pp. 30–35; Johanna Fernandez, "The Fire

This Time: Harlem and Its Discontents in the 1990s," vol. 3 (1996–1997), pp. 32–37; Bill Fletcher Jr., "Black Studies and the Question of Class," vol. 4 (1997–1998), pp. 38–40; Joy James, "The Future of Black Studies: Political Communities and the 'Talented Tenth,'" vol. 4 (1997–1998), pp. 36–38; Maulana Karenga, "Black Studies: A Critical Reassessment," vol. 4 (1997–1998), pp. 40–44; Kamala Kempadoo, " 'Sandoms' and Other Exotic Women: Prostitution and Race in the Caribbean," vol. 3 (1996–1997), pp. 48–54; Martin Kilson, "Black Studies Revisited," vol. 4 (Academic Year 1997–1998), pp. 44–46; Manning Marable, "Black Studies and the Black Intellectual Tradition," vol. 4 (1997–1998), pp. 3–8; Brian Meeks, "The Political Moment in Jamaica: The Dimensions of the Hegemonic Dissolution," vol. 3 (1996–1997), pp. 39–47; Leith Mullings, "Culture and Afrocentrism," vol. 1 (1994–1995), pp. 28–30; Barbara Ransby, "Afrocentrism, Cultural Nationalism, and the Problem with Essentialist Definitions of Race, Gender, and Sexuality," vol. 1 (1994–1995), pp. 31–34; Nikhil Pal Singh, "Toward an Effective Antiracism," vol. 3 (1996–1997), pp. 62–70; and "Prophetic Alternatives: A Dialogue with Cornel West and Manning Marable," vol. 2 (1995–1996), pp. 39–46.

Published in *Souls: A Critical Journal of Black Politics, Culture and Society:* Beverly Xaviera Watkins and Mindy Thompson Fullilove, "Crack Cocaine and Harlem's Health," vol. 1, no. 1 (Winter 1999), pp. 36–48; "Race in American Life: A Conversation with John Hope Franklin," vol. 1, no. 3 (Summer 1999), pp. 73–87; and Manning Marable, "Race and Revolution in Cuba: African-American Perspectives," vol. 1, no. 2 (Spring 1999), pp. 6–17.

Henry Louis Gates Jr., "A Call to Protect Academic Identity from Politics," and Manning Marable, "Scholars Must Act Upon, Not Just Interpret Events," first appeared in the *New York Times,* April 4, 1998.

Note

1. St. Clair Drake, "In the Mirror of Black Scholarship: W. Allison Davis and *Deep South,*" in Institute of the Black World, ed., *Education and Black Struggle: Notes from the Colonized World,* Monograph no. 2 (Cambridge: Harvard Educational Review, 1974).

Dispatches from the
Ebony Tower

Introduction: Black Studies and the Racial Mountain

Manning Marable

> *We younger Negro artists who create now intend to express our individual dark-skinned selves without fear or shame. If white people are pleased, we are glad. If they are not, it doesn't matter. We know we are beautiful. And ugly too. . . . We build our temples for tomorrow, strong as we know how, and we stand on top of the mountain, free within ourselves.*
> —Langston Hughes, 1926

> *Black History cannot help but be politically oriented, for it tends towards the total redefinition of an experience which was highly political. Black History must be political, for it deals with the most political phenomenon of all, the struggle between the master and the slave, between the colonized and the colonizer, between the oppressed and the oppressor. And it recognizes that all histories of peoples participate in politics and are shaped by political and ideological views.*
> —Vincent Harding, 1970

Behind the concept of African American studies is essentially the black intellectual tradition, the critical thought and perspectives of intellectuals of African descent and scholars of black America, and Africa, and the black diaspora. That black intellectual tradition can be characterized by three great points of departure. First, the black intellectual tradition has always been descriptive, that is, presenting the reality of black life and experiences from the point of view of black people themselves. Instead of beginning the logic of intellectual inquiry standing on the outside of the lived experiences of the people, the black intellectual tradition at its best has always presumed the centrality of black life. The scholar was a participant-observer who was challenged to undertake a thick description of cultural and social phenomena. Scholarship was therefore grounded in the very subjective truths of a people's collective experience. It is from this experience that historical knowledge can be constructed that accurately describes and defines the contours of consciousness and identity.

The black intellectual tradition has, second, been corrective. It has attempted to challenge and to critique the racism and stereotypes that have been ever present in the mainstream discourse of white academic institutions. Our intellectual tradition has vigorously condemned and disputed theories of black people's genetic, biological, and cultural inferiority. It has attacked the distorted representation of blackness found in the dominant culture. It has challenged Eurocentric notions of aesthetics and beauty that, all too often, are grounded in an implied, or even explicit, contempt for the standards of blackness.

And, finally, the black intellectual tradition has been prescriptive. Black scholars who have theorized from the black experience have often proposed practical steps for the empowerment of black people. In other words, there is a practical connection between scholarship and struggle, between social analysis and social transformation. The purpose of black scholarship is more than the restoration of identity and self-esteem: it is to use history and culture as tools through which people interpret their collective experience, but for the purpose of transforming their actual conditions and the totality of the society all around them. This common recognition of the broad social purpose of intellectual work did not mean that black scholarship must be a kind of narrow advocacy or a partisan polemic with no genuine standards of objectivity. Black scholars within the classical tradition placed great emphasis on their methodologies and fostered rigorous approaches to the collection and interpretation of data. But the high standards they sought to maintain, despite their woefully inadequate research funding and material resources, did not contradict their belief that new knowledge could in some way serve and empower those people with whom they shared a common culture, heritage, and struggle. Thus black studies was never simply the scholarship of intellectuals who just happened to be black, nor was it the research about the black experience by just anyone of any random ethnic background and ideological bias. Black studies was never a subcategory of some race-based ideology but a critical body of scholarship that sought over time to dismantle powerful racist intellectual categories and white supremacy itself.

The intellectual currents of what would become African American studies first developed more than two centuries ago, in what James P. Garrett has termed the "nascent period" of the tradition. Under the early leadership of ministers such as Richard Allen, African Americans developed a network of African Free Schools and a number of church-supported educational institutions, including Wilberforce University in 1856. In the "conceptual period" of black studies, from Reconstruction through the Great Depression, more than one hundred public and private postsecondary institutions for African Americans were established.[1] It was from these often underfunded and politically vulnerable segregated colleges that several generations of black intellectuals produced the classical body of scholarship that now defines the field.

Foremost of his group was the great scholar-activist W. E. B. Du Bois. Trained at both Fisk and Harvard, Du Bois was thoroughly familiar with what constituted the standards and norms of white scholarship. He deeply believed that studies of the black experience should be scientific and rigorous. But Du Bois also knew that to be a Negro, living in the age of Jim Crow segregation, required a different kind of commitment and approach to the study of social phenomena. Du Bois's 1899 study, *The Philadelphia Negro*, notes Martin Kilson, "was one of the first urban sociological surveys in America and is a classic in the urban sociology of blacks."[2] For about fifteen years Du Bois regularly sponsored research conferences on topics relating to the black experience at Atlanta University, producing a series of edited volumes that form the modern foundations of black studies.

At Tuskegee Institute, at the beginning of the century, Monroe Work initiated a massive study of the socioeconomic, educational, and political conditions of African American people. Beginning in 1912, he edited and published the *Negro Yearbook*. This became a major source of data for scholars doing work on the contemporary African American experience. More significantly, Work also kept a massive clipping file on lynching and other forms of random racist violence against black people across the South. In nearby Nashville, Tennessee, sociologist Charles S. Johnson conducted a series of scientific investigations into the social development and political economy of blacks in the South. In 1944 Johnson initiated the Race Relations Institute at Fisk University, attempting to put scholarship into public policy practice. Other influential research in the fields of sociology and anthropology was produced by African American scholars such as Horace Mann Bond, author of *The Education of the Negro in Al-*

abama: A Study in Cotton and Steel, published in 1937, Allison Davis, whose 1941 book, *Deep South: A Social Anthropological Study of Caste and Class,* coauthored with Burleigh B. Gardner and Mary R. Gardner, was the best ethnographic survey of race relations under Jim Crow segregation published in the 1930s and 1940s, E. Franklin Frazier, author of *Negro Youth at Crossroads* in 1940 and many other influential studies, St. Clair Drake, who produced *Black Metropolis: A Study of Negro Life in a Northern City* in 1945, and Oliver Cromwell Cox, who in 1948 authored the most richly detailed theoretical study of black America and U.S. race relations produced in the first half of the twentieth century, *Caste, Class and Race.* In the area of literature there was the explosion of creative works during the Harlem Renaissance by artists such as Zora Neale Hurston, Langston Hughes, Jean Toomer, Countee Cullen, Claude McKay, and Nella Larsen. Literary criticism and what today is termed cultural studies was represented by Alain Locke's *The New Negro* in 1925 and J. Saunders Redding's *To Make a Poet Black,* published in 1939.[3]

In the field of history, Harvard-trained historian Carter G. Woodson established in 1916 the Association for the Study of Negro Life and History and founded the first academic journal devoted to the examination of the black experience, the *Journal of Negro History.* To reach thousands of black public school teachers and a general audience, Woodson launched *Negro History Bulletin* and initiated Associated Publishers. Rayford Logan, who succeeded Woodson as the editor of the *Journal of Negro History,* produced several influential volumes on the history of race relations, including *What the Negro Thinks* in 1944 and *The Negro in American Life and Thought: The Nadir, 1877–1901* in 1954. John Hope Franklin's masterful saga of the historical sojourn of African American people, *From Slavery to Freedom,* was published shortly after the Second World War, in 1947, and followed in 1956 by *The Militant South,* which presented a black interpretation of the significance of white supremacy in Southern culture and history.

There was also an influential group of what may be termed "organic intellectuals," drawing from Antonio Gramsci's concept—African Americans who were not formally trained in traditional universities but who had a critical understanding of their world and communicated their ideas to black audiences. For decades, J. A. Rogers published a weekly newspaper column devoted to the examination of "little known facts about black history," which regularly reached hundreds of thousands of readers. Arthur

Schomburg, a black Puerto Rican bibliophile, donated his vast personal collection of books and manuscripts to the New York Public Library, which led to the creation of the Schomburg Library in Harlem in 1940. The most brilliant among this group was Cyril Lionel Robert James, Trinidadian Marxist, Pan-Africanist, historian, and cricketer. There is no more powerful history in the English language, in my judgment, than James's classic study of the Haitian revolution, *The Black Jacobins*, first appearing in 1938. *Beyond a Boundary*, drawing upon James's autobiographical reflections and thoughts about race, colonialism, and the game of cricket in the West Indies, was in many respects the first volume of modern cultural studies. What all these black intellectuals shared was a passionate commitment to the equality and humanity of people of African descent. They knew that any intellectual investigation into the heart of black life and culture had to be interdisciplinary, that is, the tools of scholarship could not be narrowly confined by the parameters of so-called disciplines fostered by white intellectuals. The black intellectual tradition questioned and challenged disciplinary boundaries from the beginning, and, of course, the best example of this is the life and thought of Du Bois—trained as a historian yet making vital contributions to the fields of sociology, political science, economics, literary criticism, and the creative arts.

The strong interest of these black intellectuals in linking their scholarly production to the lived experiences of black people says something about their understanding of the nature of knowledge. Who produces knowledge, and what is the social utility of certain types of knowledge? Can knowledge be a form of private property, or should it be freely disseminated? Such questions, especially for people who are oppressed, are not abstractions. The classical scholarship in the black intellectual tradition suggests that knowledge exists to serve the social welfare of black people and, by extension, humanity as a whole. Therefore, knowledge should not be seen as a commodity, even in a capitalist environment. Access to learning and to educational institutions should be made universal. Thus black studies must also be an oppositional critique of the existing power arrangements and relations that are responsible for the systemic exploitation of black people. In 1969 anthropologist St. Clair Drake articulated this perspective:

> The very use of the term Black Studies is by implication an indictment of American and Western European scholarship. It makes the bold

assertion that what we have heretofore called "objective" intellectual activities were actually white studies in perspective and content; and that a corrective bias, a shift in emphasis, is needed, even if something called "truth" is set as the goal. To use a technical sociological term, the present body of knowledge has an ideological element in it, and a counterideology is needed. Black Studies supply that counterideology.[4]

In the quarter-century following the end of World War II, African American studies was transformed from a discourse and body of scholarly work confined largely to racially segregated institutions, to a vibrant curriculum and hundreds of programs fighting to change white higher education. One can identify at least five important factors that contributed to this transition. There was, perhaps foremost, the transformation of the global status of black and third world people in the United States and internationally. Anticolonial and independence movements erupted across Asia, Africa, and the Caribbean. The newly formed United Nations created a forum for these emerging nations, which had struggled for years against Western colonialism. These developments prompted the establishment in the U.S. between 1948 and 1971 of nine Title VI National Resource Centers in African Studies. Significantly, eight of these federally funded centers were located at white major institutions, including UCLA, Northwestern University, and the University of Wisconsin at Madison.[5] Many of the new political leaders of independent African states, such as Nnamdi Azikiwe and Kwame Nkrumah, and the theoreticians of Pan-Africanism such as George Padmore, had been educated in black American universities and were widely known by African Americans. Dialogues across the black Atlantic grew more frequent, as symbolized by the 1956 Congress of Negro Writers and Artists held in Paris. Foreshadowing much of the political language of black studies, Frantz Fanon argued that third world people have to reclaim the study of their own history and culture in order to emancipate themselves: "The plunge into the chasm of the past is the condition and the source of freedom."[6]

The rise of the cold war and the global competition between the Soviet Union and the United States, contributed to the impetus for the new interest in black culture and history. The Soviet bloc astutely attacked U.S. credibility on issues of democracy and freedom by pointing to the American system of Jim Crow segregation at home and U.S. support for colonialism abroad. The United States Information Agency countered by subsidizing tours of black cultural groups and lectures by prominent black

Americans throughout the third world. Through programs such as the Peace Corps in the early 1960s, the U.S. government attempted to display altruism and benevolence in underdeveloped nations.

Within the United States the preconditions for the growth of black studies were both demographic and political. Between 1945 and 1965 over three million Negroes left the South and migrated to the northeast, northcentral, and western states. This vast migration changed the racial composition of major U.S. cities and gave greater political clout to the black electorate. Black elected officials and civil rights activists aggressively pushed for affirmative action policies, and the opening of publicly funded colleges and universities to more African American students. The black freedom movement, in both its civil rights phase, 1955–1965, and black power phase, 1966–1975, championed the desegregation of white civil society and the empowerment of black people within previously all-white institutions. The change in the racial composition of U.S. colleges was very dramatic. In 1950, for example, only seventy-five thousand Negroes were enrolled in American colleges and universities. In 1960 three-fourths of all black students attended historically black colleges. By 1970 nearly seven hundred thousand African Americans were enrolled, three-fourths of whom were at white colleges. Most of these white institutions were ill-prepared for the eruption of black student protest they would encounter between 1968 and 1972.

At San Francisco State University the student strike of 1968–1969 forced the establishment of the Division of Ethnic Studies and full-fledged departments of black, Asian, Chicano, and Native American studies. San Francisco State's Black Student Union drafted a political statement, "The Justification for Black Studies," that would subsequently become "the seminal document for developing black studies departments at more than sixty universities." The objectives listed in the document included "to oppose the 'Liberal-Fascist' ideology rampant on campus whereby college administrations have attempted to pacify Black Student Union demands for systemic curriculum by offering one or two courses in Black history and literature," "to prepare Black students for direct participation in Black community struggles, and to define themselves as responsible to and for the future success of that community," "to reinforce the position that Black people in Africa and the Diaspora have the right to democratic rights, Self-Determination and Liberation," and "to oppose the dominant ideology of capitalism, world imperialism and White supremacy."[7] At Yale University, in the spring of 1968, nervous administrators tried to get ahead of the protest curve by hosting a national symposium on black studies. Unfortunately, Yale provost Charles Taylor addressed the audience with a series of anachronistic questions: "Is the special study of the black experience intellectually valid? Is it educationally responsible? And, is it socially constructive for blacks and whites?"[8] Student strikes and takeovers of administration buildings soon followed at Harvard, Northwestern, and dozens of other universities. In the most publicized campus conflict, black students seized control of the student union building at Cornell University and were widely depicted with firearms.[9]

The struggles for black studies on white campuses soon extended into academic organizations. In October 1969, at the annual meeting of the African Studies Association (ASA) in Montreal, a group of black scholars and graduate students denounced the organization's "complexion," "activities," and "direction." In a well-publicized statement the ASA was denounced for

> perpetuat(ing) colonialism and neocolonialism. . . . African peoples will no longer permit our people to be raped culturally, economically, politically and intellectually merely to provide European scholars with intellectual status symbols of African artifacts hanging in their living rooms and irrelevant and injurious lectures for their classrooms.[10]

In May 1970, at a conference at Howard University, the African Heritage Studies Association (AHSA) was formed, "dedicated to the preservation, interpretation and academic presentation of the historical and cultural heritage of African peoples both on the ancestral soil of Africa and in diaspora in the Americas and throughout the world." Black studies scholar Milfred Fierce recalled that the audience was "electrified . . . with chants of 'It's Nation Time,' and 'We Are an African People.'" For Fierce the founding of the AHSA "ranks among the most significant and eloquent expressions of Pan-African unity at an intellectual gathering to take place on U.S. soil."[11]

The principal architects of these new black studies programs were frequently young men and women in their twenties and thirties. Many were doctoral students, some of whom would never complete their terminal degrees. Most had been involved in black cultural and political protest activities and organizations. Although the "cultural nationalists," represented by intellectuals like Maulana Karenga and, for a time, Amiri

Baraka, and the "revolutionary nationalists," who identified with black radicals like George Jackson and militant formations such as the Black Panther Party, were constantly at odds, there was also a remarkable degree of consensus across ideological boundaries. At the Yale University symposium in 1968 Karenga declared that the university "is not basically an educational institution—it's a political institution. . . . It is basically a political thing, and it provides identity, purpose, and direction within an American context."[12] To Karenga's left, Robert L. Allen, author of the influential 1969 study *Black Awakening in Capitalist America*, made the same point. The American university, Allen observed in 1974, was a "political institution" that functions as a "servant of the bourgeois order, preparing an academic and professional elite that can 'manage' America on behalf of the white power-holding classes."[13] The immediate challenge thus was the construction of a militant black institution inside a conservative white institution that was for all practical purposes hostile to its existence. The urgent tasks of institution building required blacks to conceive of their curricula and research paradigms in new ways. In 1970 political scientist Ronald Walters insisted that "Black life has been distinctive enough and separate enough to constitute its own uniqueness that the ideology and the methodology of Black Social Science rests."[14] Black studies was a useful "tool" for the maintenance of "black identity," noted educators James R. Rosser and E. Thomas Copeland in 1973:

> The educational ideology, goals, and objectives of Black Studies must be illustrative, not only of emphasis on the revitalization of the black intellectual tradition, but also of a commitment to the eradication of weak egos, perceptions of incompetence and educational skill problems in general. If such is not possible within predominantly white schools, then maybe Black Studies should not exist at such schools.[15]

Like the historically black colleges, the successful black studies program should endeavor to cultivate and maintain an intimate relationship with the African American community. Nathan Hare, a faculty leader of the Black Studies revolt at San Francisco State and cofounder of the journal *Black Scholar*, emphasized in 1978 that black educational institutions must draw their strength from the black masses. "We must take our skills to the black community," Hare insisted,

We must wed the black community and the educational process. We must transform the black community and make it relevant to the educational endeavor at the same time as we make education relevant to the black community. We must bring the community to the campus and the campus to the community. Because education belongs to the people and the idea is to give it back to them.[16]

In the span of three short years, from 1968 to 1971, hundreds of black studies departments and programs were initiated, many espousing the blend of black nationalist militancy and idealism outlined above. It is not clear exactly how many programs were established. Robert L. Allen estimates there were approximately 500 colleges and universities that "provided full-scale Black Studies programs" by 1971. Up to 1,300 institutions as of 1974 offered at least one course in black studies.[17] Another estimate places the number of black studies programs peaking at 800 in the early 1970s and declining to about 375 by the mid-1990s.[18] Yet opposition to the institutionalization of African American studies programs, as well as black cultural centers and offices of minority affairs, never entirely disappeared. For example, Columbia University, which is located near the heart of Harlem, recruited Charles V. Hamilton, coauthor with Stokely Carmichael of the militant manifesto *Black Power*, to its political science department in the late 1960s. Hamilton was hired as a noted proponent of black studies.[19] But Columbia, for whatever reasons, failed to establish a formal program and core faculty in African American studies until 1993. Black studies scholar James Jennings cites two other examples from the early 1970s. At Brooklyn College, part of the City University of New York, "students were *physically assaulted* [Jennings's emphasis] by racist whites in a cafeteria because these Black and Puerto Rican students had chosen the Studies program as their major." At Hunter College, "there was major resistance by the administration to the demand for Black and Puerto Rican Studies. Professors would discourage their students from any connection with Black and Puerto Rican Studies."[20]

There were also several prominent African American scholars who vigorously opposed the creation of such departments. Perhaps the most vocal critic was Harvard political scientist Martin Kilson. In a 1973 article published in the *Journal of Black Studies*, Kilson raised a series of concerns. Black studies frequently fostered racial separation, and, in Kilson's view, "in the white colleges, both private and state, where now over seventy percent of all Afro-Americans in college are in attendance, the exclusion of whites from Black Studies is unjustified." Kilson felt that it was "doubt-ful" that a "large segment—perhaps the majority—of black students who become school teachers should major in Black Studies." Kilson criticized African American studies departments that permitted black undergradu-ate students to administer curricula: "Quite frankly, this is utter non-sense." All faculty appointments, Kilson insisted, should never be made in black studies *without the curricular control of an established discipline*" (Kilson's emphasis). Black studies faculty without such disciplinary-based credentials "will be dilettantes at best, and charlatans at worst."[21] Even St. Clair Drake, a strong defender of black studies, worried about the "anti-intellectual bias among some of the most committed students. . . . There are intellectual tasks associated with the Black Revolution just as there are with any revolution; and these tasks are important as the 'street tasks.'"[22]

There is a tendency for some veterans of the African American studies departments and black cultural centers to mythologize the actual origins of the majority of these programs, placing their development somewhere in the long sweep of black revolution, perhaps between Angela Davis's firing at UCLA for being a member of the Communist Party and the pris-oners' uprising at Attica. In truth, the militant student confrontations ex-perienced at Cornell, Harvard, Berkeley, and other major research uni-versities that initiated black studies departments was not always the norm. At many private liberal arts colleges and smaller state universities modest African American studies interdisciplinary programs were fre-quently started without controversy or conflict. Most liberal white facul-ty in the late 1960s and early 1970s were prepared to accept black studies as a legitimate part of the college curriculum. However, they opposed the notion that the black experience could only be researched or taught by African Americans or that whites should be excluded from black studies classes or black cultural centers. They rejected what they felt was the high-ly political content of black studies and sought to steer the new programs toward traditional standards of white scholarship. A 1974 study by Elias Blake Jr. and Henry Cobb reviewed twenty-nine black studies depart-ments and programs and found that most were "academically oriented," with one-third of those queried identifying "the development of tools of inquiry for research and publication" as their "major objective." Only three programs included the goal "to fashion a black identity" in their curricula. Most of these programs were structurally weak and underfund-ed, with few tenured faculty or administrators who possessed experience in academic management. Blake and Cobb's study found that "nearly all the programs surveyed . . . did not (have) the stability that might have been expected. . . . The inability to operate on the basis of long-term plans created an atmosphere of impermanence."[23]

The vast majority of black studies units in the 1970s were interdisciplinary programs, not formal departments. In most institutions they lacked the ability to tenure their own faculty. Their curricula were based frequently on an eclectic menu of courses initiated by faculty who were hired and/or tenured in traditional disciplinary-based departments. The director or chair of the African American studies major was often a faculty member tenured or appointed in a traditional department who was subsequently given release time to coordinate the interdisciplinary program. By the mid-1970s some of the early radicals and cultural nationalists who had initiated some programs were being eased out, replaced by black academics with more mainstream credentials. In 1974 Robert L. Allen warned that the black studies movement was "now fighting a rearguard battle; its very survival on campus is in doubt." Part of the problem was that "some schools simply took all their courses touching upon race relations and minority groups, lumped them together and called this potpourri Black Studies." But Allen also identified the growing interest of foundations and the federal government as a threat to the integrity of African American studies:

> By selecting certain programs for funding while denying support to others, government agencies and foundations could manipulate the political orientation of these programs and the direction of academic research. With hundreds of such programs competing for limited funds, effective control of the future of Black Studies was thereby shifted away from black scholars and students, and instead . . . to the funding agencies—college administrations, government and foundations. Departments which were thought by the establishment to be dangerously independent or radical could thus be crippled or destroyed without the necessity of resorting to violent repression.[24]

The standard for what a "responsible" black studies unit should look like in the 1970s and early 1980s, from the vantage point of liberals in higher education, was Yale University's Afro-American Studies Program. Yale had been the first elite university to adopt black studies, in December 1968, but developed the new program along traditionally liberal norms. The major required students to concentrate in a traditional discipline relevant to black studies. The Ford Foundation applauded Yale's "high faculty standards" and its focus on "serious academic study and teaching."[25] Harvard's "radical" black studies department, which was led by Ewart Guinier, was largely boycotted and isolated by the university's administration and other departments. In 1980 historian Nathan Huggins was appointed to chair Harvard's Afro-American studies department, moving it rapidly away from the militant program created by Guinier. The Ford Foundation soon provided funding for the development of the W. E. B. Du Bois Institute for Afro-American Studies at Harvard. By 1982 Ford was generously supporting two senior scholars and residents for postdoctorates and a major lecture series at the Du Bois Institute. That same year Huggins was invited by the Ford Foundation to write a comprehensive survey of the entire field of black studies. Published in July 1985, the Huggins report reflected the triumph of the liberal multiculturalist version of black studies. With confidence, Huggins observed that "since the decline of interest in black studies in the mid-seventies, supporters have seldom talked of autonomy. . . . Most of those that started with separatist notions either expired or moderated their positions."[26] Huggins's administrative and ideological interventions laid the groundwork for the appointment of Henry Louis Gates Jr. as chair of the department of Afro-American Studies and director of the W. E. B. Du Bois Institute in June 1991.

One is tempted to say that the decline of militancy and radicalism in black studies programs was inevitable, given the conservative nature of most academic institutions. Such an interpretation would ignore the changing political context in which African American studies programs functioned by the late 1970s. The 1978 Bakke decision was the first decisive legal step away from affirmative action and race-based "quotas"; the urban rebellions of the late sixties had been quelled; many prominent black rebels had exchanged their dashikis for polyester suits and were either running for public office or employed by corporations or the government. With the election of Ronald Reagan in 1980, the ideological and political environment for African American studies specifically, and for black people in general, became far more repressive. The Reagan administration inspired or directed attacks on black higher education at nearly every level. The programs and policies that quickly fell under assault included minority scholarship programs, financial aid for low-income students, and culturally diverse curricula. Federal courts challenged the existence of historically black colleges and universities for their racial composition. The number of African Americans who were enrolling in doctoral programs across the country began to decline significantly. Many institutions no longer aggressively enforced equal opportunity or affirmative action measures. By the early 1990s the far right had begun to aggressively attack the concept "political correctness" to undermine nearly all the multicultural initiatives for reform within higher education.

Moreover, despite the decade-long hegemony of black power, this recent renaissance of black nationalism was the exception, rather than the rule, in expressing the core ideology of the black middle class. Throughout the twentieth century, with some important exceptions, the bulk of the African American middle class has been inclusionist or liberal integrationist. The liberal integrationists always assumed that blacks had to succeed in the context of white institutions and Euro-American standards. They perceived academic training as a prerequisite to the goal of managerial, technical, and professional advancement. The liberal integrationists generally rejected all forms of racial separatism such as the establishment of separate all-black dormitories and cultural centers and the creation of autonomous black studies departments. They disagreed with the argument that African American studies could not be taught by white Americans. And they insisted that "academic standards" should not be held hostage to the political agendas of black militants.

Although this liberal multiculturalist current seemed to disappear during the height of the black power movement, a significant number of black educators who completed doctoral programs during these years generally supported these views. Even in the context of black studies programs, a number of integrationist-oriented black teachers and scholars were employed, especially at white private liberal arts institutions and smaller state colleges. At dozens of these institutions black studies curricula and programs did not reflect the militancy of black nationalism and racial separatism. These kinds of African American studies programs easily coexisted with well-established and traditionalist white academic departments. Conversely, such interdisciplinary programs often lacked real academic coherence or intellectual integrity. The core required courses were sometimes taught by faculty who had little intellectual commitment to black studies as a field of scholarly inquiry. One recurrent problem was that disciplinary-based departments always recruit, promote, and tenure their faculty on internal criteria, which might have a tenuous connection to the interdisciplinary scholarship, publications, and research of African American, Latino, and/or ethnic studies.

Those black studies programs that maintained an ideological orienta-

tion toward black nationalism, in both its cultural and revolutionary nationalist tendencies, also underwent profound institutional change. As
early as 1970 a twenty-eight-year-old scholar at UCLA, Molefi Asante,
initiated the *Journal of Black Studies*, which quickly became the major
publication of the field. The African Heritage Studies Association was
largely superseded by the National Council of Black Studies (NCBS),
founded in 1975. By 1990 NCBS claimed more than two thousand individual members and over one hundred institutional members. Its members were actively involved in multicultural curriculum reform from elementary school grades through graduate school.[27] However, for Abdul
Alkalimat, a leading radical social theorist and political activist, both the
Journal of Black Studies and NCBS "were not created as part of the radical negation of the mainstream or through direct active struggle." Both
were in Alkalimat's view "insulated . . . from the dynamics of the Black
liberation movement. They fell into idealism, ideological dogmatism and
a careerist machine of circulating leadership posts and awards among a
small group of loyalists."[28]

The nationalist-oriented African American studies group included a
number of the field's most prominent and influential intellectuals. A short
list of them would include James Turner, longtime director of Cornell's
Africana Studies and Research Center, Ivan Van Seritma, professor of
African Studies at Rutgers University, founding editor of the *Journal of
African Civilizations* and author of *They Came Before Columbus: The
African Presence in Ancient America* (1976), Asa G. Hilliard, professor of
education at Georgia State University, and author of many books, includ-
ing *Testing African American Students* (1987), Tony Martin, history pro-
fessor at Wellesley College since 1973, well-known for his 1976 major
study *Race First: The Ideological and Organizational Struggles of Marcus
Garvey and the Universal Negro Improvement Association* and, more recently, for his highly publicized and controversial pamphlet, *The Jewish
Onslaught: Dispatches from the Wellesley Battlefront*, University of
Maryland political scientist Ronald Walters, a key interpreter of African
American politics and adviser to Jesse Jackson and the rainbow coalition,
and the late John Henrik Clarke, professor of black studies at Hunter College and author of many volumes in black history and culture. Unques-
tionably, however, two intellectuals in this group have been most pivotal
as interpreters and political forces in the development of black studies—
Maulana Karenga and Molefi Asante.

Karenga was the principal proponent of black cultural nationalism in the 1960s, the creator of Kwanzaa, the Afrocentric cultural ritual and celebration that has been adopted by millions of African Americans. Karenga's first major intervention in the field was his *Introduction to Black Studies*, which in the 1970s and 1980s was perhaps the most widely used text of its kind. He was a frequent contributor to the *Black Scholar*, the *Journal of Black Studies*, and the other academic publications. Karenga denounced Huggins's 1985 report, claiming that "for all its pretensions and in spite of his previous scholarship, [it] is little more than European hagiography masquerading as history, and an unscholarly melange of personal preferences posing as meaningful analysis." In his 1988 essay, "Black Studies and the Problematic of Paradigm," Karenga identified seven key "contributions" that African American studies makes:

> (1) to humanity's understanding of itself, using the African experience as a paradigmatic human struggle and achievement; (2) to the university's realizing its claim of universality . . . (3) to U.S. society's understanding itself by critically measuring its claims against its performance and its variance with a paradigmatic just society; (4) to the rescue and reconstruction of Black history and humanity from alien hands, and the restoration of African classical culture on and through which we can build a new body of human sciences and humanities; (5) to the creation of a new social science, more critical, corrective, holistic, and ethical . . . (6) to the creation of a body of conscious, capable, and committed Black intellectuals who self-consciously choose to use their knowledge and skills in the service of the Black community

and (7) to make a "contribution to the critique, resistance, and reversal of the progressive Westernization of human consciousness, which is one of the major problems of our times."[29]

Molefi Asante built and chaired for nearly fifteen years what became the largest African American studies department in the United States, at Temple University. He authored and edited more than three dozen books and 250 articles and edited the *Journal of Black Studies*. But Asante's greatest impact was ideological. In his 1980 book, *Afro-Centricity: The Theory of Social Change*, Asante proposed a philosophical construct for the development of the entire field of African American studies. "Afrocentricity," at its most simple expression, is the intellectual perspective that begins "from the standpoint of the agency of African people and the centrality of Africa in its own story."[30] Thus Asante's critique of the Huggins report begins with the observation that "Black Studies is not merely the study of Black people" but a philosophical and cultural approach to the interpretation of social reality that takes as its starting point the perspectives and interests of people of African descent.[31] "The Afrocentrist will not question the idea of the centrality of African ideals and values but will argue over what constitutes those ideals and values," Asante explained in 1990. "The Afrocentrist seeks to uncover and use codes, paradigms, symbols, motifs, myths, and circles of discussion that reinforce the centrality of African ideals and values as a valid frame of reference for acquiring and examining data."[32] In hundreds of public lectures on universities and within black communities, Asante and his growing constituency of educators pushed the view that "African Americans should be viewed not as objects or victims, but as actors and subjects of history."[33] Textbooks and curricula developed around Afrocentric themes were implemented in hundreds of schools. In 1991 the Baltimore public school system began "infusing Afrocentric studies throughout all courses in kindergarten through fifth grade." In Detroit that same year several all-black male academies were established, using an explicitly "Afrocentric curriculum."[34] New academic publications such as the *Journal of Pan-African Studies*, initiated by the Pan-African Studies Department of California State University at Northridge in 1998, were dedicated to the pursuit of "Afrocentric theory, methodology, and analysis."[35]

As the debate about "multiculturalism" and cultural diversity erupted in both higher education and public school systems, the theory of Afrocentricity—more commonly called by some supporters and many detractors "Afrocentrism"—began to generate intense criticism. Liberal historian Arthur Schlesinger Jr. denounced Afrocentricity as reverse racism: "If a Kleagle of the Ku Klux Klan wanted to use the schools to disable and handicap black Americans, he could hardly come up with anything more effective than the Afrocentric curriculum." Diane Ravitch, the Bush administration's assistant secretary of education, attacked the Afrocentric curriculum, making the ridiculous (and racist) assertion that "part of what school is for is studying the society in which you are going to live. You don't study your own race."[36] One major newspaper editorialized that "Afrocentrism betrays the very clientele it claims to serve. . . . It hucksters shoddy goods that burden the maltutored with lifelong grievance against the supposedly racist refusal of whites to see gold where, in fact, there is only dross."[37] One *San Diego Union Tribune* black columnist complained in 1995 that "Afrocentrism, which is a disguised name for reverse racism, is attempting to overtake the black community. Even many of our African American churches have brought the lie that for self-esteem, we must have Afrocentric-based principles."[38] These shrill attacks only had the effect of greatly enhancing Afrocentricity among millions of black people.

But frequently even the proponents of Afrocentricity argued about the definition and meaning of the concept. Howard University Medical School professor Keith Crawford defines "pure Afrocentricity" as a "philosophy which has evolved as African peoples began to understand their relationship with God and Nature, and the experiences of human existence."[39] The editors of the *Journal of Pan-African Studies* suggested that "Afrocentrism is not yet a scientifically based paradigm, nor yet a set of associated theories. Its adherents and advocates simply need to rein in the rhetoric, muzzle the egos, and do the hard core research."[40] Karenga has candidly recognized several frequent criticisms about Afrocentricity, including charges of its "dogmatic" character, its denial of the genuine diversity and pluralism within African cultures and societies, and its "static" and "monolithic" categories of historical and social analysis.[41] Other criticisms of Afrocentricity focus primarily on its tendencies toward racial essentialism, or what might be termed a racist pseudoscience of the black experience. Political controversies surrounding the black studies department of the City College of New York, chaired by Leonard Jeffries, led some to unfairly associate Afrocentrism with anti-Semitism.[42] Afrocentric scholarship rarely came into constructive dialogue with new bodies of research—women and gender studies, queer studies, postcolonial studies, postmodernism—and was hostile toward radical interpretations of social reality, most specifically Marxism.

In everyday language, *Afrocentrism* has come to mean a positive black consciousness that is anchored in the knowledge of African culture and history. Leith Mullings makes this point very well in her chapter, "Reclaiming Culture: The Dialectics of Identity." Afrocentrism can be expressed in rituals, styles of dress, values, and kinship relations. It can be equated with certain kinds of political mobilization, such as the Million Man March in October 1995. But in some black studies departments efforts to systematize Afrocentricity as a comprehensive philosophical system, based on a "shallow, non-scientific homogenizing of disparate African cultures," in the words of James P. Garrett, have served as ideological cover for what is basically an extremely conservative middle-class approach toward black education. Garrett accuses the "culturalists," or proponents of black cultural nationalism, with turning some departments into "quasi-feudal enclaves which refuse entry to non-black students and faculty as well as to 'ideologically impure' sectors of the Black community." These programs "graduate acolytes and sycophants, while simultaneously and consistently trying to discourage and isolate those students who wish to pursue an independently critical, analytical scholarship."[43]

Abdul Alkalimat has suggested that the conflict between the two dominant currents in African American studies, the inclusionist liberal integrationists and the Afrocentrists, is more illusory than real. Focusing on the work of both Gates and Asante, Alkalimat argues:

> What unites both of these approaches is that they are not interested in the relationship between their ideas and the historical context of social and political conflicts in which they live and work. Gates wants us to examine the text and not the context and Asante wants us to primarily concern ourselves with ancient Egypt for our orientation. Neither of these approaches helps us to clarify the crisis facing Africa nor that facing the American people. Both represent an ideological retreat by a new Black middle class that has been unable to find the courage to link up with the masses of Black people fighting to survive.[44]

Throughout the twentieth century and into the present, there has also been a third ideological tendency within black public discourse and inside the struggles to define the African American community. Leith Mullings and I have characterized this tendency as "transformation," the collective efforts of black people neither to integrate nor self-segregate but to transform the existing power relationships and the racist institutions of the state, the economy, and society. This transformationist or radical perspective begins with the assumption that racism exists not merely at the ideological level but has become an integral factor in the construction of the U.S. political economy and the social class hierarchy of the country. Thus to dismantle institutional racism will require much more than simply assimilating the values and interests of the white professional and managerial classes within African American life and social organization; it cannot be achieved by flights of fantasy to ancient Egypt. It necessitates the building of a powerful protest movement, based largely among the most oppressed classes and social groups, to demand the fundamental restructuring of the basic institutions and patterns of ownership within society. Toward this larger goal, the building of black institutions is an essential process, in providing the resources for African American people to survive and resist. Black intellectuals therefore have a special obligation to utilize their skills and resources to contribute to the liberation of their people.

These radical ideas were consistently expressed in the political life and scholarly work of W. E. B. Du Bois. Many of the central scholars in the black intellectual tradition shared these views as well, including C. L. R. James, St. Clair Drake, Oliver Cromwell Cox, and E. Franklin Frazier. A radical black perspective on issues of gender was developed through the writings of Anna Julia Cooper, Ida B. Wells-Barnett, Claudia Jones, Ella Baker, Angela Davis, and Barbara Ransby. The black radical perspective on internationalism and Pan-Africanism is reflected in the thought and political activities of Du Bois, James, Paul Robeson, Walter Rodney, and Amilcar Cabral. A radical analysis of black spirituality and faith extends from George Washington Woodbey to James Cone and Cornel West. Within the most radical tendency of black nationalism, similar ideas found expression through the militant activism of Cyril V. Briggs, Malcolm X, and Kwame Ture (Stokely Carmichael.) And among the writings of lesbian, gay, and bisexual intellectuals a black radical perspective is expressed through the powerful writings of Audre Lorde and Barbara Smith.

Within African American studies the radical or transformationist perspective was represented in the late 1960s by the Institute of the Black World (IBW). IBW was originally conceived as an "Institute for Advanced Afro-American Studies" in which "the work of Du Bois could find a renaissance," according to historian Vincent Harding. In the summer of 1968 the institute for Advanced Afro-American Studies was planned to be part of the Martin Luther King Jr. Memorial Center. A nucleus of progressive black scholars joined Harding in this process, including political scientist Bill Strickland, Stephen Henderson, Councill Taylor, A. B. Spellman, Lawrence Rushing, and Gerald McWorter (Abdul Alkalimat.) Within a year the renamed Institute of the Black World had come into increasing conflict with the King Center, and divisions developed among the original planning group. McWorter, Spellman, and Rushing left the institute, and by the fall of 1969 a core senior research staff was developed that included Harding, Strickland, historians Lerone Bennett and Sterling Stuckey, sociologist Joyce Ladner, and education scholar Chester Davis. In November 1969 IBW hosted a national working conference on black studies, inviting the directors of thirty-five major departments and programs to discuss models "towards an education appropriate to our struggle."[45]

Throughout the 1970s IBW represented the most progressive model of what African American studies could have been. Breaking its affiliation with the King Center, IBW faced a continuous struggle to finance its researchers and staff. Given its limited budget, the range of activities and public programs it initiated was truly remarkable. IBW's "Black-World-View" news column was widely distributed to black media, schools, prisons, and community groups. IBW's massive library of audiotaped lectures and manuscripts documented the ideas and research of several generations of scholar/activists. Harding and Strickland were influential in helping to draft the National Black Political Convention's Preamble and Black Agenda, adopted at the Gary Black Convention in March 1972. IBW established ongoing contacts with Vietnamese, Cuban, and other third world groups. It conducted summer institutes and seminars for teacher training and educational programs that reached prisoners' study groups, housing projects, and black caucuses in religious denominations. IBW's international network of associated scholars included Walter Rodney, C. L. R. James, and Robert Hill, the editor of the definitive study of the collected papers of Marcus Garvey and the Universal Negro Improvement Association. Howard Dodson, who was for a number of years the director of IBW's administrative staff, later became the head of Harlem's Schomburg Center. Harding's magnificently crafted history of the black freedom movement in the nineteenth-century United States, *There Is a River*, published in 1981, has become a standard text in both African American studies and American history.[46] Alkalimat became the founder of People's College at Fisk University, authored a widely read introductory text in African American studies, served as the director of black studies programs at the University of Illinois and later at the University of Toledo, and was a leading figure in black activist organizations and movements, from the African Liberation Support Committee in the 1970s to the Black Radical Congress. However, by the early 1980s, IBW could no longer sustain itself financially, and the center was forced to close.

The history of IBW provides both the exception as well as the rule regarding radical black studies. When IBW's radical research agenda and political activities became clear, most foundations and other external funders rejected overtures for support. The center lacked permanent connections with major research universities, which could have subsidized graduate fellowships and resident scholars. IBW's accomplishments are also exceptional, because most parallel efforts to construct radical African American studies programs have not succeeded. The reasons offered by progressive black scholars for this failure are varied. The majority of black socialists and Marxists are not logically drawn into academic careers in universities. Some are involved in trade union and labor organizing; many can be found doing community-based work around police brutality, public education, health care, and women's issues. Their involvement in a wide variety of local and national formations, from Brooklyn's Audre Lorde Center to the Black Radical Congress, often takes priority over other concerns. Many are social workers, teachers, and public employees or work in nonprofit organizations. When black leftists do manage to circumvent the various political roadblocks in graduate school, and after their subsequent employment at colleges and universities, they are rarely tenured. Even tenured and productive research scholars have been subjected to political harassment. Angela Y. Davis, one of the most influential and prolific black feminist scholars, has only recently been the object of a right-wing campaign to remove her from the University of California at Santa Cruz. There are several important academic journals of the black left, notably the *Black Scholar* and *Race and Class*, but most university presses would not aggressively solicit manuscripts from black leftists.

A more complicated factor lies in the nature of black studies as an intellectual project. Marxists believe that there is a close relationship between knowledge and power. As C. L. R. James observed, "All political power presents itself to the world within a certain framework of ideas."[47] Those who exercise state power and control society's resources would be truly foolish to encourage and support a kind of scholarship that seeks their removal from power. Black socialist intellectuals strive to place the voices and struggles of black people at the center of our interpretations of history and social reality. But to "correct" history requires more than "black" history. It also requires the insights drawn from critical interpretations of gender, sexuality, class, and ethnicity. African American studies, like most black formations and institutions, is constructed along the terrain of society's racial mountain. That special vantage point yields important truths and insights black people have learned about the American experience, one many white Americans refuse to accept or acknowledge to this day. But an intellectual project that deliberately confines the parameters of its inquiry to the racial mountain alone will be of little value in the larger effort to transform society. This careful balance between the particular and the universal is what distinguishes the work of scholars like W. E. B. Du Bois and Anna Julia Cooper and public leaders such as Robeson and King. They uncompromisingly fought for the perceived interests of black people, but in a language that addressed the totality of society's concerns. As Vincent Harding once declared, "Negro History Week becomes passé, for we move toward controlling the total definition of society."[48]

As we enter a new century, African American studies is experiencing a new wave of popularity. Most major universities now recommend as part of their core curricula or distribution requirements a menu of multicultural courses that usually includes black studies. The most prominent program today is Harvard's W. E. B. Du Bois Institute for Afro-American Studies, directed by Henry Louis Gates Jr. With the recruitment of social theorist Cornel West from Princeton University in 1994 and the appointments of prominent sociologists William Julius Wilson and Larry Bobo several years later, Gates constructed a formidable intellectual enterprise. Wilson is widely considered the most influential social scientist of his generation, the author of several important works including *The Declining Significance of Race* in 1978 and *The Truly Disadvantaged* in 1987. West's popular 1992 collection of essays, *Race Matters*, became a standard text in hundreds of colleges. Gates established his reputation with the publication in 1988 of *The Signifying Monkey: A Theory of Afro-American Literary Criticism*, which was followed by a constant stream of anthologies, collections of essays, and the autobiographical *Colored People*. With Harvard philosopher and cultural studies scholar K. Anthony Appiah, Gates edits *Transition*, a lively intellectual journal. Gates's commentaries appear regularly in the *New Yorker* and the *New York Times*. Like most prominent public figures, Gates has his share of critics. He has been criticized for his public celebrity image—"more like that of a movie star than an academic"—and for several controversial essays he has written, such as a 1992 attack against "black anti-Semitism" published in the *New York Times*.[49]

However, to paraphrase Martin, "Where do we go from here?" Perhaps in the quest for public acceptance and influence within the academic and political mainstream we have lost our way. Fundamental social change is usually achieved at the boundaries of society and not from the center. The classical black intellectual tradition was largely constructed at the margins of white society, in segregated black institutions with close proximity to the daily struggles of African American people. It was no accident that the character of black intellectual work was frequently passionate, informed by the urgent tasks of black survival and resistance. This was true throughout Africa and the black diaspora. Walter Rodney was a rigorous, careful scholar and historian of West Africa and the Caribbean, but he was also a major revolutionary political leader in his native Guyana before he was assassinated at the age of thirty-eight. Eric Williams wrote *Capitalism and Slavery* in 1944 and assumed the leadership of the independence movement in Trinidad and Tobago a decade later. Even after Julius Nyerere was named prime minister of independent Tanganyika in 1961 he continued to write and publish works on popular education and culture that were adopted into curricula and community development programs worldwide. The real meaning of Du Bois's life and thought is that there must be an active dynamic link between serious scholarship and the concerns of the black community.

More than a quarter-century ago Robert L. Allen posed a series of questions confronting the future of African American studies. "The critics are right," Allen admitted, "when they note that politics is a fundamental problem for the development of Black Studies. But the question is not politics or no politics, but rather it is *which* politics? Whom will Black Studies serve?" Allen suggested two basic choices ahead for the field. "Will it be truly democratic in its intellectual and political vision, or will it become 'political' and acquiesce to a narrow, elitist and bourgeois view of education?"[50] The scholarship of African American studies must reflect the full diversity and conflict of theoretical perspectives that currently exist. No voices should be suppressed in the pursuit of knowledge. The liberal multiculturalists of one tendency in black studies must engage in a critical conversation about the substance and meaning of their scholarship and research with those who do not fully share their views. Conversely, Afrocentricity will only be taken seriously as an intellectual project when its proponents critique the paradigm's tendencies toward ahistoricism and essentialism.

Yet the old "integrationist versus black nationalist" debate that characterized much of black social and political discourse of the twentieth century is rapidly being superseded by new social forces. Globalization, cyberspace technology, and the mass assimilation of commercialized popular culture make the politics of both racial essentialism and liberal integrationism irrelevant and anachronistic. The racial mountain offers only a partially privileged terrain from which we must interpret and engage with universal cultures and issues affecting the entire globe. That new inquiry and level of analysis and debate should not occupy a space utterly detached from the lived experiences of the African American people. Black studies will continue to be challenged to become once again not merely another methodology for interpreting the black world but an intellectual project that seeks its transformation.

Notes

Several students at the Institute for Research in African-American Studies at Columbia University were largely responsible for the background research essential in preparing this essay. John McMillian, a doctoral candidate in history, identified a number of important sources. Sherell Daniels and Patrick Guarasci also significantly contributed to this work. As frequently occurs in my work, some of the key ideas expressed here come from anthropologist Leith Mullings.

1. James P. Garrett, "Black/Africana/Pan-African Studies: From Radical to Reaction to Reform?—Its Role and Relevance in the Era of Global Capitalism in the New Millenium," *Journal of Pan-African Studies*, vol. 1, no. 1 (Fall-Winter, 1998–1999), pp. 150–151.

2. Martin Kilson, "Reflections on Structure and Content in Black Studies," *Journal of Black Studies*, vol. 3, no. 3 (March 1973), p. 298.

3. Ibid., pp. 298–299. In this essay Kilson mentions many of these works, as well as others, that established the modern black intellectual tradition.

4. St. Clair Drake lecture at Brooklyn College, September 23, 1969, cited in Ronald Bailey, "Black Studies in Historical Perspective," *Journal of Social Issues*, vol. 29, no. 1 (1973), p. 104.

5. Milfred C. Fierce, *Africana Studies Outside the United States: Africa, Brazil, the Caribbean* (Ithaca: Africana Studies and Research Center, Cornell University and Ford Foundation, 1991), Monograph Series no. 7, pp. 5–6.

6. Vincent Harding, *Beyond Chaos*, p. 14.

7. Garrett, "Black/Africana/Pan-African Studies," pp. 160–162.

8. Amstead L. Robinson, Craig C. Foster, and Donald H. Ogilivie, eds., *Black Studies in the University: A Symposium* (New Haven: Yale University Press, 1969), p. 3.

9. See Ernest Dunbar, "The Black Studies Thing," *New York Times Magazine*, April 6, 1969, p. 25.

10. "Statement" and "Statement of the Black Caucus," dated October 15, 1969, "The African Heritage Studies Association," *Black World*, vol. 19, no. 9 (July 1970), pp. 20–21.

11. Ibid., pp. 22–24; and Fierce, *Africana Studies Outside the United States*, p. 7.

12. Maulana Ron Karenga, "The Black Community and the University: A Community Organizer's Perspective," in Robinson, Foster and Ogilvie, *Black Studies in the University*, pp. 37–38.

13. Robert L. Allen, "Politics of the Attack on Black Studies," *Black Scholar*, vol. 6 (September 1974), p. 6.

14. Ronald Walters, quoted in Bailey, "Black Studies in Historical Perspective," p. 107.

15. James R. Rosser and E. Thomas Copeland, "Reflections: Black Studies—Black Education?" *Journal of Black Studies*, vol. 3, no. 3 (March 1973), p. 290. Also see Herman Hudson, "The Black Studies Program: Strategy and Structure," *Journal of Negro Education*, vol. 41, no. 4 (Fall 1972), pp. 294–298.

16. Nathan Hare, "War on Black Colleges," *Black Scholar*, vol. 9 (May/June 1978), p. 18.

17. Allen, "Politics of the Attack on Black Studies," pp. 2, 5.

18. See Thomas J. LaBelle and Christopher Ward, *Ethnic Studies and Multiculturalism* (Albany: State University of New York Press, 1996), p. 78.

19. In the late 1960s Hamilton reviewed about forty black studies proposals for departments and programs at a number of universities. He reached various conclusions about the value of African American studies to the pursuit of excellence in higher education. "Black studies, some proposals state, will bring about a new spirit of cooperation between blacks and whites," Hamilton noted. "Black studies will instill a sense of pride in black students who will study and learn about their heritage and history. They will develop a sense of identity." Curiously, none of these proposals would be implemented at Columbia University for more than twenty years. See Charles V. Hamilton, "The Challenge of Black Studies," *Social Policy*, vol. 1, no. 2 (1970), p. 16.

20. Interview with James Jennings, "A Look at Black Studies Today," *Forward Motion*, vol. 4, no. 4 (February-March 1985), p. 10.

21. Kilson, "Reflections on Structure and Content in Black Studies," pp. 300, 303, 306–309.

22. St. Clair Drake, quoted in Bailey, "Black Studies in Historical Perspective," p. 103.

23. Elias Blake Jr. and Henry Cobb, *Black Studies: Issues in Their Institutional Survival* (Washington, D.C.: U.S. Department of Health, Education, and Welfare, 1974), pp. 3, 9.

24. Allen, "Politics of the Attack on Black Studies," pp. 2, 5.

25. Jack Bass, *Widening the Mainstream of American Culture: A Ford Foundation Report on Ethnic Studies* (New York: Ford Foundation, 1978), p. 8. Also see John W. Blassingame, ed., *New Perspectives on Black Studies* (Urbana: University of Illinois Press, 1971).

26. Nathan Huggins, *Afro-American Studies: A Report to the Ford Foundation* (New York: Ford Foundation, 1985), p. 45.

27. Fierce, *Africana Studies Outside the United States*, p. 8.

28. Abdul Alkalimat, "Black Power in U.S. Education: Ideology, Academic Activism, and the Politics of Black Liberation," *Africa World Review* [London], (May-October 1992), p. 15.

29. Maulana Karenga, "Black Studies and the Problematic of Paradigm:

The Philosophical Dimension," *Journal of Black Studies*, vol. 18, no. 4 (June 1988), pp. 396, 406–407.

30. Molefi Asante, review of Microsoft *Encarta Africana*, edited by Henry Louis Gates Jr. and K. Anthony Appiah, H-NET Discussion List for African American Studies, February 3, 1999, <H-AFRO-AM@H-NET.MSU.EDU>.

31. Molefi Asante, "A Note on Nathan Huggins," unpublished manuscript, quoted in Karenga, "Black Studies and the Problematic of Paradigm," p. 403.

32. See Molefi Asante, *Kemet, Afrocentricity, and Knowledge* (Trenton, N.J.: Africa World, 1990).

33. From speech by Molefi Asante at Alabama State University, quoted in Monique Fields, "Founder of Afrocentricity Aims to Dispel Myths," *Montgomery Advertiser*, April 10, 1996.

34. Dennis Kelly, "Afrocentric Studies: A Concept Rooted in Controversy," *USA Today*, January 28, 1992.

35. See the premier issue of the *Journal of Pan-African Studies: A Journal of Afrocentric Theory, Methodology, and Analysis*, vol. 1, no. 1 (Fall-Winter, 1998–1999).

36. Kelly, "Afrocentric Studies."

37. Tom Teepen, "By Distorting Black History, Afrocentrism Just Tarnishes Its Legacy," *Minneapolis Star Tribune*, February 27, 1996.

38. Carlotta Morrow, "This Afrocentrism Is Reverse Racism," *San Diego Union-Tribune*, November 12, 1995.

39. Keith Crawford, "Defining Afrocentrism: One Perspective," *Journal of Pan-African Studies*, vol. 1, no. 1 (Fall-Winter 1998–1999), p. 30.

40. "Afrocentricity: What It Is, What It's Not, and What It Yet May Be," *Journal of Pan-African Studies*, vol. 1, no. 1 (Fall-Winter 1998–1999), p. 18.

41. See the second revised edition of Maulana Karenga, *Introduction to Black Studies* (Los Angeles: University of Sankore Press, 1993).

42. "A is for Ashanti, B is for black . . . ," *Newsweek* (September 23, 1991).

43. Garrett, "Black/Africana/Pan-African Studies," p. 169. Garrett continues: "During the past 20 years, the culturalists have repeatedly used Black Studies as a platform to declare themselves national and international cultural analysts and icons. They have adopted traditional African rituals, male dominated elder-chair/worship, created artificial hierarchies, employed redundancies and catechisms, promoted festivals and conferences (while supporting a cottage industry of African clothing and attire, cosmetics, drum performances and book displays), all of which have been critical in cultivating and nurturing the high level of influence they claim and maintain. Self-praise and self-aggrandisement have become characteristic of many such departments and programs. However, the main role the culturalists have played has been to deflect Black Studies from confronting the established American social order, that is, to focus seriously and relentlessly on the rapidly deteriorating social/economic conditions the masses of Black people face domestically and globally" (pp. 169–170).

44. Alkalimat, "Black Power in U.S. Education," p. 15.

45. Vincent Harding, "Introduction," in Institute of the Black World, ed., *IBW and Education for Liberation* (Chicago: Third World, 1973), pp. iii–ix.

46. For a generational overview of the political activities and research projects of IBW, see Institute of the Black World, ed., *Education and Black Struggle: Notes from the Colonized World, Harvard Educational Review*, Monograph no. 2 (Cambridge: Harvard Educational Review, 1974).

47. C. L. R. James, "African Independence and the Myth of African Inferiority," in Institute of the Black World, ed., *Education and Black Struggle*, p. 34.

48. Harding, *Beyond Chaos*, p. 27.

49. See Cheryl Bentsent, "Head Negro in Charge," April 1997, <http://www.bostonmagazine.com>; and Franklin Foer, "Henry Louis Gates, Jr.: The Academic as Entrepreneur," April 11, 1997, <http://www.slatemag.com>. The most recent controversy involving Gates was generated by the publication, with coeditor K. Anthony Appiah, of *Encarta Africana,* a "comprehensive encyclopedia of black history and culture." Critics such as Asante questioned its selection of topics, its "uneven scholarship," and the exclusion of a number of contemporary black scholars and writers who reflected a different "perspective or orientation" than that of the editors. See Molefi Asante, "Review of Microsoft *Encarta Africana,* from <H-AFRO-AM@H-NET.MSU.EDU>.

50. Allen, "Politics of the Attack on Black Studies," p. 7.

PART ONE

Theorizing the Black World:
Race in the Postcolonial,
Post-Civil Rights Era

1

Toward an Effective Antiracism

Nikhil Pal Singh

First let us face what the Negro question is. It is an eco-nomic question; it is a political question; yes, so it is; but it is primarily a question of human relations, but not in the common sense of those words. . . . That is where we must begin. There is involved here a revolution in rela-tions comparable only to the revolution which will emancipate labor and the revolution which will emanci-pate women.
—C. L. R. James, American Civilization, *1950*

At the dawn of the twentieth century, in the shadow of the failure of Re-construction in the United States, W. E. B. Du Bois stood before the first Pan-African Congress in London and offered his startling prophecy that the "problem of the twentieth century is the problem of the color line."[1] Several years before, in front of the American Negro Academy, Du Bois delivered what at the time was his more celebrated and widely known paper, "The Conservation of Races" (1897). Addressing his audience in unequivocally nationalist accents, Du Bois spoke for "his people," those with whom he was "bone of the bone and flesh of the flesh," those he would later describe as living within the "Veil."[2] Not mentioning the color line as such, Du Bois instead emphasized another point, that "the Negro people as a race, have a contribution to make to civilization and humanity which no other race can make."[3]

As he composed his most famous work, *The Souls of Black Folk* (1903), a few years later, Du Bois deftly combined these two distinct appeals. Ad-vocating neither the assimilation, and consequent erasure of "Negro" distinctiveness, nor the preservation of an absolutist and damaging conception of black difference, he doggedly attacked the color line while refusing to denigrate those who had lived their lives within it and had been defined by it. Subtly weaving the civilizationist appeals of nineteenth-century black nationalism with an insistence upon what Albert Murray has called the "incontestably mulatto" character of American culture, Du Bois effectively negotiated the double bind presented by U.S. racism at the turn of the century.[4] Resisting both the segregationist implications of insisting upon black autonomy and self-activity and the assimilationist tendency to denigrate the cultural practices and history of ex-slaves, Du Bois instead asked that the nation and the world recognize the freedman as a "coworker in the kingdom of culture."[5]

This work of nearly a century ago marks the beginning of one man's immense discursive labor of racial reconstruction, spanning the decades of postemancipation disenfranchisement and imperial conquest as well as the subsequent era of decolonization and the modern civil rights movement. Yet, today, as we sit on the threshold of the twenty-first century, the condition of poor communities of color, and black communities in particular, is as dire as at any time in recent history. Standing in the shadow of the failure of the Second Reconstruction in black America, do we take courage from Du Bois's observations and insights about the first, or simply despair?[6] To whom do we address ourselves today, when calling for solutions to the crisis of black politics and theory, black life in America? Where is the "color line"? Where are the empires? How do we identify and how do we confront the calamity that befalls this generation of "black folk"? Most important, what do we make of the fact that that "crisis" of which we speak—one of Du Bois's preferred metaphors for describing what it meant to be black at the turn of the last century—today appears not as an exception but as the rule?[7]

We have many answers to these questions, most of them unsatisfactory if not misleading. Commentators of diverse political stripes, for example, have seized upon the argument that the explicit politics of racial redress, and the struggle for racial justice, make less and less sense due to race's "declining significance" in the face of deepening class oppression and (intraracial) class polarization.[8] Others, more disingenuous, have argued that in order to again gain influence, American liberals and leftists must put aside racial questions altogether, since by aligning progressive ideas under the banner of antiracism liberalism has done little more than alienate itself from a "silent majority" of Americans and initiate a "backlash" that has pushed this country on a more or less continuous rightward course since the late 1960s.[9] Finally, and perhaps most ingeniously, on the ascendant right it is imagined that the legacies of antiracism (i.e., antipoverty programs, affirmative action, and voting rights legislation) are now the real obstacles to achieving a truly "color-blind" America as well as being the crutch that continues to hinder black bootstrap self-discipline and progress.[10]

Despite their differences, these positions comprise what amounts to a quite remarkable consensus, indicating that we may have entered a neoracist, if not a *postracist* age, in the United States, a fact that may hold some keys to understanding the current difficulties of black politics and theory.[11] The range of arguments enumerated above represents the disorganization and wholesale raiding of the at least partially sedimented resources of *antiracist* theory and practice over the past forty years, if not longer. Although enlightened elites (especially in the academy) may pay homage to a hollow multiculturalism, or denounce the most egregious manifestations of hate speech and overt discrimination, contemporary politicians invariably fashion their appeals to justice, fairness, and expansive neutrality by consistently repudiating even the slightest suggestion that "race" might be a matter of public concern. The 1995 omnibus crime bill, for example (one of the few issues related to poor people of color where the state is still *willing* to spend money), could not even bear a whisper on behalf of racial justice in its repudiation of the justice-in-sentencing provision for death-row prisoners who are disproportionately black. Meanwhile, the state of California, already in the forefront of anti-immigrant hysteria, now stands poised to overturn all forms of affirmative action to the applause of America's pundits. In a stunning turnabout, today *antiracism* is depicted as something akin to the boy who cried wolf, while *anti-antiracism* has become the sheep's clothing of "common sense" and fair play.

In the face of these influential and popular formulations, even our most articulate and empowered spokespersons have been reduced to making tepid pleas to what is left of the liberal conscience that "race matters."[12] I do not necessarily fault these efforts. They are an attempt, however insufficient, to hold the line against the combined assaults of neoliberal social policy and neoracist common sense that have accumulated over the past two decades. Nonetheless, it is quite clear that a great deal more needs to be said and done. In Harold Cruse's words, the "crisis in black and white" is still a crisis of social theory, although today it is also a crisis of politics and one of memory.[13] The political demand for color-blindness, heard from all quarters of American public opinion today, is a demand to *erase the memory of the struggles against racism*; it is also an inadvertently apt description of how racism itself persists in all its forms, in ways we often have difficulty *identifying*. But let us make no mistake: right now we are in the midst of what Mike Davis correctly views as the most "drastic devaluation" of the citizenship of poor people of color in the United States since the end of Reconstruction, as what is left of the welfare state is slowly absorbed "by the police state."[14] In the face of this, there is little in the way of an effective antiracist challenge in sight.

It is in this sense that I argue that the racial "crisis" that characterizes our own moment should be understood, at least in part, as an impasse of antiracism as a political project. Before going any further, I would like to say a few things about the word *crisis* itself as a way of describing America's racial predicament. Crisis generally refers to a moment of exceptional or extraordinary danger. Yet when we recognize just how regularly it appears as the defining term within discussions of "race" in America—Du Bois's or Cruse's or our own—then we must ask ourselves why we persist in believing that it effectively defines or differentiates any one of these moments. The term *crisis* implies that a situation of normality exists *in comparison*, either as a precedent or as an expected resolution lying in wait in the future. Racism, however, as something that disrupts, dismembers, and disfigures black life worlds in America is, as Derrick Bell puts it, a "permanent" feature of U.S. society, constitutive of its normal reality and comprising its normative history.[15] Paradoxically, the term *crisis*, as one that denotes a historically exceptional circumstance, is a remarkably *ahistorical* way of depicting the dilemmas of black politics and theory. Here, again, the crisis is not the exception but the rule.

Yet, while racism and the racial crisis are not exceptional, they have not been unchanging. Rather, they have been shaped by both organic and conjunctural social processes that have produced dramatic changes in the nature and scope of racial ideologies and significant changes in the social relations of "dominant and subordinate social groups who recognize themselves in terms of 'race.'"[16] The point that needs emphasizing is that racism, and hence the notion of race itself, is historically produced. Contemporary racial discourse binds together the legacies of racism and antiracism in structuring racial identities and the forms and horizons of social struggle. Antiracism, in this sense, must also be understood as a "permanent" feature of American life, comprising *a history of continuous struggle*, beginning with the efforts to abolish racial slavery, against the just as continuous and perhaps more forceful reinventions of racism in the twentieth century. Indeed, antiracism might actually be the one *indispensable* feature of every significant progressive social struggle that has occurred in the United States. It has, for example, been central, to a greater and lesser extent, within every significant invention and reinvention of American radicalism, including abolitionism, feminism, populism, and in various ways helped to pave the way for the rise of the C.I.O., the Popular Front, the New Left, and the cultural struggles for radical democracy in our own time.[17]

In its current incarnation, however, antiracism is an increasingly inadequate frame, too thinly descriptive and too narrowly construed to encompass the ways in which the struggles against racism have informed emancipatory politics and provided a rich source of radical meaning and history, theory, and practice over the past two centuries.[18] In its contemporary guise, antiracism is presented simply as a *negation* of the political and institutional structures of discrimination that comprise a given racist complex, frequently in the name of "color-blind" universalism, citizenship, and equality. This form of antiracism, which I call *antiracist universalism*, tends prematurely to dissolve race in its earnest desire to transcend racism. Indeed, this form of antiracism has frequently had great difficulty distinguishing its attacks on the color line from its discomfort and even antipathy toward the real objects of racial discrimination. What antiracist universalism has had the hardest time coming to terms with is the legacy of racially coded difference itself. Failing to eradicate this difference once and for all, its bewildered idealism often turns into vengeful resentment against those who initially evoked concern. Thus, in the end, even the most well-intentioned proponents of this position have turned against it, implicitly or explicitly reproducing the oppressive interrogative long at the center of America's relation to its black people, namely, "How does it feel to be [the] problem?"[19]

The bind that is presented to those who remain committed to antiracist politics is that antiracist universalism today has passed into anti-antiracism, and even postracism. When arch-conservatives can announce (in the past tense, of course) that the "one real success of modern liberalism was its opposition to segregation, and its support of the Civil Rights Movement and decolonization,"[20] then it should be clear that the resources of antiracist universalism have been largely exhausted and denuded of their critical power.[21] Indeed, this was prophesied over forty years ago by Ralph Ellison in his incisive critique of Gunnar Myrdal's *American Dilemma: The Negro Problem and Modern Democracy*, still the definitive instance of post-WWII antiracist universalism. As Ellison pointed out, Myrdal and others who proposed that the "American Creed" held all the solutions to the problem of racism and racial subjection operated under the arrogant delusion of what Frantz Fanon called "unilateral decrees of universality."[22] As a result, they could scarcely apprehend the fact that black people, in Ellison's words, had "made a life on the horns of the white man's dilemma."[23]

Myrdal, for example, argued that the "Negro Problem" was a great stain on the American democratic fabric, echoing earlier critiques of slavery as a "peculiar" rather than the defining institution of the American Republic. Furthermore, he maintained that the postwar situation made it imperative that the United States finally complete "the main trend in its history," or "the gradual realization of the American Creed," in order to assume its proper role as world leader.[24] According to Myrdal, the "American Creed" was the Americanization of the Enlightenment legacy, or the defense of human universality, equality, and formal freedom. Far from disproving the notion that the Enlightenment had entered a glorious new incarnation with the advent of the "American Century,"[25] the "Negro Problem" was the single glaring *exception* to the otherwise justifiable claim of the United States to be (as Myrdal put it) "humanity in miniature."[26] Ironically, while mounting what was at the time a remarkably comprehensive critique of segregation and discrimination, the very occasion of *An American Dilemma* was intended to prove that America contained their transcendence.[27] At the same time, and this is what irked Ellison, the Hegelian reading of United States history as essentially integrationist completely elided the complex and enduring centrality of black presence and expressive culture in the United States, *in spite of* American racism, not to mention the American Creed.

Ellison recognized that "double vision [w]as the necessary antidote to the double-consciousness imposed on African-Americans" by American racism.[28] As Du Bois had demonstrated so powerfully in 1903, American racism has always presented a double bind for African Americans, negating black humanity in both assimilationist and segregationist accents: *today's appeal to be color-blind and yesterday's enforcement of the color line*. Ellison understood that in order to be effective antiracism could not rely on strategies of transcendence but needed to subvert and transform the structure of the double bind itself. At his most subversive he saw that antiracism had to develop an immanent critique of American claims to universality and the implicit and explicit forms of racism it upheld. Ellison's insights can thus lead to a more radical conception of antiracism skeptical of the claims of antiracist universalism, and especially its promise of color-blind citizenship. While not necessarily renouncing the practical humanist goals associated with the latter, *radical antiracism* also addresses itself to what Ellison called the "blackness of blackness" and to the fact that the problem of the color line invariably raises the question of human emancipation in its broadest, most universal aspects.[29]

Ellison's cultural elitism and his embrace of American exceptionalism, often related in a condensed form in his political and aesthetic disagreements with the left wing and more overtly political black writers like Richard Wright, has tended to obscure the fact that he presented what was perhaps the most profound and devastating critique of the ascendancy of antiracist universalism available from within the confines of cold war America. At the height of the cold war, however, with black radical leaders like Paul Robeson and W. E. B. Du Bois held in a state of virtual confinement and under strict surveillance because of their Communist affiliations, it was Wright and not Ellison who most thoroughly developed the political implications of this position and the "double vision" necessary to uphold it.[30] "Isn't it clear to you," Wright asked defiantly from his own self-imposed exile in France, "that the American Negro is the only group in our nation that consistently and passionately raises the question of freedom?" He added, "The voice of the American Negro is rapidly becoming the most representative voice of America and of oppressed people anywhere in the world."[31] Finally, in an ironic formulation, Wright inverted the emphasis of *An American Dilemma*, casting the problem of universality from the vantage point of the black, the oppressed, and the unfree. "The history of the Negro in America," he summarized, "is the history of America written in vivid and bloody terms . . . the history of Western Man writ small. . . . *The Negro is America's metaphor.*"[32]

Wright's and Ellison's midcentury (re)formulations of antiracist universalism are important because they come at perhaps the most significant juncture in the history of the modern American "racial formation" and are sophisticated reflections on the problem of antiracism in our own time.[33] What is worth remembering—and what I want to emphasize here—is that in its current dominant form antiracist universalism is primarily a product of the immediate post-WWII period and the cold war that followed. Indeed, I would argue that the postwar period might be characterized in its entirety by the combined and uneven efforts on the part of the corporate-liberal state, in dialogue and in struggle with antiracist movements, to (re)construct American nationality on a nonracial basis. The postimperial geopolitical ambitions of the "American Century" and the domestic imperative to eradicate the "American Dilemma," as Newt Gingrich has astutely recognized, have, in other words, been intimately bound up with one another. This period marks the formal dismantling of American apartheid, in law and in official state practice, as well as the mass organization of black and white Americans in antiracist social movements. The last fifty years have witnessed an "expenditure of immense psychic, political and intellectual energy" in an effort to make the "Negro problem," and hence the "Negro," disappear.[34] The unstable, nominal fulfillment of this process, emblematized in the achievement of the preferred, ostensibly "ethnic" rather than "racial" name *African American,* telescopes a profoundly complex and ambiguous series of transformations.[35]

The current impasse of antiracism as a political project, in other words, is not simply a result of the explicit Reagan era attacks on the legacies of the racial liberalism of the 1960s but an outgrowth of the initial, highly contradictory efforts of the Keynesian welfare state to resolve the so-called American dilemma between the 1940s and the late 1960s. The fact is that post-WWII social policy around "race" was a mass of failures and contradictions. The national-symbolic impetus toward desegregation in the military and the schools, for example, coexisted with the state's underwriting of a geography of apartheid (euphemistically called suburbanization) that provided one of the important material underpinnings for the contemporary racist complex.[36] Meanwhile, the cold war, despite the pressure it exerted to end European colonialism and to reform the national image abroad, principally acted as a screen for the institution of the global political and economic prerogatives of the United States and for the (re)imposition of domestic hierarchies.[37] Not the least of the effects of this was the pacification of militant trade unionism, the defeat of the C.I.O., and the dissolution of the promise that the unparalleled, sustained economic growth that was the central feature of this period would also result in the integration of a permanent black working-class population into the productive and distributive circuits of the U.S. economy.[38]

In this context Wright's conclusion that the "Negro is America's metaphor" contains a profound insight, namely, that the symbolic and

thematic centrality of "racial" division in America consistently under-
writes the characteristic forms of political domination in American society, specifically the concrete marginalization of actual black people. Indeed,
as recent work on blackface minstrelsy shows, the elaborate metaphoriza-
tion and consumption of blackness in American popular culture by white
performers and audiences has actually been a persistent mechanism
through which racial hierarchy, social distance, and economic accumulation have been secured and recognized and, at the same time, disavowed
and concealed.[39] Ironically, the rendering of the Negro Problem in the
United States as the American dilemma possesses a similar structure, reen-
acting what may be the most characteristic form of American racism since
the Early Republic, in which the "Negro" becomes simultaneously the em-
bodiment and the disfiguration of America's democratic dreams and pretensions.[40] The figuration of the dilemma (like the aforementioned crisis)
thus paradoxically shores up, and even consolidates, America's (implicitly white) *self-identity*, while the "Negro" (recalling Fanon once again) exists as the degraded currency of the "comparison."[41] This remains as true
today as at any other time in American history—in spite of formal equality—as an unmistakably racial discourse about crime and welfare is at the
center of political reflections and judgments about the state of American
society, even for those who loudly proclaim that "race" doesn't matter. To
this Wright would have offered the following rejoinder: there has never
been a "Negro problem" in America, only a "white problem."[42]

What might be most important about the 1960s is that it represented a
series of attempts to transform the normative staging of race within American culture. As Wright anticipated, the extension of the metaphorical va-
lences of black struggles beyond the United States had, in fact, strained the
nation form, and with it the self-assurances of American self-identity. For
a time, at least, it seemed as though black people in struggle had seized
control of "racial" assets, the fund of metaphor, symbolism, and imagery
that have always been central to the construction of American peoplehood, wrenching, if not rupturing, the self-containing, self-perpetuating
logic of America's dilemma. From James Brown's galvanizing "Say it
Loud, I'm Black and I'm Proud" to the redolent phrase "Black is Beautiful," to the startling imagery of bare feet and black fists raised in protest
at the Mexico Olympic Games, to the oxymoronic saliency of the Black
Power concept itself, the cultural politics of the 1960s were thus centered
around a series of dramatic and potentially liberatory transvaluations of
the signifying content of blackness.[43] Policy elites and official commenta-

tors, for example, noted with alarm the fact that the sixties "black movement had as surprising a resonance abroad as at home."[44] While, at home,
black struggles were the basis for a different kind of comparison, becoming the "trigger struggle," or switch point, for a host of other minority discourses and contestations and a relay station for emancipatory impulses
of decolonization from around the world.[45] In the end, it is this uniquely
subversive, insistently traumatizing legacy that has been the least understood, and most devalued, in the revisionism that characterizes the current conjuncture. At the same time, this legacy remains to a greater and
lesser degree most alive in the racial politics of cultural performance and
in the critical reworking of antiracist theory and practice today.[46]

Of course, I don't want to completely downplay the immense struggles
against Jim Crow in the South during this period, but I think it is important that we acknowledge that the central achievement of the civil rights
movement, namely, the formal conquest of citizenship rights by African
Americans, appears in retrospect to be something of a Pyrrhic victory.
This was recognized by civil rights activists working in the South relatively early on as nonviolent efforts to expand black voting power were
thwarted in Birmingham, Albany, and by the national Democratic Party
machine.[47] It became even more apparent once the movement began to
confront the more durable and immovable obstacles of de facto apartheid
in northern cities and suburbs. This has become even clearer today as
whatever value accrues to formal citizenship is depreciated under the
pressures of inegalitarian deficit reduction and remanded under the aus-
pices of excessive policing and punishment. If the civil rights era was
characterized by struggles *over the terms* of black assimilation into the
American polity and its public spheres (including various black nationalist and revolutionary positions that contested the unilateral lure of assimilation as a ruse and a trap), the post–civil rights era has given way to a
paradoxical process. On the one hand, the past thirty years has resulted in
the growth of a sizable (if not entirely stable) black "middle class," comprising anywhere from 30 percent to 50 percent of America's black population.[48] At the same time, this period has witnessed the structural and
political reconstitution of racial alterity through the decimation of urban
aid programs and the concomitant expansion of a prison-industrial-
complex.[49] The ideological mirror and justification for the latter processes is the ever renewable figure from the American national imaginary
of the black "anticitizenry," today populated by criminals, drug users,
predatory youth, teen mothers, and "welfare queens."[50]

The most farseeing theoreticians of Black Power foresaw many of these developments, understanding that symbolic equality would provide little genuine sustenance for working-class racial migrants and do little to counteract the ravages of "racial capitalism" that had already systematically "underdeveloped" black America.[51] Even as the legal edifice of segregation was being dismantled by government decree (beginning as early as the end of World War II), a much more enduring and pervasive structure of spatial apartheid was being inscribed into the social landscape as the divide between urban ghettos and suburban idyll.[52] As Jim Crow subjugated blacks in the South, the 1.5 million black migrants who came North between 1900 and 1950 had their life chances curtailed and confined by "a hardening color line in employment, education, and especially housing," a division violently enforced by riot, pogrom, and hate strike.[53] Moreover, while white communal violence was central to the initial construction of black ghettos in urban areas, their perpetuation and extension since World War II has been carried out by more "civilized" means and with possibly greater consequences. I am referring to the familiar story of "red-lining," restrictive covenants, and "neighborhood improvement associations," the impact of which has never been sufficiently calculated. What might even be more startling about the post-WWII period, however, is the degree to which the Federal government itself, acting according to principles formulated under the New Deal, actually promoted and subsidized the massive expansion and elaboration of the racial geography that defines the U.S. today.[54]

The current tendency to dismiss or repudiate what are often deemed the excesses of Black Power in the 1960s occurs without an attempt to adequately theorize or historicize the black radicalism of the sixties in light of the social transformations characteristic of the post-WWII racist complex.[55] The most radical instances of Black Power rhetoric—for example, declarations like "the city is the black man's land" or variations on the idea of the black ghetto as an "internal colony" of the United States— might actually be seen as entirely prescient and real responses to an existing situation.[56] No migrant group has experienced the depth and duration of residential segregation that has been imposed upon black internal migrants within the United States. Although black militants during the sixties may have made seemingly contradictory demands that the state underwrite greater black inclusion in the polity by enlarging the black share of the social surplus, while at the same time emphasizing their own categorical opposition and apartness from the dominant public sphere (Black

Power's "double-vision," perhaps), it seems clear (especially in light of the sorry tale of "urban renewal" and black-led city government) that the most interesting and creative instances of Black Power grew out of a justified and widespread feeling that formal state-sanctioned channels of racial redress had been exhausted.

To take the Black Panther Party as an example: while it may be that it was the very possibility of state-aided integration and assimilation into the polity (i.e., the Civil Rights and Voting Rights Acts as well as the "War on Poverty") that gave such a powerful charge to their refusals and contestations,[57] the Panthers' dramatic performance of their own noncitizenship, and even anticitizenship (especially their open resistance to policing), necessarily implied a wholly different region of identification. The emphasis on "power," "community control," and the like then, as vague and ill-defined as these notions often were, were nonetheless meaningful responses to what Eldridge Cleaver cleverly disparaged as the hypocritical half-hearted attempt "to citizenize the Negro."[58] More than anything else, the Panthers and others resignified "blackness" in all its geopolitical and intrapsychic density. Indeed, I would argue that the party's much discussed and often criticized emphasis on "violence" may actually have more to do with its repudiation of the violence that came with the imperative of black assimilation itself, namely, the internalization of the frontiers of the nation and an "inhabiting of the space of the state" as the place where black people "have always been—and always will be at home."[59] This was essentially the argument of *An American Dilemma* and the intellectual foundation of a modern civil rights discourse that posited the end of racism as the telos of American history. Yet it is this kind of faulty historicism that cripples us whenever we try to come to terms with "the time of the now" or the spatial strategies of the contemporary racist complex that hollow out the meaning and substance of black nationality and citizenship in the United States today.[60]

This said, I would not necessarily want to defend the internal colony thesis as an answer to the contemporary incarnation of America's racial "crisis." Indeed, if there is a flaw in the notion that the ghetto is an internal colony, it is that its prospects for "liberation" and "self-determination" seem slim, if not already co-opted by New Right discourses about "enterprise zones," tight discipline, and low-wage austerity as the preconditions for urban aid and the promise of future development. As James Blaut suggests, the structural ghettoization of racial and/or colonial migrants in the U.S. might be more fruitfully considered as a kind of internal *neocolonialism* or, perhaps more accurately still, as the internalization of neocolonialism. Although ghettoized areas lack the ability to press for self-determination as "formal politico-geographic units," like neocolonies all over the world, the issue of self-determination is moot, as it has provided few, if any, answers to the relations of exploitation and oppression that continue to underdevelop some parts of the world and overdevelop others.[61] What the internalization of neocolonialism reveals is that the nation-states of the Enlightenment are places where the idea of common citizenship no longer seems to hold sway (if, indeed, it ever did). The world today, as Etienne Balibar writes, is now revealed as one that is "traversed by a shifting frontier—irreducible to the frontier between states—between two humanities which seem incommensurable, namely the humanity of destitution and that of 'consumption,' the humanity of underdevelopment and that of overdevelopment."[62]

What I would emphasize is that just as there was an ongoing relationship between decolonization and antiracist universalism during the cold war, there is currently a relationship between the reconstruction of forms of neocolonial and postcolonial domination in the world system and neoracist and postracist domination within the United States. In fact, I would go so far as to say that the entire period since 1945 marks the general extension of an American model of imperialism that has from the outset been built upon the premise of free trade, open markets, and internal colonization—one of the reasons why it has been and remains so difficult to name. The advantage of the internal colonization perspectives developed during the 1960s is not that they are accurate in every historical or sociological detail but that they accurately depict a world in which uneven development and racially defined subordination and oppression coincide. These relations, moreover, have been spatially and temporally defined, as ghettoized areas are excluded from sharing in social surpluses, the site of superexploitation, underemployment, and "underdevelopment," and become points of maximum displacement of official and unofficial forms of social violence. Du Bois himself recognized this connection at the onset of the American Century when he argued that Europe's own "colonies" were, in effect, "the slums of the world."[63]

The shift to varied terrains of cultural politics and the intensification of the "culture wars" since the 1960s is at least in part the result of the profound disorganization of progressive political forces and a reflection of widespread despair about meaningful political options at the tail end of the American Century, which is also the era of transnational capitalism.

Progressive cultural politics and cultural struggle, however, must be theorized in relation to the many insights of the Black Power period. Indeed, I would argue it has primarily been through the agency of feminist and antihomophobic *critiques* of Black Power that it is once again possible to understand black liberation in the terms put forth by C. L. R. James in the epigraph to this essay—namely, not as an isolated, or self-contained, political struggle but as a universal one. As we reinvent an effective antiracism today (out of what I hope I've shown are ample insights from the past), we must draw from the resources inherent within those universalities that present themselves as alternatives to a capitalism that today unilaterally declares its own, even as it everywhere "radiates disaster triumphant."[64] In the face of this there can be no retreat into a narrow politics of nationalism. A sectarian black nationalism, in particular, while providing what are in many ways the simplest responses to the sustained attack on "race" as a meaningful political category, holds few answers to the living complexities of racial subordination today.

Finally, I believe that effective political struggles must relink antiracist theory and practice to the rethinking of the thresholds of citizenship and "nationality" in the international arena, through a politics of human rights, and in subnational, local, and institutional spaces of the nation-state: the housing project, school, and prison. At the same time, we must recognize that the contemporary racist complex appears not only as a spatial order but as a crisis of public spending, one that consistently presents itself in "racial" guises as questions of "illegality" and "welfare." Today a line is being drawn through the very concept of citizenship itself, and black people are not the only ones cast out of the net, only to be represented as subcitizens; so are newer immigrants, poor women, the homeless, the sick, and "deviant." In keeping with the call for doubled and redoubled vision, we must also fight today for a robust concept of social citizenship, one that is not dictated by imagined fiscal constraints and finance capital but by and for ourselves. In this struggle the intellectual and political resources of antiracism are indispensable, and still requisite to a belief in humanity.

Notes

A version of this essay was previously published in Ned Landsman et al., *Beyond Pluralism* (University of Illinois Press, 1998).

1. George Sheperson, "Notes on Negro American Influences on the Emergence of African Nationalism," *Journal of African History*, vol. 1, no. 2 (1960), p. 307.

2. W. E. B. Du Bois, *Souls of Black Folk* (New York: Vintage, 1990), p. 4.

3. W. E. B. Du Bois, *W. E. B. Du Bois Speaks: Speeches and Addresses, 1890–1919*, ed. Phillip Foner (New York: Pathfinder, 1970), p. 84.

4. Wilson Moses, *The Golden Age of Black Nationalism* (New York: Oxford University Press, 1987); and Albert Murray, *The Omni Americans: Black Experience and American Culture* (New York: Da Capo, 1970), p. 22.

5. Du Bois, *Souls of Black Folk*, p. 4.

6. Manning Marable, *Race, Reform, and Rebellion: The Second Reconstruction in Black America, 1945–1982* (Jackson: University Press of Mississippi, 1984).

7. Here I am paraphrasing Walter Benjamin's "Theses on the Philosophy of History." "The tradition of the oppressed," Benjamin writes, "teaches us that the 'state of emergency' (i.e., the 'crisis') in which we live is not the exception but the rule. We must attain to a conception of history that is in keeping with this insight. . . . The current amazement that the things we are experiencing are 'still' possible in the twentieth century is not philosophical. This amazement is not the beginning of knowledge—unless it is the knowledge that the view of history which gives rise to it is untenable." Walter Benjamin, *Illuminations*, ed. Hannah Arendt (New York: Schocken, 1969), p. 257.

8. William Julius Wilson, *The Declining Significance of Race: Black Politics and Changing American Institutions* (Chicago: University of Chicago Press, 1980).

9. Thomas Byrne Edsall and Mary D. Edsall, *Chain Reaction* (New York: Norton, 1991). See also David Roediger's useful critique of these positions in "The Racial Crisis of American Liberalism," in his *Toward the Abolition of Whiteness* (New York: Verso, 1994), p. 122.

10. As Antonin Scalia stated in his opinion overturning state-based redistricting efforts to ensure black political representation: "In the eyes of government, we are just one race here. It is American." This formulation is perhaps most reminiscent of the Americanization rhetoric of the WWI era. Quoted in Jeffrey Rosen, "The Color-Blind Court," *New Republic*, July 31, 1995, pp. 19–25.

11. The notion of postracism is alluded to but not fully explained in a provocative aside by Etienne Balibar. Etienne Balibar and Immanuel Wallerstein, *Race, Nation, Class: Ambiguous Identities* (New York: Verso, 1991), p. 9. Manning Marable has also attempted to describe this phenomenon under the rubric "non-racist racism." See Marable, *The Crisis of Color and Democracy: Essays on Race, Class, and Power* (Monroe, Me.: Common Courage, 1992).

12. Cornel West, *Race Matters* (Boston: Beacon, 1993).

13. Harold Cruse, *Rebellion or Revolution* (New York: William Morrow, 1968), p. 27.

14. Mike Davis, "Who Killed L.A.? Political Autopsy," *New Left Review*, no. 197 (1993), p. 25.

15. Derrick Bell, *Faces at the Bottom of the Well: The Permanence of Racism* (New York: Basic, 1992).

16. Paul Gilroy, "One Nation Under a Groove," in David Theo Goldberg, ed., *Anatomy of Racism* (New York: Routledge, 1990), p. 263.

17. This point is developed in an exemplary manner by C. L. R. James in his until recently unpublished manuscript from 1950, *American Civilization* (London: Basil Blackwell, 1994), from which I have taken my first epigraph.

18. See, for example, Paul Gilroy's powerful critique of a simple form of antiracism as it has been developed in England, "The End of Anti-Racism," in James Donald and Ali Rattansi, eds., *"Race" Culture and Difference* (Newbury Park, Cal.: Sage, 1992). As Gilroy writes (in a formulation that echoes James in remarkable ways), "The anti-racism I am criticizing trivializes the struggle against racism and isolates it from other political antagonisms—from the contradiction between capital and labor, from the battle between men and women. It suggests that racism can be eliminated on its own because it is readily extricable from everything else" (193).

19. This is, of course, the famous query with which Du Bois begins *Souls*.

20. Newt Gingrich, "New York City Address," Hilton Hotel, March 24, 1995.

21. I do not, however, mean to suggest that overt forms of formal white supremacy and racial hatred have disappeared. If anything, the racist wing of the burgeoning militia movement and the recent round of black church burnings suggest the contrary. The point is that the "official" condemnations of this sort of activity are now always already in place.

22. Frantz Fanon, *Toward the African Revolution* (New York: Grove Press, 1967), p. 31.

23. Ralph Ellison, *Shadow and Act* (New York: Signet, 1963), p. 301.

24. Gunnar Myrdal, *An American Dilemma: The Negro Problem and Modern Democracy*, vol. 1 (New York: Pantheon, 1944), p. 3.

25. The "American Century" in my usage essentially applies to the brief but explosive decades after World War II dominated by an expanding, globally influential and domestically prosperous corporate-liberal American state. In my view the American Century lasts roughly from 1945–1973. The reasons for its eclipse are too complex to detail here. Suffice it to say, this period is marked by the global ascendancy of U.S. monopoly capitalism, the dismantling of most of the old European colonial empires, and the "virtuous circle" of intensive accumulation and domestic economic growth and prosperity within the U.S. itself. The term, of course, was first coined by Time, Inc. chairman Henry Luce, in 1941. Also see Michel Aglietta, *A Theory of Capitalist Regulation: The U.S. Experience* (London: Verso, 1979).

26. Gunnar Myrdal, *An American Dilemma: The Negro Problem and Modern Democracy*, vol. 2 (New York: Pantheon, 1944), p. 1022.

27. Frederick Keppel, representing the Carnegie Foundation, the sponsors of the study, argued that "to review the most serious race problem in

the country is an idea singularly American." *An American Dilemma,* 1: xlviii.

28. T. V. Reed, *Fifteen Jugglers and Five Believers: The Literary Politics of Social Movements* (Berkeley: University of California Press, 1993), p. 58.

29. See the interesting discussion of Ellison's cultural politics in Reed's *Fifteen Jugglers and Five Believers,* p. 65. One of the most succinct articulations of "double-vision" during this period was offered by the great black composer Duke Ellington, who in 1944 called upon black people to embrace a "strategy of dissonance." For black people, as Ellington put it, "Dissonance is our way of life in America, we are something apart; yet an integral part." Mark Tucker, ed., *The Duke Ellington Reader* (New York: Random House, 1994).

30. In fact, the idea of "double vision," as Paul Gilroy tells us, was actually Wright's reformulation of Du Bois's notion of "double-consciousness." I am suggesting, however, that in spite of Ellison's Americocentrism, and his desire to distance himself from Wright, the two men were in many ways much closer than is often apparent today. See Paul Gilroy, *The Black Atlantic: Modernity and Double-Consciousness* (Cambridge: Harvard University Press, 1994).

31. Richard Wright, *White Man Listen!* (New York: Anchor, 1957), p. 101.

32. Ibid., p. 72 (my emphasis).

33. The concept of racial formation comes from Michael Omi and Howard Winant, *Racial Formation in the United States* (New York: Routledge, 1986).

34. I am indebted here to Cedric Robinson's felicitous phrasing, used in a different context to describe the historical *creation* of blackness: "The creation of the Negro was obviously at the cost of immense expenditures of psychic and intellectual energies in the West." Cedric Robinson, *Black Marxism* (London: Zed, 1983), p. 5.

35. I would suggest that African American as a substitute for "Negro," or "black," is a part of a normative post-WWII process of ethnicization. In other words, it is an attempt (however fraught) to fold "racial" difference into a concept of ethnicity, by substituting a signifier of geographic/national difference for the signifiers of "racial" difference. A uniquely American neologism, ethnicity in this sense should be understood as the preferred concept for describing relative difference, a kind of difference that ultimately doesn't threaten the overall integrity and coherence of properly national belonging or contradict the imperative of assimilation. Of course, the designation *African,* as it is placed in front of the dominative *American,* can still only satisfy this imperative in partial and ambivalent ways in the context of the ongoing underdevelopment of Africa within the world system.

36. See Douglas Massey and Nancy Denton, *American Apartheid: Segregation and the Making of the Underclass* (Cambridge: Harvard University Press, 1993); and Mike Davis, *City of Quartz* (New York: Verso, 1990). It is

probably time I defined what I mean by racist complex. Following Balibar, there are three interdependent phenomena that comprise a given racist complex: a conception of history, or what he calls a "historiosophy," a social and material structure of discrimination, and a set of relations to identity constituting institutions (i.e., the national state). Modern suburbia encompasses all three, with its there-goes-the-neighborhood rationalization of white flight, its concrete forms of racial value coding or discrimination (home ownership, taxation subsidies, infrastructural investment, and zoning restrictions), and its ongoing vexed relationship with central state authority whenever the latter does not uphold the interests of what is imagined to be the "suburban nation" (namely, spending tax dollars on the urban poor, i.e., blacks, Latinos, etc.). Etienne Balibar, "Migrants and Racism," *New Left Review*, vol. 186 (1993), p. 11.

37. Among the many useful works I have relied upon for thinking about cold war hierarchies, domestic and global, are Mike Davis, *Prisoners of the American Dream* (New York: Verso, 1984); George Lipsitz, *A Rainbow at Midnight: Class and Culture in Cold War America* (Bloomington: Indiana University Press, 1994); L. S. Stavrianos, *Global Rift: The Third World Comes of Age* (New York: William Morrow, 1981); Joel Kovel, *Red Hunting in the Promised Land* (New York: Basic, 1994); and Gerald Horne, *Black and Red: W. E. B. Du Bois and the Afro-American Response to the Cold War* (Albany: SUNY Press, 1986).

38. In light of this, C. L. R. James's insight from 1948 can only be viewed as prophetic: "The independent Negro Movement must find its way to the proletariat. . . . If the proletariat is defeated, if the CIO is destroyed, then there will fall upon the Negro people in the U.S. such repression, such persecution, comparable to nothing they have seen in the past. We have seen in Germany and elsewhere the barbarism that capitalism is capable of in its death agony." C. L. R. James, "The Revolutionary Answer to the Negro Question in the United States," in *The C. L. R. James Reader*, ed. Grimshaw (London: Basil Blackwell, 1992), p. 188.

39. Eric Lott, *Love and Theft: Blackface Minstrelsey and the American Working Class* (New York: Oxford University Press, 1993); David Roediger, *The Wages of Whiteness: Race and the Making of the American Working Class* (New York: Verso, 1991); and Alexander Saxton, *The Rise and Fall of the White Republic* (New York: Verso, 1990).

40. As Balibar argues (following Jacques Derrida), racism is the supplement of nationalism. Hence my argument, glossing Wright, is that the "Negro" is America's supplement, which is to say that which makes possible, and yet at the same time threatens to undo, the position of the dominative citizen-subject of the United States. Blackness in America, in other words, has been constituted as the boundary of hegemonic citizenship, serving as both its limit and condition. This is what Balibar defines under the rubric of the "paradoxes of universality," which is something that Ellison, Du Bois, and Wright

each grasped in their own way long ago. See Balibar and Wallerstein, *Race, Nation, Class*, p. 97.

41. Frantz Fanon, *Black Skins, White Masks* (New York: Grove, 1967), p. 211. I am indebted to David Lloyd, "Race Under Representation," *Oxford Literary Review*, vol. 13, no. 1–2 (1991), pp. 63–94, for this insight.

42. Wright, *White Man Listen!* p. 99.

43. Kobena Mercer, "1968: Periodizing Politics and Identity," in Lawrence Grossberg and Cary Nelson, eds., *Cultural Studies* (New York: Routledge, 1992), pp. 424–449. As James Brown recalls, "In 1968, after I came out with 'Say it Loud, I'm Black and I'm Proud,' it was all over. The dark-skinned man had all of a sudden become a cosmopolitan." See James Brown and Bruce Tucker, *James Brown, the Godfather of Soul* (London: Fontana and Collins, 1988), p. 124. Following upon this, we might see 1968 as a moment when "blackness" as a sign of oppositionality and resistance "travels" literally and figuratively in unprecedented ways. Yet, as Mercer cautions, the circulation of a revalued blackness was by no means restricted to the province of oppositional politics. After all, 1968 was also the year that James Brown accepted an invitation to play at Richard Nixon's inauguration, assented to Nixon's description of Black Power as "black capitalism," and allied himself with the state's own engagement in the struggle to define difference, so as to relocate, and in effect domesticate, its potentially insurgent movement.

44. These are the words of Daniel Patrick Moynihan, who did more than any other policy analyst or scholar-pundit to lay the public policy groundwork for the racist reaction that effectively ended the Second Reconstruction. Quoted in Sheila Collins, *The Rainbow Challenge: The Jackson Campaign and the Future of U.S. Politics* (New York: Monthly Review, 1986), p. 57.

45. R. Radhakrishnan, "Toward an Effective Intellectual—Foucault or Gramsci," in Bruce Robbins, ed., *Intellectuals, Aesthetics, Politics, and Culture* (Minneapolis: University of Minnesota Press, 1990), p. 59. Radhakrishnan credits Jesse Jackson with formulating the idea that black struggles in America are "trigger struggles." According to him, Jackson's vision of a rainbow coalition pointed to the possibility of moving beyond a politics of discrete representation and alliance to the articulation of a new "oppositional bloc," which is close to my view of a robust antiracism at the center of the reinvention of political radicalism in the United States. Clearly, there are also more explicit links to the late 1960s contained in this idea, especially considering that the first notion of a "rainbow coalition" was not Jackson's but Black Panther leader Fred Hampton's. Hampton developed a coalition between the Puerto Rican Young Lords, the Young Patriots (a white youth gang), the SDS, and the Black Panther Party in Chicago—a promising moment in the late 1960s, worth reconsidering. Hampton was, of course, murdered by the Chicago police a few months later. See my "Black Liberation in the Theater of Nationality: The Black Panthers and the 'Undeveloped Coun-

try' of the Left," in Charles E. Jones, ed., *The Black Panther Party Reconsidered: Reflections and Scholarship* (Baltimore: Black Classic, 1998).

46. I am thinking of the work of scholars far too numerous to name here but centering around innovative efforts at rethinking questions of "race" that have emerged from cultural studies. Following upon the pathbreaking work of Stuart Hall, and the so-called Birmingham School, this group includes Paul Gilroy, Andrew Ross, Eric Lott, Tricia Rose, Hazel Carby, and bell hooks.

47. Clayborne Carson, *In Struggle: SNCC and the Black Awakening of the 1960s* (Cambridge: Harvard University Press, 1981).

48. For the statistics and outlook of the new black middle class see the special issue of the *New Yorker*, "Black in America," April 29 and May 6, 1996. See also Manning Marable, "The Paradox of Integration: Black Society and Politics in the Post-Reform Period, 1982–1990," in Marable, *Race, Reform and Rebellion*.

49. Mike Davis points out that the 64 percent cutback in Federal aid to cities since the 1980s, combined with postsixties white flight, suburbanization, and the production of so-called edge economies, has intensified conditions of unemployment and underdevelopment affecting black urban dwellers, producing conditions of "spatial apartheid." See Davis, "Who Killed L.A.?" p. 14.

50. The notion of black people as "anti-citizens . . . enemies rather than members of the social compact," comes from David Roediger's fine work. See Roediger, *The Wages of Whiteness*, p. 57.

51. See Robinson's *Black Marxism* for the notion of "racial capitalism"; also see Manning Marable, *How Capitalism Underdeveloped Black America: Problems in Race, Political Economy, and Society* (Boston: South End, 1983).

52. Davis, *City of Quartz*, ch. 3.

53. Massey and Denton, *American Apartheid*, p. 30.

54. George Lipsitz, "The Possessive Investment in Whiteness," *American Quarterly*, vol. 47, no. 2. I have also relied upon Kenneth Jackson, *Crabgrass Frontier: The Suburbanization of the United States* (New York: Oxford University Press, 1985); and Massey and Denton, *American Apartheid*, especially chapter 2, "The Construction of the Ghetto," pp. 17–59.

55. One of the most egregious examples of this is Hugh Pearson, *In the Shadow of the Panther: Huey Newton and the Price of Black Power in America* (New York: Addison-Wesley, 1994).

56. James Boggs and Grace Lee Boggs, "The City Is the Black Man's Land," *Racism and Class Struggle* (New York: Monthly Review, 1971); and Robert Allen, *Black Awakening in Capitalist America* (Trenton: Africa World, 1990 [1970]).

57. Davis makes this point in *City of Quartz*, chapter 5.

58. Eldridge Cleaver, *Post-Prison Writings and Speeches* (New York: Vintage, 1970).

59. Balibar and Wallerstein, *Race, Nation, Class*, p. 95.

60. See Benjamin, "Theses on the Philosophy of History"; and Singh, "Black Liberation in the Theater of Nationality."

61. James N. Blaut, *The National Question: Decolonizing the Theory of Nationalism* (London: Zed, 1987).

62. Balibar and Wallerstein, *Race, Nation, Class*, p. 44.

63. W. E. B. Du Bois, "Human Rights to All Minorities," in *W. E. B. Du Bois Speaks: Speeches and Addresses, 1920–1963*, ed. Phillip Foner (New York: Pathfinder, 1970).

64. Theodore Adorno and Max Horkheimer, *The Dialectic of Enlightenment* (New York: Verso, 1979).

2

The Political Moment in Jamaica:
The Dimensions of Hegemonic Dissolution

Brian Meeks

Me nuh know how we and dem a go work it out
... For me nuh have no frien' in a high society
　　　　　　　　—Bob Marley, "We and Them,"
　　　　　　　　　　　　Uprising Album, *1979*

Freeman and slave, patrician and plebeian, lord and serf,
guildmaster and journeyman, in a word, oppressor and
oppressed, stood in constant opposition to one another,
carried on an interrupted, now hidden, now open fight,
a fight that each time ended, either in the revolutionary
reconstruction of society at large, or in the common ruin
of the contending classes.
　　—Karl Marx and Friedrich Engels, The Manifesto of
　　　　　　　　　　　　the Communist Party

In 1993 P. J. Patterson, the newly elected leader of the People's National Party (PNP), romped home in Jamaica's twelfth general election since universal adult suffrage with a decisive mandate of fifty-two out of a possible sixty seats and some 60 percent of the popular vote. While there were widespread criticisms of corrupt practices,[1] particularly in troubled urban constituencies, leading to an initial boycotting of parliament by the opposition Jamaica Labour Party (JLP), and while there was a remarkably low turnout at the polls,[2] there was, nevertheless, a widespread feeling that the victory represented something of a renewal in Jamaica's political life. Prime Minister Manley had, after all, retired a year before, ending his family's four-decade presence in the uppermost echelons of the country's politics. Patterson was, in the shade-conscious reality of Jamaica, unambiguously black, and was perceived as representing the younger and far more confident majority of Jamaica's people. He was also, and importantly, from a rural constituency and therefore seen as being relatively untainted by the violence and corrupt practices that tarnished virtually all previous political leaders, based as they traditionally were in the strategic and troubled Kingston metropolitan area.

The Economic

A year later the picture could not be more different. There appears to be widespread despondency and disaffection, led by the seemingly endless economic crisis that has afflicted the country for the past twenty years. The Jamaican dollar, which stood at 5.5 to the U.S. dollar in 1989 when Edward Seaga's JLP lost power, plummeted to 29 to 1 in late 1991, then stabilized at 22.5 after a celebrated initiative by elements in the private sector. In mid-1993, following deflationary budget cuts, it again began to tumble and is today at a temporary plateau of some 33 to 1 U.S. dollar. While Jamaica has been lucky to avoid hyperinflation of the Latin American variety, its rates of inflation have been consistently high. The relatively low figure of 14.9 percent in 1992 was transformed the following year, as the free fall of the dollar contributed to a rate of 40.6 percent, far above the targeted figure of some 11 percent.[3] The popular opinion is that the real rate, insufficiently captured in the basket of goods used by the statisticians, is much higher than this.

Since its return to power in 1989, the nominally democratic socialist People's National Party government has followed textbook neoliberal policies, including an accelerated divestment of nationally owned assets, relaxed import duties, a liberalized foreign exchange regime, high interest rates, and tight fiscal policies.[4] This has been largely predicated on the current World Bank and International Monetary Fund policies, which assume that if Jamaica and other similar developing economies could only get the liberalization equation "right" then it could achieve sustained growth and travel the path to success of the Southeast Asian Newly Industrializing Countries (NICs).[5] One of the problems, however, is that this at best problematic policy has been followed inconsistently. In

1992, in the months preceding the general elections, duties were dramatically lowered on imported automobiles; tax rates were lowered and liberal wage increases granted to elements in the public sector. This typical vote-buying tactic contributed, in effect, to a wave of money printing and laid the basis for the subsequent round of devaluation and inflation that is still feeding through the system today.

It is perhaps too early to say that the government, based on its own criteria, has failed, but, at best, the results are disappointing. While there are increasingly large reserves of foreign exchange held in local private accounts, the actual flow into the official banking system was reduced by 50 percent in the last half of 1993, though it is now on the increase again. Largely due to a high and subsequently deflationary interest rate policy, the new minister of finance, Omar Davies, has been able to preside over the first positive net international reserves position for the country in two decades.[6]

What is evident, however, is that if one focuses on the statistics that would point toward future growth, the picture is not encouraging. Jamaica, particularly in the wake of the long North American recession, has not been an attractive target for foreign investment, and there has been no massive inflow of new capital. Despite the positive performance of some nontraditional exports like the garment assembly industry, which itself is now threatened by the new North American Free Trade Agreement (NAFTA), the downturn in bauxite/alumina exports with the saturation of the world aluminum market has meant that export growth has been sluggish. Imports, on the other hand, encouraged by the reduction in automobile duties and spurred on by an abysmal public transport system, have skyrocketed. In 1993 the balance of visible trade moved from the already bad figure of - US$872.8 million to - US$1,120.7 million.[7] The saving grace to the frightening and mushrooming negative balance of trade picture has been tourism, which, quite remarkably, has grown consistently through the recession and increased its earnings from some US $794.2 million in 1992 to US $902.1 million in 1993.[8] Alongside this the inherently difficult-to-estimate informal economy—legal, semi-, and illegal—has provided a steady flow of resources to sections of the population that might otherwise have been further impoverished.[9]

Nevertheless, it is fair to say that poverty is alive and well in Jamaica. Consistently high interest rates—the policy followed to mop up excess liquidity and undermine the black market in foreign exchange—have served to increase the disparity between rich and poor, already one of the most notoriously wide in the region.[10] Between 1986 and 1991 the lowest paid 40 percent in Jamaica received, on average, 15.9 percent of the national income, compared with a figure of 19 percent in Barbados, to use a nearby example. For the same period the UNDP found that 80 percent of rural Jamaicans lived below the poverty line, compared with 39 percent in Trinidad and Tobago, 70 percent in the Dominican Republic, 50 percent in St Lucia, and 25 percent in Grenada.[11] The incongruity of the 'Two Jamaicas' is evident to even the most casual observer. The lifestyles of the wealthy in the salubrious communities of Cherry Gardens and Norbrook, and along the North Coast, with their Mercedes Benzes, BMWs, and shopping junkets to Miami, rival anything to be found in the United States, along, of course, with perfect weather. Descriptions of parties like the following, held by an American entertainment executive, are common items on the social pages of the daily newspapers:

> The rich and the famous have been flocking to the elegant Round Hill Hotel, Hanover, to soak up the winter sunshine, to rest and to party. Like the big fortieth anniversary bash for the founder of MTV Bob Pittman . . . crystal chandeliers dangling from trees, bare footed waiters dressed in top hats, tails and black ties, complemented by a fabulous Jamaican cuisine of baby lobsters, avocado and fruit. . . . The men went dressed to kill, in their black ties and sarongs—bare footed. So did the ladies, also bare footed in their splendid evening gowns of silk and satin and their head wraps that gave them a charming Madame Pompadour grace and elegance.[12]

But a few miles away are the notorious Montego Bay ghetto communities of North Gully and Glendevon, mirror images of the far larger and more violent garrison communities of Kingston, like Rema, Concrete Jungle, and Tivoli Gardens. And, a few miles from these is the even more desperate Riverton City, where thousands of people live literally on the city dump and many survive by a daily schedule of picking through the refuse for spoilt food and saleable junk. One further statistic is, perhaps, of note: since 1970, according to the UNDP Human Development Index, Jamaica, while remaining a "middle-income country," has had, with the exception of Romania, the greatest fall in standard of living of any country in the world.[13]

There has undoubtedly been a long and drawn-out economic trauma, the end of which is not yet in sight, but the crisis of the present moment is by no means purely an economic phenomenon. Accompanying it is a crisis of will, of direction, of ideas, and of conflicting values, that can be roughly captured under the heading of what I call "hegemonic dissolution."

The Political

Politically, postwar Jamaica has been characterized by the existence of one of the tightest, most impermeable, and consistent two-party systems in the hemisphere.[14] There have been twelve general elections, eleven of them seriously contested by both major parties, and, apart from the first in 1944, when independents as a group actually outvoted the losing PNP, no third party has made any significant inroad. Each party succeeded the other in a two-term, roughly ten-year cycle, with the loser never getting less than 40 percent of the national vote. The system was underwritten by a number of features, including clientelism, extreme Westminster centralization of power, the absence of an effective back bench, the exclusion of third parties, and the absence of a strong, independent civil society.

Its success and relative longevity have derived from a series of unwritten pacts and compromises between the largely brown-skinned and educated upper middle classes who actually controlled state power and the black working and lower classes who voted for them and occasionally engaged in internecine warfare in the rank and file of either party.[15] These centered around: a) access to resources and the use of these resources to consolidate power. Once in power, the government (the patron) was expected to use its position to provide contracts, housing, land, work, access to visas, and other scarce benefits to its supporters at all levels of society; b) the acceptance of the principle of succession, which meant that at least every ten years there would be a change that the losing party would, despite sharp contestation and rancor, accept and thus allow the former opposition party a chance to eat from the pie; and c) the existence of accessible and charismatic leadership, so that the leader, in classic Weberian manner, would not simply rule according to bureaucratic and constitutional norms but would maintain an extensive level of contact with his supporters, not only to facilitate the distribution of benefits, but to strengthen the notion of a unified and popular party with common national interests. This last factor led to the consolidation of a tight system (based on the historical and charismatic roles played by the elder

Manley and Bustamante, perceived and celebrated as national heroes and cofounders of the nation), the real role of the trade union affiliates of the two parties in improving the lot of the working class, and the significant improvement in the quality of life of the people arising out of the postwar social reforms, which have been felt especially in education, health, and housing.[16]

In retrospect, the high point of this system was the year 1980 when, ironically, over eight hundred died during the months before the elections.[17] While there was undoubtedly a cold war dimension to the urban (and increasingly rural) violence, as both sides relied to some extent on their international alliances for tactical and political support, on reflection 1980 was the last election in which the great majority felt that the government was a prize, that the process of supporting a party and winning an election was the vehicle that would bring a "better" life, whether defined as the mythical future of socialism or the mythical past of plentiful 1960s capitalism. The JLP won that election in a landslide, using the slogan of deliverance and promising the people that money would soon "jingle in their pockets." By 1982, however, the polls showed that the government had become a minority[18]—a position in which it would remain for the entire decade, but for an opportune moment in 1983, when, temporarily boosted by the murder of Maurice Bishop and the invasion of Grenada, it swept back to power in a snap election, boycotted by the opposition PNP.

At the time sensitive commentators saw this early shift from the JLP as the beginning of a new phenomenon of shorter-term governments, with a five- rather than a ten-year cycle. But few, if any, could have recognized it as the beginning of the collapse of the pact of 1944, the intricate set of rules that developed between the two parties and, within the parties, between the leaders and their supporters. This collapse is not yet complete, but all the signs point in that direction. Among the most outstanding are:

a) The undermining of the resource base available to successive governments, which has enabled them to be effective patrons, distributing largesse to needy clients. The main factor accelerating this has been the IMF-inspired structural adjustment agreements that have significantly reduced the size of government and, consequently, its effective role in the wider society.

b) The natural exhaustion of the two-party cycle. Transition from one party to the other, with the accompanying slogans of redemption, has occurred too often without any significant change, and the population is no longer willing to listen to promises of "better" and "deliverance," which are never fulfilled.

c) The retirement of Michael Manley from the positions of prime minister and leader of the PNP in 1993 ended the last link in the old charismatic chain that connected him to his father and to his cousin Bustamante on the other side of the fence. The populist connection never existed for Seaga (who, even at the nadir of PNP support in 1981, trailed behind Manley in the polls), and it does not seem to be emerging for Patterson.[19]

By the mid-eighties the onset of a sea change was quite evident, when Stone's polls showed that, compared with 1971, when 87 percent of the electorate were loyal party voters and only 13 percent issue voters, by 1986 only 48 percent considered themselves loyal to the party, and 52 percent had become issue voters.[20] A poll done in 1994 by Stone's organization a year after his death suggests that this new configuration is consolidating. Asked "Which party would you vote for?" 26 percent supported the governing PNP, 29 percent were for the opposition, while a large bloc of 45 percent remained uncommitted.[21] A further indicator that the two-party system is in mortal crisis has been the failure of the opposition to significantly increase its support out of the dire social and economic difficulties faced currently by the majority of the people. On the first anniversary of the PNP's electoral victory, the JLP declared a "day of shame" and called on the people to stay away from work to protest what it considered the illegitimate 1993 elections and the deteriorating economic situation. Apart from some incidents of gunfire and a few roadblocks in established JLP strongholds, the day passed without any significant popular mobilization.[22]

But if the moment is characterized by the collapse of support for the two traditional parties, it is also one in which a radical alternative has failed to assert itself in the popular imagination. An effective organized left does not exist in Jamaica today, nor is there any other radical force of a populist or religious kind on the immediate horizon. The Workers Party of Jamaica (WPJ), the communist left of the seventies and eighties, fell apart toward the end of the last decade. Indeed, the major debates in the WPJ, influenced by the tragic collapse of the Grenada Revolution, preceded the historical collapse of the communist bloc and centered on the broad issues of the role of the market versus central economic control, the legitimacy of democratic centralism as an appropriate policy, both within the party and in the state, and the relative emphasis placed on "national" factors, such as race, as opposed to "internationalist" or purely class factors. If the specific reasons the WPJ collapsed in the late eighties were to be isolated, they would include:

a) The failure to make any serious headway, despite being in existence for more than a decade, in elections—the decisive benchmark of success in Jamaican politics. No national or local government seat was ever won by the WPJ, a factor that ultimately led to demoralization and recrimination. This failure can in turn be accounted for in 1) the impermeability of the two-party system, where the fact of fifty years of tradition passed on through families and communities effectively excluded any third force; 2) the existence of armed "garrison" communities, excluding the possibility of peaceful organization in those poorest communities in which the class-based appeal of the WPJ might have been greatest; 3) the "wasted vote syndrome," which in a first-past-the-post constituency system works against small third parties without significant geographic concentration; and 4) persistent fear of communism among broad cross-sections of the Jamaican population, enhanced by cold war propaganda, which provided, perhaps, the most effective inoculation against radical political movements.
b) For its own part, the WPJ harbored unrealistic notions of imminent revolution that often led to dogmatic textbook Leninist methods of organization, which, on the back of the already daunting list of constraints, served to further isolate the party from mainstream politics.[23]

The Social

In a context where both major parties have lost support, where the two-party project is increasingly discredited, and where there is no clear radical alternative to the system, the third dimension of the crisis seems fairly obvious—that is, the collapse of the social project of 1944. Accompanying the unwritten political pact that surrounded the 1944 electoral arrangements was an entire series of social arrangements, which are more visible in their moment of collapse than they were while functioning

properly. These would include an acceptance of social cues from the dom-
inantly brown middle classes, including notions of decency in language,
dress, and manners. To speak English fluently was to be decent, to speak
Jamaican patois was not just different but bad. These arrangements were,
of course, welded onto the older plantation hierarchies of color and class
in a complex structure. Carl Stone, in typically blunt manner, described it
as such:

> Jamaica has always been South Africa without Apartheid. The brown
> man and the red man have always assumed social superiority over the
> blacks in every sphere of activity, and blacks have always played up to
> these powerful colour and ethnic interests to get by in the society. The
> red man and the brown man have been taught to believe that they are
> the natural leaders and that black people's role is really to follow their
> leadership.[24]

Thus, it was not impossible for a very dark person to be upper class, but
this would have to be demonstrated by an overcompensation in manners
and language, for the person would have to be on constant guard in case
he or she were mistaken for someone from a lower-status position.[25]

The converse of this social leadership was that the middle was expected to play an active role in Jamaica's social and political life. The
classic example of this was Norman Manley's Jamaica Welfare[26] of the
thirties, an organization that sought to build community structures in
the rural areas, often with tremendous sacrifice from its middle-class leadership. The perception today is that the middle class has largely retreated
into its suburban enclaves, with houses individually guarded by security
guards, cars air-conditioned with tinted windows, effectively insulating
them literally and metaphorically from the rest of Jamaica. This development was captured by a columnist in the *Gleaner*:

> There are certain areas in this country, where a poor, black man cannot
> walk, without calling attention to himself, and with the risk of being
> detained and arrested. The only difference between us and South Africa
> is that our people don't have to carry passes. . . . Like South Africa with
> its sprawling ghettos physically juxtaposed to the affluent white com-
> munities, so is Jamaica. The beautiful "members only" Constant Spring
> Golf Club elegantly sits next to Cassava Piece "ghetto" with a mere
> barbed wire fence separating the two.[27]

The economic crisis, the collapse of the political project, the growing psychological independence of the subordinate classes, and the shelving of social leadership by the middle classes are the conditions under which a moment of hegemonic dissolution has emerged. Using hegemony, in the Gramscian sense, to mean effective leadership and control of the direction of society, we can argue that the social bloc in charge of Jamaican society is no longer ruling over a people convinced of its social superiority and its inherent right to, using the popular Jamaican phrase, "run things."[28]

There is sharp contestation[29] over a wide sphere of social and economic issues. At the mercantile level higglers, referred to as Informal Commercial Importers (ICIs), are competing head-on with the traditional Syrian and Chinese merchant classes in the lucrative dry goods trade. At the level of language there is a practical battle for dominance between English as the lingua franca and Jamaican. This is perhaps most evident in the shift to Jamaican (as opposed to Jamaican English) as the dominant norm in popular music. If the classical protest reggae music of the seventies, reaching its apogee in the works of Bob Marley, oscillated between standard, if biblical, English appeals against "Babylon" and more overtly patois statements, the currently popular "dance hall" form has largely abandoned the tradition of resorting to the occasional refrain in standard English.[30]

In terms of dress and popular fashion, the growing disparity in normative trends is again evident in the dance hall, where unconventional modes of dress, often involving colorful and daring cut-outs and highly unconventional patterns, suggest that the cues of what is considered high fashion are neither coming from the traditional middle classes nor, for that matter, from a purely North American context. Instead, they are being distorted and reinvented through the lens of the urban ghetto experience into something not only peculiar but also in an adversarial position to traditional fashion.

In the music itself an increasingly sharp rift is emerging between "uptown" and "downtown," with the latter adhering to dance hall and the former either completely hostile to reggae or counterposing the more traditional "classical" forms to the current "debased" dance hall rhythms. Contestation is sharp and extends beyond the lyrics and rhythms to the actual volume of the music played. In a pointed dance hall piece, popular DJ Shabba Ranks along with the singing group Home T argue that loud music and the dance hall are the poor people's means of entertainment:

Some have satellite, some have video
but poor people have nowhere to go . . .
Dance hall business is all we know.[31]

Then, even more ominously, the verse suggests that the alternative to loud music, if it is suppressed, will be guns and violence:

If yu nuh wan' dem fi go bus' no shot
Low di soun' system mek it nice up di spot.[32]

The tremendous significance of the dance hall as an alternative space, removed from the restraining confines of (high) society, is captured in this observation from music critic and social observer Jean Fairweather Wilson:

D. J. Man, a charismatic figure, strides and struts the stage, making periodic leaps into the air as if possessed. He dominates the space, ruling his kingdom with a microphone, as his subjects hearken unto his voice. The microphone is a rod of correction. It is a gun. It is a conductor of electricity. It is a symbol of the power his listeners crave, want to identify with or need to affirm in themselves. "Dance Hall" is about power.[33]

At the level of gender the collapse of the project of 1944 can also be seen as the collapse of a dominant male project. Women, against tremendous odds and despite continuing resistance, are coming into their own in Jamaican society. They now constitute 38 percent of all private sector executives, compared with 21 percent twenty years ago. At the University of the West Indies, in all faculties except natural sciences, where they are only slightly outnumbered, women constitute the clear majority. In the Critical Management Studies Department women outnumber men by a ratio of nearly three to one.[34] In the dance halls, to use that fertile cutting edge example again, women arrive at dances in groups. They dance together unless one asks a man to dance with her. If any aggressive man tries to enter the group unrequested, he is liable to be attacked, including use of the weapon of choice—acid—which many revelers carry as protection. Again, Fairweather Wilson amplifies this dimension:

Our genuine dance hall women leaders who originate from downtown, typically, have a measure of economic power and independence. Some achieve this through lucrative activities as Informal Commercial Importers. Some have become successful by way of dressmaking and other business concerns. These women can afford to buy themselves the most fabulous finery, successfully competing with the well kept women of the dons. They often go out by themselves, in posses, dressed in their garments of liberation. They can certainly afford to pay their own bar bills. This level of economic independence has implications for the man-woman relationship. It seems to me that the on-going power struggle between man and woman has taken on some new dimensions in the dance hall culture.[35]

In the sphere of manners there is an almost tangible dissolution of accepted modes and norms. It is felt perhaps most acutely in the increasing failure to form cues of any kind. The Jamaican public has never been particularly sympathetic to the concept of "lining up," but the little that did take place in the past is fast disappearing. This example, given by a *Gleaner* columnist, speaks eloquently to the moment:

> Stand in any line, anywhere in Jamaica! Someone will try to push in front of you. If you object it is you who will be berated. . . . I remember being in the express line of a corporate area supermarket, under a sign which read "One to Ten Items Only." A well-dressed woman with a cart full of groceries pushed in front of me. I objected, firstly because she didn't wait behind me and secondly because she had many more than ten items. . . . She took a deep breath and treated all those within earshot to a vocabulary more appropriate to a construction site. Her tirade ended with the trump card "Yu t'ink dis a Sout' Africa white gal?" Even worse, everyone else in the line took her side, suggesting I should join some other line if I didn't like the way this one was being run while the cashier stared off into space.[36]

The example is poignant because it brings so many of the features of the moment into sharp focus. The collapse of middle-class hegemony has meant the collapse of the reflexive deference to persons of fairer complexion but it has also meant the collapse of deeper universalistic norms of respect for other individuals that are the underpinnings of any functioning civilization. The baby is in danger of being thrown out with the bathwater. The glue that held Jamaica together is in a process of terminal meltdown.

The result of all this is hegemonic dissolution or, as Obika Gray suggests, "dual social power."[37] In some respects this moment is akin to the dual political power that is one of the definitive features of a mature revolutionary situation. The old hegemonic alliance is unable to rule in the accustomed way, but, equally, alternative and competitive modes of hegemony from below are unable to decisively place their stamp on the new and fluid situation. What is definitely absent is an effective populist political organization that might provide leadership and perhaps also steer the people in the direction of more traditional hierarchical channels. There is also, in the new unipolar world order, no permissive world context or international conjuncture that would facilitate the success of a national revolutionary upsurge. In this critical respect as well the present moment is quite different.[38]

Three Instances

Three "case" studies help to illuminate the facets of the present conjuncture. In each case extensive source material from the daily papers is used to suggest the immediacy and poignancy of the situation. Each incident occurred in 1994 and involves sharp, often violent, confrontations between the people and authority. In none of the cases is there—at least in the short run—an outright solution. People are aggrieved, they fight, and in the end they either lose or arrive at some compromise. Underlying them all, though, is a sense of anomie, of drift, and of the decay of binding relationships on all sides. The first case involves the squatter community of Flankers on the outskirts of the tourist city of Montego Bay. On Saturday, March 12, the *Gleaner*'s headline proclaimed, "Squatter Fury Erupts Out West":

> The depressed community of Flankers erupted in fury yesterday as a result of a pre-dawn demolition raid against squatters. Enraged residents told the *Gleaner* that police were accompanied by armed thugs who began tearing down houses, vandalizing furniture and stealing money. Residents retaliated with stones until the police and their companions retreated downhill to the main road. Five persons were reportedly shot and several infants were affected by tear gas. . . . As the disturbances spread, persons started mounting roadblocks with stones, old vehicles and burning tyres. Schools and shops closed and tourists

were advised to stay in their hotels. At the Eastern exit of town, traffic was backed up all the way to Rosehall and a vociferous crowd surged along the main road by Flankers hurling abuse at the police.

Inspector Steadman Roach, who led the demolition team, was pelted and knocked flat with rocks and wounded. He left the scene in a police car under cover of reinforcements who attempted to disperse the crowd by firing in the air. Burning barricades reappeared as soon as they were removed by the police team, which at one stage included Colonel Trevor Macmillan, Commissioner of Police. Joe Whitter, owner of the property, had his Fort Street office set afire. . . . The crowd spotted Mr. Whitter in a rental car by a roadblock near Wexford Court. They swarmed the car and almost turned it upside down before Mr. Whitter was rescued by the police.

Back at Flankers shortly before noon, the Commissioner of Police arrived and was escorted by a hysterical crowd to the Flankers All Age School. . . . Colonel Macmillan, after calling for strict observance of the law, told the people that the information he had received indicated that the police had acted improperly and Inspector Roach had been relieved of his duties with immediate effect, pending the outcome of an investigation which would be done by an independent team from Kingston. "I want a report by Monday, I give you my word, my word is my bond, that where the police have acted illegally, they will be highly disciplined."[39]

The second case involves a shift from the West to the arguably even more beautiful eastern end of the island. Again, it involves a question of right and a clash between vested propertied interests and aggrieved people who invoke traditional rights of access in opposition to the formal right to own property. The *Sunday Gleaner* of April 3, a mere three weeks after the Flankers incident, noted in a headline that "Vandals Wreak Havoc at Blue Lagoon":

Vandals invaded the premises of the Blue Lagoon, Portland, between Friday night and yesterday morning, smashing and destroying five boats. Another boat is reported missing. The vandals also emptied an undetermined quantity of gasoline into the Blue Lagoon. At least two fishermen lost their boats and equipment in the wave of destruction.

The vandalism followed eviction notices served three weeks ago on twelve squatters who had been occupying the site for some time.

On Friday, a crowd of some 25 persons converged on the Lagoon property shouting death threats at the owner Valerie Marzouca. They also painted the walls and pavements with threats and obscene slogans.

On Friday, police continued with their investigation to determine the identities of persons instigating threats and vandalism.

In a statement to the *Gleaner* on Friday, Mrs. Marzouca said that "it would appear that property owners in Jamaica no longer have any rights to their properties in the face of public indiscipline and anarchy."[40]

In the third incident we return to the West, to the sleepy fishing village of Green Island and a tragic incident resulting from a common example of excessive force used by members of the Jamaican police force. On September 2 the *Friday Herald* headline noted "Green Island Protest Leaves One Dead":

Green Island, the fishing town midway between Lucea, Hanover and Negril, the tourist resort in the West, remained calm last night after two days of protest sparked by the police shootings which left one dead and twenty residents detained by the police.

Dead is Keisha Johnson, 17, a student of Green Island Comprehensive High School. . . . She was killed yesterday, the second day of rioting in the town, following an incident on Tuesday between the police and some residents in which an elderly woman was reportedly beaten by two officers. . . . Eyewitness [*sic*] told Universal Press Services (UPS) that Miss Johnson was shot fatally when she intervened after the police held her uncle Johnny Whitmore in her yard. The policeman's gun reportedly went off and hit her in the chest and arm. . . . The killing sparked protests by residents who described it as "police brutality." . . . Disorder broke out on Tuesday around noon, residents said, after a number of persons who were seeking medical attention at the local health centre attempted to shelter from heavy rainfall in a building which is under construction. The police were called after an incident developed between the foreman of the construction site and residents. . . . The residents said that without warning the police started raining blows on a number of persons on their arrival. It was alleged that a young girl who saw her grandmother being hit by the policeman intervened by using her umbrella to hit the policeman. The scene became a free for all with the police using force and the residents retaliating. By afternoon residents had blocked the main road leading to and from Negril, forcing traffic to divert.[41]

Three common factors are evident in otherwise spatially distinct and unconnected incidents. The first is the willingness of the state—often in close cooperation with vested interests—to resort to force before attempting moral suasion. The second is the complete absence of any fear or respect for the dominant strata, evident in the physical attack on Whitter, the contempt shown for Marzouca, and, in a different kind of incident, the willingness of the unnamed young girl to wield an umbrella in defense of her elderly grandmother against the armed forces of the state. The third feature, as previously suggested, is the inability of the aggrieved to prevail. The incident flares up; roads are blocked and tires burned; important officers of the state arrive and the incident peters out until the next instance. Those "above" are losing the moral authority with which they have ruled effectively for five postwar decades. But those "below" do not have the tools, worldview, or organization to present a credible alternative to that rule.

There are, perhaps, three broad possibilities. First, an authoritarian government comes to power either within or outside the constitution and seeks to reimpose order, good manners, and decency via coercive measures. Already the reintroduction of the long-shelved policy of flogging criminals,[42] the strong support across wide sections of society for the use of the death penalty,[43] and the long tradition of recorded instances of excessive use of force and police brutality in Jamaica[44] all suggest that an authoritarian solution is not completely out of the question in the future. The second option would entail a process of democratic renewal, which would recognize the potential in the present conjuncture for unleashing the creative energies of the Jamaican people and seek to funnel the present, admittedly chaotic, moment in a positive direction of national consensus and popular inclusion.[45] There is really also a third alternative, which is Marx and Engels' oft-quoted "common ruin of the contending classes," an option that no one wishes to contemplate; but the experiences of Yugoslavia, Lebanon, Somalia—and Haiti, closer to home—suggest that it is not impossible if the political and social situation continues to drift and no clear social force is able to assert its dominance.[46]

But to address the second, which is my favored option, it would have to include the following:

a) A democratically constituted constituent assembly to rewrite the constitution. A rewrite is at present underway, but insufficient attempt has been made to really include the broadest sections of the population, including simplified summaries of the existing document and an explanation of the implications of various options;[47]

b) among the issues that would have to be examined in any popular rewrite, the first would have to be the overarching powers of the prime minister, which would require checks and balances, perhaps along presidential lines, while trying to avoid the pitfalls of grid-locked ineffective government;

c) the inclusion of an element of proportional representation, perhaps in the upper house, which is now nominated, to avoid the "do or die" reality of a winner-takes-all system, with its inherent potential for confrontation, and yet maintain an element of constituency-based responsibility in the lower house;

d) a system of recall for nonperforming members of parliament, designed to avoid frivolous excesses, yet sufficiently effective to allow greater popular control over representatives;

e) a concerted, if belated, attempt to "level the economic playing field" through more transparent means of access to government lands, bank loans, and other financial instruments;

f) a national cultural renewal based on a reappraisal of popular culture and language and its greater acceptance through the public media and other avenues of discourse; and

g) the arrival at a consensus on the economic and social path for the country, with the recognition that certain social services and economic institutions will not be tampered with by successive governments for narrow partisan advantage, along with the identification of clear economic priorities, clustered around the things that Jamaican people do well (especially in the areas of entertainment, sports, and services).

A case is not being made for the uniqueness of these developments in Jamaica. Politics and the state are under siege throughout the world. Informal economies have grown along with the growth of cookie-cutter governments advocating textbook structural adjustment. Poverty is not Jamaican, just as the rebellion in Chiapas cannot be totally isolated from the Venezuelan riots or from the Sendero uprising in Peru.[48] While not adhering to a Wallersteinian interpretation of these events as symptoms of one coalescent and coherent world system, it would be simplistic and blind not to see the similarities and underlying causalities that connect them all.[49] The question really is—in a world without sharply differentiated and competitive poles—how do we reinvent a notion of popular change that will carry us beyond structural adjustment, lead to a genuine advance in democracy, empower people, and ultimately provide a better life for everyone?[50] In other words, is change possible? Will it come from above or below? Are there real people on the ground able to lead such a renewal?

All crises provide the opportunity to look forward and look back. This sketch of the present Jamaican crisis suggests that the answer is not at all predetermined, but the clues to its possible direction are to be found on the outskirts of Montego Bay, next to the pristine Blue Hole of Portland, and in the throbbing dance halls of Kingston—and, indeed, in every town in Jamaica—on Saturday night.

Notes

1. Dissatisfaction with the elections was substantial. A year after, albeit in a period when the new government's popularity had begun to wane, 44 percent of those polled felt that the election had not been free and fair, compared to 31 percent who answered in the affirmative and 25 percent who were unsure. See Stone Poll in the *Gleaner*, March 17, 1994, p. 3.

2. The 59 percent turnout of registered voters in the 1993 elections was the lowest since the first universal adult suffrage election in 1944. Within this context, however, the PNP had its largest ever majority, breaking the 60 percent mark for the first time. For its part, the Jamaica Labour Party faced its worst defeat since 1955. See the *Sunday Gleaner*, March 27, 1994.

3. See *Statistical Bulletin: Consumer Price Index, June 1994*, Statistical Institute of Jamaica.

4. For a thoughtful and critical examination of the possible models and the prospects for Jamaica's economy, see Donald Harris, "The Jamaican Economy in the Twenty-First Century: Challenges to Development and Requirements of a Response," in Patsy Lewis, ed., *Jamaica: Preparing for the Twenty-First Century* (Kingston: Ian Randle, 1994) pp. 13–52. It is important to note that Harris recognizes that for the economy to move forward there must be a "workable truce" and a "social pact" (p. 40), precisely what is missing in Jamaica today.

5. When the Jamaican economy is measured against the criteria required prior to "take off" on the Southeast Asian path, it falls short. Gerald Tan suggests that among the critical factors necessary before industrialization can be considered are 1. an efficient agricultural sector; 2. rapid, prior growth in exports; 3. a clear prior shift to the manufacturing sector; 4. little industrial unrest; 5. low rates of inflation; 6. an efficient public administration; and 7. a stable political climate. Jamaica's performance on the economic dimensions is bad or, at best, anemic. On the more political criteria, it cannot claim low levels of industrial unrest. The public administration is poor, and, while par-

liamentary democracy is entrenched, it is difficult to describe the current political climate as stable. See Gerald Tan, "The Next NICs of Asia," *Third World Quarterly*, vol. 14 (1993), pp. 57–74.

6. In September 1990 the Net International Reserves figure showed a deficit of US $552.3 million. In December 1993 it went into the black and has been on the increase for every month since then. See *Statistical Digest, March/April 1994*, Bank of Jamaica, Kingston, p. 82.

7. See *Statistical Digest, March/April 1994*, p. 84.

8. Ibid., p. 90. The irony, of course, is that tourism, with its relatively lavish display of wealth and luxury, is expected to perform as the growth industry in a society beset with chronic unemployment and dire poverty. The potential for disruption of the crucial foreign exchange lifeline, as Jamaicans have experienced on many occasions, is enormous.

9. The item "Private Transfers" in the official statistics gives some indication of the potential size of the informal economy. In 1993 this item amounted to some US $267.8 million, or roughly a third of the earnings from tourism. This is only the tip of the iceberg, for it does not include the vast number of private transfers that are not recorded, the earnings from itinerant musicians on the international circuit, and, of course, the illegal earnings from drug lords and posse members. See *Statistical Digest*, p. 90.

10. Interest rates, which hovered at around the 19-percent level in 1988–1989, shot up to 35 percent in 1992 before reaching the unprecedented level of 52 percent in the early months of 1994. More recently, there has been a gradual decline. See *Statistical Digest*, p. 50, and the *Gleaner*, February 2, 1994, for a report of the government's policies to stem the slide of the dollar.

11. See *Human Development Report, 1994* (New York and Oxford: Oxford University Press, 1994), p. 164.

12. *Daily Gleaner*, March 11, 1994, p. 40.

13. See *Human Development Report 1993* (New York and Oxford: Oxford University Press, 1993), p. 103.

14. For a critical assessment of the main features of the Jamaican political system in the mid to late seventies, see Carl Stone, *Democracy and Clientelism in Jamaica* (New Brunswick, N.J. and London: Transaction, 1983). For a later critique of Stone's work, see Carlene Edie, *Democracy by Default: Dependency and Clientelism in Jamaica* (Boulder: Lynne Rienner, 1991).

15. For an assessment of the path to power of the brown middle classes, see Trevor Munroe, *The Politics of Constitutional Decolonization: Jamaica, 1944–1962* (Kingston: Institute of Social and Economic Research, 1972).

16. The genuine improvement in the conditions of life of the people, spurred on by British Fabian policies and a booming economy for much of the postwar period, is still being felt, although it has been severely undermined in recent times. The 1994 *Human Development Report* could still find that among developing countries Jamaica's life expectancy was ranked eighth, its infant mortality rate was fifth in terms of lowest number of deaths,

its adult literacy rates second, and its access to safe water first. See *Human Development Report, 1994*, p. 102.

17. See, for example, Michael Kaufman, *Jamaica Under Manley: Dilemmas of Socialism and Democracy* (London: Zed, 1985); Michael Manley, *Struggle in the Periphery* (London: Writers and Readers, 1982); and Evelyne Huber Stephens and John Stephens, *Democratic Socialism in Jamaica* (Basingstoke: Macmillan, 1986).

18. See Carl Stone, *Politics vs. Economics: The 1989 Elections in Jamaica* (Kingston: Heinneman, 1989), p. 27.

19. In his poll of July 1981 Carl Stone asked his sample who was the most outstanding leader in Jamaica. Only 29.2 percent supported then Prime Minister Seaga, while 33.4 percent supported Manley. See Carl Stone, *The Political Opinions of the Jamaican People* (Kingston: Blackett, 1982).

20. See Stone, *Politics vs. Economics*, p. 108.

21. See the *Sunday Gleaner*, March 27, 1994.

22. See the *Gleaner*, March 31, 1994. It can be argued, with some justification, that it is still too early in the PNP's term of office to conclude that the JLP is no longer a viable alternative. Only time will conclusively prove this, but the absence of popular response to the JLP in the face of undoubtedly some of the most traumatic developments in the economy is a telling factor.

23. For a discussion of some of these issues, see Rupert Lewis, "Which Way for the Jamaican Left?" *Third World Viewpoint*, vol. 1 (May 1993).

24. Carl Stone, *The Stone Columns: The Last Year's Work* (Kingston: Sangster's, 1993), p. 96.

25. For a sensitive discussion of the peculiarities of class and color in Jamaica, see Rex Nettleford, *Mirror, Mirror: Identity, Race and Protest in Jamaica* (Glasgow: Collins and Sangster, 1970).

26. For a good description of the early welfare and grassroots development movement in Jamaica, see D. T. M. Girvan, *Working Together for Development* (Kingston: Institute of Jamaica, 1993).

27. *Sunday Gleaner,* March 20, 1994.

28. See Antonio Gramsci, *Selections from Prison Notebooks* (London: Lawrence and Wishart, 1986). For a more current, less "economically bound," though controversial, reinterpretation of hegemony, see Ernesto Laclau and Chantal Mouffe, *Hegemony and Socialist Strategy: Toward a Radical Democratic Politics* (New York and London: Verso, 1989).

29. It is not that there is no broad recognition that something is wrong. In February Patterson's prestige was boosted immensely when he hosted a national conference on "values and attitudes." The topics discussed by the large turnout of delegates ranged from crime to the family and the question of gender. The real rift probably exists between a trend that imagines traditional moral and religious values simply need to be reimposed, and the society will return to the good old days, and a view closer to that expressed here, which recognizes a more profound conjunctural crisis, requiring more broad-

based strategies to address it. See *Report on the National Consultation on Values and Attitudes* (Jamaica Information Service, April 1994).

30. For a more detailed and technical discussion of the current trends in "dance hall" or "dj" music, see Carolyn Cooper, *Noises in the Blood: Orality, Gender, and the "Vulgar" Body of Jamaican Popular Culture* (London and Basingstoke: Macmillan, 1993).

31. Shabba Ranks, *Mr Maximum*, Pow Wow Records, 1982.

32. Ibid.

33. Jean Fairweather Wilson, "Dance Hall: Sifting the Truths," *Sunday Gleaner*, April 17, 1994.

34. See *Student Registration, Mona, 1993/4 and 1992/3 as at 3/11/93*, UWI Academic Board document AB (M), p. 10.

35. Ibid.

36. Diana Macaulay, "Wrong But Strong," *Gleaner*, February 2, 1994.

37. See Obika Gray, "Discovering the Social Power of the Poor," *Social and Economic Studies*, vol. 43, no. 3 (September 1994).

38. See Walter Goldfrank, "Theories of Revolution and Revolution Without Theory," *Theory and Society*, vol. 7, nos. 1 and 2 (1979); and Brian Meeks, *Caribbean Revolutions and Revolutionary Theory: An Assessment of Cuba, Nicaragua, and Grenada* (London and Basingstoke: Macmillan, 1993).

39. *Gleaner*, March 12, 1994. One of the ironies of the "Flankers Rebellion," which is what it has come to be called in the popular domain, is that the landowner, Mr. Whitter, far from being an exemplar of the fair-skinned landed elite, is a self-made black man who made his wealth as an immigrant in Britain.

40. *Sunday Gleaner*, April 3, 1994.

41. *Friday Herald*, September 2, 1994.

42. See "Flogging Is Back: Judge Orders Punishment After Twenty Year Lapse," *Gleaner*, August 9, 1994.

43. See "Hang Them: KSAC Backs Call to Get Tough With Convicts," *Gleaner*, August 10, 1994.

44. See "Jamaica Leads in Police Brutality," *Gleaner*, June 6, 1994. The position advocating draconian and extraconstitutional measures has by no means triumphed, but it is growing. In a recent conference former deputy governor of the Bank of Jamaica and now World Bank economist Gladstone Bonnick argued that "the society should be prepared to give up certain freedoms it has enjoyed in the past but which have been abused by criminals. . . . The freedom of movement at all hours of night and day from one area to another may have to be reconsidered." Gladstone Bonnick, "Crime and Violence: Implications for Economic Expansion," in Lewis, *Jamaica*, p. 158.

45. See, for example, Trevor Munroe's call for fundamental institutional change in the *Gleaner*, April 10, 1994, and repeatedly in his book, *For a New Beginning: Selected Speeches, 1990–1993* (Kingston: Caricom, 1994).

Munroe, former general secretary of the WPJ, is now a member of a loose alliance called the New Beginning Movement, composed of former (and some standing) members of the two major parties as well as independent individuals. The NBM has made important statements on the need for transparency and greater democracy in national life, but the impression is that even this group, composed as it is of many people who have been tainted by the old politics, may be trailing behind the mood of the people and the current tendency to disconnect from "official" organizations.

46. The trend toward the "common ruin" option is perhaps most evident in the crime statistics. If 1980, the year when the country almost descended into civil war and eight hundred people were murdered, is used as a benchmark, then the current picture is frightening. In 1993 the gun was used in 4,385 crimes and 653 people were murdered. The difference with 1980 is that in that year most of the violence could have been attributed to the partisan battle for political power, whereas the shift in 1993 has been to random acts of violence and domestic incidents. This statistic may provide cold comfort to those who have lost members of their family or friends, but it does underline the drift away from an organized state to some notion of anarchy. See the *Gleaner*, January 20, 1994.

47. Carl Stone's thoughtful 1992 report to the Jamaican government on the possible reform of Parliament touches on most of the critical areas requiring reform, including the examination of proportional representation, the abandonment of the prime ministerial system, and the strengthening of constituency representation. Initially met with a lukewarm response from both government and opposition, the report has been increasingly embraced as the depth of political decay becomes more apparent. Yet, despite the acknowledgment of the need for change, the whole process remains largely divorced from the day-to-day existence of the vast majority of the people. See Carl Stone, *Report of the Stone Committee Appointed to Advise the Jamaican Government on the Performance, Accountability, and Responsibilities of Elected Parliamentarians* (Kingston: Bustamante Institute of Public and International Affairs, 1992).

48. Burbach argues that Chiapas is the first "postmodern" rebellion, not only because it has occurred after the end of the cold war, but because of the particular level of popular involvement and the relationship between leaders and led. To this extent, the present political moment in Jamaica might also be considered postmodern. The "people" are asserting themselves in national life in unprecedented ways without traditional political leadership in a flanking movement around the state apparatus and beyond national boundaries. See Roger Burbach, "Roots of the Postmodern Rebellion in Chiapas," *New Left Review*, vol. 205 (May/June 1994).

49. For a recent attempt to analyze the ideological dimensions of the "world system," see Immanuel Wallerstein, "The Agonies of Liberalism: What Hope Progress?" *New Left Review*, vol. 204 (March/April 1994).

50. For an extensive discussion of the possibilities for democratic transition for developing countries in the New World Order, see Shahid Qadir, Christopher Clapham, and Barry Gills, "Democratization in the Third World: An Introduction," *Third World Quarterly*, vol. 14, no. 3 (1993). Indeed, the entire volume is devoted to a discussion of democratic alternatives.

3

Sandoms and Other Exotic Women: Prostitution and Race in the Caribbean

Kamala Kempadoo

Two different approaches often surface when the subject of prostitution is broached by progressive scholars. The most common revolves around an analysis of the capitalist political economy, stressing notions of the commodification of the body and migration into the sex trade due to processes of underdevelopment, displacement, and dispossession. Sex work is, in this perspective, defined as a response by poor women to macroeconomic forces and structures. A second approach, articulated by radical feminists, situates prostitution as the ultimate expression of patriarchy. In this reading it is a constituent part of the sexual politics of rape and a form of "sexual slavery" in which women are the victims of violence and sexual terrorism. A representation of helpless, passive female populations is invariably produced through this analysis.

In this paper I argue for a different approach. Situations in the Caribbean, and across the globe, illustrate that prostitution is conditioned not only by economic and patriarchal interests but also by constructs of race, ethnicity, and nationality. Hence, I propose that we need to address relations of power based on these constructs in any contemporary analysis of the sex trade. Furthermore, I enter the discussion with the assumption that in order to fully apprehend the sex industry today we need not only an analysis of structural forces but also an examination of the way in which women and men, as sexual agents, organize and understand their everyday practices and of the intersection between macro- and microstructuring principles. In the following I first sketch a situation in the Caribbean that illustrates some of the complexities embedded in the sex trade, elaborate on the notion of exoticism as an ideology that underpins the present-day sex trade, both in the Caribbean and globally, and finally identify some of the ways we can begin to think about social change in relation to prostitution.

Prostitution in Curaçao

In 1949 the largest single brothel in the Americas opened on the Dutch Caribbean island of Curaçao. It was the result of deliberations between the chief police inspector, the minister of health, fathers of the Catholic Church, and the head of U.S. military forces on the island. It was approved by the colonial governor on behalf of the queen of the Netherlands and was financed by the Dutch Savings Bank. The rationale was to regulate prostitution on the island for the purpose of catering to the sexual needs and demands of various single men on the island—sailors, the U.S. military, Dutch marines, and migrant workers employed by the Royal Dutch Shell company—and to protect local womanhood from the "physical and psychological consequences of an evil" (*Aanbieding*).

An enclosed sex house with one hundred rooms, a police department to control activities within the brothel, and a government medical service to monitor prostitutes for sexually transmitted diseases were established. Hugo Bakhuis, a local businessman, was permitted to run the sex house under a hotel license, and women from other Caribbean territories were recruited to work at the "hotel" for three months. The sex house was christened Campo Alegre (the Happy Camp), continues to operate today under the name Mirage and is still in the hands of the Bakhuis family. Since 1949 around twenty-five thousand women, initially mainly from Cuba and Venezuela, today almost exclusively from the Dominican Republic and Colombia, have registered and worked in the brothel. They apply by letter to the immigration department for permission to work at the "hotel." The selection process is handled by a female administrator attached to the Vice and Morals Police Department and the women are registered so that they must attend a weekly medical checkup at a designated clinic. They may return again to the brothel after a year. During the time of my fieldwork in 1993, around 250 letters of application per month were arriving on the desk of the administrator; only 35–40 would make it through the selection process. Around 50 percent of the final candidates had worked at Campo previously. The women who are licensed to work in the brothel are invariably in their early twenties, "light-skinned" (i.e., brown or "mulatto"), with silky or bleached blond hair, and slim: the proverbial image of the sensual, sexy Caribbean woman. Few are full-time prostitutes. The majority incorporate a stint of sex work into their lives as domestic or factory workers, teachers, traders, mothers, and wives. Some are hoodwinked into the work, and arrive in Curaçao without being aware of what it was they applied for, but equally as many know what *Campo* stands for.[1]

Campo/Mirage is just one part of the sex work scenario on the island today. Small hotels are scattered around Willemstad, relying on the sexual labor of women who visit the island for two to three weeks on tourist visas—from Trinidad, Suriname, Haiti, Venezuela, Jamaica, and Aruba. They visit the island primarily to buy household and electronic goods or clothes in the Free Trade Zone as part of their trading activities in the region. Few women in this sector have pimps, and they manage to work quite independently. Escort services are also in operation, one of which is owned by two young Curaçaoan brothers who also run a restaurant and catering business. They offer female sexual services exclusively to tourists, "VIP's," and traveling businessmen. A majority of the escorts are white Dutch women who are employed on a part-time basis and hold other jobs elsewhere. Curaçao also has a substantial number of male prostitutes who mainly cater to male clients and who associate in closed parties or occasionally work in drag on the street. Much more hidden are the men who sell sex to women, mainly at the tourist resorts, working from beaches and bars.[2]

The sex trade on the island is also intertwined with the drug trade. The Dutch Antilles are transshipment points for cocaine from Colombia to the U.S. and Europe; some of the substance remains and is dealt and consumed on the island. Base—a derivative of cocaine, similar to crack—is widely smoked. Users—particularly women ranging anywhere from age fourteen into their sixties—sell sexual services cheaply from the street in order to obtain the drug. At the same time, men regularly pay prostitutes to use drugs with them (particularly in Campo) and/or the women take to cocaine or base to relieve the stress and strain of prostitution.

In short, Curaçao has a range of activities that exploit and profit from female sexual energies, several of which are supported and legitimized by the state. According to police officers, there are as many women working in the streets and small hotels as there are in Campo/Mirage at any given time, selling sex predominantly to men. About half the prostitutes are monitored by the police and department of health; others work clandestinely. The majority are Latinas, commonly referred to as *Sandoms,* a name derived from the capital of the Dominican Republic, Santo Domingo. Almost all are foreigners to the island and are located in extremely vulnerable positions. Even if documented and on the island with licenses to work in Campo, there are few avenues for support in cases of conflict with clients, sex hotel owners, or the police. They face isolation because of the hours they must work and the stigma that surrounds women in prostitution. Many are dependent on middle men for papers, letters of application, permits, airline tickets, travel arrangements, and accommodations. There are also various health risks specific to the job. Clients who bribe them to have sex without condoms are undoubtedly one of the greatest hazards in an era of AIDS and the HIV virus.

While prostitutes are continuously under scrutiny by government authorities, their clients are completely ignored. Nevertheless, simple calculations over the years have led to estimates of a minimum of ninety thousand paid visits per year to Campo alone. This figure probably doubles if the women are to make any profit and triples if the clandestine trade is taken into account. And although prostitution was initially legalized to cater to male visitors and migrants, by 1993 the majority of the paying clients were Curaçaoan and other Caribbean men of all classes.

Sexual Labor

Prostitution in the Caribbean, both state-regulated and clandestine, is not unique to Curaçao, even though the organization in Campo may be specific to the Dutch legal and colonial context. Historical studies by Fernando Henriques (1965), on race, sexuality, and prostitution, and by Hilary Beckles (1989) and Barbara Bush (1990) on slavery, for example, uncover various prostitution practices in the region. Studies of contemporary Jamaica, Haiti, the Dominican Republic, Aruba, Barbados, Suriname, Cuba, and Belize also point out that informal and more formal sex work and prostitution are common occurrences (Harrison 1991; Chanel 1994; Kalm 1975; Press 1978; O'Carroll-Barahona et al. 1994; Strout 1995). These and studies of other forms of sexual relations in the region indicate that paid sex is an integral part of the social fabric of Caribbean life, as much embedded in the societies as, for example, "outside," "visiting," "common-law," or even *"mati/kambrada/*lesbian" relationships (Abraham van der Mark 1973; Dann 1987; Wekker 1992).

In an extensive survey of women in the English-speaking Caribbean carried out from 1979 to 1982 and elaborated by Olive Senior in 1991, reliance by women on their sexual labor was defined as a way many working women "make do," constituting just one of the many "sources of livelihood" that they can and do use. Women in prostitution whom I interviewed in Curaçao also stressed this aspect of their involvement; in the wide range of their income-generating activities and strategies to provide and care for family, household, and selves, they defined sexual labor as one of their multiple resources. The notion of prostitution as work is also reflected in the new terms that are emerging in the region, such as *trabajadoras sexuales* in the Dominican Republic, *sekswerkers* in Suriname, and *jineteras* in Cuba. Stephanie Kane argues, on the basis of extensive research, that "recognized prostitution in Belize is a gender-specific form of migrant labor that serves the same economic function for women as agricultural work offers to men, and often at better pay" (Kane 1993:972).

The interpretation and redefinition of prostitution as "work" in the Caribbean echoes experiences and perspectives in various parts of the world. In recognition of this phenomenon various scholars have argued for a conceptualization of prostitution as a form of labor that begins with the premise of the employment of sexual energies for production and reproduction of human social life in both material and nonmaterial ways (Pheterson 1989; Sturdevant and Stolzfus 1992; White 1990; Raghuramaiah 1991). Thus, as a human resource, sexuality is seen as a way to nourish and sustain life—organized for pleasure, material gains, and procreation (Troung 1990). Given the particularities of specific political, economic, and cultural contexts, there is little claim to a universality in the social organization of sex in this conceptualization of prostitution. Nevertheless, studies of women's lives in capitalist-dominated societies point out that sexual labor is also exploited for capital accumulation: commodified, bought and sold for wages, thus constituting a basis for sex businesses that include brothels, sex centers, theaters and nightclubs, the pornography industry, and massage parlors. Mobilization of female sexual labor for the revitalization and renewal of male labor and military forces has also been identified in various contexts, such as in the Philippines, Korea, Indonesia, and Belize. Simultaneously, sex work has become an important source for financial support of the household or family of the prostitute. Taking all these aspects into account, sex work can be equated with any other human activity that contributes to the production and reproduction of capital and labor.

While it is often claimed that prostitution is the oldest profession, analyses of gendered relations of power within the sex industry point out that women overwhelmingly provide the labor while men profit—as managers of businesses, pimps, organizers of the sex trade, middle men and procurers, and as the party in the sexual interactions that gains pleasure and power. Drawing on larger patterns of masculinist hegemony, prostitution relations also reflect deeply embedded devaluations of the nonmale and nonmasculine in a variety of cultural contexts, in some instances distorting or exacerbating traditional religious practices and precolonial organizations of sex. Thus, prostitution thrives today on wide-scale control and exploitation of female sexual labor.

Race and Sex Work

A recurring theme in studies of the history of race and sex in the Caribbean concerns the intertwining of ideologies and practices that situated a woman of mixed African/European descent (the mulatta) as the object of white male sexual desire and fantasy, constituting her as the sexual servant, concubine or mistress, and whore (Henriques 1965; Bush 1990). This historical pattern is still very much alive in the tourist industry, where women are often portrayed in advertisements and promotional materials as "sensual mulattoes" (Dagenais 1993; Bolles 1992). However, it is as equally pernicious in the sex trade, upheld by governments as well as the broader male population. Reports from Haiti, for instance, suggest that a racist ideology continues to condition preferences by Haitian men for Dominican women. Dominican women are considered exotic and more professional than Haitians and, in the words of a pimp, are preferable because "they more closely approximate to Western standards of beauty" (Chanel 1994). In a similar vein, a sex tourist to Cuba states:

> The girls that are the easiest to find are usually black and from Oriente. I think the girls in the Dominican Republic, who are all mixed race, are more beautiful than these Cuban girls. But the black Cuban girls do not have the same dark complexion as the Haitians. (*World Sex Guide*, July 1995)

Elsewhere, the Cuban racial-sexual hierarchy is described as one where "fair-skinned, fine-featured, 'shopping girls,'" are the highest priced sex workers, with mulatta and black women in the lower echelons of the sex trade, working for predominantly Spanish and Italian tourists (Cooper

1995). In Belize "brothels tend to hire exclusively young 'Spanish,' 'clear-skinned' women . . . who come from the neighboring Central American republics" to cater to "the needs" of British soldiers, male tourists, and "Belizeans of all classes and ethnic backgrounds" (Kane 1993:971–972).

Similarly, formal and informal regulations in Curaçao not only exclude black Haitian women from Mirage but favor "light-skinned" Sandoms and other Latinas. Or, as a male respondent assured me: "If she's light colored, then she is sexually attractive to this population." A popular image in Curaçao is of women in the Dominican Republic being specially trained and groomed to provide sexual pleasure to men and thus being particularly suited to sex work. On the island Haitian women are perceived as "too black" and "unhygienic" (Lagro and Plotkin 1990). While "light-skinned" women thus dominate the sex trade in the region, it is white European women who form the elite among sex workers, with Afro-Caribbean women concentrated among the lowest-paid and the street-walking population.

Long-standing colonial racist hierarchies are reinforced through these "preferences," reassertimg the undesirability of "blackness" and the privilege of "whiteness." The patterning has produced a situation where, on the one hand, a specific category of Caribbean womanhood is targeted to sustain local economies and businesses, and, on the other hand, color and race define a woman's sexual capital. It is obviously rooted in colonial legacies and racial hierarchies that promote white superiority and power. However, in the context of today's sex trade in the region, where the largest proportion of the clients are black and other men of color, we need to interrogate this issue further, for it would seem that, in spite of black struggle, independence movements and reappreciations of blackness, particularly since the 1950s, there is still a very fundamental issue of racism that undergirds sexual relations and desire. Frantz Fanon's analysis in *Black Skin, White Masks* (1952) of the devaluation of black masculinity and need for a decolonization of the black mind in relationship to sexuality and whiteness seems to be still relevant in this context. Along similar lines, a black revolutionary noted in the late 1960s in Curaçao:

> At Campo Alegre I have noticed that there are only white women, and the Black woman who might be among them has to work double the hours to make the same money as her white colleagues. . . . I have seen how our revolutionaries and young men who are full of Black Power are the first in the line to go to bed with a white woman, or to marry a

white woman. . . . I have noticed that when they screw a Black woman she becomes their whore, but if they screw a white woman, it's as if she has done them a favor. . . . Why is our Black woman used by the white man and rejected by the Black man? (*Vito*)

Ongoing explorations into social constructions of black masculinity, femininity, and sexualities may begin to unpack other dimensions of this racialized dynamic within the sex trade. It may also lead to a fuller apprehension of an apparent "underrepresentation" of Haitian and other African women in the trade, despite the fact that they come from nations that, "objectively," constitute the world's poorest.

Exotic Women

Compounding the issue of racism in the trade is the employment of sexual labor of foreign migrant women. In Curaçao state regulations were very deliberately set up to "protect" Dutch Caribbean womanhood from what was perceived as degradation, dishonor, and immoral promiscuous behavior and to license foreign women for prostitution. The classic madonna/whore dichotomy was therefore defined along not only racial and cultural but also national lines. Surveying the global arena on this count, it becomes quickly apparent that this phenomenon is not specific to Curaçao.

Despite the difficulty of quantifying underground criminal activities, various research and news reports indicate a heavy reliance in the global sex trade on migrant/foreign women. Between 1932 and 1945 around 200,000 Asian women were forced into brothels for the Japanese army as so-called comfort women (*New York Times,* August 31, September 1, 1994; Howard 1995). Approximately 80 percent of this population was Korean (Howard 1995; Hicks 1995). In 1991 70 percent of the estimated 150,000 sex workers in Japan were Filipino (Korvinus 1992). In the same year young Afghan refugee women worked as sex workers in Pakistan, where another 200,000-odd women from Bangladesh were also involved. Sri Lanka had approximately 70,000 young women in the sex trade, many of whom had been sold into marriage or sent to Greece, Lebanon, India, Pakistan, and Cyprus. An estimated 17,000 of these young Sri Lankan women worked in Kuwait as prostitutes (Korvinus 1992).

Observations in China signal increasing numbers of Eastern European, Russian, and Vietnamese prostitutes in Beijing—foreign women who are reported to be more "skilled" than their Chinese counterparts and considered more attractive in the trade (*BBC World Service Report*, April 28, 1994). The world's largest red-light district, in Bombay, India, which according to recent estimates involves anywhere from 100,000–600,000 women, relies predominantly upon migrant female labor, around 50 percent of which originates in Nepal (Friedman 1996; Barry 1995). In the late 1980s around 60 percent of the prostitutes in the Netherlands were from third world countries, with an increasing number also originating from Eastern Europe (Brussa 1989; Altink 1995). Fifty percent of the approximately seven thousand prostitutes in Paris, France in the early 1990s were "immigrants" (Barry 1995). In the U.S. women of color comprise between 30 and 40 percent of the prostitute population (*Gauntlet* 1994:17). Conversely, men stationed in or visiting countries such as Korea, the Philippines, Thailand, and Belize are provided with organized rest and relaxation facilities or sex tours that depend on the participation of local women (Sturdevant and Stolzfus 1992; Enloe 1993). In short, large proportions of women in the global sex trade have been, and continue to be, culturally, nationally, or ethnically different from their clients.

Exploitation of "alien" labor and "foreign" bodies in the international sex trade therefore requires much more attention than it has hitherto been given. The overrepresentation of "other" women and the hierarchies of race and color within the trade seem to suggest that there is no straightforward correlation between economic conditions and prostitution or patriarchy and prostitution. Simply put, not all poor women are likely to end up in the sex trade. Rather, their entrance into the business, and the conditions under which they work, vary according to local, regional, and international relations of power along gendered, economic, national, and ethnic divides in which there is much variation. In Curaçao, for example, these factors combine to produce notions of the desirable Sandom whore.

Sexualization of the racial, ethnic, or cultural Other, and the simultaneous oppression and vicious exploitation that accompanies the sex industry, is reminiscent of the practice and ideology of exoticism of earlier colonial and imperialist projects. The Noble Savage of the Americas, Sable Queens of Africa, Tahitian Beauties through Captain Cook's lenses, stereotypes of the sensual Oriental Temptress, and French artistic representations of the Black Venus are a few of the representations (Said 1979; Kabbani 1986; Rousseau and Porter 1990; Bush 1990). Encounters with cultures and societies that differed from Western European bourgeois norms and values produced various ideologies of non-Western peoples living in idyllic pleasure, splendid innocence, or paradiselike conditions as purely sensual, natural, simple, and uncorrupted beings.

Simultaneously, the societies were defined by Europeans as backward, inferior, and uncivilized, requiring guidance, government, and development. The eroticization of women of the different cultures was an integral part of this movement, whereby their sexuality was defined as highly attractive and desirable yet was related to the natural primitiveness and lower order of the Other. Exotic cultures, and particularly their women, thus became sites where sex "was neither penalized, not pathologized nor exclusively procreative" (Porter 1990:118). Womanhood among the colonized thus represented uninhibited, unbridled sensuality and sexual pleasure for the colonizer. Exoticism in its various expressions brought legitimacy to European rule and is distinguished from other racisms in that it fostered the illusion of admiration for, and attraction to, the Other while enacting murder, rape, violence, and enslavement. That sex industries today depend upon the eroticization of the ethnic and cultural Other suggests that we are witnessing a contemporary form of exoticism that sustains postcolonial and post–cold war relations of power and dominance.

Toward a Change

Whenever the subject of challenging and changing the injustices and oppressions that are glaringly obvious in the global sex industry is raised, deep-seated moral judgments about sex begin to surface. From Marx and Engels to the present-day abolitionist movement (in the guise of an international network against trafficking in women), sexual intercourse is equated with the highest form of intimacy and love, both of which are firmly grounded in notions of the body as a sacred site. Kathleen Barry makes this point: "Sexual experience involves the most personal, private, erotic, sensitive parts of our physical and psychic being" (Barry 1984: 267). A certain claim to universally shared morals, codes, and experiences speaks from this position. Rarely do radical feminists or socialists include notions of sex for pleasure in the absence of love or as an honorable "source of livelihood." Yet it is precisely these two facets that women in the sex trade talk about in the light of social change. Prostitutes stress the need to understand sex and sexual arrangements in specific cultural, class, and religious contexts, to strip away the stigmas attached to sex work, to decriminalize prostitution, to end the trafficking of persons for prostitution, and to legitimize sex work. Building settings in which both women and men are able to engage in various sexual relations on the basis of equality, dignity, and respect is of utmost importance to this movement (Troung 1990; Pheterson 1989:40–42).

This approach is all the more relevant in the case of the Caribbean, where the history of sexual relations is far less confined to monogamous marriages and ideologies of "romantic love" than in fully Europeanized societies and includes a range of sexual arrangements. The centrality of sexual praxis to Caribbean social life suggests that if we are serious about envisioning alternatives for social change in the Caribbean, we need to pay more attention to this arena in women's and men's lives and to integrate analyses of sex and sexuality into our political and theoretical work. We may find that the dominant values of sex as intimacy and love hinder rather than sustain broader visions of sexual and gender equality and justice and that we need to redefine and reconceptualize older paradigms and approaches to prostitution.

Second, as I have argued here, contemporary forms of prostitution and sex work are also complicated by hierarchies of race and ethnicity as well as exploitations of "the exotic." Thus, apart from identifying and empowering alternative definitions of sex work, a deconstruction of racialized and ethnicized genders and sexualities is also necessary. This part of the struggle—as Audre Lorde (1984), Cornel West (1993), and bell hooks (1993) point out—has not been a strength among black progressive scholars. Various masculinist racist myopias, narrow neo-Marxist paradigms, or an unwillingness to examine and uncover personal complicities and actions has meant there is little critical scholarship about sexual relations and race within black communities or societies, particularly from a perspective that affirms and empowers black female sexuality.

Third, the conceptualization of prostitution as sexual labor enables us to make links to international divisions of labor and to support broader working peoples' struggles for change. As a vital part of national, household, and community economies and trade, sex work can be compared to other informal sector activities in which women are increasingly concentrated. As various researchers have established, structural changes since the mid-1970s in the organization of production and investment in the formal global capitalist economy have greatly impacted on women's work, particularly in third world countries. The displacement of female populations from their already scarce arenas of formal employment and an even further concentration in unorganized, casual, or informal sectors is widely recognized. The spread of Maquiladora in Mexico or Export Processing Zones in countries such as Malaysia, Sri Lanka, or the Dominican Republic or the rise in home work in Britain attests to this rearrangement in international relations of production and the intensification of the exploitation of female labor (Deere et al. 1990; Rowbotham and Mitter 1994). The sex trade has also flourished, with large numbers of "exotic" Southeast Asian women and Caribbean Latinas appearing in Europe's sex industry by the mid-1980s, working in conditions comparable to that of indentured laborers—as prostitutes, strippers, porn stars, erotic dancers, telephone sex workers, or escorts—forever working to pay off a debt to a hotel or club manager, boyfriend, lover or husband, travel agent, or impresario.

Running counter to this trend are a variety of initiatives by women as "minuscule entrepreneurs" in trading, street vending, food processing, farming, shopkeeping, and other similar ventures (McAfee 1991; Haniff 1988; St. Cyr 1990). In this surge of activity older patterns of women's work are revitalized and extended, new areas explored and established, and traditional systems, values, and ideologies are sometimes challenged or redefined. It is also in this flexible, casual, and informal sector that women are organizing in cooperatives, self-employment associations, unions, and various networks to resist exploitative and oppressive relations and, in the process, shaping and defining new democratic movements and people-centered development processes (Sen and Grown 1987; Bolles 1993; Women's Feature Service 1992; Mitter 1994). While most of the attention in the last few years has centered on women's resistances and struggles in agriculture, garment production, domestic work, Export Processing Zones, textile industries, and so forth, the emergence of sex workers' organizations in, for example, Ecuador, Suriname, Brazil, Thailand, the Dominican Republic, or Zimbabwe indicates that third world and black women in the sex industry are also engaged in collective struggles for change (Pheterson 1989; ENDA 1993; O'Caroll 1994). We may want to listen more carefully to these initiatives and movements in order to redefine and broaden our political and theoretical perspectives on prostitution.

Notes

1. Of the forty-six persons involved with the sex trade whom I interviewed in-depth during fieldwork in Curaçao in 1993, nineteen were women engaged in "illegal" or clandestine sex work.

2. For further details on the workings of the brothel and the broader sex trade in Curaçao, see Kempadoo (1998) and Martis (1999).

References

Aanbieding. 1943–1944. Staten van Curaçao, 1. Zittingsjaar 1943–1944–12.
Abraham van der Mark, E. E. 1973. *Yu'i Mama: Enkele Facetten van Gezinsstructuur op Curacao*. Assen: Van Gorcum.
Altink, Sietske. 1995. *Stolen Lives: Trading Women Into Sex and Slavery*. London: Scarlet.
Barry, Kathleen. 1984. *Female Sexual Slavery*. New York and London: New York University Press.
———— 1995. *The Prostitution of Sexuality*. New York and London: New York University Press.
Beckles, Hilary. 1989. *Natural Rebels: A Social History of Enslaved Black Women in Barbados*. London: Zed.
Bolles, A. Lynn. 1992. "Sand Sea and the Forbidden." *Transforming Anthropology* 3:30–34.
———— 1993. "Doing It for Themselves: Women's Research and Action in the Commonwealth Caribbean." In Edna Acosta-Belen and Christine E. Bose, eds., *Researching Women in Latin America and the Caribbean*, pp. 153–174. Boulder: Westview.
Brussa, Licia. 1989. "Migrant Prostitutes in the Netherlands." In Gail Pheterson, ed., *A Vindication of the Rights of Whores*, pp. 227–239. Seattle: Seal.
Bush, Barbara. 1990. *Slave Women in Caribbean Society: 1650–1838*. Bloomington: Indiana University Press.
Chanel, Ives Marie. 1994. "Haitian and Dominican Women in the Sex Trade." Trans. Cathy Shepherd. *CAFRA NEWS* 8 (June):13–14.
Cooper, Marc. 1995. "For Sale: Used Marxism." *Harper's Magazine*, March.
Dagenais, Hugette. 1993. "Women in Guadeloupe: The Paradoxes of Reality." In Janet H. Momsen, ed., *Women and Change in the Caribbean: A Pan-Caribbean Perspective*, pp. 83–108. Bloomington and London: Indiana University Press.
Dann, Graham. 1987. *The Barbadian Male: Sexual Attitudes and Practice*. Caribbean: Macmillan.
Deere, Carmen Diana, Peggy Antrobus, Lynn Bolles, Edwin Melendez, Peter Phillips, Marcia Rivera, and Helen Safa. 1990. *In the Shadows of the Sun: Caribbean Development Alternatives and U.S. Policy*. Boulder: Westview.
ENDA. 1993. "Sex-Workers, Health, and Human Rights in Africa." Report of the VII Conference on AIDS in Africa held in Yuounde, Cameroun, December 7–9, 1992. Dakar: ENDA.
Enloe, Cynthia. 1993. *The Morning After: Sexual Politics at the End of the Cold War*. Berkeley: University of California Press.
Fanon, Frantz. 1970 [1952]. *Black Skin, White Masks*. London: Paladin.
Friedman, Robert I. 1996. "India's Shame." *Nation*, April 6.

Gauntlet: Exploring the Limits of Free Expression, no. 4 (1994).

Haniff, Nesha Z. 1988. *Blaze a Fire: Significant Contributions of Caribbean Women.* Toronto: Sister Vision Black Women and Women of Color Press.

Harrison, Faye V. 1991. "Women in Jamaica's Urban Informal Economy: Insights from a Kingston Slum." In Chandra Talpade Mohanty, Ann Russo, and Lourdes Torres, eds., *Third World Women and the Politics of Feminism,* pp. 173–196. Bloomington and Indianapolis: Indiana University Press.

Henriques, Fernando. 1965. *Prostitution in Europe and the Americas.* New York: Citadel.

Hicks, George. 1995. *The Comfort Women: Japan's Brutal Regime of Enforced Prostitution in the Second World War.* New York and London: Norton.

hooks, bell. 1993. "Dreaming Ourselves Dark and Deep: Black Beauty." In *Sisters of the Yam: Black Women and Self-Recovery.* Boston: South End.

Howard, Keith, ed. 1995. *True Stories of the Korean Comfort Women.* London: Cassell.

Kabbani, Rana. 1986. *Europe's Myths of Orient.* London: Pandora.

Kalm, Florence. 1975. "The Two 'Faces' of Antillean Prostitution." Paper presented at the American Anthropological Association Meeting, November.

Kane, Stephanie. 1993. "Prostitution and the Military: Planning AIDS Intervention in Belize." *Social Science Medicine* 36:965–979.

Kempadoo, Kamala. 1998. "The Migrant Tightrope: Experiences from the Caribbean." In Kamala Kempadoo and Jo Doezema, eds., *Global Sex Workers: Rights, Resistance, and Redefinition,* pp. 124–138. New York: Routledge.

Korvinus, Berthy. 1992. "Grenzeloze Sexuele Uitbuiting." Report from the Conference of the Asian Women's Human Rights Council held in Seoul, Korea, December 1991. Werkgroep Mensenrechten Raad van Kerken in Nederland.

Lagro, Monique and Donna Plotkin. 1990. *The Suitcase Traders in the Free Zone of Curaçao.* Port of Spain: Caribbean Development and Co-operation Committee, Economic Commission for Latin America and the Caribbean.

Lorde, Audre. 1984. "Uses of the Erotic: The Erotic as Power." In *Sister Outsider,* pp. 53–59. New York: Crossing.

McAfee, Kathy. 1991. *Storm Signals: Structural Adjustment and Development Alternatives in the Caribbean.* Boston: South End.

Martis, Jacqueline. 1999. "Tourism and the Sex Trade in St. Maarten and Curaçao, the Netherlands Antilles." In Kamala Kempadoo, ed., *Sun, Sex, and Gold: Tourism and Sex Work in the Caribbean,* pp. 201–215. Boulder: Rowman and Littlefield.

Mitter, Swasti. 1994. "On Organizing Women in Casualized Work: A Global Overview." In Sheila Rowbotham and Swasti Mitter, eds., *Dignity and Daily Bread,* pp. 14–52. London and New York: Routledge.

O'Carroll-Barahona, Claris, Juanita Altenberg, Dusilley Cannings, Christel Antonius-Smits, and Ruben Del Prado. 1994. *Needs Assessment Study Among Street-Based Female Commercial Sex Workers in Paramaribo, Suriname.* Paramaribo: National AIDS Progamme.

Porter, Roy. 1990. "The Exotic as Erotic: Captain Cook in Tahiti." In G. S. Rousseau and Roy Porter, eds., *Exoticism in the Enlightenment*. Manchester: Manchester University Press.

Pheterson, Gail, ed. 1989. *A Vindication of the Rights of Whores*. Washington: Seal.

Press, Clayton M., Jr. 1978. "Reputation and Respectability Reconsidered: Hustling in a Tourist Setting." *Caribbean Issues* 4 (April):109–119.

Raghuramaiah, K. Lakshmi. 1991. *Night Birds: Indian Prostitutes from Devadasis to Call Girls*. Delhi: Chanakya.

Rousseau, G. S. and Roy Porter, eds. 1990. *Exoticism in the Enlightenment*. Manchester: Manchester University Press.

Rowbotham, Sheila and Swasti Mitter. 1994. *Dignity and Daily Bread: New Forms of Economic Organizing Among Poor Women in the Third World and the First*. London and New York: Routledge.

Said, Edward. 1979. *Orientalism*. New York: Vintage.

Sen, Gita and Caren Grown. 1987. *Development, Crises, and Alternative Visions: Third World Women's Perspectives*. New York: Monthly Review.

Senior, Olive. 1991. *Working Miracles: Women's Lives in the English-Speaking Caribbean*. London and Bloomington: James Currey and Indiana University Press.

St. Cyr, Joaquin. 1990. *Participation of Women in Caribbean Development: Inter-Island Trading and Export Processing Zones*. UN Economic Commission for Latin America and the Caribbean.

Strout, Jan. 1995. "Women, the Politics of Sexuality, and Cuba's Economic Crisis." *Cuba Update* (April/June).

Sturdevant, Saundra Pollock and Brenda Stolzfus, eds. 1992. *Let the Good Times Roll: Prostitution and the U.S. Military in Asia*. New York: New Press.

Troung, Than Dam. 1990. *Sex, Money and Morality: The Political Economy of Prostitution and Tourism in South East Asia*. London: Zed.

Vito, November 23, 1969.

Wekker, Gloria. 1992. " 'I Am Gold Money' (I Pass Through All Hands, But I Do Not Lose My Value): The Construction of Selves, Gender, and Sexualities in a Female Working-Class, Afro-Surinamese Setting." Ph.D. diss., University of California.

West, Cornel. 1993. "Black Sexuality: The Taboo Subject." In *Race Matters*, pp. 83–91. Boston: Beacon.

White, Luise. 1990. *The Comforts of Home: Prostitution in Colonial Nigeria*. Chicago: University of Chicago Press.

Women's Feature Service. 1992. *The Power To Change: Women in the Third World Redefine Their Environment*. London: Zed.

World Sex Guide. 1995. Cuba report, July.

4

Race and Revolution in Cuba: African American Perspectives

Manning Marable

The historic Abyssinian Baptist Church of Harlem was packed to over-flowing on Sunday night, October 22, 1995. A flood of dignitaries managed to make their way into church: Congressman Charles Rangel, Congressman Jose Serrano, and Congresswoman Nydia Velasquez; Minister Conrad Muhammad, leader of Harlem's branch of the Nation of Islam; Afrocentric scholars John Henrik Clarke and Leonard Jeffries; and radical feminist scholar-activist Angela Y. Davis. Reverend Calvin O. Butts welcomed his audience of thirteen hundred people and described Abyssinian's guest of honor as "one of the great leaders in the world."[1] Reverend Butts added that it had been long the tradition of his church "to welcome those who are visionary and revolutionary and who seek the freedom of all of the people around the world." Harlem black nationalist activist Elombe Brath informed his audience that the daughter of the keynote speaker was among the demonstrators denouncing his presence in New York City. Her behavior was "hardly" what one might expect of "family." But, after all, Brath smiled, "Castro has family right here . . . among us!" The audience roared with approval.[2]

Fidel Castro had come home to Harlem. Everyone in the audience knew about, and many remembered from personal experience, Castro's controversial visit to the United Nations thirty-five years earlier. Now part of Harlem's folklore, Castro was celebrated for staying at the Hotel

Theresa, at the corner of 125th Street and Seventh Avenue. Other world dignitaries who had traveled uptown to caucus with Fidel included Nikita Khrushchev, Gamal Abdel Nasser, and Jawaharlal Nehru. Castro reminded his audience that his 1960 delegation had first been expelled from a fancy midtown hotel. "We were happy to have the heart of Harlem as our neighbors," Castro declared. "We could see the city's discrimination, it was so very obvious. As President Lincoln said, 'You can fool the people some of the time—you can fool not all of the people all of the time.'" Castro honored his African American audience by adding: "You were never deceived. We were never deceived." There was thunderous applause.[3]

Now Castro had returned to the United States and once more had been snubbed. He observed that he was not welcome at a reception President Clinton had just hosted for other world leaders at the New York Public Library in midtown Manhattan. New York's conservative mayor, Rudolph Giuliani, had also excluded Castro from attending a host of dinners and public receptions. "The Mayor says I was a demon, and a demon couldn't be invited to dinner," Castro explained. "So I said I'll go hungry the first day in New York." But Castro added, "as a revolutionary, I knew I would be welcome in this neighborhood." Castro was even appropriately attired for the occasion. Downtown at the United Nations he had worn a conservative dark suit. For the Abyssinian audience, he put on his olive green fatigues. The president of Cuba laughed, "How could I go to Harlem in my business suit?" The United States had maintained an illegal embargo against his country for thirty-five years, but the Cuban people would defend their revolution. Castro's voice rose defiantly, "We will never change because we are right."[4]

The enthusiastic acclaim Fidel Castro received that evening was absolutely genuine. No white political leader, not even President Clinton, would ever come as close to receiving this kind of approval from literally every sector of the African American community. To Nation of Islam minister Conrad Muhammad, Castro was respected for "maintaining the dignity of his nation and his dignity as a world leader." Castro's visit was "one of the few occasions when we don't see a man bowing down and kissing the feet of America."[5] Across the ideological spectrum of black American politics, Fidel was not viewed as just another third world politician. Only Nelson Mandela of South Africa surpassed the moral authority and political credibility that Castro could claim within black America.

For generations, African American leaders have felt a deep affection for the people of Cuba and their historic struggles for self-determination.

Cuba and black America are, by most criteria, very different societies. Yet they also share certain common historical experiences and social characteristics. These social and historical similarities form the context for an ongoing political dialogue between the people of both nations. The exchange has frequently been sympathetic and in concert with acts of political solidarity. But it has also been filled with misunderstandings and ambiguities. Adding to the confusion is that Cubans and African Americans often use identical language to describe a racial issue or concept, but they generally mean very different things.

The most obvious characteristic the two societies have in common is their histories of racialization. Cuba and the U.S. are both "racial formations," societies constructed over hundreds of years with different kinds of racial hierarchies that were first developed in slave economies. What separates the two societies, however, is how the dynamics of racial domination and black resistance evolved over time. This is admittedly something of an oversimplification, but a proper starting point is found by examining the different meanings and definitions of "race." In the North American context race as a social force generally had a two-dimensional or dual character. As it historically evolved, race was simultaneously imposed from without and constructed from within. That is, race in the U.S. represented a political economy of exploitation and subordinate sets of social relations largely coded by phenotype or skin color. To be "black" was to be overdetermined by sets of social and economic structures of domination, which were rationalized and justified by an elaborate ideology of white privilege. Yet, for African Americans, "race" was also a site of resistance. The designation of racial inferiority, imposed from without, gave the oppressed a very different and potentially creative perspective on the nature of power and how the society actually worked. In this sense the category of race generated a series of modes of struggle, from expressions of cultural resistance to outright rebellion. From within the confines of the racialized social body, black Americans found a freedom to challenge the social order in ways that most whites could barely conceive.

Cuba, by way of contrast, evolved a definition of race that was in certain respects one-dimensional. Blacks, whites, and everybody in between conceived of race as a social hierarchy that confined a segment of the society to the bottom rung. Blackness was therefore something to be avoided, overcome, transcended. Even to people of African descent, blackness represented a kind of stigmatization. Thus the best way to approach the issue of racial differences was by not talking about race at all. Moreover, in countries like Cuba and Puerto Rico, a popular cross-race nationalism had developed by the late nineteenth century. Blackness by itself did not prohibit individuals of talent and ability, such as Antonio Maceo, from assuming leading positions in the struggle for national independence. In short, race mattered, but Cuban nationalism usually trumped race. Conversely, American nationalism was so intertwined with white supremacy that it is impossible to imagine an African American Maceo assuming the role of George Washington or Ulysses S. Grant. In the U.S., to be "all-American" is presumed to be "white."

The Cuban model of race relations was influenced by its distinct historical and social development. Compared to other slave societies in the Americas and the Caribbean, Cuba's economic development occurred relatively late. It was only in the nineteenth century that Cuba took the place of Saint Dominique as the center of sugar production in the Western hemisphere. The expansion of the sugar industry depended upon labor, and this was the primary factor behind the massive importation of Africans into the country. Between 1811 and 1870 about 550,000 slaves were shipped into Cuba, or roughly the number that was transported to all of Spanish America in the previous century. The physical conditions for Cuban slaves were, by all accounts, horrific, and mortality rates on the sugar plantations were extremely high. But the legal and cultural structure for organizing race relations in Cuba, compared to the United States, was in many respects more liberal. In 1872 Cuba's racial composition included 287,000 African slaves, 107,000 mulattoes and free blacks, and 306,000 whites. Through the system of *coartación*, many Africans were permitted to purchase their freedom.[6] Mulattoes and free blacks still experienced extreme discrimination and economic liabilities. But they did not encounter the same virulent ideology of white supremacy and racial prejudice that was all too common in the United States.

Throughout much of the nineteenth century antislavery activists in both the United States and Cuba recognized the similarities between their respective slave societies and drew mutual support from each other. For example, at the outbreak of Cuba's Ten Years' War (1868–1878), African American leaders quickly rallied behind the movement for independence against Spain. They recognized that the most prominent general of the revolutionary forces, Antonio Maceo, was black, and they also understood that this struggle would inevitably lead to the abolition of Cuban slavery. The great African American abolitionist Frederick Douglass declared that "the first gleam of the sword of freedom and independence in Cuba secured my sympathy with the revolutionary cause," and he urged young black Americans "to join their fortunes with those of their suffering brethren in Cuba."[7] In 1872 the Cuban Anti-Slavery Society was founded in New York City with the leadership of black abolitionist Henry Highland Garnet. The chief theoretician and political leader of the Cuban independence movement, Jose Martí, was personally close with black activists such as Garnet, and he frequently attacked the policies and practices of U.S. racism against African Americans and American Indians.[8]

A second factor that helped to foster links between Cuba and black America was the connection of both to the black Caribbean. Toussaint L'Ouverture and the Haitian revolution of the late eighteenth and early nineteenth centuries inspired a series of slave conspiracies and insurrections in the U.S., including those of Gabriel Prosser, in Virginia in 1800, and Denmark Vesey, in South Carolina in 1822. There was among black Americans a recognition of racial solidarity through the struggles of the Haitian masses as well as those of other black populations in the Caribbean region. Such linkages would become even more important a century later, as hundred of thousands of Afro-Caribbean poor and working people migrated to both the United States and Cuba in the desperate search for employment. Over 80,000 Jamaicans migrated to Cuba between 1919 and 1931. Another 140,000 black migrants, mostly from the Caribbean, entered the U.S. between 1899 and 1937. Historian Winston James estimates that by 1930 nearly one-fourth of Harlem's population was of Caribbean origin.[9] This black Caribbean diaspora was a vast international network where political ideas and protest organizations moved broadly across geographical boundaries.

One example of the intricate connections between the black Caribbean, black America, and Cuba was represented in the black nationalist international movement of Marcus Garvey. Garvey's Universal Negro Improvement Association (UNIA) was founded in Jamaica in 1914 but soon developed a mass base of supporters throughout the United States. The UNIA also moved to establish contacts with the Afro-Cuban community. By the time Garvey visited Cuba in March 1921, there were already 25 UNIA branches across the island. When sectors of the Cuban press criticized Garvey's appeals to black solidarity and pan-Americanism as antithetical to Cuba's supposed tradition of nonracialism, his response said a good deal about the racial outlook of at least some Afro-Cubans. Garvey declared that it was

> a mistake to suppose that I want to take [all] Negroes to Africa. . . . Each Negro can be a citizen of the nation in which he was born or that he has chosen but I see the building of a great state in Africa which, featuring in the concert of the great nations, will make the Negro as respectable as others. . . . Cuban Negroes will be favored by the building of this African state because when this state exists they will be considered and respected as descendants of this powerful country which has enough strength to protect them.[10]

Although the UNIA, at the height of its influence in Cuba, claimed fifty-two branch organizations, historical evidence indicates that the bulk of Garvey's local converts to black nationalism were workers from the non-Hispanic Caribbean, frequently of Jamaican background. Winston James observes that "Afro-Cubans would sometimes attend the meetings of the Garveyites, but seldom joined the organization." Most of Cuban representatives at the UNIA's international conventions "had surnames like Collins, Cunning and Taite."[11] Despite the somewhat limited appeal of Garvey, the U.S.-backed Cuban dictator, General Gerardo Machado, left nothing to chance. Garvey's newspaper, the *Negro World*, and the UNIA chapters were viciously suppressed. In 1930 Garvey himself was barred from ever visiting the island again. Machado sternly declared that racism did not exist in Cuba and that "the propaganda of Garvey is prejudicial to society in Cuba."[12]

A third element in the African American–Cuba relationship was the parallel struggle that oppressed people in both societies had waged for political democracy and, to a lesser extent, self-determination. In the United States blacks were deliberately barred from legal citizenship for more than two centuries, and for nearly one hundred more years were effectively blocked from exercising their full constitutional rights. The black freedom movement that emerged in this context emphasized the redefinition and expansion of the concept of democracy and questioned the deeply flawed institutions of U.S. representative government that rationalized and even celebrated white supremacy. In short, the practical experiences of being black in racist white America have taught African Americans that the United States had no monopoly on the true meaning of political freedom and that other societies should have the right to decide for themselves what their political institutions should look like. In Cuba, after centuries of Spanish domination, the United States claimed its own hegemony over the island and its people. Cuba was defined as part of "America's backyard," and its political institutions and economic system were expected to conform to U.S. interests. Thus the insurgent democratic movements that emerged in twentieth-century Cuba also developed ideologies that were intensely critical of the U.S. model of political democracy.

Intellectuals, artists, trade unionists, and many others in Cuba and black America actively corresponded with each other and closely followed major political events in each country. One excellent example is provided by the great Cuban poet Nicolás Guillén, who maintained extensive contacts with African American artists and writers such as Langston Hughes.[13] Just as important, the struggles of the African American people served to inspire Cuban progressives. For instance, in 1931 when nine young black men were framed for the rape of two white women in Scottsboro, Alabama, and were threatened with execution, Cubans participated in the international campaign to save their lives. Mirta Aguirre's 1935 poem presents a powerful antiracist critique of U.S. society:

> Scottsboro en Alabama
> Scottsboro en Yanquilandia.
> Es un hierro puesto al fuego
> y elevado en las entrañas de una raza.
> Nueve negros casi niños, sin trabajo
> Dos mujeres, prostitutas.
> Ley de Lynch, capitalismo, burguesía,
> las tres K del turbia historia
> Y a los pies del monstruo enorme de mil garras,
> nueve negros casi niños.
> Scottsboro en Alabama,
> en la tierra imperialista: Yanquilandia
> es un manto de martirio y es un manto de vergüenza
> que cobija las dos razas.[14]

A new phase in Cuban-black American relations began on January 1, 1959, with the flight of dictator Fulgencio Batista to the Dominican Republic and the triumph of the Cuban revolution. The massive economic and social reforms initiated by the new government had the greatest positive impact upon Afro-Cubans who were disproportionately represented at the bottom of society. The revolution's explicitly antiracist agenda was clearly stated by Fidel Castro in a televised speech on March 22, 1959. Outlawing racial discrimination in public accommodations, in the work-place and schools, Castro declared that "nobody can consider himself as being of a pure, much less superior, race."[15] Black American opinion at the initial stages of the Cuban revolution was generally favorable. In early 1959 the *Amsterdam News* published a series of articles documenting the prospects for the revolution and its implications for black people, both inside Cuba and the United States. One remarkable essay by John Young III, "The Negro in Castro's Cuba," located the significance of events in Cuba within the civil rights struggles then occurring throughout the South:

> It is a mark of his destiny that in the present world struggle between Russia and the United States for friendship of colored peoples, the mantle of leadership has fallen upon the shoulders of the American Negro. This leadership has made him increasingly sensitive to injustice wherever it may occur in the world. It logically follows, therefore, that Cuba, with a great Negro population, should draw the active interest that has been manifested in Harlem during the present crisis. Then, too, the Batista injustices of lynching and police state are so remindful of the identical practices now prevalent against the Negro in the South.[16]

As hundreds of thousands of mostly white upper- and middle-class Cubans fled into exile in the U.S., many black Americans began to interpret this exodus in distinctly racial terms. In 1959 journalist Ralph Matthews, writing for the *Baltimore Afro-American* observed: "Every white man who cuffs, deprives and abuses even the lowest colored person, simply because he is white and the other colored, should have seared upon his consciousness the fact that it is possible for the tables to be turned. Castro has proved it in our time."[17]

In July 1960 a group of African American writers and activists—including John Henrik Clarke, LeRoi Jones (Amiri Baraka), Julian May-field, and Harold Cruse—were invited to Cuba to "see for ourselves what it was all about," as Cruse later wrote. In his *Crisis of the Negro Intellectual*, Cruse captured the contradictory feelings of some African Americans about the turbulent situation in revolutionary Cuba. "I was admittedly pro-Castro, but there were too many Communists around acting imperious and important," Cruse complained. "Yet we were treated with such overwhelming deference, consideration and privilege, it was difficult to be critical." The delegation made the long journey from Havana to the Sierra Maestra mountains to attend the July 26 national celebration of the revolution. Cruse recalls:

> We were caught up in a revolutionary outpouring of thousands upon thousands of people making their way up the mountain roads to the shrine of the Revolution, under the hottest sun-drenching any of us Americans had ever experienced. Jones and I stood shoulder-to-shoulder in a Cuban rebel army truck, packed to its side-ribbings with liberated Castroites whose euphoria we could feel profoundly, but not experience. . . . Our reward was the prize of revolutionary protocol that favored those victims of capitalism away from home.[18]

Despite being swept up in the spirit of revolution, Cruse was still troubled by the question "What did it all mean and how did it relate to the Negro in America?"[19]

LeRoi Jones, representing a younger, more militant black generation, came away with very different impressions than Cruse. In his classic 1960 essay, "Cuba Libre," Jones recounted his experiences traveling through revolutionary Cuba. At the July 26 rally, surrounded by thousands of people, the North American delegation was introduced to Castro on the speaker's platform. Jones grasped Fidel's hand and, through an interpreter, explained that he was a poet from New York City. Castro was amused and asked Jones what the U.S. government "thought about my trip. I shrugged my shoulders," Jones states, "and asked him what did he intend to do with this revolution." Jones continues:

> We both laughed at the question because it was almost like a reflex action on my part; something that came out so quick that I was almost unaware of it. He twisted the cigar in his mouth and grinned, smoothing the strangely grown beard on his cheeks. "That *is* a poet's question," he said, "and the only poet's answer I can give you is that I will do what I think is right, what I think the people want. That's the best I can hope for, don't you think?"[20]

Two months after the delegation's visit to Cuba, Castro came to New York City to speak at the opening of the fifteenth session of the United Nations General Assembly. Although thousands of supporters greeted Castro upon his arrival, the U.S. government set severe travel restrictions on the entire Cuban delegation, forbidding it from leaving Manhattan. After refusing to give a $20,000 security fee demanded by the management of the midtown Selburne Hotel, the Cuban delegation immediately relocated to Harlem's Hotel Theresa. Thousands of black and Latino Harlemites surrounded the hotel, cheering and carrying pro-Cuba signs. Late on the evening of September 19, Malcolm X dropped by the Hotel Theresa to extend his personal greetings. The two leaders conversed for about an hour. Castro assured Malcolm that the new Cuban government was firmly committed to uprooting racism. "On racial discrimination," Castro stated, "we work for every oppressed person." Castro emphasized the growing political solidarity of the newly emerging countries of Africa and Latin America, and praised African Americans for their leadership and struggles for political rights. "Negroes in the U.S. have more political consciousness, more vision than anyone else," he declared.[21] Malcolm was deeply moved by Castro's sincerity. One reporter present at the meeting recalled that "Malcolm also expressed that it was good to see [Fidel] continue his struggle for all black people." In a subsequent conversation with Cuban journalist Reinaldo Penalver, Malcolm observed, "I am very interested in Cuba and also because the only white person that I have really liked was Fidel."[22]

In April 1961, when anti-Communist Cuban exiles, supported by the CIA, attacked Cuba in an attempt to overthrow the Castro government, a number of prominent African Americans spoke out against the invasion. One group of black scholars and political activists—including W. E. B. Du Bois, LeRoi Jones, John Henrik Clarke, Shirley Graham, Harold Cruse, and Robert F. Williams—issued an appeal, "Cuba: A Declaration of Conscience by Afro-Americans," which was published in the *Afro-American* on April 22, 1961. Black Americans "have the right and duty to raise our voices in protest against the forces of oppression that now seek to crush a free people linked to us by bonds of blood and a common heritage," the statement declared. "Thanks to a social revolution . . . Afro-Cubans are first-class citizens and are taking their rightful place in the life of the country where all racial barriers crumbled in a matter of weeks following the victory of Fidel Castro." The anti-Castro forces were denounced largely in racial terms, drawn more from the U.S. context than from Cuba itself. "Now our brothers are threatened again—this time by a gang of ousted white Cuban politicians who find segregated Miami more congenial than integrated Havana." The statement concluded with an assertion that the black freedom movement in the United States was directly linked to the struggles of revolutionary Cuba: "Afro-Americans, don't be fooled—the enemies of the Cubans are our enemies, the Jim Crow bosses of this land where we are still denied our rights. The Cubans are our friends, the enemies of our enemies."[23]

Other black intellectuals interpreted events in Cuba as the historical culmination of revolutionary movements throughout the Caribbean. C. L. R. James, in his 1962 essay entitled "From Toussaint L'Ouverture to Fidel Castro," observed, "What took place in French San Domingo in 1792–1804 reappeared in Cuba in 1958." James was also optimistic that the triumph of Castro had created the objective conditions for shattering U.S. capitalist hegemony in the Americas and the Caribbean. In his 1961 letter to American friends, James predicted: "the Cuban Revolution has brought the actual concrete social revolution to the American hemisphere for the first time. . . . [It] has unloosed the process of capitalist disintegration in the Western hemisphere."[24]

In retrospect, it was literally impossible for the new revolutionary government to erase hundreds of years of racial inequalities and injustices in the span of several months or years. The new antidiscrimination laws, land reform, and the mass literacy campaign all had the greatest impact upon black Cubans. It is not surprising, therefore, that Afro-Cubans provided the revolution with its greatest constituency of supporters. But the ideology of black inferiority and white privilege could not be shattered simply by government edicts. It would require a deeper cultural transformation, the radical restructuring of the hegemonic ideas about race, color, and class that defined social reality for most Cubans. Black Americans, coming from their own very different racial formation, generally did not appreciate the enormous difficulties the Cubans faced in the construction of a more racially just social order.

The first prominent African American activist who became bitterly disillusioned about Cuba was Robert F. Williams. Williams had gained national attention in 1959 for promoting the idea of armed self-defense for the black community in Monroe, North Carolina. Following a shoot-out with a unit of the state's National Guard, Williams ultimately went into exile in Cuba. Upon his arrival, Williams promptly declared that the revolution had successfully eliminated racism. Yet Williams's nationalistic, racially separatist views inevitably came into conflict with his Cuban hosts. Williams began to criticize the Cuban government for refusing to permit blacks to develop their own political associations based on race.

For their part, the Cubans believed that black American nationalism had little or no relevance to their situation and that race-based politics was inherently divisive and reactionary. Within several years, when he departed for Communist China, Williams bitterly announced that "power in Cuba was in the hands of a white petite bourgeoisie."[25]

Even more problematic was Eldridge Cleaver, former convicted rapist and Black Panther Party minister of information, who arrived in Havana in late 1968. Cleaver immediately alienated his hosts by attempting to initiate a chapter of the Black Panther Party inside Cuba. Cleaver managed to recruit some African American exiles who had hijacked their way into the country as well as other dissidents. After a hunting trip, he kept the weapons to be used for his insurrectinonary plans. Undoubtedly, the Cubans were disturbed by Cleaver's schemes and instrumental in transporting him to a new home in exile in Algeria. Years later, after Cleaver renounced his revolutionary past and embraced born-again Christianity and conservative Republicanism, he harshly repudiated his links with Cuba. "The white racist Castro dictatorship is more insidious and dangerous for black people than is the white regime of South Africa, because no black person has illusions about the intentions of the Afrikaners, but many black people consider Fidel Castro to be a right-on white brother," Cleaver complained. "Nothing could be further from the truth."[26]

Despite these and other problems raised by African American revolutionaries inside Cuba, the vast majority of black activists in the U.S. continued to have generally favorable opinions of the Castro government. This feeling was reinforced by Cuba's decisive support for African liberation movements in the 1970s and 1980s. When the Portuguese pulled out of Angola in 1975 and civil war erupted, the Cubans threw their support behind the Marxist-oriented Popular Movement for the Liberation of Angola (MPLA). The Cuban government sent thirty thousand combat troops into the conflict, enabling the MPLA to defeat the South African-backed forces led by Jonas Savimbi. Three years later the Cubans dispatched twenty thousand troops to Ethiopia to assist a beleaguered Marxist regime in its border conflict with Somalia. Cuban medical personnel, teachers, and technicians were sent throughout the black world, from the social democratic government of Michael Manley in Jamaica to the New Jewel Movement regime of Maurice Bishop in tiny Grenada. Cuba's material solidarity with anticolonialist movements and radical states throughout the black diaspora became a major factor in the steady deterioration of U.S.-Cuban bilateral relations. In the early 1980s the

Reagan administration imposed tougher sanctions against Cuba, including tightening the economic embargo and establishing Radio Martí, a U.S. government-funded media propaganda program aimed at Cuba. These international developments elevated Cuba's stature even among moderate U.S. black leaders, who held little regard for Communism but appreciated the enormous sacrifices made by Cuba to assist struggling black nations. That Cuba's internationalism was largely funded by Soviet economic assistance equaling $3 billion by the mid-1980s was largely irrelevant to most black Americans. What was abundantly clear was that Cuba's interventions in southern Africa were decisive in the efforts to topple the white-minority apartheid regime in South Africa.[27]

The collapse of Soviet Communism abruptly ended the bipolar superpower conflict and eliminated the context for Cuban internationalism across the black and third worlds. More than 80 percent of Cuba's foreign trade in 1988 was with the Soviet Union and Eastern Europe. The demise of this trade plunged Cuba into an economic free fall, termed the "special period." Shortages of manufacturing and agricultural equipment, plus a lack of foreign exchange, produced a decline of Cuba's gross domestic product by 50 percent in only four years. Out of necessity, U.S. dollars were decriminalized and freely permitted to circulate among the general population. Corporate investment from Europe, Canada, and Mexico was eagerly solicited. By 1997 there were over three hundred Cubans who registered as private entrepreneurs with the government. New resort hotels were rapidly constructed to cater to a thriving tourist business.[28]

All of these changes have had profound racial consequences inside Cuba. Prostitution is once again flourishing in major cities, and it is now virtually impossible to enter or leave a major hotel or nightclub without encountering prostitutes. To an uncomfortable degree, the Cuban state is now promoting sex tourism, marketing the bodies of black and mulatto women especially for European guests. The restrictive policies of the U.S. have also accelerated new problems of racialization. For example, about one hundred thousand Cuban American exiles, who are overwhelmingly white, now travel to Cuba annually. They send over $1 billion to their relatives in Cuba each year.[29] In effect, the Cubans who are largely white, and who are related to people whose sole political objective is the destruction of the Cuban state, are receiving massive amounts of money. This group's new-found affluence means that Cubans who have remained loyal to the revolution, especially Communist Party members, government officials, and generally the Afro-Cuban population, are increasingly economically disadvantaged. In a similar way, the U.S. policies toward the Catholic Church in Cuba are deliberately designed to reinforce new racial divisions. Under the rubric of humanitarian aid the U.S. government and private groups are funneling resources into the Catholic Church, fully recognizing that this has always been a Spanish, mostly white, upper-class institution. As of 1998, of Cuba's 250 priests, roughly one-half were foreigners and only two were black. During Pope John Paul II's 1998 visit to Cuba, an anti-Castro exile group seized the opportunity to distribute baseball-card-sized images of the Virgin of Charity. Although always historically depicted as colored, these images, financed by grants from the U.S. government, show the Virgin of Charity as a white woman.[30]

The Cubans have generally become more candid over the years about the shortcomings and contradictions of race that still exist within their society. At the Communist Party's Fifth Congress in October 1997, party members were "reminded to be vigilant against racism."[31] The number of Afro-Cuban leaders on the party's twenty-eight-member political bureau increased from three to six. Nor has Cuba forgotten its special relationship with black America. In May 1990 the Casa de las Américas hosted a conference on the theme "Malcolm X Speaks in the 90s," which attracted a number of African American political activists, journalists, and scholars. On the final day of the symposium, Castro made an appearance and gave a brief but very moving personal statement. "We have always been in solidarity with the struggle of black people, of minorities, and the poor in the United States," the Cuban leader declared. "I think that in these times we need that friendship more than ever, and we need your solidarity more than ever. And we fully appreciate it, because we understand that one has to be very courageous to organize a rally supporting Cuba in the United States." Castro expressed regret for not spending more time talking with Malcolm X during his 1960 visit to New York City, but was "grateful" to the African Americans for their participation "in the seminar in remembrance of Malcolm X. Now, more than ever," Castro emphasized, "we have to remember Malcolm X, Che [Guevara], and all the heroes of the struggle and the cause of the peoples."[32]

More recently, the Cuban government and people have extended their solidarity as part of an international campaign to free African American political activist and journalist Mumia Abu-Jamal, who is currently on death row in Pennsylvania. In 1995, as black activists in the United States mobilized to force a stay of execution, the Cubans responded in kind. Black American journalist Rosemari Mealy observes: "From Havana to

Las Villas, from Oriente to Camaguey, the message upon the lips of the
Cuban people echoed: '¡No Ensombrezcas, Philadelphia!' (translated:
Don't Put a Death Shroud On Philadelphia!)." The National Union of
Cuban Writers and Artists, the Federation of Cuban Women, the Union of
Cuban Journalists and Writers, and many other organizations became ac-
tively involved in the solidarity campaign. Cuban journalist Carlos Castro
Sanchez initiated a petition and open letter denouncing the "political per-
secution" of Mumia Abu-Jamal "because of his ideas and his writings."
When the temporary stay of execution was granted, Cuba's press and
radio "jubilantly announced" the decision. Mealy also quotes a poem that
captures the essential connection between the historic struggles of African
Americans and the Cuban revolution:

> When powerful nations threaten us
> with their demagoguery and war machines,
> when our freedom fighters face death at
> the hands of the state,
> We listen to Cuba when she pierces the
> walls of the propaganda
> with the truth . . .
> while challenging without fear
> her enemy.
> We have observed Cuba reaching out to the world
> through acts of active solidarity.
> It is understandable how a Cuban child
> would hold my hand and tell me emphatically—
> "Mumia will be free!"[33]

In June 1997 the Institute for Research in African-American Studies, Columbia University, sponsored a delegation of African American scholars
and writers on a nine-day research mission to Cuba. The fifteen-member
delegation was hosted by the Center for the Study of the Americas in Havana. The goal of the delegation was to engage in a critical exchange between black Americans and representatives of Cuban cultural, academic,
and government institutions. There were four major themes of concern
that the delegation addressed: the changing role of race and the status of
Afro-Cubans within society, issues of gender and the status of Cuban
women, the socioeconomic impact of market-oriented policies and the

growth of private investment, and debates about human rights, political pluralism, and the future role of the Cuban Communist Party. The Cubans were extraordinarily frank in their discussions with us. Nothing was defined out of bounds. We challenged our hosts at every turn, especially on the issue of race.

For black America, Cuba remains part of the imagined community of the black world, a contradictory yet hopeful site of how race might be transformed, if not entirely dismantled, as a social force.

Notes

1. Joe Bragg, "President Fidel Castro Received Hero's Welcome to Harlem," *New York Beacon*, November 1, 1995. Butts had first met Castro in 1984, when he was part of a delegation of theological scholars attending a conference in Cuba.

2. Castro's daughter, Alina Fernandez Revuelta, officially defected from Cuba in 1993, during the severe economic crisis of the "special period." Fernandez had been a model and public relations director for a Cuban fashion company. She is now a prominent spokesperson for anti-Castro Cuban extremist groups. See Alina Fernandez Revuelta, *Castro's Daughter: An Exile's Memoir of Cuba* (New York: St. Martin's, 1998).

3. For news coverage of Fidel Castro's speech at Harlem's Abyssinian Baptist Church, see Cathy Connors, "Sí, Sí, Sí . . . ! Harlem Welcomed Fidel!" *New York Amsterdam News*, October 28, 1995; Hugh R. Morley, *Record*, October 23, 1995; and Juan Forero, "Castro Criticizes the West," *Star-Ledger*, October 23, 1995.

4. John F. Harris, "Harlem Warmly Embraces Castro," *Washington Post*, October 23, 1995.

5. Bragg, "President Fidel Castro."

6. Ronald Segal, *The Black Diaspora* (New York: Farrar, Straus and Giroux, 1995), pp. 83–85.

7. Lisa Brock, "Introduction," in Lisa Brock and Digna Castaneda Fuertes, eds., *Between Race and Empire: African-Americans and Cubans Before the Cuban Revolution* (Philadelphia: Temple University Press, 1998), p. 8.

8. Ibid., p. 9.

9. Winston James, *Holding Aloft the Banner of Ethiopia: Caribbean Radicalism in Early Twentieth-Century America* (London: Verso, 1998), pp. 12, 29.

10. Thomas Fernandez Robiana, "Marcus Garvey in Cuba: Urruita, Cubans, and Black Nationalism," in Lisa Brock and Digna Castaneda Fuertes, eds., *Between Race and Empire: African-Americans and Cubans Before the Cuban Revolution* (Philadelphia: Temple University Press, 1998), pp. 120–121.

11. James, *Holding Aloft the Banner of Ethiopia*, p. 196.

12. Brock, "Introduction," p. 9.

13. See Keith Ellis, "Nicolás Guillén and Langston Hughes: Convergences and Divergences," in Lisa Brock and Digna Casteneda Fuertes, eds., *Between Race and Empire: African-Americans and Cubans Before the Cuban Revolution* (Philadelphia: Temple University Press, 1998), pp. 129–167. Also see Edward Mullen, ed., *Langston Hughes in the Hispanic World and in Haiti* (Hamden, Conn.: Archon, 1977).

14. Mirta Aguirre, "Scottsboro," in Carmen Gomez García, "Cuban Social Poetry and the Struggle Against Two Racisms," in Lisa Brock and Digna Casteneda Fuertes, eds., *Between Race and Empire: African-Americans and Cubans Before the Cuban Revolution* (Philadelphia: Temple University Press, 1998), pp. 230–231.

The English translation of Aguirre's "Scottsboro" is as follows: Scottsboro in Alabama / Scottsboro in Yankeeland. / It is an iron put to the fire / and lifted into the belly of a race. / Nine blacks almost children, out of work / Two women, prostitutes. / Lynch law, capitalism, bourgeoisie, / the three Ks of shady history / And at the feet of the enormous monster with a thousand claws, / nine blacks almost children. / Scottsboro in Alabama, / in imperialist territory: Yankeeland / is a cloak of martyrdom and a cloak of shame / that covers the two races.

15. Segal, *The Black Diaspora*, p. 234.

16. Van Gose, "The African-American Press Greets the Cuban Revolution," in Lisa Brock and Digna Casteneda Fuertes, eds. *Between Race and Empire: African-Americans and Cubans Before the Cuban Revolution* (Philadelphia: Temple University Press, 1998), pp. 273.

17. Ibid., p. 226.

18. Harold Cruse, *The Crisis of the Negro Intellectual* (New York: William Morrow, 1967), pp. 356–357.

19. Ibid., p. 357.

20. LeRoi Jones, "Cuba Libre," repr. in Rosemari Mealy, ed., *Fidel and Malcolm X: Memories of a Meeting* (Melbourne: Ocean, 1993), p. 71.

21. Ralph D. Matthews, "Going Upstairs—Malcolm X Greets Fidel," *New York Citizen-Call*, September 24, 1960, repr. in Mealy, *Fidel and Malcolm X*, pp. 41–44.

22. Interviews with Jimmy Booker and Reinaldo Penalver, ibid., pp. 48, 58.

23. "Cuba—A Declaration of Conscience by Afro-Americans," *Afro-American*, April 22, 1961, repr. ibid., pp. 79–80.

24. James would later be troubled by Cuba's growing dependency on the Soviet Union. He attended the Cultural Congress held in Havana in January 1968 and reported on the event several months later in London in a paper entitled "Cuba Report." After this report James was virtually silent about his attitudes on Cuba and Latin America until his death in 1989. An excellent dis-

cussion of James's evolving views about Cuba is provided in Santiago Colas, "Silence and Dialectics: Speculations on C. L. R. James and Latin America," in Grant Farred, ed., *Rethinking C. L. R. James* (Cambridge: Blackwell, 1996), pp. 131–163.

25. Williams's highly critical appraisal of the Cuban revolution is presented in Carlos Moore, *Castro, the Blacks, and Africa* (Los Angeles: UCLA Press/Center for African Studies, 1988). Moore has become the most controversial black nationalist opponent of the Cuban government. He was originally born in Oriente of black West Indian parents. Moore was one of the endorsers of the 1961 "Declaration of Conscience by Afro-Americans" in behalf of Cuba.

26. On Eldridge Cleaver's misadventures in Cuba, see Moore, *Castro, the Blacks, and Africa*; see also Kathleen Route, *Eldridge Cleaver* (Boston: Twayne, 1991).

27. See William M. Leo Grande, *Cuba's Policy in Africa, 1959–1980,* Policy Papers in International Affairs no. 13 (Berkeley: University of California, 1980); and Jorge Domiquez, *To Make a World Safe for Revolution: Cuba's Foreign Policy* (Cambridge: Harvard University Press, 1989).

28. William M. Leo Grande, "From Havana to Miami: U.S. Cuba Policy as a Two-Level Game," *Journal of Interamerican Studies and World Affairs*, vol. 40, no. 1 (April 1, 1998), pp. 80–101.

29. Maria T. Padilla, "The Pope's Visit: Political Dissent Raises Accusations of Intolerance," *Orlando Sentinel*, January 11, 1998.

30. Alfred L. Padula, "White Exile Elite Runs Cuba Policy," *Portland Press Herald*, March 29, 1998.

31. Lori S. Robinson, "Race and Revolution," *Emerge*, vol. 9, no. 6 (May 1998), pp. 51–57.

32. Mealy, *Fidel and Malcolm X*, pp. 59–61.

33. Rosemari Mealy, "Cuba—In Defense of Mumia," in S. E. Anderson and Tony Medina, eds., *In Defense of Mumia* (New York: Writers and Readers, 1996), pp. 214–218.

5

The Fire This Time: Harlem and Its Discontents at the Turn of the Century

Johanna Fernandez

In December 1995 a blazing spotlight descended upon Harlem, albeit temporarily, in response to a controversial dispute that led to a fire which consumed a clothing store on 125th Street, Harlem's main thoroughfare. Following a series of small demonstrations protesting the policies of the Jewish-owned Freddy's Fashion Mart, Roland Smith—a black Harlem vendor—ran into Freddy's screaming, "It's on now! All blacks out!" The angered man fired his gun and set fire to the store, leaving eight dead, including himself.

The incident was sparked by a dispute over plans for a next-door expansion by Freddy's that would displace the Record Shack, a small black-owned business that had been in Harlem for nearly two decades. The tragedy was immediately cast in black and white by the media and by politicians like New York Mayor Rudolph Giuliani, who proclaimed that the Harlem fire was caused by racism against Jews.[1] However, as the storyline of this tragedy unraveled, the incident appeared more complicated and the class divisions within Harlem's black community more manifest.

Freddy's subleased part of its space to the Record Shop and leased from the United House of Prayer for All People, a predominantly black church located in Central Harlem. The landlord, in this case the church, agreed to evict Sikhulu Shange, owner of the Record Shop, because it was bidding for the tenant who would pay the highest rent. However, a Buy Black campaign that Reverend Al Sharpton and Morris Powell, leader of the

125th Street Vendors Association, led against Freddy's in the weeks prior to the incident did not denounce the self-interested policies of the black church. Instead, Freddy's became the target of often race-baiting protests while the church remained in the background. The circumstances surrounding this incident highlight the multiplicity of divergent interests among blacks in Harlem and the persistence of a black nationalist strategy—at least among a section of blacks—and its limitations in addressing problems of injustice, economic inequality, and racism in New York City.

Despite the attention the neighborhood attracted in the aftermath of the fire, the fatal flames of the Harlem Fire seem not to have been fierce enough (to the safekeepers of New York) to command an investigation of the conditions that led to this social explosion. However, the circumstances and events that detonated this tragedy provide a case study of the poverty, joblessness, and despair that have made a tinderbox out of modern-day Harlem. That Freddy's fire occurred in the midst of an immense social crisis cannot be overstated. Social tensions, like the ones that led to this recent tragedy, are either created or exacerbated by the objective conditions that surround them. Roland Smith snapped, ironically killing five Latinos, an Indian, and a black man under the pressure of a capitalist system that discriminates against minorities, lays off workers without regard to their household responsibilities, and creates pockets of poverty alongside immense wealth in cities like New York.

The overarching constant in Harlem is its poverty, and the statistics are jarring. According to figures from the 1990 census, 44 percent of families with children under eighteen years of age in Harlem live below the poverty level, the minimum income deemed necessary to meet the most basic needs of a household according to the federal government.[2] Furthermore, the unemployment rate, at 18 percent, is among the highest in the nation.[3] In 1991 a study by two Harlem Hospital doctors concluded that Harlem may be the place with the sickest people in the United States. The same study concluded that black adult males in Harlem are less likely to live until the age of forty than young men in Bangladesh, the poorest country on earth.[4] The mortality rate in this part of the city is more than twice that of whites in the United States and 50 percent higher than that of all blacks nationwide.[5] In 1994 *New York Newsday* reported that between 1993 and 1994 the infant mortality rate in Harlem increased by 40 percent.[6]

The fatal consequences of Harlem's poverty figures are alarming. Harlemites are dying from treatable conditions such as cancer, heart disease, alcoholism, pneumonia, and diabetes for lack of access to proper and adequate medical care. A horrifying 5 percent of women with cancer in Harlem are diagnosed early enough to be treated as opposed to 42 percent of African American women and 52 percent of white women nationwide.[7] Tuberculosis cases are reaching epidemic proportions, as the risk of contamination is thirty-five times greater in Harlem than in more affluent sections of the city. Accordingly, tuberculosis cases are four times higher in Harlem than in the rest of New York City.[8] The dearth of basic equipment in Harlem Hospital—the community's sole public health facility—wheelchairs and stretchers and cleaning supplies, detergents, mops, and brooms—complicate minor medical problems and contribute to the spread of disease.[9]

Although many historians have suggested that the flight of the black middle class during the 1960s sounded the death knell of the community, a look at the cuts in public housing programs initiated during Jimmy Carter's administration and intensified during the Reagan years can take us from a description to an analysis of what has happened in Harlem during the last two decades. For example, the crisis of tuberculosis can be attributed to a decrease in federal spending on tuberculosis control from more than $15 million to less than $5 million between the late 1960s and the early 1980s.[10] The current health crisis in Harlem—where 85 percent of the community is medically underserved—will magnify exponentially in the next few years, especially since Mayor Giuliani's administration reduced Harlem Hospital's budget by $30 million as of July 1995. Already the number of doctors and physician assistants have decreased by 20 percent and at least 467 hospital workers have been laid off.[11]

The chronic health crisis in Harlem is but one of a number of serious concerns in the community and is compounded by the presence of other social problems. Fully one-third of the residential buildings in Harlem are abandoned or vacant and "four thousand 'old law' tenements, those declared unfit for human habitation in 1901, are still occupied."[12] Current policies that advocate the easing of government regulations in order to establish a less restrictive market are responsible for the deterioration and fatal collapse of a building in Central Harlem in March of 1995 that claimed the lives of three people and seriously injured six.[13] Similarly, national cuts in education account for "savage inequalities" that produce low levels of achievement: a mere 40 percent of students in Harlem perform at or above grade level.[14]

The most recent response to the problem of poverty and unemployment in Harlem is the Empowerment Zone. Spearheaded by Harlem Representative Charles Rangel, the logic of the Northern Manhattan Empowerment Zone is to rebuild the poorest parts of Washington Heights, a predominantly Dominican neighborhood, and Harlem by providing $250 million in tax incentives to corporations that set up outlets on 125th Street. In addition to rewarding corporations that invest in Harlem, the project proposes to spend $300 million over a ten-year period in job development, job training, housing, and rehabilitation programs. However, concrete proposals for such programs are not as forthcoming as those for corporate initiatives, and even if a concrete program were in place one would have to perform mathematical acrobatics to glean the proposed creation of 55,000 jobs out of a $300 million-dollar budget.[15]

Propelled by the residual trickle-down-economics ideology of the 1980s, which Democrats have since bought wholesale, the Empowerment Zone is incapable of addressing the chronic structural problem of poverty in the inner city. The failure of urban development initiatives is tied to their intrinsic logic. Premised on the myth that poverty can be overcome by the development of a competitive business sector in the ghetto, they fail to address the roots of poverty: unemployment, low wages, poor housing, inadequate education, and lack of access to health care. The Empowerment Zone initiative is merely an incarnation of the failed Enterprise Zones, the urban development project of Jack Kemp, former secretary of housing and urban development under Ronald Reagan, which benefited the business sector but did little for the lives of poor urban populations in the 1980s.

Many community leaders and politicians are enthusiastically anticipating that the empowerment zone will revitalize America's poor urban sectors. At first glance this project may appear to some to be a panacea— after all, it proposes to create 55,000 jobs in Harlem over a ten-year period by giving zone corporations a $3,000 tax credit a year for each community person employed. But a closer look at the project proposals and at the problems in Harlem yield a soberer projection of the Empowerment Zone's impact on the Harlem community.

Although the industries (mainly retail and service sector) that are being wooed into Harlem promise to open permanent jobs numbering in the tens and twenties each, the jobs that will be available follow the national trend of the past two years, which has seen a creation of low-wage jobs with absolutely no benefits. Furthermore, the $300 million to be allocated over ten years for community development is but a drop in the roaring ocean of poverty, made more furious recently by millions of dollars in cuts to public spending. The job openings at Duane Reade, for example, or the Body Shop cannot annul the enormous social impact of over fifteen years of cuts in social spending, which have worsened the conditions of housing and public schools and have decimated whole wards and departments at Harlem Hospital.

Furthermore, the public discourse that has anchored the proposed revitalization of Harlem praises the integration of the urban poor into the mainstream economy through the introduction of commodity markets in the ghetto. In the midst of substandard public schooling, threatened hospital privatization, and dilapidated apartment buildings Harlem residents should rest assured that freedom is coming their way: now they can choose between the Gap and Footlocker. Not only does the Empowerment Zone project intend to give Harlem a face-lift while its sick body remains untreated, it also intends to capitalize on the much touted "black purchasing power." About Walt Disney's incentive to build a mall in Harlem, the Wall Street Journal writes, "The project offered them a rare chance to build a beachhead in one of the nation's last densely populated neighborhoods that isn't already overrun with stores. 'What is so appealing about Harlem is that there are so many young professional and young families. There isn't a huge amount of retail for that community, but there is strong demographics,' said Thomas A. Heymann, President of Disney's store operations." Disney recently signed a contract to start building its upscale retail and entertainment complex, Harlem USA, on 125th Street and Frederick Douglas. The mall proposes to house a multiplex cinema, a rooftop skating rink, a jazz hall, a bowling alley, and a health club among other stores and stands to be the largest commercial employer in Harlem, with five hundred workers.[16]

The social impact of the Empowerment Zone on the Harlem community is yet to unfold. At worst, Harlem could be designated the last frontier in New York City and gentrification would punctuate the end of the century that gave birth to Harlem's black community.[17] What is certain, however, is that the Empowerment Zone will shower an economically devastated area with consumer goods. Whether consumerism will tame the consciousness of poor working-class people in Harlem and pacify the rage produced by a savagely unequal society remains to be seen. However, New York City's police chief decided to take no chances. Since large glittery shops on 125th Street could potentially signal danger in the event of a riot, a recent memo ordering more police patrols on 125th Street, in public housing and transit stations in Harlem, has been the subject of local news and community concern.[18] The mixed blessings of the Empowerment Zone will be felt instantaneously, as the incidence of police brutality against black youth is sure to increase with increased police presence.

Among the more visible outcomes of the Empowerment Zone initiative are the escalating rents on 125th Street, which have, in turn, generated ever increasing instability and financial trouble among small black-owned Harlem businesses such as La Famille, Lucky Spot, Oasis, the Get About, and Stake N' Take. Since 1994 large corporate entities like Duane Reade, Foot Locker, Ben and Jerry's, Rite-Aid, Blockbuster, and the Body Shop have successfully bought out businesses and made it increasingly difficult for small stores and specialty shops to survive. The black-owned Record Shack, protagonist in the dispute that led to Freddy's fire, fell victim to the property-upgrading mandates of the Empowerment Zone, as it, too, was unable to pay higher rent.[19]

That black officials and community leaders are enthusiastic about the Empowerment Zone and the prospect of creating nonunionized minimum-wage jobs for adults with household responsibilities in New York—where the cost of living ranks highest in the country—is a confirmation of the rightward shift of the black political establishment, which twenty years ago would not have promoted corporate tax-break strategies over implementing government programs that address problems of poverty in the black community. What is most perplexing about the recent urban development proposal is that while the government is orchestrating a project that promises to create jobs it is simultaneously dismantling the largest employer in Harlem: Harlem Hospital. The net effect of this yields a decrease in the standard of living of Harlem workers, as unionized jobs with living wages and benefits are being lost to minimum wage jobs with no benefits.

For over two decades the majority of blacks in Harlem have had to contend with a coterie of "black managers of the system" who claim to be the political leaders of black America but instead represent—in and of themselves—a specific class of blacks whose interests are different from poor and working-class blacks. In Harlem black elected officials have carried out the same policies as their white counterparts, the net result of which has lowered the life chances of blacks. For example, in 1990 Mayor David Dinkins called for unprecedented budgetary cuts to New York's public hospitals, which threatened to close Harlem Hospital's burn unit, the only burn center in all of Northern Manhattan and the best burn unit in the city. Fortunately, the center was saved after a series of militant protests by unionized hospital workers. That same round of cuts also led to the disappearance of the Midwifery Services Department, which provided prenatal care to adolescents and other women's health services.[20] Disenchanted with Dinkins and the Democrats and doubtful that a trip to the ballot box would make their lives any better, poor and working-class blacks stayed home during the 1993 elections and Mayor Dinkins lost to his Republican challenger, Rudolph Guiliani. Despite the persistence of racism in all levels of society, American capitalism has accommodated a section of blacks, making elected and appointed government officials of some and business professionals of others. The black middle class can thank the civil rights struggles for gains such as affirmative action, which allowed it to grow in size and income. But while the gains of the civil rights movement signaled a tremendous improvement in the lives of blacks, it did not uproot the system of capitalism, whose survival, historically, has depended on keeping people confused and divided on the basis of racism and other forms of discrimination. Therefore, the persistence of racism alongside the gains of the civil rights movement allowed for a managerial class of blacks to reap the benefits of the system and to add a bit of color to the dominant class, while the majority of blacks have continued to suffer from economic and political oppression.

The profound changes brought about by the movements of the 1960s are reflected in the fact that class polarization is now greater among blacks than whites.[21] Differences in the daily experience of poor and working-class blacks versus that of upper-class blacks have resulted in a difference of opinion with regard to the way in which social problems are perceived and should be remedied. In short, the objective financial improvement of a group of African Americans has translated into a rightward shift in consciousness. In the absence of the need to fight against segregation or the right to vote—which previously impeded the advancement of the black middle class—there are no objective interests pushing middle-class blacks to address the issues (like layoffs, police brutality, and cuts in social spending) that are devastating the lives of the majority of blacks.

In Harlem this phenomenon is increasingly visible. Black managers have placed the fate of the community in the hands of the system. Enamored of private enterprise, they continue to support policies that, by default, perpetuate a status quo that condemns 33 percent of African Americans nationwide to a life of poverty. Among the most prominent and well-endowed black leaders in Harlem is Trade Union president Stanley Hill of D.C. 37. In December of 1995 Hill signed a contract on behalf of municipal workers that excluded job security for public hospital workers and thereby made it easier for the city to go forward with its privatization plans for Harlem and Kings County Hospitals if it chose to do so.[22] Not too far from Harlem Hospital sits the president of Harlem's City College of New York, Yolanda Moses, who oversaw tuition increases and cuts in financial aid that forced three thousand mainly black and Latino students to leave school between August 1995 and May 1996. As of the spring semester of 1996, City College had disbanded ten departments. The four departments that fall under the Ethnic Studies rubric at City College— African American, Latino, Asian, and Jewish studies—were among the ten casualties. Despite the fact that the elimination of ethnic studies only saved $140,000, President Moses personally authorized its dismantling.[23]

Recently appointed by Mayor Giuliani, Empowerment Zone director Deborah Wright, a graduate of Harvard Business and Law Schools, has joined the ranks of black managers. Recently Wright told the *Daily News* about the insights she obtained growing up as the daughter of a preacher in a poor community. She said that she grew up "where people cared about each other and supported each other without the extensive structure we've come to believe that government must provide."[24] Clearly, this black woman promises to ruffle no feathers in Harlem. The list of Harlem's Talented Tenth continues: Percy Sutton, director of the now defunct Harlem International Trade Center, was among the leaders of the Harlem Urban Development Corporation (HUDC), which was forced out of business when it was unable to account for $100 million in tax dollars; Wanda Goodloe, Governor George Pataki-appointee and director of the Harlem Community Development Corporation that replaced HUDC; Harlem congressman Charles Rangel; and director of Harlem Hospital Linnette Webb. These people represent what Manning Marable calls the "Black Managerial and Professional Elite." Given their class position, they are vested in negotiating the terms of black oppression and exploitation, not in taking the radical measures necessary to end them.

To consider the grim events of December 8 without unearthing the chain of social offenses that helped incense Harlem's shopping strip is to misrepresent the process of history. The kindling for this fire was gathered over the many years of assaults on the Harlem community. But the kindling was finally lit in October 1994 when Giuliani's Quality of Life campaign succeeded in enforcing New York's antivending laws on 125th Street, thereby destroying the livelihood of hundreds of mainly black Harlem street vendors and displacing several hundred others onto an enclosed and much less lucrative space on 116th Street.[25] Interestingly, Roland Smith was one of the six hundred vendors that were expelled from Harlem's main shopping strip.

A series of factors converged on 125th Street, all of which increased racial tensions. While the majority of people in Harlem are black, approximately 50 percent of the businesses on 125th Street are owned by whites. As store owners, a disproportionate number of whom are white,[26] and a mayor with a bad record on racial politics joined against the vendors, tensions between vendors and store owners inevitably took on a racial dimension. However, the legitimate outpouring of anger by vendors against the discrimination that prevents black entrepreneurs from obtaining low-interest bank loans, which would allow them to set up their own shops, can gloss over the clash of competing economic interests that cross racial lines in Harlem. For example, while a small group of frustrated vendors rallied along with Powell and Reverend Sharpton to save the Record Shack, earlier Shange, the owner of the Record Shack, had lined up against the vendors, along with other shopowners who believed their clientele was being taken away by the vendors.

The conflict between vendors and store owners revolved around a debate in which the latter protested that they were losing over $300 million in profits to the vendors and the former argued that for over fifty years vendors had worked to make 125th Street a vibrant strip the outcome of which inevitably brought business to store owners. Thus the policy to remove the vendors was not driven by racial politics alone. Economic concerns inspired the endorsement, by both black and white business owners, of the vendors' removal. But the initiative to clear 125th Street of what one player in Harlem politics called "unfair competitors who pay no rent or taxes"[27] was also the logical conclusion of the Empowerment Zone project, which is forced to clear up the streets in order to lure corporate chains onto 125th Street.

In the end, the conflict that was tragically exposed by Freddy's fire, although articulated in racial terms, involved economic issues that concerned economic expansion and the heightened competition on 125th Street as a result of the Empowerment Zone initiative. After all, behind this incident was a church that owns a $25 million estate, among other assets, and that has launched a $178 million project to renovate and expand its holdings.[28] The black nationalist strategy of Reverend Al Sharpton and Morris Powell, however, emanates from a politics that uses antiwhite sentiment to bolster black capitalism, such as that of the United House of Prayer for All People. In a radio program the Reverend Al Sharpton said that "we will not stand by and allow them to move this brother so that some white interloper can expand his business on 125th Street." Similarly, Powell stated that "we are not going to stand idly by and let a Jewish person come into black Harlem and methodically drive people out of business."[29] Reverend Sharpton's and Powell's remarks are not only anti-Semitic but also distort what is really happening on 125th Street. After all, the changes that are threatening small black-owned businesses on the strip were spearheaded by Congressman Charles Rangel and supported by the black political establishment. The assumption of Reverend Sharpton's campaign is that all blacks have the same economic interest, when in fact they do not. The campaign imagines a community among blacks that simply does not exist, even, and perhaps especially, in Harlem.

Given the magnitude of the attacks on the Harlem community, that only Freddy's has been the receptacle of community frustration, however misdirected that frustration may have been, is surprising. The reason the protests against Freddy's did not get a hearing beyond a handful of people is due to the character of the grievances that were voiced by the leaders of the Buy Black campaign. Unlike Harlem's Don't Buy Where You Can't Work campaign of the 1930s, comprised of a broad coalition of people and community organizations including whites in the Communist Party, Reverend Al Sharpton used an antiwhite message that did not appeal to the vast majority of Harlemites.

The broad support for the Don't Buy Where You Can't Work campaign resulted from the fact that jobs and the fight against racism were its rallying cry. A campaign centered around the fight for decent jobs and against racism in present-day Harlem, where socioeconomic conditions are sadly not unlike Harlem in the 1930s in the midst of the Great Depression, has a better chance of attracting the numbers of people necessary to impact real change. A collective initiative of this kind could have generated the necessary social pressure that would have forced the United House of Prayer for All People, which, according to the *New York Times*, has "grown into an unusually prosperous religious organization with extensive and growing real estate holdings in cities across the country,"[30] to negotiate with the small black-owned Record Shack.

What is clear about Freddy's fire is that none of the players in this tragedy turned political ball game ever raised the concerns of the majority of poor and working-class blacks in Harlem. At a moment when the contradictions within the black community are starker than ever, it is important to unravel the complexity of racial divisions in American society. With every day that passes upper-class blacks are becoming increasingly wedded to the status quo and to entrepreneurial capitalism. At the same time, the black nationalist response to the conflict of race in this country fails to appreciate the objective and real class differences that exist within the black community.

Despite the persistence of racism in American society and its devastating ramifications for blacks in urban communities, the statistics of the last two decades defy the dominant conception that the basic divide in American society is the one between blacks and whites. At the same time that the wages and benefits of working people in this country have witnessed unprecedented declines since the post–World War II economic boom, the language and image of race is being fanned and used by political leaders to conceal what is, in essence, the inability of the free market to meet the most basic needs of the majority of people in this country: employment, nutrition, health care, housing, and education.[31] Although the prospects for multiracial unity in this country may seem bleak to some, it is important to keep in mind that the internal contradictions of capitalism demand layoffs and cuts in social spending that impact the lives of people of all races and create the objective conditions for a multiracial working-class movement that can challenge racism and fight for an egalitarian future.

Notes

The author would like to gratefully acknowledge the discussions she had with Manning Marable, Joan Parkin, Curtis Stokes, and Lee Sustar that helped in the development of this article.

1. Although the conflict between blacks and Jews has its specific history, conflicts between blacks and Jews often find a place within the dominant framework of American racial politics—black/white—because Jews are considered "white" and because Jews in the United States have successfully assimilated into the hegemonic mainstream.

2. *Demographic Profiles: A Portrait of New York City's Community Districts from the 1980 and 1990 Censuses of Population and Housing* (New York Department of City Planning, 1992), pp. 292–297.

3. Catherine Newman, "What Scholars Can Tell Politicians About the Poor," *Chronicle of Higher Education*, vol. 41, no. 41 (June 23, 1995), pp. B1–B2.

4. E. R. Shipp, "For the Sickest Patients, an Ailing Hospital," *New York Times*, April 7, 1991, pp. 1, 29.

5. Harold P. Freeman, "Women's Health Hearing," *House Committee on Energy and Commerce, Washington, D. C.: GPO, 1994*, April 23–24, 1990.

6. "A Call For Action on Infant Deaths," *New York Newsday*, November 5, 1994, p. A6.

7. Phillip R. Lee, "Health Care Reform (Volume XIII) Hearing," *House Committee on Ways and Means* (Washington, D.C.: GPO, 1994), February 7, 1994.

8. Diane Seligsohn, "The New Underclass and Re-Emerging Disease," *World Health*, vol. 6 (November-December 1994), pp. 25–27.

9. J. Zamgba Browne, "Proposed Hospital Budget Cuts Spur Massive Protest," *Amsterdam News*, May 5, 1990, p. 2.

10. David Hage, "Business: Weeding Out Waste," *U.S. News and World Report*, vol. 116, no. 1 (January 10, 1994), pp. 51–53.

11. Mark Torres, "Hospital Layoffs Mean Less Services," *Harlem News: Newsletter of the Community Health Forum*, vol. 2 (July 24, 1995).

12. Kristin Helmore and Karen Laing, "Exiles Among Us," *Christian Science Monitor*, vol. 78, no. 244 (November 13, 1986), pp. 1, 21–24.

13. Kevin McCoy, William Bunch, and Juan Forero, "Harlem's Owner Has Spotty Record," *New York Newsday*, March 22, 1995, p. A4.

14. Micheal Kramer, "Hope Grows in Harlem," *Time*, October 10, 1994, p. 41.

15. Peter Grant, "She Zones in on Job, Rejuvenating Biz in Harlem," *Daily News*, April 8, 1996, p. 23.

16. Laura Bird and Mitchell Pacelle, "Disney Makes Bet on Harlem Renaissance," *Wall Street Journal*, June 6, 1996, pp. A2, A9. See also Thomas Lueck, "Disney Plans to Open Store in Harlem," *New York Times*, June 6, 1996, pp. B1, B3.

17. Before the 1900s blacks in New York City lived in the area between West 20th and 60th Streets, known as the Tenderloin District. During this period the living conditions of all blacks—poor, middle, and upper middle class alike—were abominable. At the turn of the century the convergence of a series of events led to the birth of a black community in Harlem: the riots of 1900, in which many blacks were killed, prompted the black middle class to aggressively seek living accommodations elsewhere; the increased migration from the South demanded a place where recently arrived blacks could settle; and cheap, vacant and extravagantly built apartments were available in the northernmost part of the city as a result of land development and speculation by realtors that was disproportionate to the actual value of property, especially since Harlem was inaccessible by public transportation. The transfer of black residents from the Tenderloin District to Harlem was made possible in large part by A. Philip Payton, a black realtor who convinced landlords that he could fill their otherwise empty Harlem apartments with well-educated

black tenants. See Jervis Anderson, *This Was Harlem: A Cultural Portrait, 1900–1950* (New York: Farrar Straus Giroux, 1991), pp. 13–14, 147–150; and Gilbert Osofsky, *Harlem: The Making of a Ghetto* (New York: Harper and Row, 1983), pp. 88–91.

18. David Kocieniewski, "Police Propose Assault on 125th Street Crime," *New York Times*, May 29, 1996, p. B3.

19. Angela Ards, "Fifth Avenue, Uptown: Searching for the Promised Land," *Village Voice*, December 26, 1995, pp. 15, 17.

20. Jonathan Ewing, "Midwife Services at Harlem Hospital Will Be Severely Reduced by New Budget," *Amsterdam News*, July 6, 1991, p. 4.

21. Sharon Smith, "Twilight of the American Dream," *International Socialism* (Spring 1992), p. 20; and Bart Landry, *The New Black Middle Class* (Berkeley: University of California Press, 1987), p. 229.

22. Steven Greenhouse, "Public Employees Vote Five-Year Deal in New York City," *New York Times*, February 9, 1996, p. A1.

23. Joan Parkin, "Blackout: How the CCNY Administration and CUNY's Board of Trustees Shut Down Ethnic Studies," *Advocate*, vol. 4, no. 8 (June 1996), pp. 8–9.

24. Grant, "She Zones in on Job," p. 23.

25. Jojo Sarpong Kumankumah, "Showdown on 125th Street," *New York Newsday*, July 11, 1994, pp. C1+.

26. Ards, "Fifth Avenue, Uptown," p. 17.

27. A quote by Malcolm Barksdale, financial adviser of the United House of Prayer for All People, in Ards, "Fifth Avenue, Uptown," p. 15.

28. Douglas Frantz and Brett Pulley, "Harlem Church Is Outpost of Empire," *New York Times*, December 17, 1995, pp. 49, 51.

29. "Radio Excerpts in Harlem Store Dispute," *New York Times*, December 14, 1995, p. B4.

30. Frantz and Pulley, "Harlem Church Is Outpost of Empire," p. 51.

31. Between 1987 and 1992 alone, 5.6 million U.S. workers who had been working with their employers at least three years lost their jobs. Yet, during this same period, affirmative action and immigration—two clearly racialized wars—were targeted by the media and by the government as major public policy problems and were posited as the primary reasons why working-class whites were losing their jobs. The language of race has also been used to justify cuts in social spending. The image of the "black welfare queen," for example, was successfully manipulated by Democrats and Republicans alike to tear down a system that services a majority white population. See Paula Mergenhagen, "Job Benefits Get Personal," *American Demographics*, vol. 16, no. 9 (September 1994), p. 34.

6

Crack Cocaine and Harlem's Health

Beverly Xaviera Watkins and
Mindy Thompson Fullilove

Harlem is one of the most famous urban all-black communities in the United States. In its early years Harlem prospered and gained international recognition as a center of African American music, art, and literature. Between 1960 and 1990 four disparate forces—suburbanization, economic decline, epidemic disease, and municipal public policy—transformed Harlem from a functional "urban habitat" to a deurbanized area with a hyperconcentration of poor people with serious health problems.

In 1990 Colin McCord and Harold Freeman published a special article in the *New England Journal of Medicine* that described the relative risk of death for Harlem residents in comparison with other areas of New York City. Harlem had the highest rate of age-adjusted mortality from all causes. The rate was more than double that of U.S. whites and was 50 percent higher than that of U.S. blacks living in other areas. Cardiovascular disease, cirrhosis, homicide, neoplasms, and drug dependency were the five major causes of death. Homicide, cirrhosis, and drug-related deaths accounted for 40 percent of excess mortality in Harlem, suggesting a corresponding excess burden of substance abuse-associated morbidity. They concluded, "Black men in Harlem were less likely to reach the age of 65 than men in Bangladesh."[1]

Zip code-level data for all New York City hospital admissions, covering 1989–1990, released by the New York State Health Systems Agency (HSA), complement McCord and Freeman's analysis. HSA found that the five Harlem and East Harlem zip codes were ranked among the "top ten" (out of a total of 168 citywide) with respect to substance abuse admissions; three of the five were ranked among the highest ten with respect to hospital admissions for psychosis (much of which was drug related); and two of the five were ranked among the top ten with respect to HIV and cirrhosis admissions.

In 1996 the unique nature of the problems of Harlem was underscored by A. T. Geronimus and colleagues, who compared mortality rates for white and black Americans living in poor or more prosperous communities in four parts of the United States.[2] They found that men and women living in Harlem had the lowest likelihood of surviving to age sixty-five (37 percent for men; 65 percent for women). The authors note:

> The situation in Harlem was particularly dire. Comparison of the estimates by McCord and Freeman with ours shows that in Harlem mortality among women relative to that nationwide has not improved since 1980, whereas mortality among men has deteriorated. On the other hand, groups that might have been expected to have excess mortality rates equivalent to or higher than the rates in Harlem did not.

Their findings suggest that social factors in addition to race and income are needed to explain excess mortality in Harlem.

The crack cocaine epidemic of 1985–1995 significantly contributed to the decline of health in the Harlem community. Crack was both a direct and an indirect cause of excess morbidity and mortality. Lives were lost as a result of crack use and crack-related violence. In the course of crack use many addicts contracted and died from AIDS and other illnesses. The adverse health effects of the crack epidemic included increases in rates of sexually transmitted diseases, respiratory conditions, and psychological problems. The epidemic also caused social disruption that undermined the community fabric and, in turn, further aggravated health. In order to describe the contributions of crack to ill health in Harlem, this chapter will review the general features of the crack epidemic and will relate stories of the epidemic as recalled by Harlem residents.

The Crack Cocaine Epidemic

Few people in the United States, other than those involved in the drug underground, recognized the emergence of a smokable form of cocaine. The first mention of crystallized cocaine occurred in an early 1970s guide to illegal drug use entitled *The Gourmet Cokebook*.[3] It next appeared in 1981, as a footnote in another underground publication, David Lee's *Cocaine Handbook*.[4] That same year, the near-death experience of comedian-actor Richard Pryor introduced the practice of smoking cocaine, in this case "freebasing," to the general public.[5] However, the process of reconstituting cocaine for smoking was not fully understood.[6] Freebase, the base-state form of cocaine without adulterants, was not clearly distinguished from crystal cocaine, the form that contains the impurities and filler from the hydrochloride as well as from the processing products. Even among many users, particularly at the street level, the two were considered equivalents.[7] In the mid-1980s the unadulterated smokable cocaine rock form became known as "crack" because of the crackling sound made by dissolving the cocaine hydrochloride in water and sodium bicarbonate (baking soda).[8]

Crack first received media attention in 1984. The *Los Angeles Times* reported that in "South Central, cocaine sales explode with $25 rocks."[9] It would be almost a year before the term *crack* appeared in print. On November 17, 1985, while covering a story on a drug treatment center, a *New York Times* reporter discovered that this "new form of cocaine, known as crack, was for sale in New York City."[10] Two weeks later a *Times* headline read, "A New Purified Form of Cocaine Causes Alarm as Abuse Increases."[11] As crack moved north from Miami, west from New York and Washington, D.C., and east from Los Angeles, intense national media coverage followed.[12]

According to a 1988 Drug Enforcement Agency (DEA) report, the availability of crack was first reported in Los Angeles, San Diego, and Houston in 1981. Crack was localized in those areas until 1985, when crack use became a serious problem in New York City. According to the DEA, "Crack cocaine literally exploded on the drug scene during 1986 and was reported available in 28 states and the District of Columbia."[13] The presence of crack was attested to by street surveillance, emergency room visits, and arrest records. For example, crack arrests accounted for 72 percent of all New York Police Department Narcotics Division cocaine arrests during the first seven months of 1987.[14]

Political Response

Fueled by the media, political campaigns, and the national elections, illicit drug use and associated crime, in particular crack-related crime, dominated public policy debate between 1986 and 1990. By the summer of 1986 *Newsweek* had declared crack "an authentic national crisis," comparable to the civil rights movement, the Vietnam War, and Watergate.[15] Crack had become widely available in U.S. cities and was largely concentrated in inner-city areas.

On July 15, 1986, the Committee on Governmental Affairs' Permanent Subcommittee on Investigations held a hearing "to examine a frightening and dangerous new twist in the drug abuse problem—the growing availability and use of a cheap, highly addictive, and deadly form of cocaine known on the streets as crack."[16] Senators William Roth, William Cohen, Lawton Chiles, Sam Nunn, John Glenn, and Alfonse D'Amato convened the "Crack" Cocaine hearings. In turn, each promoted crack as "an egalitarian drug, attracting users of all races, colors and creeds, all walks of life and income, and all degrees of dependence."[17] The hearings clearly established that crack use had reached near epidemic proportions and required immediate combative measures aimed at treatment, prevention research, and education.[18]

The following month, on August 4, 1986, President Ronald Reagan announced a new antidrug policy. The governmental response focused almost exclusively on interdiction and eradication of the drug supply. On September 14, 1986, in a nationally televised address, Reagan, determined to begin "a sustained, relentless effort to rid America of this scourge by mobilizing every segment of society against drug abuse, declared a "War on Drugs."[19] The next day *Time* magazine ran a ten-page story entitled, "Fed Up and Frightened, the Nation Mounts a Crusade Against Drugs."[20] On October 27, 1986, the first Anti-Drug Abuse Act was enacted. Of the $1.7 billion allocated, approximately 86 percent went to law enforcement, prisons, and interdiction, and 14 percent went to treatment, education, and prevention.[21] In addition, an annual White House Conference for a Drug-Free America was established. Over the next two years drug use and sales increased, and social, legal, and medical problems proliferated.

At the time little was known about the long-term outcome of addiction to crack, but even short-term use produced important physical consequences, including cardiovascular complications (heart attack, stroke), pulmonary complications (chronic cough, aggravation of asthma), and psychiatric complications (paranoia, depression). A. Washton, M. S. Gold, and A. C. Potash warned, in 1986, that addiction to crack was growing at alarming rates. They noted that "during the past three years, a growing epidemic of cocaine use in the United States has resulted in widespread physical, psychiatric, and social problems that have alarmed medical experts, parents, and law enforcement officials."[22] The brief duration of the drug effect and rapid onset of compulsive use made this drug an ideal product from the prospective of drug marketers. Washton and colleagues called it a "self-marketing product" that "assures the dealer a reliable clientele and a high profit margin."[23]

The Second War on Drugs

Drug abuse, in particular crack use, remained at the forefront of social issues during the 1988 presidential election campaign. As a result, on October 22, 1988, Congress enacted a second antidrug abuse act. This time $2.8 billion—a $1 billion increase—was set aside to bolster antidrug efforts.[24] The focus on eradication and interdiction of the drug supply continued. However, 50 percent of the first year's budget and 60 percent of each year's thereafter were allocated to demand reduction. The 1988 legislation also created two new government offices, the White House Office of National Drug Control Policy, which was responsible for the annual National Drug Control Strategy, and the Office of Substance Abuse Prevention, which focused on treatment and prevention. This new drug policy placed an emphasis on severely penalizing crack users and dealers.[25] Steven Belenko, an antidrug policy researcher, argued that "what distinguished this anti-drug campaign was its strong emphasis on a single drug—crack cocaine."[26] He stated that the policy was driven by four assumptions about the effects of crack: (1) Crack is rapidly and strongly addictive, (2) crack users become irrational and exhibit bizarre and violent behavior, (3) the involvement of youth in crack dealing means more chaotic and violent distribution networks, and (4) crack is linked to promiscuous sexual activity. In turn, crack "is viewed as the quintessential 'hedonistic' drug and as such is in polar opposition to the prevailing white Protestant conservative morality of America."[27]

Public Concern

Although Reagan's antidrug campaign failed to stem the growth of drug use and related illegal activity, it succeeded in generating an unprecedented level of public concern.[28] The 1989 National Drug Control Strategy contained the following statement in its introduction: "One drug—crack—has stubbornly resisted our prevention efforts. Crack's stranglehold on hundreds of thousands of young Americans is tightening. To date, the crack plague has been concentrated in our central cities, but it has begun to spread to small suburbs and small towns."[29] The idea that crack was extending into nonurban middle-class areas terrified the public.

In the mid-1980s it was rumored that crack was so highly addictive that one-time use could cause addiction. In order to continue consumption of the drug, addicts spent their money, dispersed valuable possessions, and participated in sex for money or drug exchanges. Concurrently, those areas affected by crack reported an increase in the rates of common sexually transmitted diseases, particularly syphilis and gonorrhea.[30] In the course of binges—episodes of incessant drug use that might last up to several days—parents neglected their children, and all users neglected basic health care needs for adequate food, clothing, and shelter. As the epidemic of crack use proceeded, the violence among drug dealers for control of territory fed into a growing epidemic of gun-related homicide, predominately among young African American men.[31] The escalating violence was steadily transforming peaceful neighborhoods into war zones.

Media coverage bolstered the idea that crack was destroying America. The *New York Times* continuously ran front-page articles about crack: February 20, 1989, "After Three Years, the Crack Plague in New York Grows Worse"; May 10, 1989, "Crack Spreads Fear and Frustration, Overwhelming Hospitals"; October 1, 1989, "Crack, Bane of Inner City, Is Now Gripping Suburbs."[32] The next day, an article entitled "The Spreading Web of Crack" appeared.[33] The *Washington Post* cover stories included: June 3, 1989, "Small Towns Wrestle with the 'Scourge'"; September 22, 1989, "Drug Buy Setup for Bush Speech: DEA Lured Seller to Lafayette Park"; December 18, 1989, "For Pregnant Addict, Crack Comes First"; January 6, 1990, "She Smoked Crack, Then Killed Her Children."[34] The *Wall Street Journal* headlines read: May 4, 1989, "Spreading Plague"; July 18, 1989, "Born to Lose: Babies of Crack Users Crowd Hospitals."[35] The *Wall Street Journal*'s July article on crack babies was followed by two *New York Times* articles, one in August and another in November.[36] One of the most striking features of this coverage was the fact that, with few exceptions, the faces of crack babies were black. As the nonwhite crack user/dealer became a familiar image in U.S. news reports and magazines articles, the characterization of the crack epidemic began to change.

By 1990 crack was no longer considered an egalitarian drug. Crack use and crack-related crime were largely concentrated in poor nonwhite communities, and it appeared that the pattern would continue. In 1991 the National Institute on Drug Abuse (NIDA) reported a decline in crack use among middle-class high school and college students. Crack subsequently lost its place on the national agenda. The 1991 National Drug Control Strategy, a 122-page document, mentioned crack only three times, once in the introduction. By contrast, a year earlier, in the 90-page 1989 National Drug Control Strategy, crack had been mentioned 29 times, 10 of those times in the 14-page introduction.[37] Neither crack nor cocaine appeared in the 1991 National Strategy on Emerging Drug Trends.[38]

The withdrawal of public and political support for crack research and treatment left affected communities defenseless against crack and its attendant social and health problems. All the while the actual number of people addicted to crack continued to rise.[39] In 1988 a San Francisco community leader, Shirley Gross, wrote: "Nothing in the history of substance abuse has prepared us for the devastation that is caused by the use of cocaine 'crack.' Crack has destroyed entire communities by engulfing families in the web of crack sales or use."[40] Largely African American sections of Oakland, San Francisco, and Los Angeles were "taken over" by drug dealers. Addiction and drug-related violence created massive alteration in the social conditions of these communities. The ethnographer Ben Bowser described marked changes in the Bayview-Hunter's Point community in San Francisco.[41] In particular, he signaled that drug traffickers were forming their own social systems, complete with common expectations, beliefs, values, and rules, and that women, drawn into crack-related prostitution, might be far more effective transmitters of HIV infection than were women addicted to heroin.

Crack and Health

The crack epidemic undermined health in the affected communities, most of which were poor. Crack's disastrous impact on health could be measured in the spread of sexually transmitted diseases, including HIV, and the rapid escalation of violence (handgun violence related to drug sales). In 1988 the U.S. Centers for Disease Control cited crack use, coupled with the practice of bartering sexual services in exchange for the drug, as a factor in the increase in STDs (sex tied to drugs).[42] An association between crack use and HIV infection, noted among women with pelvic inflammatory disease in New York City, was the first indication that crack use might become an important factor in the spread of HIV infection.[43] Several lines of evidence have since substantiated the fact that levels of risk behavior and infection with STDs, including HIV, are high among crack users.[44] Mary Ann Chiasson and colleagues at the New York City Department of Health examined the link between HIV infection and crack use.[45] The overall seroprevalence rate among the 201 crack users, who denied traditional HIV-associated risk behaviors, was 12 percent. The Centers for Disease Control conducted a multiyear, multisite study designed to assess HIV seroprevalence among crack users interviewed at three sites in the United States, New York, Miami, and San Francisco.[46] Women with a history of engaging in sex work associated with crack cocaine use were found to be particularly at risk.[47] The prevalence of HIV infection among crack-smoking women in the sample was reported to be 29.6 percent in New York City and 23.0 percent in Miami.[48]

The association of crack with violence was acknowledged by criminologists and other researchers throughout the country.[49] A NIDA monograph pointed out that "structural violence," that is, violence related to the control of markets, was a major cause of all violence linked to drug use.[50] An increase in the use of guns appears to follow the emergence of crack in selected cities in the United States.[51] The presence of guns leads to an increase in the risk for firearm-related homicide.[52] Guns played a critical role in the rise in the number of homicides in the United States. Although firearm-related homicide had been the leading cause of death among African American male teenagers since 1969, a marked increase was noted beginning in 1987. L. A. Fingerhut and colleagues reported that "from 1987 through 1989, the firearm homicide rate among black males 15 to 19 years of age increased 71 percent to 85.3 deaths per 100,000 population, while the death rate from motor vehicle crashes (the second leading cause of death among black teenage males) fell 3 percent to 26.5 per 100,000."[53] It was also found that firearm-related deaths were concentrated in core metropolitan areas.[54]

Individual Life Stories: Crack's Impact on Harlem

As the epidemic progressed, it became clear that compulsive crack use would have a tremendous impact on users, their families, and the larger communities within which the epidemic was embedded. Harlem, like so many other poor, inner-city communities, lacked the economic and social resources necessary to ward off crack's destructive forces. Harlem's hollowed out landscape of abandoned and deteriorating buildings provided an optimal setting for the crack trade. Dealers quickly converted vacant structures into crack houses—twenty-four-hour centers for crack consumption, sale, and distribution.[55] Absentee landlords made it easy for crack dealers to set up shop in occupied dilapidated buildings. Residents recalled how buildings and entire blocks became overrun with crack dealers and users, leaving many frightened, isolated, and disillusioned. The social effects of crack were related to three factors: the growth of the drug culture, drug-related prostitution, and the collapse of family and community functioning. The dramatic social changes that Harlem underwent as a result of crack-related activity contributed to a significant health decline. Unfortunately, the Harlem community has not been able to fully recover from the disastrous effects of the epidemic. Interviews with Harlem residents provide a glimpse into the ways crack-related crime and violence have disrupted personal, domestic, and community social networks.

Community Decline

Survival in poor urban communities depends heavily on informal social ties.[56] When the network of social relationships and corresponding social controls that permit large numbers of people to live together are greatly disrupted, behaviors that would not normally be tolerated—like crime—increase. The presence of undesirable and illicit activity limits the movements of residents and thus decreases the frequency of social exchanges. Subsequently, neighbors become estranged from one another and feelings of togetherness and security are replaced by fear and suspicion. Trust, which had been the basis for cooperation among Harlem residents, began to erode as people struggled to protect themselves and their families against a multitude of crack-related social ills. One long-term resident described Harlem in the latter half of the 1980s as follows: "Back then [1985 to 1990] Harlem was a war zone and nobody, not even the police, they wasn't doing a damn thing about it. When you're fighting for your life, and children, and home, for one thing, you don't have time to say hello. You don't want to say hello or have your children say hello. Trust no one. Fear everyone. That's a military mentality." Residents uniformly held that isolation, fear, and mistrust caused Harlem's social fabric to unravel. A long-term resident recalled:

> Everybody in Harlem, including the police, knew where to get drugs. That's why nobody, unless they wanted to buy or sell drugs, ever went

down those blocks. The problem was that it happened so fast. It seemed like most of the blocks had drugs. And the saddest thing were the young ladies, disrespecting themselves. Crack was something else. And I don't mean the drug itself. Or at least I don't think so. I never tried it myself, you know. Anyway, what I mean is what it did to the community, to the family. People couldn't trust their own kids. It was like [pause] prison. Nobody wanted to let their children leave the house because you never knew what was gonna be waiting outside. You see, it's one thing if a stranger gets mixed up in, but now it was the man next door or the woman upstairs, or his son or daughter. People your children had been told to respect, they grew up around, they were friends with, you knew the family for years.[57]

An elderly resident recounted how crack confined her to her apartment:

The crack was the worse. It really did, that was the end. Those that could git [leave], well, the rest, peoples like me, we just had to stay inside. Crackheads would steal everything. You wouldn't even go outside soon as it got dark. It was worse than dope [heroin] . . . . Seemed like every other person, or the[ir] children, or somebody they know was on crack. . . . You couldn't even go to the elevator. Matter a fact, things got so bad I had to wait on my son to bring me groceries. He lives out there in Brooklyn. Comes to see me every weekend. He wants me to go out there with him, to live, you know, out there. . . . But I been in this here four by four since 1949. My husband died right here, and I reckon I will too. I never lived nowhere [in New York] but Harlem. Well, it was real bad like that for a good while. I'd say two or three years.[58]

Violence

Violence was closely associated with crack, and violent incidents grew dramatically as the epidemic spread. A March 1989 issue of the *Crisis*, the official organ of the NAACP, focused on the crack epidemic.[59] In an article entitled "Cocaine and Violence: A Marriage Made in Hell," Patricia A. Jones noted that, in New York City, young children were murdered because they were in the crossfire of drug-related violence.[60] She called this violence "drug terrorism" and noted, "Innocents killed in drug terrorism incidents are basically by-products of fights for market share in the drug business."[61]

When asked how crack affected everyday life in Harlem, one resident responded:

> There were periods when every week you heard about somebody getting shot, shootings every week. Do you know what that is? We all knew what was going on, so the police had to know. Why would you let a bunch of drug lords take over a community? If they tried to do it in a white neighborhood, the police would have done something. But this was a bunch of niggers killing each other. Little black kids were getting killed. We couldn't even walk down many of the streets in our own neighborhood. Can you imagine streets on the Upper East Side being controlled by drug dealers? White kids getting killed in the crossfire? Would people in that community take their lives and their children's lives into their hands every time they walked down the street?[62]

An elderly resident from the Harlem Senior Citizens Center remembered an incident of violence that resulted in several deaths:

> Right over here in the playground, up the street from the center, they was selling drugs. Stuff [crack vials] everywhere. We cleaned that park up, you know. I believe it, '91, yes, [in] '91. After some kids got killed. There was a big fight. Bullets flying everywhere, it was terrible. The candy store on the corner. They ran in there, too. Police was everywhere. After that we cleaned it up.[63]

Family Dysfunction

The nature of crack use has important implications for the communities that it affected. Crack use typically occurs during binges, which may last for days at time, that is, until the user is forced to stop because of exhaustion or lack of the financial wherewithal to continue. During the binge the need to procure and use crack overwhelms all other demands that might face the user. By necessity, kinship, work, and social duties are neglected. In pursuit of the drug, many women were forced to perform degrading sexual acts in sex-for-drug exchanges. As one woman told an interviewer in describing the ways in which she had failed her children, "It hurts, it really hurts because you really want to do it. You really want to take care of your children and everything, but the drug is just constantly—it's like a monkey on your back. I want it, I want it, I want it, I want it."[64]

One woman told of a mother's crack-induced neglect of her children and bartering of sex for drugs:

> There was a girl up on the third floor. Well, I knowed her since she was a baby. Her Momma died and then she got the apartment, you see. Well, she was living there with her childrens, one of each; they was twins. And well, they was just as sweet and clean. Then she got messed up, you see. And well, them childrens would cry all the time and be dirty. She was out doing drugs [crack], you see. Sometime she was gone all night. After a while the marshal come and put her out. She came and rang the bell a few times but I didn't answer. I don't know if I should be saying this. 'Cause, well, I didn't see for myself. But, well, they say she started staying over by 140th. She was one of them girls that goes with mens for drugs. Well, they would be right on the street in the day and they look sickly. Used to have a name for them, my grandbaby told me about it, you see. Some kind of fruit [strawberries]. I wonder what came a those childrens.[65]

Health

When asked to explain crack's impact on health in Harlem, residents pointed out the critical connection between the loss of community integrity and the rising rates of ill health.

One elderly lifetime resident responded:

> When I think of health, I think first of mental health and then physical. And obviously they're both being affected adversely. In the 1980s the critical problem was stagnation, S-T-A-G-N-A-T-I-O-N; remember the word. The economy was stagnate, then came the Reaganomics, you see, and then the cocaine, crack cocaine, as you call it. Then the mental attitude was stagnate. We had the ghetto mentality. The health problem in Harlem and the other Harlems has to do with a lack of preventive care. With crack you had the deterioration and breakdown of the community, and the breakdown of the community leads to other things. Crack was the straw that broke the camel's back, so to speak.[66]

Another resident agreed:

> Crack was not the problem. It was what came with crack, the crime, the gun fights, AIDS. You have to understand one of the special things

about Harlem. One of the reasons people stay in Harlem is people out on the street; everyone knows one another. That's not to say that you come to my house, but on a casual basis. "Good morning," "afternoon." Everyone thinks of Harlem in the way the media portrays Harlem, hoodlums, gangsters, and the like. But Harlem has a stable middle class and working class and an upper class. Just go to any subway station in the morning and you'll see the people going to work. At that time [during the epidemic], the streets were empty.[67]

The 1985–1995 crack cocaine epidemic was largely concentrated in poor, inner-city areas like Harlem. Initial fears that crack would sweep across the nation unsettled policy makers and the public. Unfortunately, ensuing public policy was shaped by a vision of the epidemic not as a health crisis but as a crime crisis. In response, an internal war was initiated, directed at controlling drug use and sales. The unacknowledged health crisis proceeded in Harlem and elsewhere. The toll of death and disease has not yet been fully assessed, and the emotional and social cost of the epidemic remains to be evaluated. But it is clear, even from a preliminary reading of the data, that drug addiction and its side effects—sexually transmitted diseases, respiratory ailments, psychological disorder, and violent trauma—all escalated as a result of the crack epidemic. Profound damage was done to family and neighborhood social networks.

As the epidemic recedes, it leaves behind a large number of addicted people who have little access to treatment or any established remedies for their problems. Crack has fallen from epidemic to endemic levels in Harlem's drug repertoire, but it has not disappeared. New cases of addiction continue to present for treatment. Other health and social sequelae continue to haunt the community: thousands of children in foster care, thousands of young men and women in the criminal justice system. The misguided policies that failed to recognize the health threats of the crack epidemic have not been rewritten.

The Harlem community bears a burden of ill health that is, in part, a result of a national failure to treat drug epidemics as health problems. The recovery of Harlem depends on correcting that failure. Prevention, in the classic models of public health, includes attention to problems that arise in the aftermath of illness. Rehabilitating victims of accidents is but one example of tertiary preventive care. In the case of Harlem, it is too late to prevent the epidemic, but it is not too late to prevent the consequences of illnesses spawned from the epidemic. A new, more health-conscious public policy is desperately needed as Harlem prepares for the future.

Notes

This work is part of a pilot study supported by NIH grant #IP30AG15294–01 to Rafael Lantigua, M.D., Columbia University, College of Physicians and Surgeons, Division of General Medicine, CALME. Funding was also provided by the SOROS Foundation, Open Society Institute. The authors wish to thank Robert Lehr Goodman, M.D., for his assistance in preparing the manuscript.

1. C. McCord and H. Freeman, "Excess Mortality in Harlem," *New England Journal of Medicine*, vol. 322, no. 3 (1990), pp. 173–177.

2. A. T. Geronimus, J. Bound, T. A. Waidmann, M. M. Hillemeier, and P. B. Burns, "Excess Mortality Among Blacks and Whites in the United States," *New England Journal of Medicine*, vol. 335, no. 21 (1996), pp. 1552–1558.

3. *The Gourmet Cokebook: A Complete Guide to Cocaine* (San Francisco: White Mountain Press, 1972).

4. Lee provides a detailed description of the freebase process. See David Lee, *Cocaine Handbook: An Essential Reference* (San Rafael, Cal.: What If?, 1981), p. 52.

5. *Time,* July 6, 1981, p. 63.

6. The type of cocaine base smoked by Richard Pryor has never been documented. It has always been discussed as freebase. My research suggests that this is true because cocaine users considered crack an inferior product. See Jim Inciardi, *Women and Crack Cocaine* (New York: Macmillan, 1993), p. 7.

7. Ibid., p. 9.

8. See P. Bourgois, *In Search of Respect: Selling Crack in El Barrio* (Cambridge: Cambridge University Press, 1995); and E. Dunlap, "Street Status and the Sex-for-Crack Scene in San Francisco," in M. S. Ratner, ed., *Crack Pipe as Pimp: An Ethnographic Investigation of Sex-for-Crack Exchanges* (New York: Lexington, 1993).

9. "South Central Cocaine Sales Explode with $25 Rocks," *Los Angeles Times,* November 25, 1984, p. C1.

10. *New York Times,* November 17, 1985, p. B12.

11. "New Form of Cocaine, Known as Crack, Is for Sale in New York City," *New York Times,* November 29, 1985, pp. A1, B6.

12. Inciardi, *Women and Crack Cocaine*, p. 9.

13. U.S. Department of Justice, DEA Cocaine Investigations Section, *Crack Cocaine Availability and Trafficking in the U.S.* (Washington, D.C., 1988), p. 1.

14. Ibid., p. 3.

15. *Newsweek,* June 16, 1986, p. 15. See closing paragraph of the preface to "The Plague Among Us," by editor in chief Richard Smith.

16. "Crack" Cocaine Hearing, July 15, 1986, Committee on Governmental Affairs, Permanent Subcommittee on Investigations, p. 1. Opening statement of subcommittee chairman William V. Roth.

17. Ibid., p. 4. Opening statement of Senator Nunn.

18. The 100 to 1 ratio is rumored to be based upon erroneous testimony. When asked the question "Is smoking crack fifty times more addictive than injecting cocaine?" during the "Crack" Cocaine Hearing, July 15, 1986, Dr. Byck replied yes. In fact, the answer was no: Dr. Byck misheard Senator Chiles and thought the comparison was to intranasal cocaine use. In their zeal to create a severe penalty, the committee decided to double the addiction rate. From Watkins interview with Robert Byck at Yale University, July 1997. See "Crack" Cocaine Hearing, July 15, 1986, Committee on Governmental Affairs, Permanent Subcommittee on Investigations, p. 28. Testimony of Robert Byck.

19. D. Courtwright, H. Joseph, and D. Des Jarlais, "Epilogue: Drug Use and Drug Policy Since 1965," in *An Oral History of Narcotic Use in America, 1923–1965* (Knoxville: University of Tennessee Press, 1989).

20. "Fed Up and Frightened, the Nation Mounts a Crusade Against Drugs," *Time,* September 15, 1986, pp. 58–68.

21. A further 1.7 billion was allocated in addition to the 2.2 billion already allocated.

22. A. Washton, M. S. Gold, and A. C. Potash, " 'Crack': An Early Report on a New Drug Epidemic," *Cocaine Addiction,* vol. 80, nos. 52–58 (1986), p. 52.

23. Ibid.

24. Due to the balanced budget, only $500 million was spent.

25. Section 6371 increased federal penalties for crack-related crime. The initial version included the death penalty for drug-related murders. On November 1, 1989, New York State penal law was amended, making it a felony to possess 500 mg. or more of crack cocaine. Minnesota followed New York and increased the penalties for crack. By 1991, half the states had passed similar laws.

26. Steven Belenko, *Crack and the Evolution of Antidrug Policy* (Westport, Conn.: Greenwood, 1993).

27. Ibid., p. 3.

28. Ibid.; David Musto, *The American Disease: Origins of Narcotics Control* (New York: Oxford University Press, 1987); Craig Reinarman and H. G. Levine, "Crack in Context: Politics and Media in the Making of a Drug Scare," *Contemporary Drug Problems,* vol. 16, no. 4 (1989), pp. 535–578.

29. White House Office of National Drug Control Policy, *The 1989 National Drug Control Strategy,* p. 48.

30. M. F. Goldsmith, "Sex Tied to Drugs = STD Spread," *Journal of the*

American Medical Association, vol. 260 (1989), p. 2009; B. Hoegsberg, T. Dotson, O. Abulafia et al., "Social, Sexual, and Drug Use Profile of HIV(+) and HIV(–) Women with PID," presented at the Fifth Annual Conference on AIDS, June 1989, Montreal, Canada.

31. L. A. Fingerhut, D. D. Ingram, and J. J. Feldman, "Firearm Homicide Among Black Teenage Males in Metropolitan Counties," *Journal of the American Medical Association,* vol. 267 (1992), pp. 3054–3058.

32. *New York Times,* February 20, 1989, p. A1; May 10, 1989, p. A1; October 1, 1989, p. A1.

33. Ibid. October 2, 1989, p. A2.

34. *Washington Post,* June 3, 1989, p. A1; September 22, 1989, p. A1; December 18, 1989, p. A1; January 6, 1990, p. A1.

35. *Wall Street Journal,* May 4, 1989, p. A1; July 18, 1989, p. A1.

36. *New York Times,* August 7, 1989, p. A14; November 24, 1990, p. A7.

37. Cocaine is referred to 69 times in the text, and cocaine 22 times in the introduction; cocaine references increased to 102.

38. Belenko, *Crack and the Evolution of Anti-drug Policy.*

39. U.S. General Accounting Office, *Cocaine Treatment: Early Results from Various Approaches,* June 1996.

40. Shirley Gross, CEO of the Bayview-Hunter's Point Foundation, San Francisco, quoted in *MIRA Crack Project: Preliminary Report,* 1988, p. 2.

41. Benjamin Bowser, "Crack and AIDS: An Ethnographic Impression," *Journal of the National Medical Association,* p. 540. Bowser conducted his ethnographic work during 1987 and 1988 in the Bayview-Hunter's Point section of San Francisco.

42. Goldsmith, "Sex Tied to Drugs," p. 2009.

43. Hoegsberg, Dotson, Abulafia, "Social, Sexual, and Drug Use Profile of HIV(+) and HIV(–) Women with PID."

44. See R. E. Fullilove, M. T. Fullilove, B. Bowser, S. Gross, "Risk of Sexually Transmitted Disease Among Black Adolescent Crack Users in Oakland and San Francisco, CA," *Journal of the American Medical Association,* vol. 263 (1990), p. 851–855; R. E. Booth, J. K. Watter, D. D. Chitwood, "HIV Risk-Related Sex Behaviors Among Injection Drug Users, Crack Smokers, and Injection Drug Users Who Smoke Crack," *American Journal of Public Health,* vol. 80 (1990), pp. 853–857; R. Rolfs, M. Goldberg, and R. Sharrar, "Risk Factors for Syphilis: Cocaine Use and Prostitution," *American Journal of Public Health,* vol. 83 (1993), pp. 1144–1148; S. K. Schwarcz, G. A. Bolan, M. Fullilove, J. McCright, R. Fullilove, R. Kohn, R. Rolfs, "Crack Cocaine and the Exchange of Sex for Money or Drugs: Risk Factors for Gonorrhea Among Black Adolescents in San Francisco." *Sexually Transmitted Diseases,* vol. 19 (January-February 1992), pp. 7–13.

45. M. A. Chiasson, R. L. Stoneburner, D. S. Hildebrandt et al., "Heterosexual Transmission of HIV-1 Associated with the Use of Smokable Freebase Cocaine (Crack)," *AIDS,* vol. 5 (1991), pp. 1121–1126.

46. B. R. Edlin, K. L. Irwin, S. Faruque et al., "Intersecting Epidemics: Crack Cocaine Use and HIV Infection Among Inner-City Young Adults," *New England Journal of Medicine*, vol. 331 (1994), pp. 1422–1427.

47. Institutes of Medicine (IOM), *The Hidden Epidemic: Confronting Sexually Transmitted Diseases* (Washington, D.C.: National Academy Press, 1997).

48. Edlin, Irwin, Faruque, "Intersecting Epidemics," p. 1426.

49. J. Fagan and K. Chin, *Violence as Regulation and Social Control in the Distribution of Crack*, NIDA Monograph no. 103, p. 36.

50. *Drugs and Violence: Causes, Correlates and Consequences*, (USD-HHS, 1990), NIDA Monograph No. 103.

51. I. Wilkerson, "Crack's Legacy of Guns and Killing Lives On," *New York Times*, December 13, 1994, pp. A1, B12, presents a chart showing the sharp rise in homicides following the introduction of crack in New York, Los Angeles, and Chicago.

52. See Fingerhut, Ingram, and Feldman, "Firearm Homicide," pp. 3048–3053.

53. Ibid., pp. 3054–3058.

54. Ibid., pp. 3048–3053, pp. 3052–3053.

55. Crack houses were also the site of many sex-for-drug exchanges. For a detailed account see M. T. Fullilove et al., "Crack Hos and Skeezers," *Journal of Sex Research*, vol. 29, no. 2 (1992), p. 282. Also see note 9. Dunlap, "Street Status."

56. R. Wallace, M. T. Fullilove and Wallace D, "Family Systems and De-urbanization: Implications for Substance Abuse," in Lowinson et al., eds., *Comprehensive Textbook of Substance Abuse*, 2d ed. (Baltimore: Williams and Wilkins, 1992), pp. 944–955.

57. B. X. Watkins, M. T. Fullilove, and R. J. Grele, "Remembering Harlem: An Oral History 1960–1990." Unpublished ms.

58. Ibid.

59. National Association for the Advancement of Colored People, *Crisis*, March 1989.

60. Ibid., pp. 17–19, 32.

61. Ibid., p. 17.

62. Watkins, Fullilove, and Grele, "Remembering Harlem."

63. Ibid.

64. Fullilove, "Crack Hos and Skeezers," p. 282.

65. Watkins, Fullilove, and Grele, "Remembering Harlem."

66. Ibid.

67. Ibid.

PART TWO

Mapping African American Studies

7

African American Studies and the "Warring Ideals": The Color Line Meets the Borderlands

Johnnella E. Butler

The Negro is a sort of seventh son, born with a veil, and gifted with second-sight in this American world,—a world which yields him no true self-consciousness, but only lets him see himself through the revelation of the other world. It is a peculiar sensation, this double-consciousness, this sense of always looking at one's self through the eyes of others, of measuring one's soul by the tape of a world that looks on in amused contempt and pity. One ever feels his two-ness,—an American, a Negro; two souls, two thoughts, two unreconciled strivings; two warring ideals in one dark body, whose dogged strength alone keeps it from being torn asunder.

The history of the American Negro is the history of this strife,—this longing to attain self-conscious manhood, to merge his double self into a better and truer self. In this merging he wishes neither of the older selves to be lost. He would not Africanize America, for America has too much to teach the world and Africa. He would not bleach his Negro soul in a flood of white Americanism, for he knows that Negro blood has a message for the world. He simply wishes to make it possible for a man to be both a Negro and an American, without being cursed and spit upon by his fellows, without having the doors of Opportunity closed roughly in his face.
—*W. E. B. Du Bois*, The Souls of Black Folk

A border is a dividing line, a narrow strip along a steep edge. A borderland is a vague and undetermined place created by the emotional residue of an unnatural boundary. It is in a constant state of transition.
—*Gloria Anzaldúa*, Borderlands/La Frontera

Quite a number of African American studies departments and programs are named for Dr. W. E. B. Du Bois, "the grand theorist of modern social thought,"[1] and his identification of African American double consciousness is the springboard for much discussion and policy making about African Americans.[2] The institutional and structural development of African American studies derived its guiding principles, structures, methodologies, and approaches from various interpretations of or responses to his construct. In this article I will examine several assessments of African American studies and projections of the direction it should take for the twenty-first century. I contend that these assessments and projections, taking place in the postmodern academic environment of women's studies, cultural studies, and postcolonial studies—and often in dialogue with these fields—posit an African American studies that will not intervene in exposing the "regime of truth" buttressed by racism that permeates our nation's psychology and social, legal, political, economic, scientific, and artistic structures. Furthermore, some imply that "excellent" and "sophisticated" African American studies scholarship will only be attained by moving away from the fact that, in both a legal and a social sense, American racialization historically and contemporarily remains modeled on racism against the African American. I observe that the varying degrees of liberatory and agentive impotence in conceptualizations and formulations of African American studies at the dawn of the twenty-first century emanate to some extent from contemporary characteristics of higher education and that, moreover, the particular positionings of African American studies in assimilationist, diasporic, pluralist, and Afrocentric camps all reflect, to lesser and greater degrees, the failure of African American scholars and administrators to engage from shared and related perspectives the ambivalences, ambiguities, and regimes of truth maintained by the self/other binary that Du Bois urged us to address in 1903 in order for the African American, in present-day parlance, to have agency. I contend then that racism and racialization perpetuate a dehumanized theoretical, methodological, scholarly, and life situation for the African American that African American studies can only begin to resolve through utilization of the Du Bois manifesto in "Of Our Spiritual Strivings" in its institutional organization, scholarly methodology, and pedagogy.

   The Du Boisean explication of African American double consciousness seeks the *disruption* of the self/other dichotomy through merging of the Negro and the American. Inherent to this merging is the ideal of shared power and cultural exchange of the best of traditions. The Du Boisean struggle is for the "self," the Negro, and the "other," the American, "the two warring ideals" to *merge* to attain "self-conscious manhood" and to lose neither of the older selves. The remainder of *The Souls of Black Folk* examines eloquently the role white power plays in maintaining the dichotomy, documenting and proposing ways for African Americans to disrupt it.

During the nineties Henry Louis Gates, Perry A. Hall, and Molefi Asante have advanced the most representative theoretical constructs for African American studies.[3] Gates and Hall reinscribe the binary opposition inherent in the ambivalence of African American double consciousness, and Molefi Asante emphasizes a reconstructed African perspective to the near exclusion of the dynamics of what George Kent so brilliantly discussed as Blackness and the adventure of Western culture.[4] These discussions parallel, at times overlap, and I believe unwittingly reinforce postmodern/postethnic scholarship such as that of Ross Posnock and Walter Benn Michaels, direct descendants of Werner Sollors, Arthur Schlesinger, and Lawrence Fuchs, who, under the guise of universality, project Du Bois's quests for universality as "deracinated" and studies of African American aesthetic expressions as the "pursuit of an essential black subject" (Posnock), and who, under the guise of a reasoned discussion of modernity and pluralism, argue for the irrelevance of race as part of anyone's historical consciousness (Michaels).[5]

Replicating the Binaries: Gates and Hall

Gates argues for an African American studies that "include[s] an emphasis upon cultural studies and public policy, as two broad and fruitful rubrics under which to organize our discipline" (7). He discusses ways to ensure permanent institutionalization of African American studies within the academy when "on the one hand, there has never been a better time to be a person of color and a member of the academy, and—on the other hand— . . . there has scarcely been a worse time to be black in America" (7). Calling for a "true proliferation of ideologies and methodologies" rather than "uniformity or conformity" in order for the field to grow, he advocates that "African-American Studies should be the home of free inquiry into the very complexity of being of African descent in the world, rather than a place where we seek to essentialize our cultural selves into stasis, and drown out critical inquiry" (8).

On the one hand, Gates hyphenates *African-American* and advocates the charting of "both the moments of continuity and discontinuity between African cultures and African American cultures." On the other, he simultaneously represents ahistorically and reductively negritude as well as Nommo, the West African principle of the life force, and pronounces both to be assimilationist and essentialist. He eschews reifying heritage and inheritance, arguing that, "so long as we retain a vocabulary of heritage and inheritance in defining our putative national cultures," the binary of the American or Western "self" and the African "other" cannot be resolved.[6]

Referring to James Baldwin's acceptance of himself as "a kind of bastard of the West" and Richard Wright's self-recognition as a black man of the West whose reactions and attitudes toward "black, brown, and yellow men" "are those of the West" (5), Gates equates identification with either side of the hyphen as a dangerous conflicting nationalism. In response, he evokes Du Bois moving across the color line as the answer to not making a sharp distinction between the West and the Rest (a distorting aside to Chinweizu's seminal study of colonialism, *The West and the Rest of Us*), which he suggests "is neither justifiable in theory nor desirable in practice."[7] Gates quotes Du Bois from "Of the Training of Black Men" (438):

> I sit with Shakespeare and he winces not. Across the color line I move arm in arm with Balzac and Dumas, where smiling men and welcoming women glide in gilded halls. From out the caves of evening that swing between the strong limbed earth and the tracery of the stars, I summon Aristotle and Aurelius and what should I will and they come all graciously with no scorn and no condescension. So, wed with Truth, I dwell above the Veil. Is this the life you grudge us, o knightly America?

In the name of the humanities, which he defines as "the study of the possibilities of human life in culture" that thrives on diversity, Gates argues for embracing "the challenges posed by (for example) African materials and the new approaches and techniques developed to deal with the varieties of African experience" as offering "an opportunity to enrich and expand the perspectives of all humanities disciplines and to aid in casting off disciplinary blinders" (6). Finally, in a distortion of a didactic joke of the sixties,[8] he calls for a "blackness without blood that we must pass on."

His advocacy for a hyphenated scholarship rather than for the disruption of the binary "African-American" reproduces binaries and results in his reductionist presentation of negritude and Nommo. He equates Baldwin's self-described cultural bastardy in relation to the West and Wright's ambivalence to cultural nationalism—"a vocabulary of heritage and inheritance in defining our putative national cultures" (5)—in terms that, in fact, will never resolve the contradiction of the hyphen.

Gates reads the Du Bois quote as if Du Bois wrote it outside the context of racism, as if Du Bois's "above the veil" meant that he had entered the realm of a "truly human, and humane version of the humanities, one that sees the West, not as some mythical, integrated Whole, but as part of a still larger whole" (6), rather than as if Du Bois were momentarily free of the veil, the dividing line, crossing and integrating the cultural color line of the conscience. Ignoring that Du Bois moves "arm and arm with Balzac *and* Dumas" (my emphasis) and omitting that Du Bois, earlier in *The Souls of Black Folk,* had argued for the merging of the American and the Negro, Gates reinforces a binary, dichotomous situation for which synthesis demands the eliding of the social construction of race and racism with heritage and inheritance in order to dwell above the veil. Thus, African American studies to Gates must address racism and inequities through policy studies and must illuminate "the possibilities" through the humanities. But African American studies must do so while engaging America and the West, as if the difficulty is minimal and not one systematically inherited that indeed divided the world into the West and the rest. While simultaneously calling for free inquiry into "the complexity of being of African descent," Gates dismisses as identity politics many of the vehicles for analyzing that complexity.

Rather than advocate an investigation of negritude, Afrocentricity, black nationalism, and the Harlem Renaissance as interrelated approaches to struggle against racism and colonization for self-determination, Gates dismisses the legacy of heritage in the effort to discredit the few Afrocentric purists who by no means define African American scholarship. Thus he fails to suggest a methodology for, as he sees it, investigating both sides of the hyphen and discredits most efforts to investigate the African side of his hyphenated African-American. He heavily implies that racism and race become concepts that are perpetuated by hyphenated (that is, distressed bastards of American culture) "African-Americans" who cannot resolve the "warring ideals" binary because they insist on investigating their heritage and inheritance and its relation to the West. Gates expects the replacement of the psychology of the "other" with the agency of "self" through the African American's *transcendence* of the imposed category of "other," the implication being that to move beyond the veil one must not investigate the "self" and its position. He presents, therefore, an African American studies that ultimately is impotent in disrupting the self/other binary because it engages the other to the exclusion of the self and the power relationships inherent between the two. Ellison demonstrates in *The Invisible Man* the futility of such a move toward liberation and its replication of oppressive binaries unless White America freely relinquishes its hegemony over the definition and place of the Negro "self"—a highly unlikely scenario.

Perry A. Hall presents an alternative to Gates's conceptualization of African American studies that incorporates an understanding of the transformative power of the past studied in relation to the present. The past for Hall is an American one, informed by African transformations in African American life. He provides a schema of interactive systematic and thematic principles for African American studies: Duality, Transformation, Historical Periodism, Quest for Freedom and Literary. In many ways his discussion of the role of class, African and African American cultural reference frames, and the quest for freedom and literacy is similar to Gates's conceptualization of the roles of cultural studies, policy studies, and the humanities. Hall sees duality "as a cardinal feature of identity among Blacks as . . . more of them experience educational and social mobility with concomitant exposure to and internalization of mainstream cultural sensibilities" (728). Hall, however, presents this duality as Euro-American form *versus* African-based essence, folk/popular *versus* high/elite (cultural traditions), and class *versus* cultural reference frame. In the effort to discuss African American aesthetic expression that results from various African transformations (slaves were Africans of differing ethnic and cultural groups and interacted as such) and African/American transformations (the complex interactions among Africans interacted with the New World "American" and continues), his conceptualization of African American culture remains dichotomous. Despite his invocation of transformation for self-determination, he evidences no mode for either synthesis or generative tension to resolve or disrupt the binary.

More important, his call for African American studies to be both multidisciplinary and interdisciplinary begs the question of how we reveal through scholarship the most accurate rendering of African American history, the most revelatory rendering of African American literature. While I agree with Hall that African American studies should exist in the academy as freestanding programs or departments *and* integrated across the curriculum, I do not agree with his acceptance of a binary relationship between the multidisciplinary and the interdisciplinary in African American studies. Hall argues that there is, for example, a way of teaching African American literature that is "strictly literature." He relegates this to English departments. Teaching the Harlem Renaissance, he argues, "from an approach that emphasizes style, form, method, and artistic merit of Renaissance poets and writers" then is,

> strictly speaking, literature (and part of a multidisciplinary approach) and not African American studies. If, however, it is presented as one of several forms of cultural reflection of the urban transformation of the Black experience of the early 20th century, accompanied by insights that detail the historical and social context as well as the sociodemographic and macroeconomic changes associated with the great urban migration of Blacks, then it is African American studies (and part of an interdisciplinary approach) and not strictly literature. (715)

Here, Hall accepts the postmodern, poststructuralist approach to literature as being interdisciplinary and appropriate to African American studies, relegating concern with aesthetics to the New Critical, formalist approach as being "strictly literature." Rather, the question should be not a choice between some notion of the separation of content, context, and form, or a separation of that which is "strictly literature" and an interdisciplinary approach, but whether an interdisciplinary approach reveals the necessary dimensions of the context and content and provides the necessary tools for illuminating the literary tropes and levels of meaning. Furthermore, should artistic merit be determined without consideration of cultural, historical, social, political, economic context?[9] Hall posits an African American studies that remains parallel to "traditional" scholarship rather than an African American studies that interrogates and redefines "traditional" scholarship. Thus the self-determination he sees resulting from African American studies' intervention in the internal colonized existence of black Americans remains elusive. The late Audre Lorde admonished us that we cannot dismantle the master's house with the master's tools; neither can we create a separate edifice within the master's house and expect the house to be dismantled and rebuilt without displacing and reconfiguring the entire house and its purpose for being. Furthermore, Hall names African cultural sensibilities "essence" when he clearly means something much more fluid and transformative. While it is clear from his text that he is not guilty of essentialism, Hall accepts binaries as they appear and reduces African American studies to a constant interaction of repeating unsolvable dichotomies despite his in many ways innovative paradigm. The "bastard" remains such, outside American culture, marginal—outside the realm of accepted scholarship, marginal.

Positing "Self," Excluding Interaction with "Other": Asante

Molefi Asante presents the future discipline of African American studies as one that investigates only the African side of the Du Boisean double consciousness. Rather than disrupting the self/other binary, Asante emphasizes a concept of the African "self" to the exclusion of an African American ethnicity or an American or Western culture with which African Americans interact. Subjectivity or agency for Asante means "totally disengaging [their] critical thinking from the traditional views held by whites," thereby "secur[ing] a better vantage point on the facts . . . and hav[ing] a better handle on your own theoretical and philosophical bases" (20). Identifying the two classes of critics of Afrocentricity as "those who are simply opposed to any African self-determination and those who favor African self-determination within the framework of European experiences (21)," Asante defines Africology:

> The groundedness of observations and behaviour in the historical experiences of Africans becomes the main base for operation in the field of African American Studies. Centrism, the operation of the African as subject (or the Latino as subject or the European as subject, and so forth), allows Africology to take its place alongside other disciplines without hierarchy and without hegemony. As a discipline, Africology is sustained by a commitment to centering the study of African phenomena, events, and persons in the particular cultural voice of the composite African people. But it does not promote such a view as universal. Furthermore, it opens the door for interpretations of reality based upon evidence and data secured by reference to that world voice. (25)

He describes the doctoral program at Temple University as having two fields, cultural aesthetics and social behavioral, from which emanate two areas of research and responsibility:

Creative, inventive, artistic, literary:
epistemic issues, ethnicity, politics, psychology, and modes of behavior;
scientific issues, history, linguistics, economics, and methods of investigation;
artistic issues, icon, art, motifs, symbols, and types of presentation

Social, behavioral, action, historical:
relationships, the living, the dead, the unborn;
cosmos, culture, race, class, gender; mythoforms, origins, struggles, victories; and recognitions, conduct, designs, signs. (28)

He sees the scholars of the future as "advanc[ing] the relocating process in theory and practice as the generalship of the field improves in the give-and-take of debate," and he welcomes to the field of study those who share its perspective, expecting "there will be those scholars of whatever cultural and racial background who will understand our abiding interest in free and full inquiry from our own centered perspective and who will become the new Melville Herskovitz and Robert Farris Thompsons" (28).

While Asante reminds the reader midway through the article that "the Afrocentric method pursues a world voice distinctly Africa-centered in relationship to external phenomena" and not "distinctly African," his use of "African" at crucial times to describe what he terms as "African society, either on the continent or in the Americas" (26) constructs an African identity that empties Africa's diaspora of the cultural syncretizations and transformations that occur(ed) within the Western context. Thus the "self" so constructed stands in diametric opposition to the European "other" and cannot engage in the disruption of the binary, for it does not acknowledge the binary. The opposite of Gates's approach to the binary that reifies the "other," Asante reifies the "self," and his paradigm begs the question of how to connect variously centered scholarships that contain significant opposing elements and varying degrees of power over one another's reality without replicating the dichotomy of difference.

African American Studies in the Borderlands

We have moved from the discourse of the color line to the discourse of borderlands. The borderlands, with its shifting boundaries that become entrenched, disappear, and are newly constituted, are contested areas, contested by both the population that controls the boundaries and also by those who have been restricted by the boundaries. The boundaries of the color line in the United States have shifted, yet racism remains and binaries that reinforce difference negatively regenerate modernity's fragmentation reinforced by postmodernism's replicative solution of the both/and binary.

Du Bois points the way for resolution of the self/other dichotomy, as does Carter G. Woodson. Both cross the fixed color line in their scholarship and theorizing and in so doing, illuminate the role of racism and ethnocentrism in "the mis-education of the Negro." In their volume, *Race Consciousness: African-American Studies for the New Century* (1997), editors Fossett and Tucker signal the borderland scholarship that African American studies needs for the twenty-first century's task of disrupting the binaries.[10] It builds on twentieth-century scholarship, which analyzes race and challenges the assimilationist theories of Park and his progeny. Yet, being of the borderlands, it contends with postethnic theories that erase race and interrogate the various cultural, social, and political significances of Blackness historically and contemporarily. Robin D. G. Kelley's introduction reminds us that the salient questions are "why the notion of a black community continues to carry weight among lots of ordinary people, why appeals to racial solidarity continue to work" rather than the criticism that black nationalists are essentialists and "trading in fictions" (11).

Correcting Gates, Hall, and Asante to address the self/other dichotomy means asserting the African American self as seeking wholeness and empowerment in contradiction to the fragmented self projected by the dominant Other. It also means recognizing the primacy of race and foregrounding race and racialization in methodology that examines the ways race and racialization are modified and modulated by intersections with class, ethnicity, gender, and sexual identity.[11] The Du Boisean dichotomous dialectic is still significant in the postmodern borderlands, but it must not be misread as simply a statement of a factual binary. Rather, Du Bois signals the borderlands when he calls for a consciousness based on a merger that he well knows and demonstrates is fraught with ethnocentrism, racism, and sexism. And he signals and lives the dogged battle of self-assertion and agency in the face of the dehumanizing "other."

Notes

1. Manthia Diawara, "Cultural Studies/Black Studies" in Mae Henderson, ed., *Borders, Boundaries, and Frames: Cultural Criticism and Cultural Studies* (New York: Routledge, 1995), p. 208.

2. All references to Du Bois are from W. E. B. Du Bois, *The Souls of Black Folk* (1903), repr. *Du Bois Writings*, ed. Nathan Huggins (New York: Library of America, 1984), pp. 364–365.

3. Henry Louis Gates, "African American Studies in the Twenty-first Century," *Black Scholar*, vol. 22, no. 3 (Summer 1992), pp. 3–9; Perry A. Hall, "Introducing African American Studies: Systematic and Thematic Principles," *Journal of Black Studies*, vol. 26, no. 6 (July 1996), pp. 713–734; Molefi Asante, "African American Studies: The Future of the Discipline," *Black Scholar*, vol. 22, no. 3 (Summer 1999), pp. 20–29.

4. George Kent, *Blackness and the Adventure of Western Culture* (Chicago: Third World, 1972).

5. Ross Posnock, "How It Feels to Be a Problem: Du Bois, Fanon, and the "Impossible Life" of the Black Intellectual," *Critical Inquiry*, vol. 23 (Winter 1997), pp. 323–349; Walter Benn Michaels, *Our America: Nativism, Modernism, and Pluralism* (Durham: Duke University Press, 1995).

6. Postcolonial theory posits the oppressed as the other *versus* the realized self of the oppressor—or the other as the nonliberated group *versus* the liberated former colonizer. The works of Homi Bhabha, Edward Said, and others emanate from this representation of the binary, which, in the African American context, reinforces the distancing from an agentive self and lessens the envisioning of self-empowerment.

7. Chinweizu, *The West and the Rest of Us* (New York: Vintage, 1975).

8. Gates warns that we must not "resurrect our own version of the Thought Police, who would determine who and what, is 'black.' He paraphrases a sixties didactic joke and states, " 'Mirror, Mirror on the Wall, Who's the Blackest One of All?' is a question best left behind in the sixties" (9). While during the sixties the questions of what and who were "black" were certainly raised, such questions were and are not peculiar to the sixties. As long as America remains racist, these questions will either surface or be implied, just as they were in the nineteenth-century black nationalist and colonization movements, the BTW/WEB debates, the Harlem Renaissance, etc. As I remember the sixties didactic joke, it was "Mirror, mirror on the wall, who's the fairest of them all? Not you, Blackie, and don't you forget it." I recall submitting to the bleak humor of that joke during my high school days and later reading it in one of Leroi Jones's works. The point was exclusion of blacks from aesthetics and aesthetic beauty by the mainstream "mirror," with quite a different meaning to a central question of the sixties than Gates's presenta-

tion would have it. That question asked who and what values would be accepted and identified as American.

9. For a brief but comprehensive discussion of the role of African American studies in teaching literature, see Tejumola Olaniyan, "The Role of African American Studies in English Departments Now," *Callaloo*, vol. 17, no. 2 (Summer 1994), pp. 556–558.

10. J. J. Fossett and J. A. Tucker, eds., *Race Consciousness: African-American Studies for the New Century* (New York: New York University Press, 1997).

11. See Johnnella E. Butler, "Transforming the Curriculum: Teaching About Women of Color," in James A. Banks and Cherry A. McGee Banks, eds., *Multicultural Education: Issues and Perspectives* (Boston: Allyn and Bacon, 1997), pp. 171–190.

8

The Future of Black Studies: Political Communities and the "Talented Tenth"

Joy James

The future of "the race" is fortunately not synonymous with the future of black or Africana studies. Fortunately, because the ways in which we, as (elite) academics, explore political communities are often limited by exclusivity (toward nonelites) and ideological conformity to neoliberal corporate structures. There are of course exceptions to the rule: where political struggles have broken with academic corporate culture in the risks taken by progressive faculty and students to bring attention to demands for feminist/multicultural studies and equity for "minority" faculty, staff, and students. Antiracist feminist challenges to policies that minimize the place and presence of feminist "third world" studies faculty/students/staff offer an important struggle (and model) to be supported by academics. This is especially true for Africana studies faculty, for we are often institutionally or self-constructed in ways that reinforce our status as an entrepreneurial caste that takes few political risks.

In individual or collective efforts (in coteries) to create new forms of political community within academe, we find that the ethic of the marketplace generally prevails. In our "day jobs" (which, for some, extend into the night hours of grading and research), amid the calls for increased productivity in student credit hours or publications, how do we explore, formulate, and foment political communities to shape black studies that challenge commodification and corporatism? This question is cogent, particularly given that black studies exists in a culture that sells "X" caps and "Che" Swatches in sites with restricted access to working-class and poor African Americans.

Our daily encounters in major research institutions that are ostensibly—especially in urban areas—gated communities socialize not only individual faculty but collective perceptions of the viable future of black studies. Work environments have an immense impact on the individual; through their physical spaces and rhetoric, they establish levels of political analyses and thresholds for political courage.

Those who shape the general perception of what black studies is and will be, and the marketing of same, are usually located in elite schools or publishing houses. This focus on the personnel at research institutions is an acknowledgment of the hierarchy of the educational industry. As the postmodern talented tenth, we share some of the characteristics and contradictions of W. E. B. Du Bois's cohort group of the previous century. For instance, there is the mixed (political) parentage of our caste. As Harvard historian Evelyn Brooks Higginbotham has pointed out, this concept for an intellectual, progressive—but nonradical—head for a mass black restive body is partly the progeny of prominent nineteenth-century white liberals who sought to counter the most egregious forms of white supremacy while managing "the race." Although the current presence of Africana studies on college and university campuses emerged out of civil rights protests fought during a mass movement era, today the "studies," having been institutionalized, struggle mostly for their maintenance and expansion, and to some degree for recognition from endowed parental authorities.

Consequently, there are occupational hazards to employment in Africana studies, or ethnic studies, if one takes seriously political community that challenges antiblack racism, (hetero)sexism, and classism in Americana culture and politics. First, there is the leadership problem of the academic talented tenth; it appears ill-equipped to support or sustain political communities with nonelites relevant to their crises. In the canon of radical black studies one reads critiques of black elite agency. Historically that elite agency has been severely criticized by the mature Du Bois— who repudiated his earlier romanticization of the talented tenth as viable political leadership for disenfranchised blacks; Ella Baker—who left hierarchical organizations such as the NAACP and SCLC to help form radical grassroots groups such as SNCC; and, Frantz Fanon—whose native intellectual transformed herself from the bourgeois into the revolutionary engagée. The canon of black radicalism, when read, reflects contemporary common sense and wariness among ostracized communities who see that employees conform for wages as well as to the expectations of their work sites. During his indictment as a "foreign agent" amid the anticommunist campaigns, which led many middle-class blacks to desert him while black militant trade unionists organized for his exoneration, Du Bois pointed out that those with the least to lose (materially) are the ones most likely to agitate for change. The question to ask black studies intellectuals is how do we form political community and share intellectual leadership with those who have virtually little to lose.

In addition to the above occupational hazard of belonging to an ineffectual leadership reluctant to counter neoliberalism, most who work in academe encounter the downsizing of political analysis even among black studies intellectuals who identify as progressives. This partly reflects the general society's garroting via media of critical political discourse. Just as democratic praxis has diminished in public life where elected officials such as President Bill Clinton function more like accountants than visionaries (and university presidents act more like CEOs than critical thinkers), faculty and directors of Africana studies programs often acquiesce to depoliticization (or, really, repoliticization into neoliberalism). In his work, *In Theory,* Aijaz Ahmad contends that "debates about culture and literature on the Left no longer presume a labour movement as the ground on which they arise; 'theory' is now seen as a 'conversation' among academic professionals." Academic debates may sever discussions of ethnicity and race, gender, class, and sexuality from the liberation movements that shaped and continue to influence the meanings surrounding these identities and social formations. In academe a self/text preoccupation and careerism may marginalize or psychologize political struggles. In the present forms of black studies it is not unusual to find writers advocating for the intellectual-interrogator as more enlightened than the activist-intellectual (we also find the inflation of literary production into a form of political "activism" without analyses of its relationship to community organizing). Professionalizing progressive discourse, validating it within academic conversations, has a lot to do with the commodification of not only black studies but black radicalism within black studies.

To counter this hazard requires new forms of political theory. Texts inform our theories about black politics, culture, letters, and, not least of all, black liberation. But so do social movements resisting the immiseration of black life. And, in ways quite different from the texts of nonactivists, the narratives and analyses of organizers who oppose human rights abuses offer a resource for retooling theory and deepening our imaginations about political community and courage. The problem is that there are few institutional incentives to retool or retrain for an Africana studies future that privileges the demands of radicals and nonelite communities.

The future of a black studies relevant to the multiplicity of nonelite black life, and the occupational hazards of its growing employment in the penal industry, requires a study of the praxes of radical organizers who channel critiques of abusive state policies into confrontations. In this context of struggle the impact of strengthening radical political communities would resonate within academic black studies. One by-product of such relations would be revitalized theory—distinct from academic theories, which Barbara Christian defines as elitist if not rooted in communal practice and Ahmad finds as deradicalizing if severed from a movement base. When black studies academics theorize, to use Christian's verb, the conditions of those most vulnerable to state violence—and social movements to confront police/military, INS detention centers, prisons, workfare, toxic waste sites—should shape our reflections.

Such theory among the ethnically marginalized encompasses the lives of nonelites, of women, poor, youths, gays/lesbians. That it is tied to the recovery of both historical and contemporary memory as a political project speaks to a major benefit for professional thinkers. What constitutes progressive theory, how to write and teach in ways that support progressive movements and critical thinking, how to think of subversive studies as more than performance politics are critical issues for the future of black studies seeking political communities outside of academic carcerals. We have the space to explore these issues in our work. Such a focus may garner a small audience, and smaller rewards, given the antiradicalism in U.S. society and academic culture. However, it provides an important opportunity to recover stories, analyses, and political visions too often displaced and forgotten and in that recovery some push for new forms of political communities undisciplined by academic civility.

The future of black studies is tied to past and present political battles. The ways in which we recall historical and contemporary events and actors in social struggles shape our perceptions of agency and political efficacy. Recalling the work of educators who technically qualified as the talented tenth elite yet engaged in caste suicide, we study Ida B. Wells-Barnett, Ella Baker, and contemporary heirs such as Angela Davis and Assata Shakur. (Critical readers in black studies can see that the future is particularly grim for political communities if the marginalization or erasure of female radicals from black intellectualism continues to be pervasive.) Reading the words of prison intellectuals and political prisoners George Jackson, Geronimo Pratt, or Mumia Abu-Jamal, we understand that these battles continue to be contextualized by state violence.

Although radicalism and activism are largely contested and discredited in university life and theory, and marginalized within Africana studies, rekindling memory as an extension of engagement brings a strong antidote to the occupational hazards of institutionalized black studies. It also broadens the visions of political community and gives perspective to overly optimistic appraisals of the transformative abilities of the talented tenth. Ensuring the viability of a progressive left future in Africana studies would have both a sobering and invigorating effect on our intellectual/political endeavors.

9

Black Studies and the Question of Class

Bill Fletcher Jr.

Good afternoon, and thank you, Joel, for that gracious introduction. I would like to begin with two notes. For one, while I agree that the question of black studies must be examined in light of very changed conditions (since the 1960s), I would not accept the term *postmodern* to describe our current era. This may seem like a minor point, but along with the term *postmodern* comes a myriad of other assumptions. The second point is on a very different note. I am particularly honored to have been asked to participate on this panel because it is very rare that black labor activists are encouraged, let alone invited, to involve themselves in discussions such as today's, with regard to black studies. Thank you again.

The struggle for black studies has historically represented an effort to alter the manner in which U.S. culture and history has been understood and, specifically, the African American contribution as comprehended by both the larger society as well as by black America. This has been the case since well before black studies came to be known as "black studies."

There has, then, been a struggle within black studies over the question of how one defines the African American contribution. This has ranged the ideological spectrum. On the one hand, there have been those who have limited themselves to the demand for the acceptance of the African American contribution *within* the parameters—unquestioned—of U.S.

This speech was delivered at the 1997 Socialist Scholar's Conference in New York City.

society, i.e., inclusion in the traditional manner in which the story of U.S. society has been told.

On the other hand, or further down the ideological spectrum, there have been those who have attempted, through scholarly and polemical efforts, to redefine and reanalyze the basic U.S. paradigm. W. E. B. Du Bois, for instance, in his monumental work *Black Reconstruction in America*, represents this tendency. In essence, Du Bois redefined, from the standpoint of the African American, a period in time and a social movement. This redefinition, I would hasten to add, should not be defined as *Afrocentric*, in the way that this term is currently understood, but rather as a materialist multilayered analysis that resurrected and thrust forward the otherwise ignored African American role.

With the revival and baptism of that which we came to know as black studies in the sixties, the movement focused on the national or "ethnic" feature of the African American freedom struggle. Culture was prominent, but so too was a nonclass view of the African American experience. And, it is this that I would like to focus upon.

Black studies shared a great deal with features of national liberation movements in the so-called third world (the former colonial world) during the same era. Brought to the fore in the midst of a worldwide upsurge against imperialism, colonialism, and traditional racism, black studies often evidenced an *explicitly* anti-imperialist character. Even where dominated by the "famous Negroes I have known" school of thought within black studies, there was often a populist flavor to black studies, i.e., an attempt to articulate an academic movement that spoke to and about black people.

While overall the movement was positive, particularly in its critique of white supremacy, the movement's blindspot with regard to class, and, specifically, working-class issues, subjected the movement to subversion by pro-corporate forces. I would also argue that the blindspot to class served increasingly to isolate and marginalize the black studies movement. Consider for a moment that, in its origins, black studies struggles often gained community support. As time went on, however, black studies as a movement, a series of institutions, and a discourse, became less and less relevant to the everyday African American. Indeed, in the interests of scholarship, such isolation was often upheld by certain proponents of and within black studies.

An interesting case in point was the ongoing struggle to defend and expand black studies at Harvard University. Under the exceptional leadership of Dr. Ewart Guinier, the Afro-American Studies Department at Harvard served as a base area for scholars and student activists alike during the 1970s. Guinier was committed to the department continuing and deepening a relationship to the larger black community, but he was also committed to articulating a vision of black studies that held black workers and African American social movements at its core. The Harvard administration created roadblocks at every opportunity, and specifically refused to permit the development of the W. E. B. Du Bois Institute (a research institute) as an integral part of the Afro-American Studies Department until Guinier retired. Harvard's vision of the Du Bois Institute, shared by several black scholars, differed radically from Guinier's in that, among other things, it was very inward looking rather than developing community linkages.

In briefly reviewing the development of black studies, I would argue that there needs to be a revolution *within* black studies and a further redefinition or refinement of our notion of black studies.

I would suggest the following. African American life and history remains a battle for human rights and self-determination, as Malcolm X so eloquently pronounced so many years ago. In that battle various class forces have contended, sometimes explicitly, other times implicitly. The class character of various social movements within black America is rarely analyzed within the black studies movement. At worst, we degenerate into personality analysis, pinning the definition of entire movements or initiatives on what the *great leader* happened to be thinking about. At best, we speak to these movements solely as ideological tendencies, as if ideology has no connections with class.

Thus, Booker T. Washington comes to be viewed as a savior or traitor, or both (vis-à-vis the African American freedom struggle), depending on one's point of view. We end up restricting ourselves to Malcolm's marvelous metaphor, the *house Negro versus the field Negro*, but our analysis goes no deeper. The result of this is that the dynamics and forces that characters such as Booker T. Washington represented, e.g., his relationship to an aspiring black bourgeoisie, or his relationship to black farmers (as a class), these factors are rarely addressed. I hasten to add that within black studies there are some who have departed from simplistic analysis and have looked much more deeply at the factors influencing the black freedom struggle; the work of Manning Marable is a case in point.

In addition to the above analytic problems the specific role and contributions of black workers are often ignored. I was personally fortunate in my exposure to black studies in that the movement at Harvard in the 1970s was led by a gentleman who was a former trade unionist and who held class as central to the African American experience. I am referring to the late Dr. Ewart Guinier, mentioned earlier in my remarks, who had been the secretary-treasurer of the United Public Workers, a CIO union that was expelled during the cold war purges of the late 1940s for allegedly being led by Communists. Dr. Guinier was also the father of Lani Guinier.

Black studies as a discipline generally ignores black workers and their efforts at self-organization. The contribution of unions in the fight for African American freedom, e.g., the Colored National Labor Union (of the 1860s), the Knights of Labor (1870s and 1880s), the Industrial Workers of the World (the Wobblies of the early twentieth century), the Congress of Industrial Organizations (in the 1930s and 1940s), has little relevance for the bulk of black studies, with, of course, the exception of the formalistic acknowledgment of A. Philip Randolph that accompanies most examinations of African American life and history in the twentieth century. Generally there is even little recognition of the struggles by black workers to desegregate various craft unions and to win equality within most unions, though when acknowledged it comes along with an implicit condemnation of unionism as a mechanism in the black freedom struggle.

I could go on and on, but let me close by saying that we now have an unusual and important opportunity to redefine black studies. Class polarization has widened within black America and eroded the basis for the old civil rights consensus. There is a struggle for the soul of black America, a struggle that pits black neoconservatives, black traditional liberals, as well as black radicals in a race to build a new and operating consensus in our freedom struggle. There is, simultaneously, a struggle in the multiethnic working class, a struggle represented at one level by the changes in the AFL-CIO and the new leadership of John Sweeney, Richard Trumka, and Linda Chavez-Thompson. There is a moment now for a reconfigured black studies to influence the development and self-conception of organized labor. There is, hopefully, also an opportunity for black studies to be influenced by a pro-working-class perspective.

Thank you very much.

10

Black Studies:
A Critical Reassessment

Maulana Karenga

From its beginning black studies has had both an academic and social thrust and mission rooted in the social theory and struggle of the sixties (Hare 1969, 1972). As an emerging discipline, black studies sheltered the assumption that the black experience clearly represented a truth worth knowing, but also one worth living and offering as a paradigm for human liberation and a higher level of human life. Conceiving of intellectual emancipation as a prerequisite and parallel support for political emancipation, black studies advocates posed the discipline as a synthesized and synthesizing enterprise that links thought and practice into a paradigm of active self-knowledge. At its best, such a paradigm represented a quest for self-realization that expresses itself as both self-knowledge and self-production. That is to say, a people critically grasping its inherent possibilities and self-consciously bringing these into being both as a distinct people and as a fundamental part of society and the world (Karenga 1997).

Certainly, we are constantly confronted with challenges of the reactionary right in response to the development of black studies and its continuing commitment to raise and pursue issues of both intellectual and social significance. And this response can be rightfully read as a central aspect of the larger effort to contain, compromise, and essentially defeat the ongoing struggle for an expanded realm of freedom both in the academy and the society. But it does not seem very useful to continue to point attention to it without at the same time saying what black studies is going to do about it. In fact, our argument is that our defense lies essentially in our development—in our maintenance of our commitment to our mission, with its dual thrust of educational excellence and social responsibility.

I advance the proposition in various writings that challenges successfully met enhance possibilities, and I see no reason why we should not take this posture with black studies. It is the history of humankind that overcoming social and natural oppositions strengthens them and pushes them further along the road to ever higher levels of thought and practice. And, therefore, we should welcome these struggles, for the struggle to defend and develop black studies offers similar possibilities of development in the academic as well as the social world. I repeat, the need of black studies to defend itself is at the same time a demand to develop itself.

Moreover, whatever unsure steps or stumbling there is or was in the past offers us a wealth of lessons for the future, which will aid a quicker pace of development. For, as an African teaching says, "To stumble is not to fall but to go forward faster." The need, then, is for bold and critical thought and planning, greater intellectual production, more vital research, effective organization, systematic exchange and development with other scholars of similar understandings of the world. And in fact, we must even dare discourse with those that oppose us. In a word, the need is for self-conscious action that not only answers critics but, more important, answers the critical question the discipline must continually raise for itself in the constant redefining and expanding of its capacity to carry out its academic and social mission (Stewart 1992).

Black studies, however, has shown a remarkable capacity for development and expansion in spite of its critics. And it must continue to do so. Few, if any, of the traditional disciplines have shown such adaptive vitality in meeting new and internal challenges to expand and change. Part of this receptivity to and capacity for change in the expansion of black studies is undoubtedly due to its relative newness, the absence of long-term entrenched contentions grown hoary and semisacred with age. Moreover, black studies is an open-textured and open-ended project, interdisciplinary and receptive to diversity, as expressed in its ability to include various subject areas and various intellectual perspectives and schools of thought (Turner 1984; *Afrocentric Scholar* 1993).

But, more important, black studies reflects also the history of the context in which the discipline emerges. It came into being in the midst of the black freedom movement as an emancipatory project that sought to be both an ongoing and profound critique and corrective, intellectually and socially. Thus, if it holds true to its academic and social mission, black studies is compelled to practice internally what it demands externally, i.e., self-criticism, self-correction, and the posing of a new paradigm of what it means to be human. The key to black studies' continued growth and expansion and its continued vanguard role in the multicultural challenge to the established order paradigm, then, is maintaining its open-texturedness, its open-ended character, which allows for and encourages the creative challenge of diversity and an intellectual rigor and relevance that disarm its severest critics and honor its original academic and social mission (Karenga 1988, 1995a). And the mission remains one, as Mary McLeod Bethune (1939) said, of our discovering the dawn and sharing it with the masses who need it most. For it is by bringing the fruits of knowledge to the masses that we contribute definitively to laying the basis for maximum human freedom and human flourishing.

What I want to do is pose five fundamental projects I think are important for this challenge: (1) the ongoing dialogue with African culture; (2) the expansion of our internal dialogue; (3) the continuous development of a new language and logic; (4) new models of social and human possibilities represented in social policy emphasis; and (5) social engagement, the practice that proves and make possible everything.

Speaking from the philosophical framework of Kawaida Theory, I would argue that the fundamental point of departure for African American studies or black studies is an ongoing dialogue with African culture (Karenga 1997, 2000). That is to say, continuously asking it questions and seeking from it answers to the fundamental questions of humankind. For example, how do we define and defend the dignity and rights of the human person in the midst of a rapidly and ever changing technological world? How do we pose and bring into being a just and good society? How do we define the human, the just, the good in a context of rampant consumerism, rented wombs, cloning, and ongoing degradation of the environment? What does African culture have to say about the spiritual and ethical void and social alienation that lead to Jonestown, Guyana or mass suicide in Rancho Santa Fe, California or the murders at Columbine High in Colorado?

Cheikh Anta Diop (1982:475ff.) has rightfully asked, What does African cultural philosophy have to offer in enhancing human reasoning and sensitivity in the world? And Kawaida Theory asks, What does black studies have to offer in the ongoing quest of African people to bring forth the best of their history and heritage and to pose paradigms of the best of what it means to be both African and human at the same time and in the fullest sense of the word? In this process it seems to me that black studies must reaffirm its original mission and rationale and constantly develop itself. For the respect it receives will inevitably be based on contributions that black studies makes as a discipline, the new knowledge that it brings forth, as well as the critique and corrective that it offers.

There are seven fundamental intellectual and social contributions made by black studies that prove its value as a discipline (Karenga 1992:15ff). The first, of course, is that black studies is a contribution to humanity's understanding itself, using the African experience as a paradigmatic human struggle and achievement. Second, it is a contribution to the university's realizing its claim of universality, comprehensiveness, and objectivity by demanding and facilitating a holistic approach to the study of truth and the class, race, and sexual contradictions, which constrain and distort that truth. Third, it's a contribution to U.S. society's understanding itself by critically measuring its claims against performance in its variance with the paradigmatic just society. It is also a contribution to the rescue and reconstruction of black history and humanity from alien hands and the restoration of African classical culture on and through which we can build a new body of human sciences and humanity (Diop 1982; Williams 1993).

The fifth is also a contribution to the creation of a new social science and humanities, more critical, more corrective, more holistic, more ethical, more inclusive. Sixth, it's a contribution to the creation of a self-conscious body of capable and committed black intellectuals who self-consciously choose to use their knowledge and skills in the service of the black community and, by consequence and extension, in the interest of a new and better society and the world (Du Bois 1996; Strickland 1975). And, finally, black studies finds its grounding and meaning in its ongoing contribution to the critique, resistance, and reversal of one of the greatest problems of our time, the progressive Europeanization of human consciousness (Reed 1997). And by that I mean the systematic invasion and effective transformation of the cultural consciousness of the various peoples of the world by Europeans through technology, education, and the media. So that at least three things occur: (1) the progressive loss of historical memory of these peoples; (2) the progressive disappreciation of themselves and their culture; and (3) the progressive adoption of a Eurocentric mode of assessment of self, society, and the world, inducing cognitive distortion and deprivation and the destruction of the human richness we find in human diversity.

The second major challenge of the discipline is to expand its internal dialogue. A discipline by its very nature is not only an organized and systematized body of research and literature created by a community of scholars who have common interests but also a process that allows for and encourages these scholars to exchange among themselves and to ask themselves critical questions about the direction, the content, and the future of the discipline itself. Such a functional internal dialogue is clearly evidenced in the development of black women's studies as a major field within the discipline (Sudarkasa 1999; Terborg-Penn and Rushing 1996; Aldridge 1992). But it also speaks to the constant self-questioning concerning further development of the field in technology (Hendrix et al. 1984), curriculum (Little, Leonard, and Crosby 1993), multicultural education (Karenga 1995a), and other areas (Gordon 1981; Stewart 1992).

Molefi Asante's (1990) position is that black studies at its best is Afrocentric, for it compels, even deems indispensable, critical dialogue internal to the culture and discipline. Clearly there are other schools of thought in Africana studies, but there is no substitute for centering oneself in one's own culture and speaking one's own cultural truth. This does not mean that we in Africana studies are going to speak about African people in isolation. On the contrary, we must and do engage in critical exchange with the rest of the world, bringing our own special cultural truth to the table. Often, labeling Afrocentric scholars relieves one of the responsibility of thinking critically about the issues engaged. In fact, what some people often do is sum up Afrocentric discourse with labels like *separatism* and *essentialism*. These, however, are merely catchwords that sometimes offer useful insights but also cultivate embarrassing illusions about having found a truth that was already discovered. What I want to stress here is that a discipline is a self-conscious system of research and communication in a defined area of inquiry and knowledge, a definite literature created by a body of scholars in an ongoing, mutually challenging, and productive dialogue. This requires that they center themselves, then, and that they begin to pose a new or definitive historical paradigm that involves both models of practice and possibility (Karenga 1988).

Third, we must continue to develop a new language and logic for the discipline so that we are not conceptually imprisoned by the logic and language of the established order. This is an important point Malcolm X made in a lecture at Harvard in which he stressed the need for an emancipatory logic that would undergird and inform emancipatory practice (Malcolm X 1968). What Africana studies does is offer an enrichment and expansion of the educational project in its stress on both critique and corrective, which both require a new language and new logic. Black studies evolved in the midst of the emancipatory struggle of the sixties that linked intellectual emancipation with political emancipation, campus with community, intellectuals and students with the masses, and knowledge in the academy with power in society. What emerged in the process of both struggles on campus and society was a paradigm of critique and corrective designed to critique and end domination, to expand the realm of freedom, to create a just and good society, and to pose a new paradigm of what it means to be human. Moreover, an Afrocentric critique, at its best, requires focus on contradictions in society, especially those of race, class, and gender, looking again not only for what is present and distorted in the discourse but also for what is absent and undiscussed, not only for codified ignorance but also for canonized illusion. In a word, we must then contest the present and pose paradigms of possibility for the future.

In fact, one of the most important achievements of black studies scholars is to have put forth contestation in Africana studies as a fundamental mode of understanding self, society, and the world. In such a process Africana studies seeks to create a space and process for students to recover, discover, and speak the truth and meaning of their own experience, to locate themselves in social and human history, and, having oriented themselves, to bring their unique contribution to multicultural exchange in the academy and society (McAdoo 1999; Hamlet 1998). Ideally what results from this critique of established order discourse and contestation over issues of intellect and life is the multicultural cooperative production of knowledge, rather than its Eurocentric authoritative allocation.

Another contribution it seems to me that black studies must make to a paradigm of a new educational project is to stress the ethical dimension in education. That is to say, to treat social problematics as life issues, as concrete issues, rather than abstract intellectual problems. The very practice of generating reflective problematics and correctives from the African experience, which is defined by oppression, resistance, and the creation and maintenance of free space for proactive practices in spite of social oppression, raises continuous ethical questions. Both oppression and resistance unavoidably generate ethical questions. Also, the stress on the ethical dimensions evolves from our ancient tradition of emphasis on civic moral education in Africa extending back to ancient Egypt with its concern for moral leadership in a just and good society (Karenga 1994). Likewise, this tradition is reflected and reaffirmed in the ethical teachings of the Odu Ifa, which stress the moral obligation "to struggle to increase good in the world and not let any good be lost" and cites as the first criterion for bringing good into the world "full knowledge of all things" (Karenga 1999:229ff.). This translates further as the moral and technical "wisdom to adequately govern the world" so that the good of work and wealth are always a shared good in both creation and benefit.

The Afrocentric stress on ethics also becomes the way to begin to integrate the disciplines, for it rightly raises questions about the relevance of knowledge and its pursuit for the human person in the human community. This means that ethical questions about the world or ethical questions of life and death are no longer safely assigned to religion, but rather that each discipline raises its own questions as well as participating in discourse on general ethics.

Finally, one of our greatest challenges is to contribute intellectually and practically to the creation of a just and good society that is self-consciously multicultural (Reed 1997). And by a multicultural society I mean a society that respects diversity and that has at least four fundamental aspects to it: mutual respect for each people and culture; mutual respect for each people's right and responsibility to speak their own special cultural truth and to make their own unique contribution to the way in which this society is conceived and reconstructed; mutual commitment to the constant search for common ground in the midst of our diversity; and, finally, mutual commitment to an ethics of sharing: shared status, shared knowledge, shared space, shared wealth, shared power, and shared responsibility for conceiving and building the world we want to live in.

Postmodern critiques do not give grounding or a sense of values or a sense of human possibility. They slash and burn, undermine and overturn, but they often leave nothing in their wake except the routine competence for criticism and the urge to fondle the familiar declarations of faith against essentialism, fundamentalism, and the host of anti-isms that serve as both a pabulum for the newly initiated and a prophetic engagement with illusion for the veteran. The essential question, then, is what framework and foundation can we offer to grasp and engage this challenge called life, this world of problem and possibility, this time of reaction and fundamental turning. As I (Karenga 1995b) noted in the *Million Man March/Day of Absence Mission Statement*, we must reaffirm our social justice tradition both intellectually and in practice. And this at a minimum means reaffirming respect for the rights and dignity of the human person, the well-being of family and community, economic justice, shared political power, meaningful political participation, cultural integrity, mutual respect for all peoples, and a constant struggle against all forces that would deny and limit these. In such a thrust black studies reaffirms its intellectual and social mission: an essential and ongoing contribution to the reconception and reconstruction of the human project and prospect.

References

Afrocentic Scholar. 1993. Vol. 2, no. 1 (May).

Aldridge, Delores. 1992. "Womanist Issues in Black Studies: Toward Integrating African Women into Africana Studies." *Journal of the National Council for Black Studies*, vol. 1, no. 1 (May), pp. 167–182.

Asante, Molefi. 1990. *Kemet, Afrocentricity, and Knowledge.* Trenton, N.J.: Africa World.

———— 1998. *The Afrocentric Idea.* Philadelphia: Temple University Press, 1998.

Bethune, Mary McLeod. 1939. "The Adaptation of the History of the Negro to the Capacity of the Child." *Journal of Negro History*, vol. 24, pp. 9–13.

Diop, Cheikh Anta. 1982. *Civilisation ou barbarie.* Paris: Présence Africaine. 1990. *Civilization or Barbarism.* Brooklyn: Lawrence Hill.

Du Bois, W. E. B. 1996. "The Talented Tenth" and "Talented Tenth Memorial Address." In Henry Louis Gates Jr. and Cornel West, eds., *The Future of the Race.* New York: Knopf.

Gordon, Vivian. 1981. "The Coming of Age in Black Studies." *Western Journal of Black Studies*, vol. 5.

Hamlet, Janice, ed. 1998. *Afrocentric Visions: Studies in Culture and Communications.* Thousand Oaks, Cal.: Sage 1998.

Hare, Nathan. 1969. "What Should Be the Role of Afro-American Education in the Undergraduate Curriculum?" *Liberal Education*, vol. 55, no. 1 (March), pp. 42–50.

———— 1972. "The Battle of Black Studies." *Black Scholar*, vol. 3, no. 9 (May), pp. 32–37.

Hendrix, M. et al. 1984. "Computers and Black Studies: Toward the Cognitive Revolution." *Journal of Negro Education*, vol. 53, pp. 341–350.

Karenga, Maulana. 1988. "Black Studies and the Problematic of Paradigm: The Philosophical Dimension." *Journal of Black Studies*, vol. 18, no. 4 (June), pp. 395–414.

———— 1992. *Introduction to Black Studies.* Los Angeles: University of Sankore Press.

———— 1994. "Maat, The Moral Ideal in Ancient Egypt: A Study in Classical African Ethics." Ph.D. diss., University of Southern California.

———— 1995a. "Afrocentricity and Multicultural Education: Concept, Challenge, and Contribution." In Benjamin Bowser, Terry Jones, and Gale Auletta Young, eds., *Toward a Multicultural University*, pp. 41–61. Westport, Conn.: Praeger.

———— 1995b. *Million Man March/Day of Absence Mission Statement.* Los Angeles: University of Sankore Press.

———— 1999. *Odu Ifa: The Ethical Teachings.* Los Angeles: University of Sankore Press.

———— 2000. *Kawaida Theory: A Communitarian African Philosophy.* Los Angeles: University of Sankore Press.

Little, William A., Carolyn Leonard, and Edward Crosby. 1993. "The National Council for Black Studies: Black Studies/Africana Studies Holistic Curriculum Model." *Afrocentric Scholar*, vol. 2, no. 1 (May), pp. 42–68.

McAdoo, Harriet Pipes. 1999. *Family and Ethnicity: Strength in Diversity.* Thousand Oaks, Cal.: Sage.

Malcolm X. 1968. *The Speeches of Malcolm X at Harvard.* Ed. Archie Epps. New York: William Morrow.

Reed, Ishmael, ed. 1997. *Multi-America: Essays on Cultural Wars and Cultural Peace.* New York: Viking Penguin.

Stewart, James. 1992. "Reaching for Higher Ground: Toward an Understanding of Black/Africana Studies." *Journal for the National Council for Black Studies*, vol. 1, no . 1 (May), pp. 1–63.

Strickland, Bill. 1975. "Black Intellectuals in American Social Science." *Black World*, vol. 25 (November), pp. 4–10.

Sudarkasa, Niara. *The Strength of Our Mothers: African and African American Women and Families, Essays and Speeches.* Trenton, N.J.: Africa World.

Terborg-Penn, Rosalyn, and Andrea Benton Rushing, eds. 1996. *Women in Africa and the African Diaspora.* Washington, D.C.: Howard University Press.

Turner, James, ed. 1984. *The Next Decade: Theoretical and Research Issues in Africana Studies.* Ithaca: Africana Studies and Research Center, Cornell University.

Williams, Selasé W. 1993. "Black Studies: The Evolution of an Afrocentric Human Science." *Afrocentric Scholar*, vol. 2, no. 1 (May), pp. 69–84.

11

Black Studies Revisited

Martin Kilson

Some Context

Viewed in either its minimum curriculum format as represented by curriculum limited mainly to those black realities associated with North American blacks or viewed in its maximum curriculum format as represented by curriculum that embraces black African societies, the Afro-American community, Afro-Caribbean communities, and Afro-Latin communities, the academic field of black studies has experienced multisided transformations since those start-up years between 1968 and 1972. Those start-up years witnessed enormous political upheaval and intellectual upheaval, a situation that while sometimes pedagogically damaging should be viewed as nonetheless developmentally inevitable. In one of my earliest commentaries on the upheaval surrounding the birth of black studies, I offered both an affirmation of the student activism that drove this field, on the one hand, while chastising the violence or violence-posturing that surrounded this activism. Writing in a special black studies monograph produced by the A. Philip Randolph Institute in 1969, I observed:

> The activity of black students on campuses across the country in behalf of Afro-American studies is welcome. Much of this activity, however, has been associated unnecessarily with violence which has no place whatever on college campuses. Violence can do no other than destroy the delicate fabric of life and work in American colleges, and will certainly prevent the establishment of Afro-American studies along viable academic and intellectual lines.

In general, while the violence surrounding the birth of black studies was quite short-lived, a tendency toward ideological rigidity in regard to the academic organization and the pedagogical execution of the field of black studies proved rather tenacious and long-lived. This situation represented a special problem for progressive and leftist African American intellectuals like myself, for while we welcomed the activism that brought American colleges—white ones, especially, but black colleges too—to incorporate black studies into their educational regime, we felt a simultaneous responsibility to tame or pluralize this ideological rigidity.

Formative Phase of Black Studies

What were some basic elements of this ideological rigidity? First, militant advocates of black studies preferred that this field be organized mainly in terms of their strongly held ideological preferences. Among these preferences, for instance, was a tendency toward the glorification of the black American experience and of African history in a manner that would serve contemporary endeavors at political activism among black Americans. My own inclination, however, was to follow the lead of that first-generation cohort of black scholars (some white ones too) who pioneered the field of black studies when it was still called Negro studies. Scholars, that is, like W. E. B. Du Bois, Carter Woodson, Charles Spurgeon Johnson, Allison Davis, Horace Mann Bond, Ralph Bunche, Rayford Logan, Melville Herskovitz, E. Franklin Frazier, John Hope Franklin, Kelley Miller, Ira de Augustine Reid, to name just a few. What many militants among black studies advocates in the formative phase failed to recognize is that the first-generation cohort of black studies intellectuals balanced within their persona both a progressive ideological commitment to black realities—to freeing those realities from oppressive white supremacist patterns worldwide and advancing their modern development—on the one hand, and a nonethnocentric or pluralistic scholarly orientation toward black realities.

Thus what the first-generation cohort of black studies intellectuals taught us, with their balanced interface with progressive ideological commitment to black realities, on the one hand, and a nonethnocentric orientation, on the other hand, was this: that the serious study of the history and contemporary experiences of black peoples—worldwide or in the United States—will produce a bewildering mixture of things that can evoke pride, criticism, ambivalence, or even revulsion. They taught us that black students, taught about the great sculpture of West African peoples, will more than likely be proud of the artistic achievement this sculpture represented, just as Anglo-American students would take pride in the works of William Shakespeare. But would these same black students consider as a source of pride the historical findings relating to the massive role of traditional ruling strata in African societies in forging the Atlantic Slave Trade? Most likely not, just as the white Anglo-American students would not likely be proud of the vicious oppression and violence perpetrated against the Irish by the English ruling class during their multicentury rule in Ireland. The history of all peoples is morally checkered!

The militant black studies advocates' belief that an academic regime in this field would produce and should produce activist cadres for black urban communities was rather shortsighted too. The academic organization of black studies was not, I believe, anything like the appropriate locale for forging political and neighborhood mobilizers. While the need for such mobilizers was genuine, their effective production should be undertaken elsewhere, I thought—in the context of black neighborhood voluntary associations, black churches, black civil rights organizations, etc. As it happened, this activist use of black studies programs proved a dead end. And this, moreover, was rather unfortunate in some respects, as the need for skilled neighborhood mobilizers was a real one and the failure of that militant segment that surrounded black studies programs in the formative phase to generate such mobilizers left a terrible vacuum in many black urban communities, among the weak working-class and lower-class sector especially. The high black homicide rate and the high rate of black-maiming-black can be attributed in part to this terrible vacuum. *One must wonder, in fact, whatever happened to all of that activistic energy and excitement that surrounded the birth of black studies programs in regard to the goal of forging neighborhood activist cadres?* Currently, it seems the vast majority of middle-class black college students have lost all connection with this aspect of the formative era of black studies, as witnessed by their fervent participation in that all-black student good-time gathering annually during spring in Atlanta—the Black Freaknik Festival! This weird outcome could not, I suspect, have been envisaged or predicted some thirty years ago, at the birth of black studies. This weird use of black middle-class resources is seventeen years old.

Maturation of Black Studies

In terms of time frame, we might place the commencement of the maturation phase of black studies from the late 1970s onward (say, 1979 onward). One measure of the maturation phase was, I think, the appointment of black scholars to head up black studies programs who were clearly scholars and intellectuals of the top rank. This occurred with the appointment of Professor Charles Davis at Yale's Afro-American Studies Department, Professor Nathan Huggins at Harvard's Afro-American Studies Department, Professor Joseph Washington and later Professor Houston Baker at the University of Pennsylvania's Afro-American Studies Department, Professor St. Clair Drake at Stanford University's Afro-American Studies Department, and Professor Claudia Mitchell-Kernan at the University of California's (L.A.) Afro-American Studies Program, to mention just a few.

What did these scholars do to initiate what I call the maturation phase in black studies? Essentially, they *disciplinized black studies,* so to speak. They slowly interlocked the structuring of the academic regime of black studies with the established academic disciplines in the social sciences and the humanities. Thus they filtered the curriculum dimension of black studies—the courses—through modes of curriculum packaging akin to those usually found in, say, regular political science courses, producing thereby such courses as "Black Electoral Politics," "Blacks in National Politics," "Black Legislators," "Politics and Society of Afro-Americans," "Black Urban Regimes," etc., etc. But an innovative thrust, curriculum-wise, evolved as well in the maturation phase, especially in the area of literary studies. This was so particularly where the field of literary studies overlapped psychological and societal areas of inquiry, producing what has amounted to a new academic discipline, that of black cultural studies. Moreover, the traditional field of literary studies was itself broadened by the penetration of this field with the works (and thus styles, aesthetics, etc.) of black American writers, African writers, Afro-Latin writers, and Afro-Caribbean writers. And, of course, the field of women's studies (gender studies), which evolved almost simultaneously with the field of black studies, has contributed in many enriching ways to the spin-off field of black cultural studies and also the established field of black studies. Women's studies has exercised this influence through its subfield of black women's studies, of course.

Interestingly enough, this penetration by established academic disciplines of black studies since the late 1970s, as well as the emergence of a major spin-off subfield of black cultural studies, has not displaced variants of black ethnocentric delineation in the black studies field. This black ethnocentric delineation of black studies goes today under the name of

Afrocentrist studies. It has also acquired a kind of parallel status with the field of black studies.

In terms of its curriculum manifestation, Afrocentrist studies is rather ideologically rigid and informed by a hyperglorification of a black realities outlook. The most prominent gathering of black scholars who function within the Afrocentrist paradigm is at Temple University, though there are smaller clusters located rather broadly at some black colleges. It should be noted, however, that given the Afrocentrist paradigms' highly emotive and hyperideological thrust, it appears to have forged a rather broad appeal at the popular level of African American society, among stable working-class and middle-class sectors no less. The appeal is of an ethnic-group-solidarity-affirming character, mainly, I believe; it is not an appeal that is translated into institution forging or systemic forging outcomes. So, over time, the Afrocentrist appeal can be expected to dissipate, assuming of course that a steady expansion of black Americans' incorporation into American social and power patterns obtains, and assuming also that this expansion is not rendered problematic by neoracist forces associated with the neoconservatism that has wide influence today among white Americans.

Concluding Note

No one, of course, can predict future trends in black studies generally with any high degree of accuracy. But one can suggest trends that might be initiated.

One trend I would like to see emerge is, in fact, a rather old trend. It relates to the early Negro studies series that W. E. B. Du Bois pioneered while he was at Atlanta University and that other scholars among the first-generation cohort of black scholars (between early 1900s and 1940s) contributed their own variants of. The Du Bois Negro studies series focused on both Negro social categories (professions, business, workers, agrarians, etc.) and on Negro institutions and their modern metamorphoses (churches, voluntary associations, professional associations, colleges, black elementary, middle, and secondary schools, etc.).

That what I view as the mature phase in black studies has not yet fashioned either broad curriculum regimes or research regimes with what I call the Du Boisean Negro studies focus baffles me somewhat—baffles me especially in light of the social mobility and overall modernization crises that have confronted the weak working class and the poor strata among African Americans. Those households that make up perhaps 40 percent of all African American households have received, of course, lots of research attention from social science scholars among blacks, but mainly with a focus toward fashioning public policy responses to intervening in the crises of joblessness, family dislocation, intrablack violence and maiming, etc., faced by these black households.

But most progressive black intellectuals have also recognized that what I call the "mobile sector" among black Americans—as contrasted with the "static sector" of weak working-class and poor households—have an obligation to fashion ways and means for intervening in the crises facing the black static sector. It is here, then, where a revival of the Du Boisean Negro studies focus in the context of our mature phase of black studies could, I think, produce important outcomes: outcomes both academic in import and operational relative to the crises facing the black static sector. The range of institutional capability associated with the black mobile sector—with its class categories and with the agencies available to these categories—is, I suggest, greater by exponential degree compared to what this institutional capability was several generations ago during Du Bois's era. Black studies programs can, in our mature phase, play a significant role in uncovering the ingredients and dimensions of this institutional capability. This is a must agenda for the years ahead.

12

Theorizing Black Studies:
The Continuing Role of Community
Service in the Study of Race and Class

James Jennings

This essay proposes that "community service" and related efforts to develop programmatic linkages with neighborhood institutions and organizations represent a key component in the theory and pedagogy of black studies. Research paradigms that include community service and civic involvement reflect the description of black studies as a discipline that is "descriptive, critical, and prescriptive," to use the words of Professor Manning Marable.[1] Attention to the pedagogy of community service on the part of scholars in black studies is important for the growth of this field of intellectual inquiry as well as for its growing impact on the analysis of political and economic issues facing black communities and U.S. urban society. Both theory and praxis are key to understanding how black life experiences have molded, and are reflected, in United States society.

Theory refers to the building of predictive and projective knowledge about the experiences of blacks in the African diaspora and how such experiences have influenced major national and global developments. The term *praxis* implies that theoretical understandings of black life experiences in this society should be informed by the experiences of blacks in ongoing political, economic, educational, and cultural struggles aimed at the expansion of racial and economic democracy. While this notion seems logical given the birth of black studies in the post-WWII period, it is resisted at some levels in higher education. Within the field of black studies, however, community service focuses on changing system-based and dominant/subordinate social and economic relations and improving living conditions for blacks, and thereby, other communities. As a matter of fact, many black studies programs in U.S. higher education were established during the 1960s and 1970s not only because of the need to examine race and political economy in urban settings but also to enhance the effectiveness of black civic participation in the interests of social and racial justice. Indeed, this is still a distinguishing feature of many black studies programs, although it is resisted somewhat, as suggested by Joy James in her article, "The Future of Black Studies: Political Communities and the 'Talented Tenth'" (chapter 8, this volume).[2]

Revisiting this traditional role of community service in the field of black studies is a timely topic in that several doctoral programs offering courses of study in black studies have been established recently. There are now doctoral programs in black studies at Temple University, the Ohio State University, the University of Massachusetts, and the University of California at Berkeley. The call for the linkage of praxis with theory, and the pedagogy of community service, is an important component of these doctoral programs. The incorporation of community service within black studies, furthermore, has been endorsed by many scholars presenting papers at recent professional and academic conferences focusing on black studies.

The relationship between community involvement, or praxis, and the development of social and economic theory has been ignored or dismissed in other disciplines. But contrasted to this mainstream bias is the idea found in black intellectual thought that scholarship must be in service to social democracy in civic life. Indeed, several black studies departments and programs across the nation have designed curricula on the basis of building theory and knowledge linked to involvement with community-level experiences, preparing students to work in a variety of civic and professional settings. The recently established doctoral programs in this field suggest, through their faculty and curricula as well as their inaugural ceremonies, that scholarship about black experiences in the U.S. should be pursued within a framework of theory, praxis, *and* community service.

Community service represents a significant component in the field of black studies because it is actually an important research tool. Thus, the call for community service is viewed not solely as public service but as a key component for certain kinds of research. For instance, some focus on community service highlights the limitations in research concepts and paradigms utilized for the study of race and class within other disciplines such as political science, sociology, psychology, and economics. These limitations are associated, in part, with the separation of theory building from praxis and community service in the organization of these fields by traditional departments and universities. This is suggested in a publication by M. E. Hawkesworth, *Theoretical Issues in Public Policy Analysis.*[3] The author notes that the field of public policy can be described as in a state of intellectual crisis because its methodology and purpose have become obfuscated with a false scientism serving no useful social purpose in advancing democracy. Mainstream scholarship focusing on the economics of poverty or race relations in the United States has not been able to help develop public policy and civic participation that can allow the United States to overcome certain kinds of racial problems. At times scholarship reflects its own industry, separated from dialogue and activism aimed at advancing social democracy. Because community service within the field of black studies is not disparaged or rejected as a component of research paradigms, it helps to inform and propel an intellectual understanding that may facilitate more effective civic responses to political and economic problems facing black communities.

In the contemporary period there are several political conditions and issues that are of particular significance in determining the social and economic status of the U.S. urban black community. The integration and utilization of community service in the field of black studies contribute to a greater understanding of the nature of these conditions and how the civic sector can respond to these issues. These major political and economic issues facing black communities include how its leadership should respond to national social policies—whether supported by Democrats or Republicans—that continue to weaken, institutionally and culturally, urban communities through the defunding of cities. Such policies include the adoption and implementation of laissez-faire or trickle-down approaches that usually focus on the development of downtown or benefits to corporate interests at the expense of neighborhoods.

Another challenge facing blacks as a group is how the nation's intelligentsia, including media, educators, scholars, and cultural leaders, continue to approach black urban communities as pathology, rather than recognize the significant cultural and intellectual contributions to U.S. society reflected in the nation's black community. A relatively new political issue for the U.S. urban black community is the status and future relations with other communities of color that are growing in number and potential social influence. Perhaps this particular issue can only be understood and responded to in the interest of advancing democracy within a context of praxis? Yet another challenge facing black communities is how to respond to the renaissance of "color blindness" as a powerful and dominant ideology protecting the social and economic status quo. This ideology is becoming increasingly popular and influential in justifying a racial order born of segregation and slavery. And certainly the growing numbers and concentration of alienated youth without linkages to cultural or socially supportive institutions in their communities are another important challenge facing black communities. While not an exhaustive listing, these are some of the basic social issues that community service pedagogy can target in the field of black studies. I propose that community service, as an integral component of black studies, is a fundamental tool for building effective theoretical frameworks and public policies.

Black Studies and the Role of Community Service

The history of black studies as a field illustrates that theory must be strongly linked to praxis, or community service. Planning and institutionalizing opportunities to pursue scholarship, praxis, and community service within an integrated framework was a major demand of students during the 1960s black cultural renaissance and black studies movement in U.S. higher education. In predominantly white universities the call for opportunities to pursue "community-based" research within programs of Afro-American studies can be summarized by the famous demands of black students at San Francisco State University in 1968. These black students, and other students as well, argued that the scholarship they were exposed to should be both informed by the everyday struggles of black people for justice and economic survival as well as useful in preparing students to make contributions to society.

The suggestion that black studies should reflect research concepts and paradigms based on community experiences is one of the strongest intellectual traditions within the black struggle for educational equality and opportunity in the United States and abroad. This is the first theme explained by Charles V. Hamilton in his classic taxonomy of black intellectual and philosophical traditions and values, *The Black Experience in American Politics*.[4] Historical and contemporary examples of how this theme is reflected in the work of a wide range of scholars can be found in William M. Banks's more recent book, *Black Intellectuals*.[5] In fact, the first editorial of the nation's first black newspaper in 1827, *Freedom's Journal*, called for black leaders to use education and scholarship as a civic and political resource aimed at the abolition of slavery and uplifting the black masses. This was an important theme of Booker T. Washington's autobiography, *Up From Slavery*, published in 1895.[6] Washington explained that he decided to pursue education in order to return to his community with skills that would help uplift blacks in the South. He argued further that this was a widely held belief in the black community; that is, those blacks fortunate enough to acquire an education were expected to return benefits to less fortunate blacks by being involved with their community and receiving training that would advance this involvement.

This theme was reflected in the activism of black journalist and anti-lynching crusader Ida B. Wells-Barnett, who went much further than Booker T. Washington regarding the professional responsibility for community service on the part of the black scholar and activist. While Washington generally felt that black scholarship could be utilized to uplift the race, such uplifting could be carried out under the social and economic order of American society. Ida B. Wells-Barnett, however, believed that the *moral* responsibility of black intellectuals meant not only trying, socially and economically, to uplift the community but also challenging a racist social order. According to Wells-Barnett, black intellectuals even had moral license to consider those social situations that might require military action in order to redress wrongs committed against blacks in America. Despite this important difference, however, in both instances scholarship and the pursuit thereof was tied to working with one's community.

The proposal that black scholarship must be put at the service of solving the social, economic, and political problems of the community was certainly a strong theme in the life of W. E. B. Du Bois. His life reflects the belief that knowledge and intellect should be informed by praxis at the service of the black community. Indeed, Du Bois's often misunderstood idea of the "talented tenth" was based on this very proposition. Du Bois certainly did not advocate that a black elite be established as in a neo-colonial bourgeoisie that would serve as a bridge or channel between powerful colonial powers and "the natives." He acknowledged that because of racism in American society it would be unlikely that the masses of blacks would be educated and thereby equipped to challenge the racial, economic, and political order. What he proposed was that those few blacks fortunate enough to break through the racial barriers of advanced education had a professional—and moral—obligation to help other blacks break down the barriers of racial exclusion in ways that would change society for the better in terms of social and economic equality.

One of Du Bois's major intellectual works, and a critical study in defining the field of urban sociology today, is *The Philadelphia Negro*.[7] This work reflected a commitment to the pursuit of scholarship within a framework of praxis and community service. Decades later, Malcolm X argued eloquently that the purpose of education was to liberate the black mind from mental slavery, but such education had to be grounded in the political and economic struggles to strengthen black communities.

Between the turn of the twentieth century and the period of Malcolm X there were many educators, activists, and scholars who insisted that scholarship that would be useful to the advancement of blacks in the United States must be grounded in praxis and community service. This is reflected in the works of St. Clair Drake and Horace Cayton, Oliver Cox, the late John Henrik Clarke, as well as the artistic contributions of individuals like Lorraine Hansberry and Paul Robeson.

There are numerous works on black life in America in the 1960s that reflect the synthesis of scholarship, praxis, and community service. Although many examples could be cited, I have found two classics particularly useful for examining the role of community service within black studies. One is Kenneth Clark's *Dark Ghetto,* published in 1965.[8] This important study, actually a sort of case study of a specific antipoverty program, HARYOU, laid the intellectual and conceptual foundation for numerous studies and books focusing on race relations and the nation's political economy today. The methodology used by Clark to produce *Dark Ghetto* reflects how community service can advance intellectual understandings of social and economic situations. Clearly, Professor Clark would not have been able to produce this insightful work about social and racial relations within and without a black urban community without his community work and experiences in the HARYOU program.

Perhaps one of the most eloquent arguments for the pursuit of community-based research within black studies is presented by Harold Cruse in his work *The Crisis of the Negro Intellectual,* also published in the mid-sixties.[9] Professor Cruse pointed to what Alexis de Tocqueville, David Truman, Robert Dahl, and many other white scholars had also concluded, namely, that the "group" is a fundamental social and cultural reality in American society. Cruse simply reminded blacks that struggles for racial and economic justice should reflect this fundamental fact of U.S. society. Black intellectuals, or the professional sector, could only be effective in the long run if they were grounded in the theories and activism necessary to advance the group or the community. Blacks who were alienated, or disconnected, from their own community were, in fact, "ahistorical" beings. Individuals, as such, have very little opportunity to do anything that will move the community forward economically and politically. The black community would not move forward, according to Professor Cruse, if they acted as a conglomeration of individuals rather than a cultural group, as have others who realized economic and political progress in the United States.

The importance of community service, and praxis, as a research tool within this field was echoed by black studies professor Abdul Alkalimat in his introduction to *Paradigms in Black Studies: Intellectual History, Cultural Meaning and Political Ideology*: "There is one profound consistency in all fundamental modes of Black social thought: a focus on change. The key issue is changing the conditions that cause Black people's historical suffering."[10] This implies that individuals educated under the umbrella of black studies must have opportunities to become involved in the challenges facing black communities, a key aspect of their education.

This fundamental role of black studies, which involves training for civic action on the part of intellectuals and students, was also captured by another black studies professor, Maulana Karenga, when he wrote in his classic work, *Introduction to Black Studies*,

> Black Studies advocates stressed the need for Black intellectuals who were conscious, capable and committed to Black liberation and a higher level of human life. They argued like Du Bois that the race would be elevated by its best minds, a "Talented Tenth" which did not sell itself for money and machines, but recognized and responded creatively to the fact of the indivisibility of Black freedom and their indispensable role in achieving it.[11]

Discussing the pedagogy of black studies, Karenga explains that a major and "early objective" of the advocates of black studies was "the cultivation, maintenance and continuous expansion of a mutually beneficial relationship between the campus and the community. . . . The intent here was to serve and elevate the life-conditions and the consciousness of the community and reinforce the student's relationship with the community through service and interaction."[12] Again, Alkalimat, in his previously cited work: "Afro-American Studies, as a field, is a partisan activity, an enterprise in which the objective is not merely to understand the world but also to help make it better." [13]

These statements are verified by many scholars examining the thoughts and writings of many black intellectuals involved with advancing education. Historians Darlene Clark Hine, Wilma King, and Linda Reed substantively illustrate this point in their collection of case studies in the struggles of black women, *We Specialize in the Wholly Impossible.* [14] This anthology shows that for many black women educators the idea that scholarship should be, and is, strongly associated with activism is a dominant one. Other examples of black women educators who based their intellectualism on community involvement are provided in the reference book by Gerda Lerner, *Black Women in White America: A Documentary History.* [15]

The importance of continuing to link black studies and a community-based research agenda was reiterated at the 1990 Annual Meeting of the National Congress of Black Faculty. The keynote speaker for the annual meeting, renowned sociologist James Blackwell, emphasized this theme in his discussion on the mentoring of black students in higher education, arguing that students needed to be trained and educated for activism. According to the minutes and resolutions of the November 2, 1990, meeting of the Council of Community Relations, this topic is important for two reasons: 1) the presence of black educators in American higher education is intricately and historically tied to black community activism; and 2) the synthesis of the community's political, social, and educational agendas with the research agendas of black scholars and teachers in academia can produce creative, significant, distinctive research projects beneficial to American society. This call does not mean that politics or political opinions take the place of scholarship. It simply means that theory is most effective, logical, and useful when it is informed by the real-life experiences of people. In fact, theory that is not informed by such experiences may not be useful in moving the black community forward socially, economically, and culturally.

Notes

1. Manning Marable, "Black Studies and the Black Intellectual Tradition," *Race and Reason*, vol. 4 (1997–1998), pp. 3–4.

2. Joy James, "The Future of Black Studies: Political Communities and the 'Talented Tenth,'" *Race and Reason*, vol. 4 (1997–1998), pp. 36–38.

3. M. E. Hawkesworth, *Theoretical Issues in Public Policy Analysis* (Albany: State University of New York Press, 1988).

4. Charles V. Hamilton, *The Black Experience in American Politics* (New York: Capricorn, 1973).

5. William M. Banks, *Black Intellectuals: Race and Responsibility in American Life* (New York: Norton, 1996).

6. Booker T. Washington, *Up From Slavery: An Autobiography* (New York: Doubleday, 1963).

7. W. E. B. Du Bois, *The Philadelphia Negro: A Social Study* (New York: Schocken, 1967 [1897]).

8. Kenneth Clark, *Dark Ghetto: Dilemmas of Social Power* (New York: Harper and Row, 1965).

9. Harold Cruse, *Crisis of the Negro Intellectual* (New York: William Morrow, 1967).

10. Abdul Alkalimat, *Paradigms in Black Studies: Intellectual History, Cultural Meaning, and Political Ideology* (Chicago: Twenty-first Century, 1990).

11. Maulana Karenga, *Introduction to Black Studies* (Los Angeles: Kawaida, 1982), p. 27.

12. Ibid.

13. Alkalimat, *Paradigms in Black Studies*.

14. Darlene Clark Hine, Wilma King, and Linda Reed, *We Specialize in the Wholly Impossible* (New York: Carlson, 1995).

15. Gerda Lerner, *Black Women in White America: A Documentary History* (New York: Pantheon, 1972).

13

A Debate on Activism in Black Studies

A Call to Protect Academic Integrity from Politics

Henry Louis Gates Jr.

The founding fathers of what we now think of as African American studies were acutely aware of the distinction between scholarship that is political and politicized scholarship. Writing in 1925, the illustrious black bibliophile Arthur Schomburg worried aloud about propaganda masquerading as scholarship: work that was "on the whole pathetically over-corrective, ridiculously over-laudatory; apologetics turned into biography," work marred at its core by "puerile controversy and petty braggadocio," work that "has glibly tried to prove half of the world's geniuses to have been Negroes and to trace the pedigree of 19th-century Americans from the Queen of Sheba."

The great black intellectual and activist W. E. B. Du Bois himself, writing in 1933, warned black scholars against "whitewashing or translating wish into fact." Closer to our own time, the sociologist Orlando Patterson memorably warned against the sort of black studies programs that utilize the "three P's approach—black history as the discovery of princes, pyramids and pageantry." Such an approach, he argued, "does violence to the facts . . . is ideologically bankrupt and is methodologically and theoretically deficient."

Would that these eloquent warnings had been heeded. Today, scholars in the field of African American studies struggle to agree on the most basic facts of our history. A vocal minority seeks the deepest truths about black America in cultist, outlandish claims about the racial ancestry of Cleopatra or the genetics of "souls." It's within this turbulent context that questions about the relation between scholarship and activism inevitably arise.

Intellectuals like Schomburg and Du Bois thought that all scholarship about "the Negro would be political," either implicitly or explicitly, given the fact that, as Schomburg put it, "The Negro has been a man without history because he has been considered a man without a worthy culture." That's why even Schomburg, a man who loved the library like life itself, argued for what he called an a priori "racial motive" in black scholarship, while Du Bois stressed that "the American Negro problem is and must be the center" of the scholarly concerns of the "college-bred Negro." Since few, if any, colleges and universities offered courses that included content about African Americans, they viewed the scholar's task—and his gift to the broader culture—as contributing to a political progress by establishing the worth of the black culture in the court of academic and public opinion.

In truth, the ideal of wholly disinterested scholarship—in any field of research—will probably remain an elusive one. But it's one thing to acknowledge the political valence of even the "purest" scholarship; it's another to demand of it immediate political utility. The ideal of knowledge for its own sake—what Robert Nisbet once called the "academic dogma"—may be unfashionable, and even unrealizable; but it should command our respect all the same. For it remains the basic rationale of the university. The scholar who analyzes the nineteenth-century slave narrative and its relation to the sentimental novel shouldn't feel guilty because her research isn't directly aiding the cause of distributive justice.

But scholars are citizens, too, and if it is wrongheaded to demand political payoff from basic research, it would be equally untenable to demand that research be quarantined from the real-world considerations that weigh so heavily upon us. Elsewhere, I've called for departments of African American studies to join with historically black colleges and universities in establishing sophomore- and junior-year summer internships for community development (through organizations like the NAACP and the Children's Defense Fund) to combat teenage pregnancy, so-called black-on-black homicide, and the transmission of HIV.

Yet those who would enlist the academy in the cause of activism must confront the awkward fact that the political views of academics can no more be regimented than their scholarly opinions. In the socialist tradition thoughtful work on the political economy of black America has been done by such scholars as Gerald Horne, Adolph Reed, and Manning Marable, who urge us to rethink the basic institutions of Western liberal democracy. In a conservative vein, such black scholars as Thomas Sowell and Walter Williams have argued that the problems of black America must be addressed primarily through voluntarist means. Obviously, both positions cannot be correct, but you can't gauge their validity by the relative compassion or commitment of their proponents. Policy disputes must be subjected to intellectual analysis, performed without a thumb on the scale. And it would be bitterly ironic if a field that was founded upon a protest against exclusion should itself become fearful of pluralism, either intellectual or political.

A typically vanguardist form of scholarly vanity is, of course, to suppose that we have a unique purchase on political wisdom, beyond the reach of ordinary citizens. Yet, in the case of African American studies, the yearning for political potency is altogether understandable. Even as the academic field has become institutionalized, black America continues to suffer massive inequities that are the legacy of historical racism. To complicate the picture further, black America has itself become enormously fissured with a widening abyss between a growing middle class and an increasingly isolated underclass. Unfortunately, many of our conventional traditional modes of analysis simply fail to engage the vexing nature of these class differentials. "People don't care that you know," a street slogan has it, "until they know that you care." But genuine progress will depend not just on caring more, but knowing more.

Public policy issues can indeed be a central concern of African American studies, as they are at Harvard, the University of Michigan, UCLA, Columbia, and elsewhere. They raise conundrums as challenging as any you'll find in the academy. Thirty years ago no one predicted the current class divide that insistently raises questions to which there are still no satisfactory answers. How do we put our people to work? How do we expand the black working and middle classes? How do structural and behavioral causes of poverty interact, and how can they be defeated?

These are among the pressing issues that public policy scholars must address if they are to generate the new analyses and policy recommendations we desperately need. But the crisis of black America can't be willed away by commitment alone. On the level of policy, of practical politics, it demands empirical and analytical rigor: in short, the string of the academic dogma.

As W. E. B. Du Bois, himself a committed activist who never abandoned the life of the mind, once wrote, "Let us not beat wings in impotent frenzy" but "rather conquer the world by thought and brain and plan."

of black Americans, born after the civil rights and black power movements, that is increasingly assaulted by the forces of unemployment, imprisonment, and social alienation.

Black studies has begun to integrate the critical perspectives of class, gender, and sexuality into its major projects. However, too many black studies programs have a tendency to focus largely on the arts and humanities and much less on political economy, public policy, and urban ethnography. This literary and cultural studies orientation should be balanced by a greater emphasis on social science.

But perhaps the greatest challenge for African American studies is not only theoretical but political: how to reduce or eliminate the destructive consequences of institutional racism and inequality in a liberal democratic state.

This is no longer just an American question. Brazil, South Africa, and other nations are also exploring the complex relationships between racial identities, inequality, and power. We need a black scholarship that recognizes that the way we think about "race" is changing because of the rapidly growing communities. "Races" are not fixed categories. Thus, an oppressed racial minority in one historical period, like the nineteenth-century Irish and Jews in the United States, could be incorporated into the white mainstream. What may be occurring here (as well as in South Africa) is a redefinition of both race and class as a segment of the minority population moves into the corporate and political establishment at the same time that most are pushed even further down the economic ladder.

Black studies is challenged to raise hard new questions about the meaning of race in American life. To do so it must construct a new analytic language and theoretical approaches toward understanding this society. We should create new black "think tanks," bringing scholars together with representatives of civil rights, labor, women's and poor people's organizations to develop public policy initiatives.

That is why many black scholars have joined feminists and labor and community activists to develop the Black Radical Congress, a grassroots political organization created to revitalize the black freedom movement. We can only advance our field of scholarship by reaffirming the connection between the intellectual work and public advocacy of Du Bois, James, Paul Robeson, and many others who established and developed black studies.

PART THREE

Afrocentricity and Its Critics

14

Afrocentricity, Race, and Reason

Molefi Kete Asante

There exists a long line of activist and intellectual precursors to the theory of Afrocentricity. Indeed, it is in these early works, organizational and theoretical, that Afrocentricity is first suggested as a critical corrective to a displaced agency among Africans. A few of the more prominent names that are used in my own corpus of work are Alexander Crummell, Martin Delaney, Edward Wilmot Blyden, Marcus Garvey, Paul Robeson, Anna Julia Cooper, Ida B. Wells-Barnett, Larry Neal, Carter G. Woodson, Willie Abraham, Frantz Fanon, Malcolm X, and the later W. E. B. Du Bois. This is not intended to be a comprehensive listing of individuals who have influenced the Afrocentric idea, but, more precisely, the aim is to identify the kind of people who have leaned in the direction of African agency as a positive statement against the deagencizing character of hegemonic Eurocentricity. Carter G. Woodson's *The Miseducation of the Negro*, first published in 1933, was one of the earliest accounts of the dislocation of the African person. Harold Cruse's *The Crisis of the Negro Intellectual* continued the description of the attitudes, behaviors, and thoughts of African intellectuals, particularly as they related their scholarship and intellectual development to the theories of whites, often the theories of racist whites. Both Woodson and Cruse are considered godfathers of the new thinking about agency (Woodson 1990; Cruse 1964).

Among contemporaries, the works of Maulana Karenga, Chinwelzu, Ngugi wa Thiong'o, J. A. Sofala, Aboubacry Moussa Lam, Terry Kershaw, Wade Nobles, Walter Rodney, Abu Abarry, Marimba Ani, Jacob

Carruthers, Kariamu Welsh Asante, Clenora Hudson-Weems, Theophile Obenga, and Cheikh Anta Diop have been most helpful and inspiring in defining the nature of the Afrocentric school of thought (Obenga 1996; Diop 1974). I hasten to add that they have all been activists, not mere armchair theorists. The principal motive behind all their works seems to have been the use of knowledge for the cultural, social, political, and economic liberation of African people by first recentering African minds. They believed that without such liberation there could be no social or economic struggle that would make sense. None wrote simply for the sake of self-indulgence; none could afford to do so, because the dispossession was so great and the myths so pervasive. Passion is never a substitute for argument, just as argument is not a substitute for passion; in the intellectual arena we may disagree over finer points of interpretation, but the overall project of relocation and reorientation of African action and data has been the rational constant in all the works of these activist scholars. I claim heir to that tradition in all its contradictions.

Although a number of writers and community activists growing out of the black power movement of the 1960s had increasingly seen the need for a response to marginality, Afrocentricity did not emerge as a critical theory and a literary practice until the appearance of two small books by the Amulefi Publishing Company in Buffalo, New York. The press published Kariamu Welsh's *Textured Women, Cowrie Shells, Cowbells, and Beetlesticks* in 1978 and my book, *Afrocentricity*, in 1980 (Welsh 1978; Asante 1999 [1980, 1987]). These were the first self-conscious markings along the intellectual path of Afrocentricity, that is, where the authors, using their own activism and community organizing, consciously set out to explain a theory and a practice of liberation by reinvesting African agency as the fundamental core of our sanity. Welsh's book was a literary practice growing out of her choreographic method/technique, *umfundalai*, that had been projected in her dances at the Center for Positive Thought, which she directed. On the other hand, *Afrocentricity* was based on my work as leader of the Los Angeles Forum for Black Artists, the UCLA chapter of the Student Nonviolent Coordinating Committee, and as director of the UCLA Center for Afro-American Studies in the late 1960s and early 1970s, as well as my observation and textual analyses of what people like Welsh and Maulana Karenga and Haki Mahdubuti were doing with social transformation at the grassroots. Based on the lived experiences of African people, and my own peasant background in Georgia, and from what I saw in North America, the Caribbean, and Africa, the Afrocentric idea had to be concerned with nothing less than the relocation of subject-place in the African world. In my view, more adamant now than ever, this was the only approach to any other liberation for a people dislocated by circumstances of white racial supremacy.

A journal titled the *Afrocentric World Review* had been published in three issues in Chicago in the 1970s. To my knowledge, however, "Afrocentric" merely appeared as a part of the title; the articles were about the political and social issues confronting African people. No attempt was made to lay out a theoretical basis for analysis. Thus, the two books *Textured Women* and *Afrocentricity* formed the early documents of what was to become the most discussed African intellectual idea since the negritude movement. They posed two important questions: How do we see ourselves and how have others seen us? What can we do to regain our own accountability and to move beyond the intellectual plantation that constrains our economic, cultural, and intellectual development? These became the crucial questions that aggravated our social and political worlds. They led ultimately to the question that Haki Madhubuti (1978) posed for the black intellectual in *Enemies: The Clash of Races*: Is it in the best interest of African people? This was a critical question in a white supremacist society where Africans were marginalized. Madhubuti, much like Harold Cruse in previous years, wanted to know whether or not a particular project led to a recentering of the interests of African people.

As a cultural configuration, the Afrocentric idea was distinguished by five characteristics:

(1) An intense interest in psychological location as determined by symbols, motifs, rituals, and signs.
(2) A commitment to finding the subject-place of Africans in any social, political, economic, or religious phenomenon with implications for questions of sex, gender, and class.
(3) A defense of African cultural elements as historically valid in the context of art, music, and literature.
(4) A celebration of "centeredness" and agency and a commitment to lexical refinement that eliminates pejoratives about Africans or other people.
(5) A powerful imperative from historical sources to revise the collective text of African people.

Essentially, these have remained the principal features of the Afrocentric critical theory since its inception, although a number of brilliant thinkers have added dimensions to the original conceptualization. By this,

I mean the works of Patricia Hill Collins, Linda James Myers, Terry Kershaw, Wade Nobles, and Ama Mazama, among others. What all these scholars have seen is the revolutionary caliber of this idea as it relates to a reordering of perspectives around questions of African action, political, economic, cultural, or social. There is a serious difference between commentary on the activities of Europeans, past and present, and the revolutionary thrust of gaining empowerment through the reorientation of African interests.

Perhaps because of the rise of this idea at a time when Eurocentric scholars seemed to have lost their way in a dense forest of deconstructionist and postmodernist concepts challenging the prevailing orthodoxies of the Eurocentric paradigm, we have found a deluge of challenges to the Afrocentric idea as a reaction to postmodernity. But it should be clear that the Afrocentrists, too, have recognized the inherent problems in structuralism and Marxism, with their emphasis on received interpretations of phenomena as different as the welfare state and e. e. cummings's poetry. Yet the issues of objectivity and subject-object duality, central pieces of the Eurocentric project in interpretation, have been shown to represent hierarchies rooted in the European construction of the political world. In fact, in *The Afrocentric Idea* (1999 [1987]), I wrote that "objectivity is a sort of collective subjectivity of Europeans." This was quite in line with Marimba Ani's observation in her elegant work, *Yurugu: An Africa-Centered Critique of European Thought and Behavior* (1994), that the reification of object is about control.

The aim of the objectivity argument, it seems, is always to protect the status quo, because the status quo is never called upon to prove its objectivity—only the challengers to the status quo are asked to explain their objectivity. And in a society where white supremacy has been a major component of culture, the African will always be in the position of challenging the white racial privilege status quo, unless, of course, he or she is co-opted into defending the status quo, which happens with enough regularity in this country.

In an extensive discussion of the subject-object speaker-audience relationship, I explained how the subversion of that configuration was necessary in order to establish a playing field based on equality. But to claim that those who take the speaker or the subject position vis-à-vis others counted as audiences and objects on the same footing is to engage in intellectual subterfuge without precedence. On the other hand, it is possible, as the Afrocentrists claim, to create community when one speaks of subject-subject, speaker-speaker, audience-audience relationships. This allows pluralism without hierarchy.

As applied to race and racism, this formulation is equally clear in its emphasis on subject-subject relationships. Of course, the subject-subject relationship is almost impossible in a racist system or in the benign acceptance of a racist construction of human relationships as may be found in the American society and is frequently represented in the literature of several scholars who have African ancestry but who are clearly uncomfortable with this fact. White supremacy cannot be accommodated in a normal society, and, therefore, when a writer or scholar or politician refuses to recognize or ignores the African's agency, he or she allows for the default position—white supremacy—to operate without challenge and thus participates in a destructive mode of human personality. If African people are not given subject place, then we remain objects without agency, intellectual beggars without a place to stand. There is nothing essentially different in this enslavement from the previous historical enslavement except our inability to recognize the bondage. Thus, you have a white-subject and black-object relationship expressed in sociology, anthropology, philosophy, political science, literature, and history rather than a subject-subject reality. It is this marginality that is rejected in the writings of Afrocentrists of the Temple Circle, a group of Afrocentric scholars who represent centered critiques of culture, race, class, language, and gender and who maintain an ongoing discourse with each other in symposia, colloquia, participating annually in the Cheikh Anta Diop Conference and the invited Afrocentric theory conference. Afrocentricity is almost definitionally a narrative of liberation, a discourse about centering, a freedom of thought and expression rooted in a necessarily perspectivist vision. I have claimed that this vision may represent an "essentialist" thrust, which I am perfectly comfortable with (though I do not speak for the circle)—to be essentialist is not to be an immutablilist.

The ancient African Egyptian term *seba*, first found in an inscription on the tomb of Antef I from 2052 B.C.E., had as its core meaning, in the *Medu Neter*, the "reasoning style of the people" (Obenga 1996). The reasoning style of Eurocentric writers often serves the bureaucratic functions of "locking" Africans in a conceptual cocoon that seems, at first glance, harmless enough; nevertheless, the reasoning supports the prevailing positions. How can an African liberate himself or herself from the racist structures? Afrocentrists take the position that this is possible and, indeed, essential, but can only happen if we search for answers in the time-space categories that are antihegemonic. These are categories that place Africa at the center of analysis of African issues and African people as agents in our own contexts. Otherwise, how can we ever raise practical questions of improving our situation in the world? The Jews of the Old Testament asked, How can you sing a new song in a strange land? The Afrocentrists ask, How can the African create a liberative philosophy from the icons of mental enslavement?

There are certainly political implications here, because the issue of African politics throughout the world becomes one of securing a place on which to stand, unimpeded by the interventions of a decadent Europe that has lost its own moral way. This is not to say that all Europe is bad and all Africa is good. To even think or pose the issue in that manner is to miss the point I am making. Yet I know, from experience, that this will be misunderstood. So let me run to say that, for Africa, Europe is dangerous; it is a five hundred years' dangerousness, and I am not talking physical or economic danger, though that history is severe enough, but psychological and cultural danger, the danger that kills the soul of a people. One knows, I surmise, that a people's soul is dead when it can no longer breathe its own air and when the air of another culture seems to smell sweeter. Following Frantz Fanon, the Afrocentrists argue that it is the assimiladoes, the educated elite, whose identities and affiliations are killed first. Fortunately, their death does not mean that the people are doomed; it only means that they can no longer be trusted to speak what the people know, because they are dead to the culture, to the human project (Karenga 1978).

Afrocentricity stands as both a corrective and a critique. Whenever African people, who collectively suffer the experience of dislocation, are relocated in a centered place, that is, with agency and accountability, we have a corrective. By recentering the African person as an agent, we deny the hegemony of European domination in thought and behavior. Then Afrocentricity becomes a critique. On one hand, we seek to correct the sense of place of the African and, on the other hand, we make a critique of the process and extent of the dislocation caused by the cultural, economic, and political domination of Europe. It is possible to make an exploration of this critical dimension by observing the way European writers have defined Africa and Africans in history, political science, and sociology. To allow the definition of Africans as marginal and as fringe people in the historical processes of the world is to abandon all hope of reversing the degradation of the oppressed.

Thus, the aims of Afrocentricity as regards the race idea are not hegemonic. I have no interest in one race dominating another; I am an ardent believer in the possibility of diverse populations living on the same earth without giving up their fundamental traditions except where those traditions invade other peoples' space. This is precisely why the Afrocentric idea is essential to human harmony. The Afrocentric idea represents a possibility of intellectual maturity, a way of viewing reality that opens new and more exciting doors to human understanding. I do not object to viewing it as a form of historical consciousness, but, more than that, it is an attitude, a location, an orientation. To be centered is to stand some place and to come from some place; the Afrocentrist seeks for the African person the contentment of subject, active, agent place.

This is neither a vain nor a vainglorious quest; it is the correct path to self-determination, self-definition, and agency. Consequently, Afrocentricity is the realization of the dreams of intellectuals and activists as different as Harold Cruse and Malcolm X, both of whom called for a new theoretical construction based on a "black perspective" to help liberate us from the jaws of a white supremacist mental shark.

The greatest victory of the Afrocentric school of thought has been the freedom to explore all dimensions of the African's presence in the world. Critics will claim that this has always been possible, but they will be mistaken. Prior to the Afrocentric revolution in thought, ideas that suggested the possibility of African agency in some historical, economic, or social context were unthought and perhaps unthinkable in the arena of Eurocentric studies. Indeed, it was impossible not because it was untrue but because Europe was seen as the only actor. One could not easily study the relationship between Swahili and Chinese sailors in a maritime history class anywhere in a Western university. Nor could a person decide to link the study of Zulu and ancient Egyptian as a possible diffusion of the linguistic influences of southern Africa in an American linguistics department. Again, this prohibition did not exist because of the lack of linkage but because of three primary reasons. In the first place, white scholars have generally refused to allow the study of any knowledge that they do not control. Second, many white scholars tend to be limited in their interest to subjects that are valuable to the European project of self-glorification and triumphalism. Finally, to view Africa as a subject in history or as the starting place for an examination of anything is anathema to those who have always ignored the role of Africa. Thus, the designations "East and West" and "Occident and Orient" are nothing more than conceptual markers in the European mind about the absence of Africa. Of course, Afrocentrists reject this construction and all other intellectual outlines that ignore the place of Africa or the role of Africans in the development of human history (Karenga 1993).

Clearly, the European slave trade is implicated in this long dismissive of Africa. We cannot change the history, but we can try to understand why Europeans and those Africans who follow them intellectually have often dismissed the contributions and activities of African people on the continent and in the Americas. They are responding to Hegel's notion that "Africa is no part of history."

In the final analysis, the issue is one of location, psychological, historical, economic, social, and moral. Where is the person located? This is the question asked by the Afrocentrists in the critique of authors, activists, politicians, and intellectuals. To know where a person is located will allow a more accurate analysis of a situation. Afrocentrists tend to appreciate agency as a key determinant in the analysis of a story, article, phenomenon, or text. Agency must not be confused with African culture or Africanity, that is, the modality of African lifestyles. Afrocentricity is not Africanity. One is devoted to a self-conscious agency and subject position in interpretation and the other is the way people live. There are many people who have Africanity but are not Afrocentric. Occasionally, those who critique Afrocentricity discover that they have barked up the wrong tree only when the Afrocentrists respond.

It should be clear that I have not exhausted the idea of Afrocentricity, nor have I attempted to identify all the Afrocentrists in this brief chapter. A number of good articles and books exist on the subject as well as scores of dissertations by promising scholars. It has been my purpose to offer a reasonable essay on the nature of the Afrocentric project as carried out within the Temple Circle. The challenge we have put to the intellectual community makes it possible for us to declare triumphantly that today you will rarely hear a professor say that "Europe is not in Africa" or that "Columbus discovered America" or that "Africans have never contributed to civilization." I cannot imagine Africology, the Afrocentric study of African phenomena transgenerationally and transcontinentally, advancing without the use of a centered theory. One can certainly study "black" people without an Afrocentric theory, but the answers one gets will be qualitatively different from those of the person who studies africologically. I am inspired by the challenges that are reflected in the research of so many new and dynamic scholars.

References

Ani, Marimba. 1994. *Yurugu: An Africa-Centered Critique of European Thought and Behavior.* Trenton, N.J.: Africa World.
Asante, Molefi Kete. 1999 [1980, 1987]. *Afrocentricity.* Trenton, N.J.: Africa World.
———— 1999 [1987]. *The Afrocentric Idea.* Philadelphia: Temple University Press.
Cruse, Harold. 1967. *The Crisis of the Negro Intellectual.* New York: William Morrow.
Diop, Cheikh Anta. 1974. *The African Origin of Civilization.* New York: Lawrence Hill.
Karenga, Maulana. 1978. *Essays on Struggle: Positions and Analysis.* San Diego: Kawaida.
———— 1993. *Introduction to Black Studies.* 2d ed. Los Angeles: University of Sankore Press.
Madhubuti, Haki. *Enemies: The Clash of Races.* Chicago: Third World.
Obenga, Theophile. 1996. *African Philosophy in the Context of World History.* Princeton: Sungai.
Welsh, Kariamu. 1978. *Textured Women, Cowrie Shells, Cowbells, and Beetlesticks.* Buffalo: Amulefi.
Woodson, Carter. 1990. *The Miseducation of the Negro.* Trenton, N.J.: Africa World.

15

Afrocentrics, Afro-elitists, and Afro-eccentrics: The Polarization of Black Studies Since the Student Struggles of the Sixties

Melba Joyce Boyd

Ancestors

Why are our ancestors
always kings and princes
and never the common people?
Was the Old Country a democracy
where every man was a king?
Or did the slave-catchers
steal only the aristocrats
and leave the fieldhands
laborers
street cleaners
garbage collectors
dish washers
cooks
and maids
behind?
My own ancestor
(research reveals)
was a swineherd
who tended the pigs
in the Royal Pigstye
and slept in the mud
among the hogs.
Yet I'm as proud of him
as of any king or prince
dreamed up in fantasies
of bygone glory.
                    —Dudley Randall

On April 4, 1968, Dr. Martin Luther King was assassinated in Memphis, Tennessee. On April 5, 1968, in Kalamazoo, Michigan, the black students at Western Michigan University occupied the Student Center Building and demanded a black studies curriculum and a scholarship fund in the face of a heavily armed National Guard. This occurrence was characteristic of sixties radicalism on college campuses and, for the most part, was responsible for the establishment of black studies on predominantly white campuses. That was over twenty-five years ago, a generation past. My history in black studies begins on that eventful day at Western Michigan University, where I was a freshwoman. In retrospect, the movement to penetrate higher education has rendered an alternative intellectualism grounded in activism.

But, to some extent, black studies has degenerated into schisms and antagonisms that confound the field today. Moreover, if it were not for social pressures clamoring for a multicultural curriculum that reflects the diversity of the American population, black studies and related "minority" studies would have faded into obscurity; however, history refuses to relent, and irony now informs university administrations that a "black" presence is essential to its social and intellectual credibility.

As a poet and a scholar who makes a living teaching at a university and writing about literature and literacy, I never expected to be accepted by most of my university colleagues. This was a given when I began my studies, since Afro-American literature was not considered significant in the annals of "great" literature. I was indifferent to this exclusion because I understood that the dream I was pursuing was beyond the limitations of cultural conventions.

It was necessary during those years of study to develop one's own theoretical approach to literature and language. Because there were few theoretical and methodological restrictions on this nascent field of study, black studies provided the intellectual freedom that was constrained in the traditional disciplines. At the same time, the absence of philosophical constraint was problematic for persons incapable of registering an ideological perspective without a "school of thought." Additionally, because of institutional racism and ideological rigidity, the academy continued to discount the validity of the field. Consequently, the cultural nationalist response was "political" in racial terms. Much of that scholarship is polemical, highly subjective, and lacking in disciplined acuity.

Other black scholars, attempting to distance themselves from the nationalists (and activists) and to promote their careers, responded whole-

heartedly to academic conformity. They approached Afro-American literature and language with the severity of an iron brace or a chastity belt—
dismantling the elements of composition without regard to creative indi-
viduality or thematic intentions. They appropriated critical dogma to
decompose the political consciousness in the literature and the black experience. These experts on black thought approached the experience my-
opically, disregarded the value of the tangible, and pursued a discursive
vocabulary foreign to the literature and experience of the people. This is
currently regarded as genius.

Because the academy remains intellectually and institutionally racist
and, in most instances, only rhetorically committed to the field of black
studies, these survival strategies continue to dominate much of our intellectual decisions. Consciously, or unconsciously, a need to secure ourselves in hostile territory results in consulting the tyranny of theories for
justification.

The cultural nationalists recognize that our dubious presence is relative
to the black community and garner support by espousing a theory that
promotes "blackness" as the center of their universe and the antithesis of
"whiteness." It is complementary, and in these unnerving times, Afrocentrism provides a belief system of certainty and an ego boost in response to
the repression and socioeconomic decline affecting black people. Currently, reactionary nationalism has entrenched all sectors of ethnic communities in America, whereby strategic retreat has resulted in paranoid,
insular thinking and internalized hatred—even hysteria—as political policy. Anti-Semitism is on the rise and is pivotal to the propaganda of the
right (including the black right).

At the same time, the elitist scholars who lead the academic power
game via the Ivy League have exploited the limitations and ideology of the
profession as they act out trickster theory and practice to secure posh positions and lucrative speaking fees. They also pose as the gatekeepers of
Afro-American culture and, to a large extent, determine who gets published and financed by the white establishment. But, as the select few exert
their privilege, the distance between these scholars and the black community is so vast in interest and experience that the "revolutionary" intentions of the student strikes in 1968 appear only as historical aberrations
in their rhetorical inflations.

Meanwhile, there are those scholars who have eked out a less grandiose
path in academe, producing research grounded in the aesthetics of our
blues culture, in full view of a need to present our expressions and experi-

ences in their respective and expansive planes of intellectual and universal intersections. These cultural workers are not concerned with impressing the exponents of Eurocentric thought by example or by insisting on a black hegemony that finds legitimacy in an ancient slave-holding society. In contrast, activist scholars are rooted in the wisdom and power of a people who invented songs and spirits capable of transcending time and space to inspire revolutions throughout centuries and continents. For sure, American slaves did not aspire to return to an Egypt in America or in Africa.

Unfortunately, the student struggles of the sixties and persistent discrimination in higher education encouraged reactionary politics and propelled the most vocal into prominence. Consequently, black studies was isolated from the core curriculum, and racism in the public sector further estranged the discipline by denying its value in public school education or its relevancy to other areas of intellectual inquiry and social life. However, with the recent crisis in our cities of explosive juvenile delinquency, scholars of black studies are consulted to determine why and how such grave circumstances exist and, more, to seek solutions.

Afrocentrism rose to prominence in the nineties because it provides a conventional explanation to chaos: a lack of identity and a need for black male role models. According to the Afrocentrics, the adoption of a consciousness centered in all things African creates "true" identity, develops self-esteem, and instills values from a worldview that founded the first civilization on the planet. Clearly, academe needs to balance its curriculum with a more encompassing world history. But in the Afrocentric haste to discard all things European or American they have also discarded that which is uniquely Afro-American.

Afro-American cultural thought has altered Old World thought in Europe and Africa. It embraces the egalitarian values of West African agrarian-based societies, the democratic consensus systems and structures reflected in traditional Native American communities, and the radicalism of the labor movement. What the Afrocentrists fail to realize, in their quest to claim civilization, is that our struggle, fundamentally and above all else, is for freedom for the common people. We do not desire to be the "new" aristocracy. Monarchies were not democracies. We aspire to a new society that does not worship royalty, racial hierarchies, gold, corporate power, or any other manifestation that demeans the human spirit.

To transcend the conventions of power and dogmatism while pursuing freedom and democracy is a difficult and arduous task. It entails an interplay of class, race, and gender issues in past and present struggles. Undoubtedly, the dream of freedom is ingrained in the memory of slavery, and it is a struggle as ancient as the Euphrates River.

Furthermore, Afro-Americans are not simply Americans of African descent. We are a multicultural people whose expressions and experiences have evolved from Africa, Asia, Europe, and, most specifically, the Americas. This fusion has created an eclectic culture, a jazz ideology. It is not a linear extension of Africa or simply the sum of its past parts. Through its dissidence, invention, and reinvention, new imaginings thrive. To ignore the diversity that resides within us is to deny the very essence that signatures our humanity.

In a momentary digression I might add that any discussion about "melanin and intelligence" or "sun and ice people" should be conducted by albinos and include the cultural perspective of the Inuit people. Clearly, anyone who would purport such a thesis failed freshman biology and has not read any of the recent studies in DNA, which blast modern racial theories back to the nineteenth-century period where they belong. More important, these extreme developments in black studies should be considered in tandem with the fundamentalist momentum that is sweeping the country in the face of economic and social crisis. It is obvious that even common sense is failing inquiry when one submits to the severity of such thoughts, which, like an occult science, simplify complexity and advocate superstition and fear. To enlist skin color to justify bigotry is not novel but rather demonstrates the way internalized oppression can create intense resentment that overrules intellectual and moral integrity.

Actually, I never expected the discipline to arrive at this point of ideological warfare. This kind of bickering plays into the hands of the ruling class and promotes the divisions that perpetuate "business as usual." And, to that end, it seems that Afrocentrism is a response that mirrors the fear black people feel in the face of that reality. That fear is real, as death and dying have become both random and commonplace in neighborhoods and in public schools. The community is under fire and desperately grasping for an elixir that eases the pain and suffering while providing the illusion of empowerment. Afrocentrism provides emotional and quick-fix solutions in this era of terror.

Similarly, black studies is a field that mirrors the deficiencies of the society and the academy. Too few scholars and institutions are dedicated to the practical application of theory, which necessitates research in realities off-campus with ample resources to investigate solutions for complex, life-threatening problems.

At the same time, intricate abstractions may engage the "holy trinity" of race, gender, and class, but they rarely extend an analysis beyond the "smart talk" into our contemporary circumstances. Furthermore, the language might as well be Greek. Even though the literature with which the Afro-elitists interface their theories is drawn from the imagery and sounds of the more oppressed reaches of our historical experience, their theoretical paradigms and ideological exchanges exclude the community, sinking in a quagmire of inferior school systems and inadequate teaching facilities and methods. However, this intellectualism is beneficial for tenure and promotion in the ivory tower.

With all due respect to my colleagues, and despite the difficulties of survival in the academy, we should regard our positions in the academy as positions struggled for and won in an ongoing revolution. We are in positions that can effect change on and off campus, if we initiate it. Our task is far easier than surviving the ocean voyage in the bowels of a slave ship, or picking cotton in the Alabama heat from sun up to sun down, or dodging bullets on the front lines of turf wars between rival gangs. We should embrace the challenge and the excitement of the future as a place where our historical claim will give testament to the power of the human spirit and the infinite reaches of the human mind. Theories for the oppressed require creative strategies grounded in empirical evidence. Neither prestigious nor glamorous, the effort is its own reward.

At this juncture in life I reflect on April 4, 1968, as the day I dedicated time and talent to struggle with the academy and to alter its intellectual and moral consciousness. But, even more so, to keep a freedom dream alive.

16

Reclaiming Culture: The Dialectics of Identity

Leith Mullings

In the last decade African Americans have once again become increasingly committed to reclaiming their culture and history. This has taken a variety of forms and is evident in phenomena as diverse as the iconization of Malcolm X, the struggle around the African burial ground in New York City, renewed interest in African hairstyles, jewelry, and clothing, mass participation in the movement for a free South Africa, and the rise of Afrocentric philosophy.

Among African Americans the term *Afrocentricity* may be used rather broadly to refer to a range of loosely integrated beliefs, practices, values, orientations, and behaviors. For some it merely signals a sense of continuity with Africa and loyalty to a community of African descent. For others Afrocentricity may be manifested in modes of dress, ritual practices, or other cultural activities. For still others *Afrocentricity* refers to recent attempts to systematize these orientations into a philosophical system of beliefs and practices. I would like to address one essential element in these various approaches—the notion of culture.

The resurgent turn toward culture is in part a reaction to the failures of liberal integration, in part a consequence of the state-sponsored destruction of the left, and in part a challenge to apologists for inequality who attribute the cause of increasing poverty to the culture of African Americans. But it also represents the continuation of a long tradition of activist social scientists such as W. E. B. DuBois, who marveled at the inherent duality of African American culture and the transformation of the African medicine owner, "a bard, physician, judge, and priest, within the narrow limits allowed by the slave system rose the Negro preacher and under him the first Afro-American institution, the Negro church" (DuBois 1961: 144). We walk in the footsteps of poets such as Countee Cullen, who pondered, "What is Africa to me?" and countless ordinary people whose everyday practices of speech, style, music, art, and ritual recall a homeland three centuries removed.

The point of departure for these diverse perspectives—the importance of the struggle for history and culture—is not at issue. "Culture is . . . the product of . . . history just as the flower is the product of a plant," as Amilcar Cabral (1973:42) poetically put it. A sense of culture and history situates the individual in time and space, plotting the places occupied by ancestors gone before and descendants yet to come. Culture provides a framework through which communities interpret their past, understand their present, and imagine their future.

Therefore, as Amilcar Cabral and Frantz Fanon have described, though from different vantage points, the dominant group's power to represent the history and culture of subaltern groups is an important tool in achieving and maintaining domination. Hegemonic cultural systems seek to impose preferences, to redefine standards of beauty, and to lay out appropriate categories of thought and action. But, perhaps most important, by interpreting the past and defining the limits of action, these ideological systems seek to depict the potential for the future, framing the boundaries for struggle. Thus the recent struggle around the African burial ground in New York City was based on the knowledge that those who control the interpretation of the past also have a major role in charting the future.

In the 1960s and 1970s attempts to confront the ideological underpinning of white supremacy within the academy were reinvigorated. Responding to the militant civil rights movement and antiwar struggles, African Americans and others fought for the establishment of black studies departments. Many ethnic, labor, and women's studies departments nurtured scholarship that produced the knowledge base for developing alternate approaches. This new body of scholarship laid the intellectual foundation for the contemporary challenge to the general curriculum, for contesting how knowledge is defined, created, and controlled, and for placing the experiences of workers, women, and people of color, rather than those of elites, at the center of the analysis. The challenge to the ideological hegemony of the dominant class—whether in the liberal form of a historian such as Arthur Schlesinger, the conservative form of an educator such as Diane Ravitch, or the many popular formulations denigrating African American history and culture from Myrdal to Moynihan—has been a critical aspect of our struggle.

But opposition to official interpretations of history and culture, particularly when linked to action, was generally met with derisive contempt or unrelenting hostility. Intolerance for rethinking history as experienced by people of color, coupled with institutional tolerance of racism, has shaped the conditions in which alternative frameworks have emerged.

Furthermore, alternative interpretations face the difficult task of disengaging from, even while critiquing, traditional categories and of rejecting the hegemonic framework that structures its own form of dissent. Indeed, one attraction of Afrocentricity is the appearance of initiating a conversation from the vantage point of another place, of creating a new space for discussion rather than accepting the categories set out by dominant culture.

Afrocentricity, then, is born of the unremitting Eurocentrism of the academy and other social institutions. Considering the large-scale invention of history from the perspective of elite Europeans, Schlesinger's charge that Afrocentricity is the "invention of tradition" (1992:86) is at best disingenuous and at worst blatantly dishonest.

I would argue, however, that though Afrocentricity represents an attempt to highlight the importance of culture, to reclaim history, and to correct the distortions of Eurocentrism, there are ways in which it is the child of Eurocentrism. Caught in its mirrorlike negation of Eurocentrism, Afrocentricity often inadvertently reflects the reductionism of traditional thinking about race and culture. Because it is, in effect, a project of negation, Afrocentricity sometimes loses its cultural compass, straying from the land of our collective memories, contemporary struggles, and hopes for the future.

There are different varieties of Afrocentricity, which I am not able to treat here as fully as they deserve, but I would maintain that the more fundamentalist versions are based on a dangerously limited notion of the nature of culture, one that is remarkably similar to Oscar Lewis's static definition of culture in his formulation of the "culture of poverty" or to the underclass theorists' understanding of culture as a set of unchanging behavioral traits. Consequently, though Afrocentric philosophers seek to reinterpret history, their concept of culture tends to be fundamentally ahistoric. Futher, despite disclaimers to the contrary, they often treat culture as independent of the social system, thereby precluding the development of the dynamic, revolutionary theory of culture necessary for achieving liberation.

Culture is not a fixed set of traits, values, or behaviors, nor is it transmitted unchanged from generation to generation, nor is it merely a set of principles. Cultures are dynamic, always developing, ever changing—as Amilcar Cabral (1973) put it, the manifestation on the ideological plane of the historical reality of people. Despite the importance of deconstructing Eurocentric representations of African history, the foundation of African American culture is not to be found in the tombs of the pharaohs.

Cultures are historically created and therefore not hermetically sealed. The contemporary world in which information moves around the globe at nearly the speed of light brings new possibilities for domination, but also fresh potential for liberation. Diasporic cultures, for example, are continually formed and reformed through constant interaction and exchange: African Americans wear kente cloth, and South Africans sing "We Shall Overcome." Just as African Americans made an important contribution to the liberation of South Africa, it is to be hoped that the new South Africa will assist African Americans in their struggle for equality.

The essence of African American culture, and therefore its resilience, lies in our people's continuing struggle for survival, continuity, and liberation. Through this process African Americans created their culture, transferring, transposing, rediscovering, and reworking elements from Africa and the Americas within the varied structural and cultural constraints of different locales. Under conditions of slavery, segregation, discrimination, and deindustrialization, our achievements have been enormous, and we need to reclaim them for ourselves and our children. Nevertheless, some aspects of culture, while perhaps initially responses to inequality, now facilitate the reproduction of domination and are an obstacle to progress. For example, many contemporary cultural expressions reflect an unfortunate valorization of the dominant society's hierarchical gender roles and accept stigmatization of African American women's lives and struggles. But the more progressive and enduring aspects of African American culture—which stand as a contribution to all humankind—are best comprehended through the lens of our people's historical struggle.

Perhaps most problematic is the tendency of Afrocentricity to reify the ideological, to treat culture as independent of the social system and as reducible to geography, climate, or environment—in this sense not entirely dissimilar to the manner in which white supremacists reduce culture to a mythical concept of race. It is important to make the comparison between cultures in which the dominant theme is individual achievement and accumulation and those characterized by collectivism and egalitarianism. But with respect to the cultures cited by Afrocentrists, this is largely a distinction between the culture of capitalism, which had its earliest and most significant development in Europe, and the culture of the village community, which, until relatively recently, existed in much of Africa. African Americans have maintained some communally oriented cultural elements precisely because of their shared historical experience of struggle. But one has only to consider an Idi Amin, a Clarence Thomas, or a Thomas Sowell to understand that we cannot reduce contrasting cultural frameworks to geography, climate, race, or ethnic identification.

While ideas can act as a material force and the struggle for power involves the struggle for interpretation, white supremacy, as we all know, is not merely a cultural or literacy project. As we are reminded every day—by the hundreds of thousands of homeless, unemployed African Americans, by nearly six in ten African American children growing up in poverty, by every African American imprisoned and executed by the state, by the young men shot down in the flower of their youth, by all our assassinated heroes—at the foundation of racism is a system of savagely unequal economic and political relations. We must, along with others, address the social relations that give rise to the power to interpret. Despite the importance of the "black is beautiful" movement of the 1960s, which sought to turn dominant symbols on their heads and to seize the interpretive initiative, cultural transformation could not be maintained without successfully challenging the institutions that produce these representations.

Culture is an important element of struggle. But it is by nature malleable and symbolic and can be deployed in different ways. For Amilcar Cabral a revolutionary notion of culture was a tool in achieving liberation. For Mangosuthu Buthelezi a reactionary notion of culture became a rationale for alliance with the white supremacists of South Africa. We cannot afford to cede the right to represent our culture and history. But those of us who are privileged to have the leisure to contemplate must place our skills at the service of social movements that critically reflect the lives, experiences, and history of our people. We must help to construct concepts that our people can use here and now to better their lives and ensure their continuity.

References

Cabral, Amilcar. 1973. *Return to the Source.* New York: Africa Information Service.
Du Bois, W. E. B. 1961. *The Souls of Black Folk.* Greenwich, Conn.: Fawcett.
Fanon, Frantz. 1963. *The Wretched of the Earth.* New York: Grove.
Schlesinger, Arthur M. Jr. *The Disuniting of America.* New York: Norton.

17

Afrocentrism, Cultural Nationalism, and the Problem with Essentialist Definitions of Race, Gender, and Sexuality

Barbara Ransby

Since the publication of Molefi Asante's book *Afrocentricity* in 1980, the ill-defined and often misdefined concept of Afrocentrism has become almost ubiquitous in the public discourse on race and African American identity. There is discussion of Afrocentric epistemology and pedagogy within academia, Afrocentric curriculum in elementary and secondary schools, Afrocentric fashion, Afrocentric spirituality, Afrocentric cuisine—and the list goes on. But, in the final analysis, what exactly is Afrocentricity?

The term has been applied so broadly and loosely as to encompass, on the one hand, the very specific mandate for authentic "African" living and thinking, as prescribed by Molefi Asante, to the crude cash crop strategy employed by national white-owned retail outlets, which now offer the purchase of Afrocentric products, ranging from fake kente umbrellas to imitation mud cloth shower curtains and underwear. In essence, the very definition of Afrocentrism is contested terrain. Even though one is hard pressed to define what Afrocentrism *is*, we should be quite clear on what it is not. It is not, for example, a specific theoretical paradigm for liberation or a prepackaged formula for a meaningful black life, as some Afrocentric writers would have us believe. Rather it is an approach, which encompasses many competing theories and visions. In the most general sense, Afrocentrism simply reflects a perspective that places people of African descent—our concerns, culture, and interests—at the center of a particular inquiry, struggle, strategy, or analysis. It certainly does not have to mean that African people are viewed in some sort of artificial historical vacuum divorced from other sets of historical experiences. In fact, in order to fully understand the experience of Africans, and, even more so, African Americans in the modern era, we must look at the dialectic of political and class struggle between people of African descent and others, and, of course, between Africans and African Americans themselves. Otherwise we are left with a very distorted and one-dimensional view of our history and, most important, one that negates the ways in which the dynamics of power and exploitation have helped to shape the African and African American experiences. Neither African Americans nor Africans have created their own history insulated from the larger evolution of world history. To employ an Afrocentric approach in studying the culture and history of African and African American people is to view people of African descent as subjects and conscious actors in the creation of history and culture rather than the passive recipients of someone else's actions. The conclusions at which various scholar-activists have arrived through this enterprise have been diverse and, at times, antithetical.

It is important to note that Afrocentrism has a long, rich, and disparate history, encompassing many distinct intellectual and political traditions. Most often cited is a group of scholars and writers who historian Darlene Clark Hine refers to as "Authentists and Originists." They include Dr. Yosef ben Jochannan, the Senegalese scholar, Cheikh Anta Diop, John Henrik Clarke, and Ivan Van Sertima. Many of the younger cultural and systematic nationalists (as Asante prefers to call himself)—including Asante, Na'im Akbar, Haki Madhubuti, and Jawanza Kunjufu—trace their intellectual roots to this group. Equally prominent among the pioneer Afrocentrists, but representing a very different perspective, is the great black intellectual and prolific writer W. E. B. Du Bois. Du Bois offered a powerful example of Afrocentric scholarship in his 1935 class analysis of the post–Civil War era entitled *Black Reconstruction*. In it Du Bois borrows heavily from the European-based Marxist tradition to formulate a very cogent and provocative Afrocentric analysis of a particular phase in U.S. history. Thus Du Bois represents a very different strain of the Afrocentric tradition than Molefi Asante and many of his Authentist predecessors, but an equally legitimate one.

Most often when we hear the term *Afrocentrism*, we think of a short list of names: a group of nationalist thinkers who see culture, narrowly defined, as the principal arena for black political struggle. One reason that the struggle over definition is so important is that the term *Afrocentrism*, applied generally, has a special resonance among African American people, and no single intellectual or political tradition has proprietary rights over it. The concept represents an oppositional stance vis-à-vis the oppressive dominance of Eurocentrism in our lives. More specifically, the systematic promotion of Eurocentrism, and the erroneous notion of white supremacy, as ideological justifications for colonialism, slavery, and modern-day racism are the material bases for African Americans' positive response to the general ideas of Afrocentrism as corrective. Since Afrocentric scholars like Asante, and the even more controversial Leonard Jeffries, have received such extensive media attention, it would be easy and unfortunate for the general public, and African Americans in particular, to assume that these individuals represent the intellectual vanguard of the struggle against racism in the academy and the only representatives of that oppositional Afrocentric tradition. They do not.

Even while it is important, on the one hand, to recognize that cultural and systematic nationalists do not hold a monopoly over the term *Afrocentrism*, it is still necessary to discuss and critique their ideas as some of the more popular versions of Afrocentricity that are being disseminated within the African American community today. First of all, Asante should be credited with the important positive contribution he has made in forcing the issue of racism in academia to the forefront of the national debate about education and the politics of scholarship. At the same time, however, this contribution should not lead us to overlook some of the major weaknesses of Asanteism. One such weakness is his subtle endorsement of essentialist arguments about race and, by extension, gender. Although, to his credit, he rejects some of the crudest theories of biological determinism, his Afrocentric paradigm, nevertheless, serves to reinforce rather than refute the idea that race is some type of ahistorical phenomenon rooted in a shared genetic heritage. Readers are told there is something intrinsically African within us, rooted in a great and distant African past, that we must get in touch with in order to know our true selves and become truly Afrocentric, something that Molefi himself has achieved but, according to him, the great black leader W. E. B. Du Bois never did. This view suggests a definition of race and ethnicity that transcends social, historical, and even cultural realities. It belies the reality of Africa itself: an immense, diverse, and complex continent. When Asante argues, "We have one African cultural system. . . . We respond to the same rhythms of the universe," is he referring to the rhythms of the Yoruba, Ibo, Hausa, Kikuyu, Ndebele, or Shona peoples? All of these African peoples have different linguistic, religious, and political traditions that are equally legitimate parts of Africa's past and present. Moreover, most Africans do not think of themselves as simply Africans. Such a broad and homogenizing categorization is a luxury more easily imposed from afar. It is also easier to view Africans as one monolithic mass, irrespective of class and politics, when one is concerned primarily with the "rhythms of the universe . . . [and] cosmological sensibilities" rather than the concrete realities of people's day-to-day lives. On the serious terrain of political struggle, for example, it is very important to understand the difference between a Nelson Mandela of South Africa and a Jonas Savimbi of Angola. One is a longtime freedom fighter for the liberation of African people, the other is responsible for the massacre of thousands of African people in order to enhance his own power. Both men are African, but they respond to very different rhythms and sensibilities. It is this fuzzy notion of race as some type of innate biological bond that leads us down the slippery slope of judging allies and enemies on the basis of the color of their skin and the texture of their hair rather than on the content of their actions.

These erroneous notions of race are predicated upon equally erroneous notions of culture itself. Culture is not something fixed, static, and ahistorical. Culture is dynamic and constantly in flux; it is a process. What were authentic and natural practices within Yoruba, Ibo, Nubian, or any other cultures centuries ago would not be, and are not, "authentic" forms of those cultures (or the surviving products of those cultures) today. This would be true with or without European intervention. Cultures change and evolve, if they do nothing else. Otherwise they atrophy and die. Afrocentrists who look back and romanticize a fixed moment in the history of ancient Egypt as the source of our salvation from our current dilemmas fail to fully appreciate this fact. This failure makes certain strains of the Afrocentric tradition essentially backward looking and conservative rather than progressive and liberating.

In addition to the problematic formulation of race and ethnicity in Afrocentric writings of cultural and systematic nationalists, their analyses of gender and sexuality are equally disturbing. While most cultural nationalists of the 1990s acknowledge the value of "complementary," if not fully equal, relationships between men and women, there is very little attention given to the special oppression of women and certainly no advocacy of women's empowerment. Asante's Afrocentric ideal of family and sexuality, steeped in virulent homophobia, is very telling about how his notions of gender factor into a larger paradigm. First of all, Asante bluntly argues that "homosexuality cannot be condoned or accepted as good for the national development of a strong people." He overlooks the reality that many black lesbian and gay activists—from Audre Lorde and Barbara Smith to Essex Hemphill and Marlon Riggs—are, or have been, at the forefront of the struggle against sexism as it impacts the lives of black women and rigidly prescribed gender roles as they constrict the lives of black men. Unfortunately, the idea of men and women stepping outside of their traditional roles in relationship to one another is somehow seen as threatening to the African American community and family. However, if we are ever to realize a society where men and women are equally respected, valued, and empowered (unlike most human societies we have known, African or otherwise), we have to step outside of "traditional" roles. We have to move beyond imposed, and often artificial, notions of family, parenting, *and* sexuality and find the courage to create new definitions of both manhood and womanhood, and how the two relate to one another.

Two Afrocentric scholars, both of whom I would place within the cultural nationalist tradition, who address more directly the issue of gender within the African American community are Haki Madhubuti and Na'im Akbar. In his book, *Visions for Black Men*, Akbar offers a scenario for black liberation and empowerment that is inescapably male-centered, despite his disclaimer that his vision "though phrased in masculine terms is not a masculine vision." In essence, it is not personhood but manhood that is defined by Akbar as strength, courage, independence, economic power, and intellectual prowess—and, perhaps most telling, the ability to act as protector of presumably weaker black women. There is nothing intrinsically liberating or revolutionary about this image of manhood. In fact, in many ways it simply emulates the definitions of white manhood and masculinity celebrated by the dominant society. In large part Akbar's vision of a resurgent black manhood hinges on a power struggle between men of European and African descent, which leaves African American women relegated to the sidelines as cheerleaders until the battle is won. This vision, of course, belies the real role African American women have played as fighters, leaders, strategists, and cultural workers in our own right throughout history.

Even more explicitly, in his book, *Black Men: Obsolete, Single, Dan-*

gerous? The Afrikan American Family in Transition, Haki Madhubuti argues that "male dominance is on the decline in the Black communi-ty . . . which places the community in jeopardy." This uncritical endorse-ment of male dominance grows out of an even greater adherence to es-sentialist notions about race and gender than are espoused by either Asante or Akbar. According to Madhubuti, "Biological and sexual roles within the human species are not interchangeable. . . . The sexual defi-ciencies and needs of men and women are, indeed, different and correlate along biological and cultural lines." Thus, men and women are locked into distinct, immutable, naturally defined roles that we must adhere to. He goes on to argue that racism and white supremacy have inhibited black men's ability to live up to their roles "as warriors, providers, hus-bands and fathers." The assertion of a patriarchal ideal as model for black manhood is seen as the key to black empowerment. Thus, the struggle for black liberation is defined narrowly and quite traditionally as a struggle between men for power and the protection of *their* (helpless and coveted) women.

Madhubuti's view of black women is not only a paternalist insult to black women's strengths and capabilities, it also, at times, borders on out-right misogyny. For example, he begins one of the key chapters of his book, *Black Men*, with a scenario in which a black policewoman callous-ly shoots and kills a black male she is about to arrest in the presence of her white male colleagues. Madhubuti concludes:

> What had been described as "justifiable homicide" was in the real world "one less nigger," murdered not by a white or Black male cop, but by a Black woman cop. Few saw the significance of this act. . . . What may be the ultimate and most profound reality of our current situation may well be that some of the mothers that bring life may indeed be the moth-ers, daughters of mothers that aid Black men and white men in the re-moval of Black men from this earth.

Thus, African American women are portrayed as the annihilators of black men or collaborators, along with white men, in the destruction of black men. It is a painfully distorted and vulgarized version of black women's role in the survival of black people, men and women. Why would Madhubuti choose such an unrepresentative example of violence in the black community, and the larger society, in which generally violence between men or male violence toward women is the rule?

At a time when African American women are under heavy assault by popular cultural forms that denigrate us as "bitches and whores," and by cuts in welfare that threaten our very survival and that of our children, such scapegoating of black women for the suffering of black men is not only offensive and misleading but dangerous and reactionary as well. It fits squarely into the conservative victim-blaming scenario propagated by most contemporary culture-of-poverty theorists. This view is also consistent with the notion that it is black men, and not black women, who are the principal targets of oppression and racism today. Black women, like the black cop in Madhubuti's scenario, are allegedly being rewarded, celebrated, and promoted, at the presumed expense of black men. Of course, nothing could be further from the truth. The reality is that in comparison to white women, white men, *and* African American men, black women are still the most exploited and impoverished group. Unemployment rates are highest among black women (if we look at those who have been forced out of the workforce entirely). And, in terms of wages, black women still earn $1.10 less per hour than the average black male. Most depressing is the situation of tens of thousands of black single mothers who receive public aid, live in dangerous and deteriorating public housing prisons, and are the principal caretakers of all black children. These women, mischaracterized as immoral, irresponsible, and lazy, have become the prototypical "undeserving poor"—a stereotype fueled by racism and sexism—which serves as justification for the erosion of a whole array of public services and minimum access to resources many fought so hard for in decades past. Any supposedly liberating vision that blames, rather than seeks to empower, these women is collaboration of the worst order.

As the great poet and activist Audre Lorde reminded us, "We cannot dismantle the master's house using the master's tools." The dismantling of the master's house is the challenge many Afrocentric scholar-activists have taken up. However, while some works have scrutinized existing paradigms on one level, they have absorbed whole the existing definitions of race, gender, and sexuality on another level. In describing the limitations and pitfalls of racial identity politics, Manning Marable warns that

> both the oppressors and those who are oppressed [are] imprisoned by the closed dialectic of race. . . . Yet, in reality, race should be understood, not as an entity, within the histories of all human societies, or grounded to some inescapable or permanent biological or genetic differences between human beings.

I would add that the same dubious and static notions readily apply to our popular conceptions of gender and sexuality as well. We internalize a language and a set of tacit and often erroneous assumptions about such fundamental concepts as nature, culture, and biology. Layered on top of these flawed assumptions are our dreams, aspirations, and battle plans for liberation and empowerment. We therefore build important structures on shaky intellectual foundations. We must, as intellectuals and political activists, take up the task of interrogating presumed truths on every level and, finally, place our confidence in the optimistic notion that politics are determined in our heads and not in our genes and by our present and future actions, not the greatness of our ancestors, as great as many of them were. We have new battles to fight.

18

Afrocentricity and the American Dream

Lee D. Baker

Over the past fifteen years many African Americans have come to embrace rather broadly defined ideas of Afrocentricity. These popular notions of Afrocentricity loosely integrate and routinely police certain beliefs, practices, rituals, or other cultural activities that signify a loyalty to (and the unity of) a community of African descent. Although the performance and intellectual elite have made Afrocentricity "almost ubiquitous in the public discourse on race and African American identity," the activities are indeed performed across class lines, ranging from sorority theme parties on college campuses to study groups in the housing projects of Louisville (Ransby 1994:31; Mullings 1994:28; Jones 1996:147).

From the pulpit to the vendor, in the classroom and in the cell block, on peoples' heads and on the Internet, African Americans are consuming and reproducing notions of Afrocentricity to cultivate a collective identity and challenge the ascendancy of Whiteness in U.S. society. President Bill Clinton has even chimed in by stating, "White Americans and black Americans often see the same world in drastically different ways" (Clinton 1995). With some twelve million people celebrating Kwanza annually, the merit of Afrocentricity lies in the Afrocentric values embraced by a large swath of U.S. society.

Anthropological Silence: The Power and Politics of Space and Place

A shift from industry to service production during the last two and one-half decades has left U.S. central cities in a wake of desperate poverty that has been compounded by an erosion of gains made during the war on poverty and the civil rights movement, fueling despair and displacement and fostering what Cornell West calls nihilism. These decades, however, also witnessed a horizon of unparalleled opportunities for African Americans and the largest growth of the black middle class in this nation's history. And it has been within this context that Afrocentricity has gained currency and generated considerable debate in and outside the academy. Anthropologists, however, have been strangely absent from both the forceful assertions and rigorous critique of Afrocentric discursive and cultural practices. Whether or not scholars weigh into the academic debate, one cannot dismiss the cultural significance of Afrocentricity during the final decades of the twentieth century.

My rationale for this anthropological silence is actually related to the many reasons why ideas about Afrocentricity have emerged in this context as a particularly salient U.S. discourse. Anthropologist Eric Wolf has long asserted that anthropology should actually be the "study of human freedom and liberation, of human possibility and necessity" (Wolf 1987:xii). Similarly, Stanley Diamond has emphasized that anthropologists need to explore how "human beings not only reflect cultural events but synthesize experience and have the capacity to react in creative and unexpected ways" (Diamond 1987:341). Even though participants in the Afrocentric project, explicitly, make, recreate, and affirm ideas of culture and history as a form of resistance and liberation, anthropologists have not been compelled to engage Afrocentricity, even though it clearly lies within the outlines painted by these venerable anthropologists.

The issues generated from the high-stakes debate land squarely within the purview of anthropological inquiry, since the contested terrain is, after all, culture—a culture "through which communities interpret their past, understand their present, and imagine their future" (Mullings 1994:28), but also a culture that "stresses its contextual, heuristic, and comparative dimensions" (Appadurai 1997:13).

I find it curious that very few anthropologists have attempted to explore, ethnographically, why notions of Afrocentricity resonate with the experience of so many African Americans or why certain African Americans gravitate to the principles of Afrocentricity to help negotiate contemporary society. While her findings will be published soon, Yvonne V. Jones is one of the only anthropologists to actually conduct ethnographic fieldwork that explores how people use ideas promoted by advocates of Afrocentricity to foster empowering notions of identity and culture.

The academic "space" where this silence becomes deafening is the discourse on place and space: the politics of identity, nationalism, and so-called imagined communities. From my perspective the Afrocentric project lies flat in the teeth of the "politics of place making and in the creation of naturalized links between places and peoples" (Gupta and Ferguson 1992:12). It is particularly glaring when Asante explains, "*Dislocation, location*, and *relocation* are the principal calling cards of the Afrocentric theoretical position" and organizes *Kemet, Afrocentricity, and Knowledge* using the spatial metaphors of "Interiors," "Anteriors," and "Exteriors." (Asante 1992:20; 1990).

In *Place and the Politics of Identity* (1993) Michael Keith and Steven Pile evoke Fredric Jameson to explain how their type of cognitive mapping is "meant *to allow* people to become aware of their own position in the world, and *to give* people the resources to resist and make their own history" (1993:3; emphasis added). The choice of verbs is interesting, but it does not explain why these postcolonial geographers and late capitalist ethnographers have not addressed Afrocentricity. It is particularly unusual in light of the examples they use to explore how "new spaces of resistance are being opened up, where our 'place' (in all its meanings) is considered fundamentally important to our perspective, our location in the world, and our right and ability to challenge dominant discourses of power" (Keith and Pile 1993:6).[1] No matter how one construes the Afrocentric project, it falls within this rubric. I do not want to suggest that no scholars associated with cultural studies have addressed Afrocentricity because Paul Gilroy and Anthony Appiah have been quite vocal (Appiah 1995:50; Gilroy 1993).

There are perhaps numerous reasons why the popularity of Afrocentricity has not been considered within anthropology. I speculate that one reason is that the Afrocentric project belies a bipolar political spectrum often demarcated by radical/reactionary, core/periphery, conservative/progressive, etc. Gupta and Ferguson observe:

> It must be noted that such popular politics of place can as easily be conservative as progressive. Often enough, as in the contemporary United States, the association of place with memory . . . and nostalgia plays directly into the hands of reactionary popular movements. (1992:13)

They point to easy examples of reactionary place making like the "frontier," or the "small town." Much more complicated, however, are examples of an imagined "Africa," or "Nation" of Islam employed as symbolic anchors to help empower African Americans in the U.S. Like many populist movements, Afrocentricity blurs easy distinctions between conservative and radical because it fosters liberation *and* fuels essentialism, empowers people *and* polices boundaries.

Although Afrocentricity's counterhegemonic potential is easily identified when George F. Will, Arthur M. Schlesinger Jr., and Dinesh D'Souza each view it as tantamount to treason. Its glaring essentialism cannot be overlooked, however, when claims are made about supercharged melanin that "helps blacks 'speak and read faster,' as well as 'glide in the air like a Magic Johnson or hit top speeds like Florence Joyner'" (D'Souza 1995: 51). I find assessing everything in between much more difficult.

How does one assess the way Marion Barry appropriated an Afrocentric perspective, along with Christian salvation, to persuade the electorate to vote him into office? How does one assess the throngs of black men held rapt by the explicit Afrocentric themes woven into nearly every speech during the Million Man March? Or how does one square the popularity of Afrocentric ideas with the gross black-white disparity over the Simpson verdict? Assessments like these complicate the spectrum laid out by Gupta and Ferguson and perhaps give pause to scholars engaged in the debates about space, place, and identity. William Julius Wilson suggests that "the vitriolic attacks and acrimonious debate that characterized this controversy" around Afrocentric perspectives has actually "proved too intimidating to scholars, especially liberal scholars" (Wilson 1996:174). Scholars who study the U.S., especially identity formation, must tackle the complicated politics this discourse cultivates. They should neither dismiss it as exclusionary essentialism nor blindly promote its virtues. We simply need more scholars who are committed to highlighting the importance of our culture, reclaiming our history, and correcting Eurocentric distortions of our experience.

Yvonne V. Jones is one anthropologist who provides a useful approach for exploring the significance of Afrocentricity by analyzing the various ways people in Louisville, Kentucky integrate its ideas into their lives. She has documented how ideas about Afrocentricity are articulated within a wide range of local practices that may

> involve the construction of a distinctive religious ideology in which Afro-Baptist tenets may be juxtapositioned with Islamic or Afrocentric beliefs and traditions, as well as the deliberate formation of an African

personality evidenced by outward symbols of dress, name changes, and participation in various social gatherings and rituals. (Jones 1997:117)

If writers coupled Jones's rich ethnographic analysis to virulent attacks aligned with intellectuals like George Will, a more balanced picture of the texture, counterhegemonic potential, and, indeed, hybridity of the Afrocentric project would emerge. While there are numerous ways to approach a cultural critique along these lines, I would like to frame my approach for explaining why Afrocentricity has emerged as an important public discourse with something like a supposition: *The complex social and cultural processes of collective identity formation that compel the majority of affluent African Americans to challenge ideas of "The American Dream" and vote overwhelmingly against their class interests lead many of these same Americans to embrace notions of Afrocentricity.*

Jennifer L. Hochschild, in *Facing up to the American Dream,* employs a mountain of survey research and opinion polls to explain the paradox she identified: that affluent African Americans are "succeeding more and enjoying it less." By the 1990s, she explains,

> well-off blacks have come to doubt the reality of the [American] dream for African Americans. They have also become increasingly pessimistic about the future of the dream in general, and more embittered about American society than white Americans expect, given their class's improved standing. (Hochschild 1995:87)

In specific ways Hochschild's research confirms Michael C. Dawson's notion of a "black utility heuristic." In *Behind the Mule* (1994) Dawson draws from rational choice theory and research on black political behavior to argue that, unlike most Americans, "it is much more efficient for [African Americans] to use the status of the group, both relative and absolute, as a proxy for individual utility" (Dawson 1994:10).

Hochschild and Dawson each view their research in terms of explaining a paradox or solving a puzzle, but both lines of thought turn on the fact that African Americans culturally construct collective, political, and social identities in ways that oppose the rugged individualism implicit in notions of the American Dream and in ways that ensure political homogeneity even while the black population is becoming economically polarized. The survey research Hochschild and Dawson marshal to solve these "riddles" actually quantifies the extent to which African Americans view themselves collectively. Afrocentric activities and rituals describe and inscribe this identity with the ideas of Umoja and the oft-recited Ashanti proverb, *I am because we are, without we I am not: I am because we are; and since we are, therefore I am.*

Central to the various approaches to Afrocentricity are symbolic representations like those that validate lived experience and confirm African Americans' unique cultural patterns and rich cultural heritage. This knowledge about Afrocentricity and its subsequent rise in public discourse has accompanied African Americans' increased civic and political agency since the civil rights movement. The agency is evidenced in the way activists have successfully pushed for Afrocentric approaches within the public school curriculum, social service agencies, and higher education. These dynamics also help to explain why hip-hop musicians, wedding planers, Kwanza caterers, and festival organizers respond to "the market" when they weave Afrocentric symbols into their consumer goods.

Historically, African Americans have often embraced ideas that explain contemporary social conditions and their unique contributions (and relationship) to the greater American experience. George M. Fredrickson, in *Black Liberation,* outlines similar dynamics with the rise of theological ideas about Ethiopianism in Jacksonian America. David Walker, Martin Delany, Alexander Crummell, and Frederick Douglass each articulated a form of the "Ethiopian myth" that expounded on the unique and civilized virtues of Christian Africans throughout the diaspora, while condemning white Americans for absconding the pillars of democracy and violating Jesus's clear directives delivered in the sermon on the mount (Fredrickson 1995:60). As Fredrickson notes, this type of theology used "an intellectually and emotionally satisfying narrative structure for black hopes and aspirations."[2]

A variety of different political, social, and cultural agendas have been promoted within the black community, and, during certain periods, some gain more currency than others. The ones that gain currency, successfully, make sense of the prevailing conditions or are simply more satisfying. While Afrocentricity offers novel approaches for negotiating contemporary society, the reasons it has emerged as a salient discourse for many Americans are the same reasons the agendas set forth by Ethiopianism, Washingtonism, Garveyism, negritude, and the black power movement all gained currency: the proponents effectively used theory and practice in an effort to combat oppression—making the object the subject, fostering agency, and cultivating subjectivity. What is new about the nineties is that many members of the growing African American professional class have subverted what Louis Althusser calls the ideological state apparatus with Afrocentric themes.

People have successfully lobbied school boards, deacon boards, and community development boards in an effort to incorporate Afrocentric perspectives within these governing bodies' respective institutions. These efforts make people working for a more inclusive and pluralist society furious.[3] The furor is often compounded by whites who impatiently point to the recent progress in racial equality, diversity of institutions, and representational curriculums; however, equally impatient blacks counter by pointing to all the inequality that remains.

The public tug-of-war has left many white Americans more sanguine about efforts to make the U.S. more inclusive and many black Americans more skeptical about making democracy work for all Americans. This tension has been accentuated because, just as whites', blacks' standards for success, equality, and justice rise as they experience some (Hochschild 1995:104). African Americans, however, cannot reasonably expect a more inclusive democracy when Rush Limbaugh and his ditto-heads, Ward Connerly and his CCRI, and William H. Rehnquist and his Supreme Court majority envision a better America with eroding affirmative action programs, draconian welfare reform, punitive immigration policies, erasure of majority-minority congressional districts, and sharp reductions in college financial aid.

Collective Identity: A Delicate Balancing Act

As the so-called black middle class adapted to the changing economy, they adopted new definitions of success. Competing with white privilege became a delicate balancing act. More affluent African Americans are increasingly pursuing success on competitive terms opposed to relative terms—characterized by an older generation and the less affluent (Hochschild 1995:142). Competitive success, for example, is the type of success achieved by a regional manager seeking a post as a V.P., but relative success is achieved by an individual doing better than, say, one's parents. By changing the criteria of success, shattering the glass ceiling with the efforts of John Henry is no longer tenable. The invisible glass ceiling actually transforms into a well-defined balance sheet where personal, social, and cultural costs must be carefully weighed against individual benefits. The bottom line: assimilation is often viewed as the price of the

American Dream. Yet that price can be negotiated by a home well appointed with African art, rhetoric about "cooperative economics," and even a Kwanza cocktail party. Various Afrocentric ideas actually play an important role on both sides of that balanced sheet.

I am not suggesting *because* affluent African Americans are jaded by the persistence of racism in the face of campaign rhetoric and civics lessons exulting principles of equality, freedom, and justice for all that many embrace notions of Afrocentricity. Nor do I want to suggest that Afrocentricity is a substitute for the American Dream. Quite the opposite, the rise of Afrocentricity is as American as hamburgers.

In 1919 William I. Thomas and Florian Znaniecki, in their classic *Polish Peasant in Europe and America,* laid out three scenarios for Polish families who immigrated to America. The first included individuals who assimilated the values and attitudes of American individualism and consumerism. Although forced to abandon Catholicism, their family, and community because they could not engage in gift giving, reciprocity, and the practices that ensured group solidarity, they successfully melted in the pot. The second scenario included individuals who tried this approach and failed. Ostracized from community and family members, they turned to crime, delinquency, prostitution, and, in the author's terms, dysfunctional behavior. The third scenario included those who embraced and reinvented Old World values and cultural practices, adapting them to the New World circumstances. With increased value placed upon the family, community, and sense of their Polish heritage, they formed business collectives, engaged in bloc voting, and turned to the traditional spiritual practices of their motherland for succor, solace, and sanity.

Although I would explain these as cultural practices of any nested subaltern, the popularity of Afrocentricity can also be seen as quintessentially American in its strategy of empowerment and self-help. Fierce in their hostility to drugs and casual sex, people who articulate an Afrocentric discourse in the public sphere are in the forefront of black self-help movements. These facts obviously have not convinced George Will and Arthur Schlesinger Jr. that Afrocentricity is not, prima facie, inimical to the so-called virtues of U.S. democracy.[4]

Afrocentricity has gained a certain currency in the nineties because it helps people explain contemporary and historical conditions and counters the hegemony of Eurocentric images. Although recognizing Derrick Bell's assertion of the permanence of racism, or experiencing the nihilism that Cornell West describes, may make Afrocentricity attractive, popular, and satisfying, many African Americans use Afrocentricity as a vehicle to nurture a collective identity (Bell 1992:xiii; West 1994:12).

The conundrum both Hochschild and Dawson explore is the fact that middle-class blacks vote against their pocketbook and challenge the precepts of the American Dream once they achieve relative standards of economic success. Although Hochschild recognized research that suggests "since 1952, well-educated blacks have consistently expressed more group consciousness than have poorly-educated blacks," both Hochschild and Dawson assume that African Americans should behave, at least statistically, like other ethnic or language minorities and reproduce patterns of rugged individualism once they have "made it" (1995:122). One can almost feel Hochschild's despair as she came to the conclusion that African Americans are not like other Americans because they tenaciously hold onto a sense of collective responsibility.

> Many middle-class blacks feel an acute responsibility to their history, their poorer fellows, their race, and each other. That sense of responsibility may not be growing, but they sense that American society will not allow them to fulfill their responsibility despite new-found wealth and power [, which] clearly *is* growing. The new frustration leads to a bitterness against other Americans, and eventually against the American Dream. (Hochschild 1995:115)

The data she uses to support this conclusion is not drawn from the research of her friend, colleague, and mentor, William Julius Wilson, but the Chicago political scientist bent on demonstrating that race is not declining in significance—Michael C. Dawson. Quoting Dawson's *Behind the Mule*, she explains, "Up to two-thirds of blacks believe that 'what happens generally to black people in this country will have something to do with what happens in your life'" (1995:123). Dawson, who is shackled by his own rational choice theory, dismisses culture all together. He argues that African Americans employ a bounded procedural rationality that explains why many African Americans are personally invested in the fate of the larger population. He suggests that this sort of rationality

> is measured not by how well humans achieve rational ends by maximizing one's own utility but by how rational the process of decision making is. . . . According to this view of rationality, the episodic intensification of racial hostility would lead African Americans to continue basing their political choices and behaviors (at least partly) on a calcu-

lation of racial group interests, even if over a short period of time race has seemed to be less of a factor in determining one's life chances. (Dawson 1994:62)

In a similar fashion, both Dawson and Hochschild reach the same conclusion, African Americans tend to construct a sense of collective identity that shapes identity.

Afrocentricity can thus be viewed as a mechanism to confirm and affirm, inscribe and describe this collective identity. It nurtures the unity "thing" that is at once policed and desired. Virginia Dominguez offers a useful perspective: "How we conceptualize ourselves, represent ourselves, objectify ourselves, matters not just because it is an interesting example of the relationship between being, consciousness, knowledge, reference, and social action, but at least as much because it is a statement about power" (Dominguez 1989:190).

Afrocentricity has emerged as a significant discourse because it not only resonates but actually becomes part of these cultural processes. Negotiating power has been central to cultural formations within the African American community. As Leith Mullings eloquently notes, "The essence of African American culture, and therefor its resilience, lies in our people's persistent struggle for survival, continuity, and liberation" (1994:29). Ultimately, this is the goal of the Afrocentric project, to advance and facilitate these cultural processes.

Notes

Thanks to Molefi Asante, Betsy Bryan, Yvonne V. Jones, Maulana Karenga, William A. Little, and Manning Marable for their support and comments.

1. Merely suggesting, however, that these scholars are rearticulating older forms of intellectual paternalism does not help explain anthropologists' absence from the debate over Afrocentricity.

2. He continues to explaine that "it also planted the seeds of Pan-Negroism, or Pan-Africanism" (Fredrickson 1995:63). There are fundamental parallels with this movement in the nineteenth century and Afrocentricity today, including the notion that Africans are just as civilized as Europeans and able to erect equally grandiose civilizations.

3. Actually, if one draws parallels to the movement to desegregate public education, virtually the same patterns are articulated with Afrocentric curriculums. There was resistance to desegregate graduate and professional schools, but, proposed at the grade-school level, that is when the perceived threat was heightened to a fevered pitch.

4. Describing African Americans who celebrate their African heritage,

James Baldwin similarly noted, "In this need to establish himself in relation to his [African] past he is most American." Asante actually lists specific "guidelines" for an Afrocentric perspective that would be welcomed by any U.S. civics teacher. These are "to be *excellent, provocative, organized, educated,* and *dependable*" (1988:41).

References

Appadurai, Arjun. 1997. *Modernity at Large*. Minneapolis: University of Minnesota Press.

Appiah, Kwame A. 1995. "Beware of Race-Pride." *American Enterprise* (September/October), p. 50.

Asante, Molefi K. 1988. *The Afrocentric Idea*. Philadelphia: Temple University Press.

——— 1990. *Kemet, Afrocentricity, and Knowledge*. Trenton, N.J.: Africa World.

——— 1992. "African American Studies: The Future of the Discipline." *Black Scholar*, vol. 22, no. 3, pp. 20–29.

Bell, Derrick A. 1992. *Faces at the Bottom of the Well: The Permanence of Racism*. New York: Basic.

Clinton, William J. 1995. "Remarks by the President in Address to the Liz Sutherland Carpenter Distinguished Lectureship in the Humanities and Sciences, Erwin Center, the University of Texas at Austin, Texas (October 16, 1995)." Web page. Available at http://www.pub.whitehouse.gov/urires/I2R?urn:pdi://oma.eop.gov.us/ 1995/10/17/8.text.1.

Dawson, Michael C. 1994. *Behind the Mule: Race and Class in African-American Politics*. Princeton: Princeton University Press.

Diamond, Stanley. 1987 [1974]. *In Search of the Primitive: A Critique of Civilization*. New Brunswick, N.J.: Transaction.

Dominguez, Virginia R. 1989. *People as Subject, People as Object: Selfhood and Peoplehood in Contemporary Israel*. Madison: University of Wisconsin Press.

D'Souza, Dinesh. *The End of Racism*. New York: Free Press.

Fredrickson, George M. 1995. *Black Liberation: A Comparative History of Black Ideologies in the United States and South Africa*. New York: Oxford University Press.

Gilroy, Paul. 1993. *Black Atlantic: Modernity and Double Consciousness*. Cambridge: Harvard University Press.

Gupta, Akhil and James Ferguson. 1992. "Beyond "Culture": Space, Identity, and the Politics of Difference." *Cultural Anthropology*, vol. 7, no. 1, pp. 6–23.

Hochschild, Jennifer L. 1995. *Facing Up to the American Dream: Race, Class, and the Soul of the Nation*. Princeton: Princeton University Press.

Jones, Yvonne V. 1996. "African-American Cultural Nationalism." In Janis F. Hutchinson, ed., *Cultural Portrayals of African Americans: Creating an Ethnic/Racial Identity*, pp. 113–137. Westport, Conn.: Bergin and Garvey.

Keith, Michael and Steven Pile. 1993. *Place and the Politics of Identity*. New York: Routledge.

Mullings, Leith. 1994. "Culture and Afrocentrism." *Race and Reason*, vol. 1, no. 1, pp. 28–30.

Ransby, Barbara. 1994. "Afrocentrism, Cultural Nationalism, and the Problem with Essentialist Definitions of Race, Gender, and Sexuality." *Race and Reason*, vol. 1, no. 1, pp. 31–34.

Thomas, William I. and Florian Znaniecki. 1918–1920. *The Polish Peasant in Europe and America*. 5 vols. Boston: Badger.

West, Cornel. 1994. *Race Matters*. New York: Vintage.

Wilson, William J. 1996. *When Work Disappears: The World of the New Urban Poor*. New York: Knopf.

Wolf, Eric. 1987. "Foreword." In Stanley Diamond, *In Search of the Primitive: A Critique of Civilization*, pp. xi–xiii. New Brunswick, N.J.: Transaction.

19

Multinational, Multicultural America Versus White Supremacy

Amiri Baraka

American culture, first of all, is Hemispheric. When we say America, we are really saying, Pan-America. Most of the people of Pan-America are brown and speak a Latino Spanish. Moreover, the official "Western" culture, of which the rightist wags and academics speak, is Europe. But Europe is not the West. I have a poem that says, "Leave England / headed West / you arrive in Newark."

The Europe "cover" to Pan-American, or even North American, culture is merely the continuation of European colonialism and slavery. In fact, from its origins, the term *Western world* meant Europe in relationship to Asia and Africa, pre-Columbus's "discovery" of el Mundo Nuevo, the New World. And that discovery, we know from experience, certainly combines Dis and Cover. The Rappers let us know what Dis/ing someone means: to disrespect them. The biggest "Dis" is that they can even make you Dis/appear.

Cover is a record company term meaning that, for instance, when Big Mama Thornton put out a record (or Big Joe Turner, or Duke Ellington, for that matter), the white supremacist–oriented record industry immediately put out a "cover," or a version, of the song by a white performer, in the first two cases, Elvis Presley and Pat Boone. Just as Vanilla Ice or Young Black Teenagers (! a white group) are beginning to do Rap.

It is very important that corporate/government powers who control American society always keep music lovers segregated. Like Confucius said, "If the people hear the wrong music, the Empire will fall." And for the broad multinational masses of the American nation to take up the sentiments of the content of Afro-American music, in this case, is to disrupt the racist national oppression that is the fundamental superstructural philosophy of the American social system, reflecting its imperialist economic base.

When we say that American education must be as multinational and multicultural as the reality of American society, we are just saying that what is taught in the schools should be the whole culture of the American people.

Americans are still remarkably unconscious about the totality, the whole dimension, of their own culture. But that is because the powers that be are determined to maintain white supremacy as the philosophical justification for the exploitation and oppression of most of the world's peoples. Certainly, in relationship to all the variety of people inside the U.S., the Eurocentric construct of so-called official Western Culture America is a racist fraud, a fraud that has held the entire culture of the world—certainly of the Pan-American world—as hostage.

The assertion that the actually very brief period of European hegemony in the world means that "European" culture (a term that could be argued with, even in the nineteenth century, since neither Germany nor Italy existed as states prior to this) is eternal and the supreme measure and description of civilization, is, of course, Nazi *diktat,* no reality to it—except as a reflection of the rise of European hegemony in the world, along with the rise of capitalism, the slave trade, colonialism, and modern imperialism.

The Greek Attic, like any culture, cannot be isolated from the whole context of its emergence and development. It is the result of what came before it, just as any other culture. But even more repressive is that since the majority of the peoples in the world are not European, then this kind of thinking is just neo-Goebbelsism, very fitting for our time, which has all the earmarks of another Weimar Republic: the last democratic government and period in German history before Hitler and fascism took power.

The very move to the right in the U.S., for instance, particularly with the fall of the revisionist USSR, has seen the rise of extreme nationalism not only in the U.S. but around the world. The attempt to maintain a mainly Eurocentric and blatantly racist curriculum in public schools in the U.S. is an attempt to maintain old slavery while calling for new slavery!

The stunning development of the retrograde trend in the U.S. of backward Negro academics, artists, politicians, as part of the whole reactionary period emerging in the 1980s, shows how so-called integration into the racist academic and social curricula of these colleges has helped shape a whole new generation of Yuppie Toms who have profited by Black struggle but who have been taught to disconnect themselves from the Black majority, ideologically as well as socially.

One reason for the alienation of Black and Latino students from public school education is the curriculum that they begin to understand by the third grade has very little to do with their lives or history. The incorrectness of the teaching methodology contributes to this as well, since these distortions and lies must be taught by rote, committed to memory, rather than learned!

And even though the rubric of the Blooms and Schlesingers speaks of Western culture, and makes obeisance to the ancient Greeks and Romans as the touchstone of their modern cultural assessment, these same white supremacists dismiss both these modern peoples as "degenerate." (More Goebbels!)

In fact, in the modern world, *Western Culture* means mainly England, France, and Germany. Spain and Italy are always neglected, and the rest of the world plunges into silent oblivion.

When you speak to those who uphold the status quo of undemocratic education and the culture of inequity, they will tell you that multicultural curricula are impossible because it's "technically impossible" to include all people's cultures in the curricula, suggesting that only the distorted paper culture of national chauvinism is "normal" (a northern sickness).

It is simply that we want the real lives of the people of our world, the whole world. American culture is the creation, for instance, of all Americans. It is the combining of all the nationalities and cultures here that is the actual national character of American culture. And no one is belittling the accomplishment of European humanism. Actually, an authentically multinational and multicultural curriculum would revalidate the authentic masterpieces of all cultures, highlight their fundamental unity, and help diminish their conflicts.

The undeveloped material life of most Americans is justified by both their absence from U.S. school curricula and distortion of their lives in them. The racial chauvinism of the so-called Literary Canon justifies the military cannon that enforced colonialism throughout the third world yesterday or the invasion of Panama, Grenada, and the destruction of Iraq today. Academic or artistic chauvinism explains economic and social exploitation.

The very underdevelopment of the Northern Colossus itself, in real terms, with millions of Americans living under the poverty line, including the majority of the Afro-American nation's children, is tragic for Black people, but it is also an economic deprivation, a lack of development of the larger U.S. itself. The lack of education and livelihood of the Black masses subtracts from the whole of the U.S. livelihood and economic development. Even though the old slavemaster continuum that Bush and U.S. imperialism favor generally has already been proven economically outmoded. The Black and minority aspects of the U.S. market detract from total U.S. prosperity, since Black Americans constitute an important part of even the U.S. monopoly capitalist market, whose potential cannot be tapped because of the low level of productive forces (including marginal education and high unemployment rates).

In the case of the almost neocolonial domination of English (Anglo-ish) culture in the U.S., it's as if the Tories at least won the cultural revolution, when you have huge English departments (even though "George Washington won the war") and American studies is tiny where it exists and Black studies is always under fire and in danger of being removed.

And it is just this Eurocentric, white supremacist cover of the real American culture that multicultural education seeks to eliminate. The Leonard Jeffries CCNY issue was not so much about what Jeffries said. (The influence of the Jewish bourgeoisie in Hollywood has been well documented already by Jews, and the influence of organized crime, including the Mafia, has been equally publicly discussed. And no one of the slightest analytical capacity can doubt the caricature of Black lives in U.S. flicks. But then, to paraphrase a writer in *Cinéaste*, look at Hollywood's distortion of Jews and Italians as well.) Jeffries had been talking about Black cultural nationalism for years and nothing happened. But, after he became a leading member of the group that put together New York's so-called Curriculum of Inclusion, by attacking him, dirt could be thrown that would *cover* the proposed new curriculum with much *dis*.

Remember, a change of curriculum would lessen the domination and influence of many vested interests within the school education *industry* and even result in the expansion of certain curriculum and teaching jobs within the education system. The development of a really democratic educational curriculum and U.S. All-People culture would reflect a movement to create a more democratic U.S. and a more equitable relationship to the rest of the world.

PART FOUR

Race and Ethnicity in American Life

20

The Problematics of Ethnic Studies

Manning Marable

Theoretical Questions on Race and Ethnicity

Any discussion about race and ethnicity as social forces within the contemporary American experience must begin from the vantage point of history. In the development of U.S. society there were three great social divisions that, from the very beginning, fostered hierarchies of power and privilege and sets of dependent relations. The first was the division between Europeans versus non-Europeans (particularly enslaved Africans and American Indians), the second was the division between capital and labor—the conflict between those privileged elites who controlled the land and productive resources versus those who lived by their labor power, and the third, the gender stratification between men and women—the superiority granted to males by the patriarchal weight of law, property ownership, political enfranchisement, and physical violence and control. Each of these great divisions contributed to the historical construction of a national identity of America that was largely defined by "whiteness": a racial category of privilege that rationalized and justified the domination and exploitation of "Others" who are non-European, poor, and/or female.

These three very different yet overlapping hierarchies of domination formed the foundations for what Michael Omi and Howard Winant have termed a "racial formation."[1] What emerged was a system of meanings, discourses, and hierarchies of power that was inherently unstable and constantly changing, as new immigrants entered the racial formation and created new interactions between groups. Nevertheless, as cultural anthropologist Faye V. Harrison reminds us, the instability of racialized institutions was "constrained by poles of difference that have remained relatively constant: white supremacy and the black subordination that demarcates the social bottom. Although whiteness and blackness have not had fixed meanings and boundaries, the opposition between them has provided the stabilizing backbone for the United States' racialized social body."[2]

In actual practice, what this has meant historically is that "whiteness" evolved as a racial category of privilege, which was accessible only to immigrants of European origin, with some exceptions. Whiteness was the entry point or passage through which Euro-Americans competed against each other for power and status. The white community was deeply stratified by class and gender inequalities, but all individuals who claimed the status of whiteness stood above the abyss of inferiority and subordination through which people of African descent and Native Americans had been made to plummet. Phenotype and physical features were used in this system as a rough symbolic indicator to determine the individual's access to resources, property, and power. But as powerful as the code of color was, class divisions still prefigured the range of possibilities for the dynamics of racialized ethnicity and gender. In short, every racial formation exists within a political economy and a class structure that does not dictate but does prefiguratively set the possible alternatives that can develop in all social relations. As modes of production develop and change, as the organization of labor and the economy move forward, the social configuration and social manifestations of race also mutate into new forms. Thus race and racism in 1895, when Booker T. Washington articulated his separate-but-equal compromise address in Atlanta, Georgia, was not the identical racial formation that was the context for Louis Farrakhan's Million Man March in Washington, D.C., one century later.

White racial consciousness became a central ideological theme in the political construction of what would become the United States. But, from the beginning, whiteness itself was vacuous and sterile as a cultural entity. As historian David Roediger explains: "It is not merely that whiteness is oppressive and false; it is that whiteness is *nothing but* oppressive and false. . . . It is the empty and terrifying attempt to build an identity based on what one isn't and on whom one can hold back."[3] By the late seventeenth and early eighteenth centuries, immigrants from mostly western European countries who came to the American continent had assimilated and constructed for themselves a new racial identity called white. After the establishment of the United States, whiteness was literally codified as part of the Constitution, particularly in article 1, section two, which defined enslaved African Americans for the purposes of taxation and representation as the equivalent of three-fifths of a human being.

Race is therefore a dynamic social construct that has its roots in the transatlantic slave trade, the establishment of plantation economies based on enslaved labor, and the ideological justification for the vast extermination of millions of indigenous Americans. White Americans have thought of themselves in terms of racial categories for several centuries. By contrast, ethnicity is a relatively recent concept. There are no references to ethnicity per se in the social science literature of the nineteenth and early twentieth centuries. It surfaced as an important social science category of analysis in the writings of sociologists during the Great Depression, as a means to describe the diverse immigrant populations largely from southern and eastern Europe. Later ethnicity was utilized to describe the development of modern European nationalism and conflicts developing between various communities defined by their cultural and social traditions. Manning Nash defines ethnicity as a set of "cultural markers" that give a collective identity to a group, such as kinship, rituals, communality, or language.[4] Anthropologist Leith Mullings also provides us with a good working definition of ethnicity: "group identification, by self or others, on the basis of phenotype, language, religion, or national origin."[5]

Because of the hegemony of race and racism in the social development of the United States, European immigrants who arrived here quickly learned that the key to their advancement and power was to claim the status of being white. In other words, during the nineteenth century race was much more powerful than what we might today call ethnicity in determining the life chances of most new immigrants. The Irish, who for centuries had been an oppressed nation, experienced severe discrimination upon their arrival. But within several generations in the United States they had become "white." They had assimilated the values of privilege and the discourses and behaviors of domination that permitted them to claim status within the social hierarchy. Conversely, immigrants from Latin America and Asia were frequently "racialized" by both legislative means and de facto segregation. For example, Chinese immigrants were subjected to legal restrictions as early as 1870. In 1875 the U.S. Congress essentially prohibited Chinese women from entering the country. The Chinese Exclusion Act of 1882 banned "idiots," "lunatics," and "Chinese laborers."

Legislation severely restricting Japanese immigration was passed by Congress in 1907 and in 1924. Asian Indians were limited from coming into the U.S. in 1917; Filipino immigration was curtailed in 1934. In 1942, after the outbreak of World War II, 110,000 Japanese American civilians were forcibly removed from their homes into detention camps. It was only with the passage of the McCarran-Walter Act that Asians born outside the country were allowed to become U.S. citizens.[6] An even more complicated racial coding process developed with Mexican Americans. After the U.S.-Mexican War of 1846–1848 the United States incorporated roughly one-half of Mexico's entire territory into its own legal boundaries. Slavery, which had previously been abolished by the Mexican government, was reestablished. Only Mexicans who were defined as Spanish or white could claim U.S. citizenship. Indians, peasants, and mestizos were treated as inferior groups.[7]

There are currently major academic disagreements over the meanings and materiality of both race and ethnicity. For example, should race be subsumed under ethnicity as a subcategory? Or is race an exceptional social category in its own right, because of its peculiar historical development, discourses, relations with culture, etc., which sets it apart from ethnicity? To what extent, if at all, should race be measured by biological, genetic, or cultural differences between groups? Can racialized ethnic minorities such as African Americans be "racists" themselves? And what of the complex relationships between racialized ethnicities—Asian Americans, American Indians, Latinos, and black Americans?

There have been many different theoretical approaches proposed to address these questions. At one end of the ideological spectrum are the racial-ethnic theorists, or the multiculturalists. One prominent example of their work is provided by Ronald Takaki. In several influential studies Takaki basically states that racialized minorities are fundamentally different from other ethnic groups because of their common history of oppression. African Americans came to this country involuntarily, in chains. Only American Indians were subjected to a deliberate policy of genocidal extermination. A common history of residential segregation, economic subordination, and political disfranchisement have created the basis for a comprehensive approach to the study of these ethnic minority groups.[8] Closely paralleling Takaki is the work of Johnnella E. Butler. Butler defines "people of color" as a social category that includes "those who have not and do not assimilate." Despite the many differences between these groups, Butler notes, "there are enough similarities in the American experiences of all these peoples to provide an imperfect yet workable construct of social organization—individual and group behavior—created by the peoples themselves and reflected in the academy." Butler defines this as a "matrix construct . . . a flexible diverse construct with multiple connections and interactions."[9]

A political economy approach to issues of race has been used by social scientists such as Robert Allen and Robert Blauner. Both argue that racialized minorities not only share uniquely different social histories from whites, but that their existence is strikingly similar to that of a colonized nation. In *Black Awakening in Capitalist America* Allen suggests that black America is an oppressed internal colony inside the United States. The capitalist economic system utilizes racism as a means to exploit black and brown labor power and to divide and confuse white workers from recognizing their true interests. Blauner's *Racial Oppression in America* argues that white ethnic groups may have experienced intolerance and exploitation, but that they were never "colonized." The structure of racial power confines African Americans and other racialized minorities to a subordinate status. The process of racial and class underdevelopment was therefore not accidental but absolutely essential in the consolidation of white power.[10]

At the opposite end of the spectrum are the cultural universalists who for divergent reasons attack or dismiss ethnic studies. The most influential "old school" universalists on issues of race and ethnicity are Nathan Glazer and Daniel Patrick Moynihan, authors of *Beyond the Melting Pot* and other works. These scholars have argued that ethnicity is not biologically based, but rather a product of social forces and voluntary choices people made about expressing their identities. As for black Americans, Glazer and Moynihan essentially proposed a universalist model, with whites as the standard, wherein blacks should strive to acquire the lifestyles, family patterns, and work habits of whites in order to diminish racial tensions. This theoretical orientation logically led Moynihan to his infamous 1965 "Black Matriarchy Thesis," attacking the matrifocal family structure of the black community as the principle cause of poverty and juvenile delinquency. Similarly, Glazer's subsequent hostility to affirmative action programs, minority economic set-asides, and ethnic studies programs reflects his universalist convictions that "color blindness" should be society's ultimate goal. Therefore, any policy compensating for the special handicaps or barriers that still impact blacks and other people of color, such as affirmative action, unjustly discriminates against innocent whites.[11]

Then there are the "new school" universalists who imply that any recognition of a unique status for racialized ethnic groups veers dangerously toward racial essentialism and separatism. Two leading intellectuals in this school of thought are Werner Sollors, a professor of Harvard's Afro-American Studies program, and Sean Wilentz, director of American studies at Princeton University. In a series of provocative works Sollors vilifies those who emphasize the discontinuities and conflicts among various racial and ethnic groups. For Sollors, "ethnicity" as a social construct is an "invention," nothing more. All Americans regardless of their respective racial or ethnic identities share far more in common with each other, culturally, socially, and politically.[12] In the *Chronicle of Higher Education* Wilentz accuses many ethnic studies scholars of depicting "the United States chiefly in terms of ethnic (or racial) identities and antagonisms and, in some cases, . . . proclaim[ing] that ethnic groups should defend their cultures from assimilation into a hegemonic mainstream 'American' civilization." Princeton's American studies program however, has taken a different approach, by emphasizing fundamental cultural commonalities rather than differences. Wilentz states:

> We fear, as the historian Arthur M. Schlesinger, Jr., has observed, that a fixation on ethnic differences presents a distorted picture of the United States as a country that is all "pluribus" and no "unum." We are equally convinced, however, that an ethnic or racial approach, narrowly conceived, does not do justice to the numerous ethnic and racial components of American culture. . . . To paraphrase the writer Ralph Ellison, "Americans are all 'cultural mulattos.'"[13]

The simple problem with Wilentz's formulation is that this "color-blind," assimilationist interpretation defies common sense and denies the crucial difference race still makes in daily life. The vast majority of African Americans are absolutely convinced that race is the fundamental division in U.S. society.

Finally, there are also social theorists of race and ethnicity who frankly do put forward essentialist and identity-bound models of cultural difference. The most influential school of thought presently expressed in many black studies programs is Afrocentricity, a concept initially developed by Molefi Asante, former chair of black studies at Temple University. The rationalization for Afrocentricity is constructed around its oppositional stance toward Eurocentrism, the cultural ideology and supremacist practices of the white West. Several extreme Afrocentrists even claim that racism is not socially constructed but rather a product of genetic or physical deficiencies among Euro-Americans. It is, therefore, not surprising that the national conversation around ethnic studies continues to be so politically charged and confrontational. People from the universities and public schools alike talk past each other precisely because there is no consensus, in abstract theory or in the real world, on what is meant by race and ethnicity.

Ethnic Studies: Intellectual Contours and Structures

Ethnic studies as a field of scholarship is the intellectual product of vast historical and social changes within U.S. society. It has evolved from different types of academic institutions, both public and private, and in some quarters still speaks the passionate language of the various social protest movements that gave it life a generation ago. Ethnic studies as an intellectual project is still in the process of evolving, but its essential character was forged in the demographic, political, and cultural transformations within twentieth-century American society that have occurred around the issue of difference.

At the dawn of the twentieth century racial discourse was largely, if not solely, framed on a bipolar model, black versus white. Ninety percent of all African Americans lived in the South, and roughly 80 percent were farmers or sharecroppers. Jim Crow segregation had been institutionalized throughout the South and was informally extended to govern race relations in the Northeast and Midwest. White insurgent movements seeking social change, such as the women suffragists, trade unionists, and middle-class Progressives, for the most part excluded Negroes. The few Asian Americans who had been permitted to remain in this country were marginalized and controlled by the same powerful forces that perpetuated black inferiority and subordination. Diversity in major U.S. cities was reflected largely through the complex patterns of European languages, religions, nationalities, and cultural traditions that had come to dominate urban life.

American universities rarely focused on racialized ethnic groups except to explore these communities as "problems"—e.g., the "Negro Problem." Black higher education was confined to about one hundred public and private academic institutions that had been constructed in the decades after the Civil War. What today is called black studies or, more accurately, the black intellectual tradition of scholarship, in the humanities, social sciences, and physical sciences was nurtured first at these underfunded but proud colleges. Interest in African affairs in the aftermath of the Second World War fostered the establishment of African studies programs and centers at predominately white institutions such as Northwestern University in 1948. Nevertheless, such programs were relatively isolated and few in number, reflecting the marginality of racialized minorities in the larger scope of American academe and civil society. The barrier of race structured the boundries of knowledge and legitimate intellectual inquiry for most white Americans.

Several events and factors were responsible for transforming the study of race and ethnicity in American higher education. As northern industrial and manufacturing jobs became available to blacks, millions trekked out of the South in the Great Migration. Hundreds of thousands of immigrants from the Caribbean came to the East Coast. In the 1940s and 1950s several million Mexicans who had frequently crossed the border to obtain work began to resettle the U.S. Southwest. By the 1960s there were substantial racialized ethnic populations in almost every major U.S. city. These demographic changes inevitably had an impact within American popular culture. Everything from professional sports and popular music to films and the media began to be profoundly shaped and interpreted through the prism of minority group cultures. The civil rights campaigns of the fifties and sixties helped to give shape and impetus to other new protest movements reflecting the demands and agendas of Chicanos, Puerto Ricans, feminists, lesbians and gays, American Indians, and many others. These profound movements for social reform, in turn, pressured predominantly white colleges and universities to open their doors to racialized ethnic minorities for the first time. For example, between 1976 and 1993 the number of Asian Americans enrolled in colleges soared from 198,000 to 724,000. By 1993 college enrollment for Latinos reached one million.

The newly arrived racialized ethnic groups on white campuses quickly demanded changes in the curriculum that reflected their own historical experiences, cultures, and respective intellectual traditions. The first institutionalized expression of these demands was in the field of African American studies. By 1969 African American studies programs had been established at over 100 colleges; within five years the number of black studies programs grew to at least five hundred. In the American Southwest over 50 Chicano studies programs had formed within a decade. In the eastern states Puerto Rican studies centers and programs were established. Most of these earlier programs were conceptually defined by the social reality of a specifically racialized experience and the cultural parameters set by the heritage and tradition of specific nonwhite populations. For example, African American studies generally focused on the cultural connections between Africa, the Caribbean, and black America, the construction of black culture and society inside the United States, and the patterns of resistance against racial discrimination.

The development of Native American studies was in several critical respects different from Black, Latino, and Asian American studies programs. The study of American Indian cultures and societies as a field of scholarship was for years dominated by white anthropologists, who frequently viewed their subjects through ethnocentric and even racist perspectives. Indians usually thought of themselves in terms of their tribal identities. All of this began to change in the 1950s, when the federal government initiated a policy called "termination," which in effect expelled more than one hundred tribes from lands promised to them by historic treaty obligations. This policy crisis pushed tribal groups toward a pan-Indian cultural identity. New organizations like the National Congress of American Indians and the United Native Americans were formed. In the late sixties the radical American Indian Movement fostered a new wave of militancy among Indians throughout the U.S. But it was not until 1980 that a group of Indian scholars met to establish the Native American Studies Association.

As a result of its development the field has two very different types of academic institutional structures: many traditional programs initiated and led by white scholars at predominantly white universities, which focus on anthropological, linguistic, historical, and folkloric themes and the more radical Indian studies programs, frequently connected with the network of tribal colleges. This second group of Indian scholars often define their research outside the boundaries of ethnic studies for the simple reason that Indians are the only "indigenous" people in the U.S. Indians are not an ethnic group, because they did not immigrate to this country. That is why much of the best new scholarship in the field, such as the outstanding work of Vine Deloria, is concerned with issues of law, such as treaty obligations and territorial rights.

As the new academic programs were established, two distinct curricular and research models emerged nationally. The vast majority were interdisciplinary undergraduate programs, which characteristically had a director and a list of affiliated faculty who were located in disciplinary-based departments. The director usually advised majors, taught the core required courses and supervised a modest program of lectures and campus-based activities. These programs almost always linked their central courses to their college's general education requirements or its core curriculum. The departments of black studies, Chicano studies, and ethnic studies were almost always located at large public institutions. At Ohio State University and Temple University, for instance, black studies had more than sixteen full-time faculty and graduate degree programs. In 1996 there were approximately forty-five black studies full departments, seventeen Chicano/Puerto Rican studies departments, and eight Asian American studies departments.

Both programmatic models of racialized ethnic studies had their own sets of problems. The departments often tended to suffer ghettoization. For example, traditional departments sometimes would not cross-list Black and Latino studies courses. The criteria for appointment, promotion, and tenure in the new departments were considered lacking sufficient academic rigor and intellectual viability. Faculty in these departments were often marginalized from the academic life of the campus community, in effect, preaching to their own racial constituency. Conversely, the interdisciplinary programs often lacked any academic coherence or intellectual integrity. The curricula were often eclectically organized, relying on faculty who had little academic relationship with each other. One recurrent problem was that departments always recruit, promote, and tenure their faculty on their own set of criteria, which rarely recognize the legitimacy of interdisciplinary scholarship, publications, and research of African American, Latino, and/or ethnic studies.

The evolution of ethnic studies programs was largely preceded by the creation of these other racial-ethnic programs. The first of the major ethnic studies departments to develop was, not surprisingly, in ethnically diverse California. The Department of Ethnic Studies at the University of California at Berkeley was founded in 1969, at the height of the antiwar and Black Power movements. It was originally conceived as an umbrella-like structure, with four interdependent programs operating within one department. Four separate majors and curricula were established, in Native American studies, Chicano studies, Asian American studies, and Afro-American studies. Within several years a number of serious problems had developed in the program. Because each major focused on a single racial ethnicity, students and faculty alike tended to function only in their narrow area of scholarly interest. There were relatively few faculty at the time who were involved in comparative research in the field of ethnic studies. Compounding all these issues was the internal competition for resources. The department's administration received its budgetary allocation and made the determination for how much each program would receive for the academic year. Cooperation between these programs suffered and sometimes broke down completely. By 1973 Afro-American studies made the decision to leave ethnic studies, and demanded the right to become a department. Several years later Native American studies also broke from ethnic studies. Although the department has for years continued to be the home of several outstanding scholars, such as Ron Takaki and Michael Omi, it has never received the full institutional support that it merits. Despite these problems, by the early 1990s the department had more than 150 undergraduate majors and a small but successful doctoral program in ethnic studies.[14]

For nearly twenty years Berkeley's Department of Ethnic Studies was the most influential model for the development of new programs. Dozens of ethnic studies academic units were initiated during these years. In 1979 Bowling Green University established a Department of Ethnic Studies, which included an undergraduate degree in three areas, Latino studies, black studies, and general ethnic studies. In 1983 Washington State University created a Comparative American Cultures Department, which within several years had ten faculty and offered curricula with concentrations in Native American, Asian American, Chicano, and African American studies.[15] Most of these ethnic studies units were interdisciplinary programs rather than departments, and they were frequently unable to exercise authority in the recruitment and tenure of their faculty or their own curricula. At a number of smaller colleges ethnic studies was offered as a minor concentration through traditional departments, such as sociology and anthropology.

By the mid-1980s the distinctive racial-ethnic composition of California's campuses was no longer confined to the West Coast. Significant numbers of Asian American students were enrolling in elite universities throughout the country. In 1983, for example, 5.5 percent of Harvard's entering freshman class was Asian American; in 1990 Asian Americans constituted 19.7 percent of the new freshman class. Asian American organizations initiated legal challenges against several institutions that were charged with carrying out discriminatory policies or quotas to restrict Asian American admissions. In 1988 the U.S. Department of Education investigated both Harvard and UCLA to determine whether they had "established illegal quotas limiting the number of Asian-American students they admit."[16] Just as the explosion of the African American student population at predominantly white institutions created the pressure to launch hundreds of black studies programs, the hundreds of thousands of new Asian American students made similar demands for diversity within their curricula. Their presence on campuses helped to promote a new approach to teaching ethnic studies, with a broader comparative and global focus.

The Department of Ethnic Studies at the University of San Diego was representative of the new directions in the field. Courses previously taught under separate academic menus of Asian American, Chicano, American Indian, and Afro-American studies were fully integrated, with emphasis on a rigorous, comparative core curriculum. By 1996 the department had nine core faculty who were all tenured or tenure-track within ethnic studies. More than twenty additional faculty in other departments taught regularly in ethnic studies. Instead of an umbrella model, where scholars focused solely on their own racial-ethnic topical fields, faculty were recruited largely on their academic interest in comparative ethnic research. The department has also begun the process to initiate Master's and Ph.D. programs. At present the department has about ninety majors, with over five hundred students enrolled in upper-level courses each academic year.

A similar transition occurred at the University of Colorado at Boulder. In 1987 an interdepartmental committee recommended the establishment of CSERA—the Center for Studies in Ethnicity and Race in America. CSERA was given the authority to recruit a series of senior scholars who in most cases would be jointly appointed with traditional departments. The selection of historian Evelyn Hu-DeHart as CSERA's director symbolized the new focus on comparative ethnicity. Born in China, Hu-DeHart's scholarship ranges from studies of Native Americans in the Latino Southwest to patterns of slavery and indentured servitude of Chinese immigrants in the Caribbean. CSERA's early years were marked by some tensions, as several faculty who had been originally hired to teach in only one racial-ethnic area resisted the new comparative emphasis. By 1995, however, CSERA had received departmental status and consolidated itself as a successful program.

Other institutions began to create parallel programs. In 1985 the University of Washington established the Department of American Ethnic Studies, which developed from an Afro-American studies program created fifteen years earlier. Curricula in Asian American and Chicano studies were enriched and expanded into degree programs. In 1988 Brown University established the Center for the Study of Race and Ethnicity in America, to support courses and research on racialized ethnic groups, and has developed an American Civilization Department with nine faculty positions. In 1996 Stanford University created the Institute for Comparative Studies in Race and Ethnicity (CSRE), which will integrate undergraduate majors in Asian American, Native American, Chicano, and comparative studies through introductory level and senior level courses. It will also develop close curricular connections with African and Afro-American studies and Jewish studies. The proposal for the establishment of CSRE states that a "comparative focus on the subjects of race and ethnicity, in the U.S. and abroad, is fundamental to all majors. . . . No individual ethnic-specific major has the capacity to provide the comparative dimension by itself." The proposal also emphasized the importance of CSRE's "global dimension. . . . CSRE goes beyond the American experience to incorporate the study of international issues and experiences."[18]

As of 1996 there were nearly one hundred ethnic studies programs throughout the United States, of which approximately thirty are full departments. The programs within this field that have been most successful have had several common characteristics. First and perhaps foremost is the issue of the undergraduate core curriculum or general distribution requirements. A number of the program's courses must be offered as an integral part of the collegewide core curriculum. Other courses should be cross-listed with traditional departments when possible. Second, successful departments avoid racialization and ghettoization. The study of race and ethnicity should not be confined solely to Latino, Asian American, American Indian, and black American students and scholars. Programs must be seen as being central to the intellectual life and academic culture of the whole community. Ideally, ethnic studies should assume a significant role in the strategic planning of a university.

Successful programs nearly always have the authority to initiate appointments and recruit and retain their own faculty. Absolute tenure control is not necessary for a department to be successful, and in many cases it has been a severe handicap. At several large black and Latino studies departments and research centers a number of faculty who were hired in the initial wave of institutionalization lacked scholarly credentials, or were never actively engaged in research. By the mid-to late 1980s many of this veteran group had been tenured but had ceased to function as intellectuals beyond their normal responsibilities as classroom instructors. Sometimes a "siege mentality" would set in, as junior faculty were admonished never to work in collaboration with traditional departments or other interdisciplinary programs like women's studies. Tenure and promotion reviews degenerated into contests over petty administrative power.

Such programs have always been part of the academic politics of American universities and are hardly unique to ethnic studies. What perhaps is most desirable is the recruitment of faculty who are both well-grounded in a traditional academic discipline and define their primary scholarship to be broadly interdisciplinary and comparative. W. E. B. Du Bois, for example, was the chief architect for modern black studies, but he was simultaneously an outstanding historian and sociologist. The detailed multi- and interdisciplinary research in ethnic studies has and will continue to generate new knowledge and innovative ways of thinking about traditional ideas. Much of the most innovative and creative scholarship is produced at the borders, the intellectual spaces between old disciplines. The life of the mind in a university should never be "fixed." What ethnic studies at its best can accomplish is an expansion of scholarly discourse and knowledge, new modes of examination and inquiry.

Inequality and the New Color Line

The central recurring dilemmas of scholarship in ethnic studies are the twin problems of cultural amalgamation and racial essentialism. I say "twin problems" because these two different tendencies nevertheless have a subterranean unity. Many advocates of diversity and the study of racialized ethnicities tend to homogenize groups into a broad political construct, "people of color." The concept people of color has tremendous utility in bringing people toward a comparative historical awareness as to the commonalities of oppression and resistance that racialized ethnic groups have experienced; our voices and visions cannot properly be understood or interpreted in isolation from one another. But to argue that all people of color are therefore equally oppressed and share the objective basis for a common politics is dubious at best. The opposite tendency, toward racial-ethnic *identitarianism,* to recall literary critic and activist Gayatri Spivak's term, encapsulates our respective racialized groups within the narrow terrain of our own experiences. In our own separate languages, from the vantage point of our respective grievances, we trust only in ourselves, cursing the possibility that others unlike ourselves share a similar destiny.

Most scholars of ethnic studies don't fall into either trap. We recognize both the profound divergences and parallels in the social construction of ethnicity. Different ethnic groups retain their own unique stories, insights and reflections, triumphs and tragedies from their sojourns through American life. None of this can take away from the deep structural parallels, especially in the processes of racial oppression, the struggles for survival and resistance, and the efforts to maintain cultural and social integrity and identity, that create the dynamic social framework that brings us together. But let us take seriously the dynamic, dialectical characteristics of social change that define the framework of American race and ethnicity. Most scholars agree that racialization is a social and historical process—that "races" are not fixed categories. They are permeated by the changing contours of class, gender, nationality, and sexual orientation. If this is true, then we must also recognize that an "oppressed race" in one historical epoch, such as the Irish or Ashkenazic Jews, can be incorporated into the privileged strata of whiteness. Racial designations of identical cultural groups may differ from country to country and in diverse places and times.

Moreover, the state always has a vested interest in the management of diversity. The U.S. government's decision in 1971 to create a new "ethnic, but not racial" category of "Hispanic," is the best recent example of state manipulation of the politics of difference. The designation Hispanic was imposed on over fifteen million citizens and resident aliens who had very different nationalities, racial-ethnic identities, cultures, social organizations, and political histories. But the government's attempt to regulate difference as a matter of public policy inevitably impacts how most people perceive themselves in daily life. Are Chicanos also Hispanics, or are they Latinos, or Mexicans who now live in territories that once belonged to them? The Hispanic category encompasses extraordinarily different groups: upper middle-class immigrants from Argentina, Uruguay, and Chile, who are phenotypically white and culturally European, black working-class Panamanians and Dominicans, the anti-Castro Cuban exiles of 1959–1961 who now form much of Dade County, Florida's ruling political elite and professional class, and Mexican American farm workers in California's agricultural districts. Which of these distinct nationalities and cultural groups will largely set the standards for what the Hispanic legal and social construct may become? As in every social construct, each group's collective identity is a product of political and social contestations, ideological conflicts, class and gender stratifications. Increasingly, it seems probable that, in the near future, some of these racialized ethnics will be incorporated into the white social category of privilege, through a combination of class, upward mobility, racial-ethnic intermarriage, residential segregation, and their assimilation of white conservative political behavior and voting patterns.

The general tendency of most people in the United States is to think about race and racism parochially, solely within a North American context and within our current moment in history. A much richer perspective about race as a social construct can be obtained from a comparative approach to the study of other racial formations. In South Africa, for example, a very different racialized society developed, with a colored group forming something of a buffer stratum between blacks and whites. Under the former regime of apartheid certain Asian nationalities, such as the Japanese, could be classified as white, while others, like the Chinese, were relegated to the lower status of coloreds. In colonial Brazil the importation of more than four million enslaved Africans was the foundation for the construction of a distinctive racialized society. Color and phenotype were important criteria for placing an individual within the racial hierarchy. But social class status, education, family background, and other elements were also extremely important in interpreting racial distinctions. For more than a century the Brazilians have used the expression "Money lightens the skin." It has been possible for a minority of Brazilian blacks to scale the hierarchy of whiteness through the acquisition of material wealth and cultural capital. Until recently, that was rarely the case in the United States. But new developments have fundamentally altered the old racial reality.

The central driving force today behind the configuration of the U.S. racial formation is immigration. In the 1980s there were 8.6 million immigrants who legally entered the U.S., more than in any decade since 1900–1910. In 1989 alone, about 1.1 million immigrants were admitted for permanent residence, the highest number since 1914. By 1996 there were five million illegal immigrants in the United States, with over 60 percent of them from Central American and Mexico. Illegal immigration has become a multibillion dollar enterprise. Nationwide, about one-third of the total growth rate of the U.S. labor force comes from legal and illegal immigration. In New York City alone, in 1990 there were 4,500 businesses that employed 50,000 illegal immigrants in sweatshop conditions. Asian American studies scholar Peter Kwong observes that much of the international traffic of immigrants is essentially indentured servitude:

"Smugglers are now charging $28,000 to bring in Indians and Pakistanis, and $8,000 to bring Poles through Native American reservations on the New York–Canada border. The cost to Southeast Asian women is years of indentured service as 'white slaves' in the prostitution industry."[19]

According to an Urban Institute study, more than 90 percent of this new immigrant population settles in urban areas where there are high concentrations of black Americans. The conditions have been created where native-born black workers increasingly find themselves in sharp competition with foreign-born nonwhites.[20] In his research on urban employment patterns William Julius Wilson found that employers usually prefer to hire immigrant Mexicans over blacks because Mexicans are perceived as more reliable. In some cities blacks complain that they have been fired or have lost low-wage jobs because they were not fluent in Spanish. Increasingly, some Latino and Asian American groups have used the laws against discrimination achieved by the civil rights movement to attack what many African Americans feel are hard-won gains. For instance, in late 1994 Tirso del Junco, the only Latino on the Board of Governors of the U.S. Postal Service, charged that African Americans were "overrepresented" within the postal service workforce. Using Los Angeles as a prime example, del Junco observed that in 1993 blacks comprised only 10 percent of the area's workforce but made up 62 percent of all regional postal employees. Latinos constituted 35 percent in the region but held only 15 percent of postal jobs.[21]

In the area of education, the gains achieved by African Americans in terms of access and opportunities during the 1960s and 1970s began to be reversed. The percentage of graduating black seniors who went on to college leveled off in the 1980s and started to descend. By contrast, 51 percent of all 1980 Asian American high school seniors had enrolled in four-year colleges by February 1982, compared with 37 percent of all white seniors, 33 percent for African Americans, and 20 percent for Hispanics. In terms of business development, the Census Bureau's 1987 Survey of Minority-Owned Business Enterprises indicated that Asian American businesses increased from 187,691 to 335,331 between 1982 and 1987, a 79 percent growth rate. The census also estimated the same year that about 6 percent of all Asian Americans owned businesses, compared to 6.5 percent of all whites, 2 percent of Hispanics, 1.5 percent of African Americans, and 1 percent of Native Americans.[22]

By 1992 38 percent of all retail outlets in Los Angeles County were owned by Koreans. Korean American businesses in Los Angeles had grown by 27 percent in the two years just before the city's massive unrest.[23] In the area of home mortgages, banks and lending institutions continued their discriminatory practices toward the great majority of racialized ethnics but treated Asian Americans very differently. According to the 1997 study by the Federal Financial Institutions Examination Council, banks, credit unions, and mortgage companies turned down 48.8 percent of all applications for home purchase loans from black Americans. The denial rates were 50.2 percent for American Indians, 34.4 percent for Hispanics, 24.1 percent for whites, and only 13.8 percent for Asian Americans.[24]

These and other striking differences in opportunities and upward mobility of racialized ethnics set the context for increasing social and legal conflicts. For example, much of the black and Latino violence in the 1992 Los Angeles rebellion was aimed squarely against Korean establishments. According to Peter Kwong, 1,867 Korean American businesses were looted and burned during the civil unrest, "representing one-half of the total lost from the riots." Most of the destroyed business had been located in Koreatown, an urban neighborhood that was 26.5 percent Asian American and over 50 percent Latino. Almost one-half of all people arrested by the police during the disturbance were Latinos.[25]

Two years later, Californians debated Proposition 187, which denied undocumented immigrants educational access and healthcare services, and the explosive politics of racialized ethnicity surfaced once again. Most local black elected officials and community leaders voiced their opposition but did relatively little to defeat the proposition. On election day Proposition 187 easily passed. Asian Americans had voted overwhelmingly for the initiative. Most black voters rejected the measure, but by a narrow margin of 53 percent opposed and 47 percent in favor. Black voter turnout was also unusually low, which also contributed to Proposition 187's victory. With the initiative's passing, black-Latino conflicts intensified in poor urban communities such as Compton, where underfunded schools, public health facilities, and social services had already reached a breaking point.[26]

Any discussion concerning these and other conflicts between America's racialized ethnics should take into account that there are significant differences—based on social class, nationality, language, and religion—that subdivide each grouping. Less than one-half of all Asian Americans are of Japanese and Chinese origin or descent. The Asian American category includes Japanese Americans, who have higher median family incomes than whites, and the Hmong of southeast Asia, who are one of the poorest U.S.

population groups. There is a significant class stratification and polarization within the Chinese community, with a growing professional and corporate elite as well as tens of thousands of working poor people. The construction of a pan-ethnic Asian American identity and cultural/political consciousness is historically a very recent phenomenon and remains extremely contested. Much of the focus surrounding Asian American studies, for example, has concentrated largely on the research pertaining to the historical and recent experiences of Japanese and Chinese immigrants. But as Indians, Pakistanis, Indonesians, Vietnamese, Arabs, Cambodians, and others increasingly enter the discussion regarding the definition of what the Asian American category should mean, this process will become even more complicated.[27]

Another factor that may come into consideration is the continuing attempt to differentiate some "model minorities" from other minorities, in what can be termed geopolitical-cultural capital. In this period of globalization corporate capital requires a multicultural, multinational management and labor force. Racialized ethnic consumer markets in the U.S. represent hundreds of billions of dollars; black Americans alone spend more than $350 billion annually. To better exploit these vast consumer markets, capital has developed "corporate multiculturalism," the manipulation of cultural diversity for private profit maximization.

In terms of the governmental, financial, and corporate interests, certain ethnic minorities are seen as being connected with powerful geopolitical countries such as China and Japan. At a symbolic level the prestige or power of a nation-state's economy in the global marketplace is inevitably transplanted into public policies, which in turn impact the representation and treatment of its former citizens or their cultural descendants. Another way of looking at this is from the disadvantaged position of the third world. Sub-Saharan Africa, with some notable exceptions such as South Africa, is an economic basket case. East Asia's "four tigers"—South Korea, Hong Kong, Singapore, and Taiwan—recorded 9.4 percent annual grown in per capita gross domestic product in the 1980s, compared to sub-Saharan Africa's annual growth rate of negative 0.9 percent. As of 1997, South Korea had a per capita income of $10,000 a year; the Congo, recently freed from thirty years' authoritarian rule by a U.S.-supported dictator, had an annual per capita income of $150.[28] Japan alone has invested billions of dollars in U.S. property, corporations, and financial markets. Power is often understood and interpreted through the prism of cultural hierarchy. Ideologically and culturally, the so-called backward peoples who have been historically identified with Africa, the Caribbean, and much of Latin America and southern Asia are at a distinct disadvantage in racist Western societies. This does not, by any means, minimize the significance of class stratification or the social dynamics of economic exploitation and conflicts generated by ethnic intolerance within third world societies.

A new racial formation is evolving rapidly in the United States, a new configuration of racialized ethnicity, class, and gender stratification and divisions. Increasingly the phenotypical, color-based categories of difference that only a generation ago appeared extremely rigid and fixed are being restructured and reconfigured against the background of globalized capitalism and neoliberal governmental policies worldwide. In a curious way, William Julius Wilson was both right and wrong in his "declining significance of race" prediction nearly two decades ago.[29] Traditional white racism, as configured by class and state forces over several centuries, is certainly declining. Its place is being taken by a qualitatively new color line of spiraling class inequality and extreme income stratifications, mediated or filtered through old discourses and cultural patterns more closely coded by physical appearance, legal racial classification, and language. What the critical study of racialized ethnicities can bring into focus is how and why these domestic and global processes are currently unfolding, and what can be done to challenge them.

Notes

Much of the background information from various ethnic studies programs throughout the country mentioned in this paper was compiled during my participation on a Columbia University advisory committee on ethnic studies. This committee had been created following campus unrest and student takeovers of several college buildings in the spring semester of 1996. Data from two unpublished documents was extremely helpful: the final report, "Guidelines and Recommendations," drafted by the committee in January 1997, and a "Report to the Special Faculty Committee on Ethnic Studies," written in September 1996 by Jorge Coronado and Maggie Garb. Also, many key ideas in this paper were conceived together with anthropologist Leith Mullings.

1. See Michael Omi and Howard Winant, *Racial Formation in the United States: From the 1960s to the 1990s*, 2d ed. (New York: Routledge, 1994).

2. Faye V. Harrison, "The Persistent Power of 'Race' in the Cultural and Political Economy of Racism," *Annual Reviews in Anthropology*, vol. 24 (1995), pp. 58–59; see pp. 47–74.

3. David Roediger, *The Wages of Whiteness: Race and the Making of the American Working Class* (New York: Verso, 1991), p. 13.

4. See Manning Nash, *The Cauldron of Ethnicity in the Modern World* (Chicago: University of Chicago Press, 1989).

5. Leith Mullings, *On Our Own Terms: Race, Class, and Gender in the Lives of African American Women* (New York: Routledge, 1997), p. 160.

6. Richard L. Worsnop, "Asian Americans," *Congressional Quarterly Researcher*, vol. 31 (December 13, 1991), p. 955.

7. M. Menchacha, "Chicano Indianism: A Historical Account of Racial Repression in the United States," *American Ethnologist*, vol. 20, no. 3 (1993), pp. 583–603; and John J. Miller, "Paragons or Pariahs? Arguing with Asian-American Success," *Reason*, vol. 25, no. 7 (December 1993), pp. 48–50.

8. See Ronald Takaki, *Iron Cages: Race and Culture in Nineteenth-Century America*, 2d. ed. (New York: Oxford University Press, 1990); and Ronald Takaki, ed., *From Different Shores: Perspectives on Race and Ethnicity in America* (New York: Oxford University Press, 1987).

9. Johnnella E. Butler, "Ethnic Studies: A Matrix Model for the Major," *Liberal Education*, vol. 77, no. 2 (March/April 1991), p. 26; see pp. 26–32. Also see Johnnella E. Butler and John C. Walter, eds., *Transforming the Curriculum: Ethnic Studies and Women's Studies* (Albany: State University of New York Press, 1991).

10. See Robert Allen, *Black Awakening in Capitalist America* (Garden City, N.Y.: Anchor, 1969); and Robert Blauner, *Racial Oppression in America* (New York: Harper and Row, 1972).

11. See Nathan Glazer and Daniel Patrick Moynihan, *Beyond the Melting Pot*, 2d ed. (Cambridge: MIT Press, 1970); and Nathan Glazer, *Affirmative Discrimination: Ethnic Inequity and Public Policy* (New York: Basic, 1975).

12. See Werner Sollors, ed., *The Invention of Ethnicity* (New York: Oxford University Press, 1989); and Werner Sollors, *Beyond Ethnicity: Consent and Descent in American Culture* (New York: Oxford University Press, 1986).

13. Sean Wilentz, "Integrating Ethnicity Into American Studies," *Chronicle of Higher Education*, November 29, 1996.

14. Butler, "Ethnic Studies," p. 32.

15. Ibid., p. 32.

16. Worsnop, "Asian Americans," p. 950.

17. Butler, "Ethnic Studies," p. 32.

18. Report on "The Purpose and Rationale of the Program in Comparative Studies in Race and Ethnicity," Stanford University, School of Humanities and Sciences, October 2, 1996.

19. Jack Miles, "Blacks vs. Browns," *Atlantic Monthly*, vol. 270, no. 4 (October 1992), pp. 41–68; and Peter Kwong, *Forbidden Workers: Illegal Chinese Immigrants and American Labor* (New York: New Press, 1997), pp. 172–173, 235.

20. Salim Muwakkil, "Color Bind," *In These Times*, March 6, 1995, pp. 15–17.

21. Peter Skerry, "The Black Alienation," *New Republic*, vol. 212, no. 5 (January 30, 1995), pp. 19–20.

22. Worsnop, "Asian Americans," pp. 950–953.

23. Peter Kwong, "The First Multicultural Riots," *Village Voice*, June 9, 1992, p. 31; see pp. 29–32.

24. "Rejections for Mortgages Stay Higher for Blacks," *New York Times*, August 5, 1997. The Federal Financial Institutions Examination Council is a coordinating body for five federal agencies. The 1997 survey covered 14.8 million home loan applications from 9,800 lending institutions.

25. Kwong, "The First Multicultural Riots," p. 31.

26. Larry Aubry, "Proposition 187 and African Americans: Harmful Shortsightedness," *Los Angeles Sentinel*, November 10, 1994; Jim Cleaver, "Passage of Prop. 187: Maybe Now the Lesson Will Hit Home," *Los Angeles Sentinel*, November 17, 1994; Charles S. Lee and Lester Sloan, "It's Our Turn Now," *Newsweek*, vol. 24, no. 21 (November 21, 1994) p. 57; Mike Davis, "The Social Origins of the Referendum," *NACLA Report on the Americas*, vol. 29 (November/December 1995), pp. 24–28; Kathryn Flewellen, "Whose America Is This?" *Essence*, vol. 26, no. 10 (February 1996), p. 154; and Joe Domanick, "The Browning of Black L.A.," *Los Angeles Magazine*, vol. 41, no. 5 (May 1996), pp. 74–79.

27. See William Wei, *The Asian American Movement: A Social History* (Philadelphia: Temple University Press, 1993).

28. Nicholas D. Kristof, "Why Africa Can Thrive Like Asia," *New York Times*, May 25, 1997.

29. See William Julius Wilson, *The Declining Significance of Race: Blacks and Changing American Institutions*, 2d ed. (Chicago: University of Chicago Press, 1980); and William Julius Wilson, *The Truly Disadvantaged: The Inner City, the Underclass, and Public Policy* (Chicago: University of Chicago Press, 1987).

21

Prophetic Alternatives:
A Conversation with Cornel West

On Thursday evening, September 8, 1994, more than five hundred people attended a lively dialogue between Cornel West, professor of religion and Afro-American studies at Harvard University, and Manning Marable, sponsored by the Institute for Research in African-American Studies at Columbia University. Professor West explored a wide range of topics in the discussion, including the controversies surrounding the firing of the Reverend Benjamin Chavis, former head of the National Association for the Advancement of Colored People, the public prominence of black nationalist leader Minister Louis Farrakhan within sectors of the black community, and the dilemma of rethinking a progressive and activist agenda within a largely conservative American political culture. What follows are selected excerpts from the actual exchange, slightly revised for purposes of style and length.

MANNING MARABLE: This inaugural conference of the Institute for Research in African-American Studies, which we have been planning for the last year, is hopefully only the beginning of a project that will involve scholars, researchers, activists, and community leaders, focusing on the challenges confronting people in the United States, particularly those of African descent, and also black people throughout the world, on a whole series of issues.

Our topic tonight—"What Are the Alternatives? Black Politics in Theory and Crisis, an International Symposium"—brings together scholars and activists from the United States, the Caribbean, from Africa, and from Europe to address several central questions: How have politics throughout the world been changed by the end of the cold war? What are the alternatives for progressive and radical democratic thinking? How do radicals rethink questions of theory and social change, given the collapse of Marxist and socialist parties and politics? What is the responsibility of black intellectuals in addressing the crisis our communities face, not only in Harlem or in the United States, but throughout the world?

... How would we begin to characterize the state of the African American community today, especially in light of recent conflicts and debates about the character and quality of black leadership? You and I both attended the National African American Leadership Summit, sponsored by the National Association for the Advancement of Colored People (NAACP), this June. We were both part of the dialogue addressing whether Louis Farrakhan, leader of the Nation of Islam, should have been invited to participate in this meeting. And, more recently, we witnessed the personal tragedy and conflicts surrounding former NAACP national secretary Benjamin Chavis, which culminated in a national media and political campaign to remove him from the leadership of that organization. What is your perspective on these recent events? Did Chavis's actions justify his removal as head of the NAACP?

CORNEL WEST: There's a lot there on the table. Let me first say, I'm just glad to be here. I'm so very happy that Columbia University had the wisdom to hire Brother Manning Marable and bring him to New York City. (*Applause.*) I look forward to this institutionalized dialogue, even as we proceed tonight, as we engage in a critical exchange with each other.

In regard to Brother Ben Chavis, certainly it is the case that anytime one steps forward to be a visible, let alone a visionary leader, one is going to be tried, one is going to be attacked, one is going to be assaulted in a variety of ways. There's no doubt that Ben Chavis did receive his number of unwarranted attacks, due to his attempt to move the most salient black organization in America in a highly progressive direction. By "highly progressive," I mean keeping the focus [of the NAACP] on the black suffering, sadness, and sorrow of the masses of black folk who are working people, working poor, but including, of course, the very poor brothers and sisters of African descent. That will and did create problems.

That does not mean that Ben Chavis himself is a saint, he's a sinner like all of us, finite and fallen. If you don't want the theoretical language—which is to say, he's going to make some mistakes and errors, personal as well as collective. But I think what was fundamentally behind the nearly unprecedented attacks on Ben Chavis had to do with him actually moving what is perceived to be a mainstream organization, which has actually been bogged down in the mire of an anemic liberalism, in a progressive direction. That's one of the reasons it was so very important we come to his defense, not to celebrate him. What is at stake is not just Ben Chavis; he signifies a movement that keeps the focus where it belongs—on black suffering—and has a broad enough vision to acknowledge that you can't just focus on black suffering, because black suffering means, then, that you're going to be focusing on the suffering of working people across the board. Therefore, the kind of coalition he was calling for from within the black community would be extended to a coalition of progressives across the board.

It's no accident that in our attempt to come to his defense in a critical, as opposed to a celebratory, manner, that it's very important he remain visible. He was able to give hope to so many people, especially young black folk, but also to progressive people across the board. We should make certain that he's not beaten down, fallen through the cracks, and therefore another example of what happens when you step up and try to be progressive and end up being smashed.

The summit process is continuing. You all know we have an office in Washington, D.C. Ben Chavis is the national secretary. We've got problems, tremendous obstacles and impediments, no doubt, but it's very important that Ben not only be perceived as bouncing back, but that he bounce back in order to sustain the kind of motion and momentum.

MARABLE: But how do we move an organization that originally evolved, basically, with a philosophy of inclusion? Back in the 1960s the politics of black liberal reform had the goal of "inclusion" within the existing system. They wanted to have representation within a structure of power of this society. But, inevitably, we discovered that we had to redefine the nature of the entire social order and that our real purpose was to bring about a democratic transformation . . .

WEST: That's right . . .

MARABLE: . . . then you have a brother Chavis, who leads an organization that has had a very different political agenda, certainly since Walter White and Roy Wilkins. You have not had the kind of radical, democratic, visionary leadership of that organization since Du Bois was in the leadership generations ago. So, in your opinion, was Chavis's strategy possible or even realistic? To democratically move the NAACP from inclusion to transformation?

WEST: I think it was possible. I think Ben did make a number of errors, but let me begin first by saying . . . of course, you and I never believed that what we fundamentally wanted was symbolic representation. We wanted freedom and self-determination. That's what sits at the center of the rich tradition of black freedom. So that if a "black face in a high place" can contribute to black freedom, fine; if not, get out of the way.

So, proceeding in that way, we say, "OK, how do we go about defining black self-determination in such a way that it keeps track of the complexities of what we're up against?" Big capital. Links between corporate elites, financial elites, political elites, and the tremendous weight and gravity of white supremacy, male supremacy, and homophobia. Okay. It doesn't provide a whole lot of space, right? And we know that the history of black folk in America is between a rock and a hard place, in terms of ensuring some sense of agency and action, so we could project possibility. I think the NAACP, even given the anemic liberalism I alluded to earlier, could possibly have been transformed, because it is in deep crisis. It was before Ben took it over, it remains so today, and what is characteristic about anemic liberalism is that it then usually finds itself open to new alternatives, if those alternatives can be articulated in such a way that the division is clear, and there are some vehicles by which that vision can actually move on the ground.

I think in many ways Ben Chavis—I love him dearly—had to come and hit the ground running, but you also have to get inside the culture of these organizations, very much like being a pastor of a church. In some ways, it's like being the pastor of a church; there's positive and negative aspects of that. But it means that when you come into a different institution you have to get a sense of the internal dynamics of the subculture within that institution. In order to do that, you have to be able to solidify your power base in such a way that when you articulate your vision you bring people along, even though they might not really want to go along as quickly as you like to go along. A good pastor knows how to do that and still be a democrat.

Ben's problem, in part, was that he was unable to solidify his social base from within the NAACP, which has old, decrepit structures and infrastructures; therefore, he's off running, and they're keeping track of him as they are organizing, consolidating their social base, and boom—they got him on something. Because there's tremendous internal struggle. Now, keep in mind, the NAACP to me is still indispensable for the black freedom struggle, even given their link to a vision I find inadequate, truncated, etc. It will always be crucial. The problem is, it won't be *the* major institution that will be on the cutting edge; one will have to bring them in, kicking and screaming, if a radical democratic vision ever takes off. But that's fine. That's what struggle is all about. That's how historical motion is generated. That's how social change takes place. You never have a blueprint, a pure ideology in which everyone subscribes to that ideology. You create these coalitions and alliances that would never have been conceived previously. But given new, historical conjunctures, they come together, and you try to seize possibility, in light of those coalitions and alliances.

So I in no way want to trash the NAACP, even as I'm highly critical of what they've actually done to brother Ben. I hope we can continually infuse progressive energies in both the organization as well as the movement Ben Chavis is now associated with.

MARABLE: Let's take a look at some of the reasons why Ben Chavis came under attack. You have said for over a year . . . many commentators who have talked about this, that had Chavis not had the contradictions of sexism, or had he not made the personal and administrative errors and mistakes he made, in effect, all of those were secondary to the fundamental question that you're raising: moving an organization from inclusion to transformation. Related to the controversy around Chavis is the continuing influence of Louis Farrakhan. How do you explain the resurgence and the powerful restatement of black nationalist separatism in 1992? We saw this evolve, peaking with the renaissance in popular culture with the Malcolm phenomenon in the early 1990s. We also witnessed the rapid growth and popularity of the Nation of Islam. In the academic sphere there has been the rise of Afrocentrism in universities. A separatist political and cultural ideology has really now taken off within broad sectors of the African American community. How do you explain this?

Second, how do you interpret the role of Farrakhan? Chavis invited Louis Farrakhan to the June summit and received much criticism for this. Many critics, including Julian Bond, deplored the invitation, arguing that

Farrakhan had no place in the dialogue with African American leadership. The media also severely criticized Chavis. What was your take on all this?

WEST: The problem with the mainstream media is that they often have tremendous difficulty keeping focus on black suffering and are much more preoccupied with white fears and anxieties. That's very true. It's very sad, actually, because you cannot engage in a dialogue with a variety of different voices of black folk without acknowledging the voice of Louis Farrakhan. It's impossible. Why? Because Louis Farrakhan's fundamental focus is on black suffering. Now you can disagree with how he understands it. You can disagree with his vision of how to overcome it. But, believe it or not, the mass media would have you think that Louis Farrakhan primarily focuses on white folk and Jewish brothers and sisters. That's not true. He gets to them after he focuses on black suffering, trying to account for that suffering.

Meaning what? Meaning that you need people who are focusing on black suffering—and it's not only white folk. We've got a number of white brothers and sisters focusing on black, brown, and yellow suffering—who have different visions, different analyses, and then try to keep one another accountable so that, of course, their high moral ground can be preserved, so that the analysis of black suffering itself does not fall into xenophobic traps. Which is to say, highlighting black suffering and downplaying somebody else's suffering.

Because Louis Farrakhan has been so thoroughly demonized by the mainstream media, just touching him—you know what I mean?—it becomes some kind of crime. Like a crime. "Heard you were in the same restaurant with Louis Farrakhan!" Something's wrong. Sit down with Jesse Helms and have a long dialogue, and you're open-minded. The important point here is, we are at a moment now in the black community where black folk are so disillusioned, so deeply discouraged about the capacity of American society to ever acknowledge black humanity. It's no accident that black nationalist voices are gaining popularity. . . . Now here I'm going to use the term *black nationalist* rather than *black separatist*. I think that's very important.

MARABLE: What's the distinction between them?

WEST: Black separatism tends to be kind of a secondary, tertiary note within a much larger, rich black nationalist tradition. There is a variety of different perspectives within the black nationalist tradition. Black nationalism has always been integral to the black freedom struggle. Now, I'm not a black nationalist, but I'm part of a struggle in which black nationalists are always there. Therefore, the fact remains, when black nationalist tendencies, voices, and organizations are gaining power, it's no accident that a Ben Chavis will be in dialogue with them. Louis Farrakhan happens to be the major articulator of that particular tendency in the black community.

Louis Farrakhan is also one of the most talented orators in the country. If you go to Madison Square Garden and you've got thirty-five thousand black folk, they come to hear someone who can speak, period. Now you ask the question, how many join his organization after he speaks? Many do, but not that many, right? The three largest black Baptist churches in Brooklyn are roughly the equivalent of his national organization. Isn't that something? The press doesn't project that. Why? Because the black folk who come to hear him come to hear someone focus on black suffering, someone who's bold, defiant of the white power structure, somebody who's going to feel free to speak his mind, whatever is on it.

You see, for people who are hungry and thirsty for freedom there is always the tendency to want to at least be in touch with somebody who's free inside himself. And one thing about Louis Farrakhan, he is free inside himself. He is. He is free. And what we need are more progressive, radical democrats to bring critique to bear on Louis Farrakhan not based on him but based on the freedom to which he claims to have allegiance. That's been the history of the black freedom struggle, for those who have been able to do that. Now, of course, there's a cost. There's a tremendous cost for doing that. Live every day under the threat of death, that's the first one. That's real. There's Louis Farrakhan, Jesse Jackson, go right down the list. Every day they live under threat of death because of the legacy, the vicious, pernicious legacy of white supremacy in this nation.

So this is serious business we're talking about. That's the first thing. The second thing is being willing to speak in such a way that people perceive in what you have to say a certain level of integrity. That's very important, because part of our problem, among so many black leaders, has been a decline in integrity, let alone courage. We feel as though we have to run so many little obstacles here and there that we're not speaking from the heart. This is true, in many ways, for progressive leadership across the board.

MARABLE: All of us are familiar with your recent book, *Race Matters.*
Let's talk about what "race" is. Now, in the United States we get
trapped into these pseudo-biological and geneticist arguments about
race. We can dispense with any kind of scientific notion of race. We
know that race is a social construction. We know that race is structured around power, privilege, ownership of resources, and is perpetuated by violence and exploitation. But then, how do we understand
the role of race within the current conjuncture? . . . How does race
matter differently today in the "Hip-Hop" generation of the 1990s,
as compared to what race was in the "We Shall Overcome" generation of the 1960s? Is part of the leadership problem that we're interpreting the character of institutional racism in the context of a generation ago, when we were trying to seek to obtain an integrated cup of
coffee, as opposed to the 1990s, when the dynamics of institutional
racism and class domination are different? That is not to say the
essence of racism has changed; rather, its manifestations are different.
Therefore, new strategies and programs challenging inequality will
be different as well.

WEST: I think you're absolutely right. Let me just add a historical note
here. Since the beginning of the human adventure there has been a variety of mythological formulations and ideological articulations that
have tried to defend power and privilege by appealing to a host of different features and traits of people. The most vicious was the construction of white supremacy. . . . I like to talk about white supremacy more than just race, per se, because it's a way of acknowledging the
degree to which it is inextricably linked to asymmetric relations of
power. It takes us back to the age of Europe, roughly 1492 to 1945.
This is a particular moment in the history of the human adventure
when this vicious construct of white supremacy is articulated in order
to degrade black bodies, in order to control and exploit them.

Now it isn't only black bodies, it's red bodies and brown bodies as well,
but it emerges at a particular moment, at a moment in which those nations
between the Ural mountains and the Atlantic Ocean are about to engage
in an economic takeoff, which is predicated on imperial and colonial expansion, in the so-called New World. Then there was 1885 in Berlin, with
Africa, but it's a larger ongoing process that is to be understood. We are
simply dealing with some of the major results, consequences, and effects
of living now, forty-nine years after this "Age of Europe," but the devas-

tation is one with which we have yet to fully come to grips; which is to say, the social costs of the so-called Age of Reason and Rationality. The underside of the voices of those human beings who were viewed as subhuman begins, slowly but surely, to move to the center of the historical stage as the decolonization process started in the middle part of this century. These people viewed the public face of European "modernity" as one of terror, horror, and hatred. The whip, the police stick, the bombs. . . . Now, people often say, "Oh, he's histrionic, might feel bad, feel self-pity," etc. We're talking about "now." The present is history. There are historical residues in the present linked to the past, and yet the present is also different. But it's different primarily because people decided at a particular moment, "We're not going to put up with this. We're going to organize. We're going to mobilize."

We need vision to do that. We need analysis to do that, and at the present moment it seems to me we need, more than anything else, a vision of hope grounded on a radical democratic tradition that keeps track of the humanity of all ordinary people such that they're able to feel as if they're having a say at the highest levels of the decision-making processes of the institutions that guide and regulate their lives. That will be very difficult, precisely because of the right-wing consolidation we're seeing, not just in this country but in Europe, and the corrupt neocolonial leadership in so-called third world nations.

By "third world" we simply mean the places where the majority of humankind—everyday folk not at all unlike ourselves—live and die. By "everyday," I just mean people who are fundamentally concerned about keeping radical democratic values alive. You see, what is distinctive about the United States is that here you actually have an experiment in democracy. And as Malcolm X said, you have "niggers," victims of American democracy. That's your scientific definition.

Malcolm's absolutely right, because what do you have? You have a democracy predicated on white supremacy. You have a democracy based in part on this profound hatred of . . .

MARABLE: The "Master Race" concept.

WEST: Very much so. . . . For 188 years they can, for the most part, bypass that black suffering I talked about before and think they are the most democratic, enlightened, tolerant, free nation in the world! You see? The hypocrisy that black freedom fighters have always acknowledged. Not until the 1960s do we actually raise the question "Is multiracial democracy a possibility?" Maybe. But there's this strong tradition in the black freedom struggle that says, "Look. American democracy simply does not have the capacity to be multiracial." That's the black nationalist claim. That's what [Marcus] Garvey used to say right in front of Liberty Hall, 138th Street, every week: "As long as there are black people in America, they will live lives of disaster and ruin. They've got to go, just like the Jews in Europe. They've proved they can't be protected. Their humanity cannot be acknowledged. Find a place where that can happen. Look around to see where you can find a place. Look in Central America, etc., look in the Middle East." Black nationalists say the same thing: "You've got to find a place where black folk can be protected, acknowledged and recognized." But the black nationalist tradition has never been able to generate a credible response to the "land" question, and therefore we talk more about states of mind than nation states.

As a radical democrat, I want to say I certainly understand the impulse behind black nationalists. There's a "Garveyite" skeleton that ought to be hanging in every radical democrat's closet, all the time, because that's the pessimism. There's not a whole lot of evidence that one could present to the black nationalists and say, "You're wrong. There's overwhelming support in white America for black humanity." There's always a slice of white brothers and sisters who are open, but they cut against the grain in their own respective ways. They get in deep trouble by going against white supremacy in their white community.

MARABLE: Let's apply the insight that you have on race and class relations inside the United States to the global dynamics that are occurring presently. Now, since 1945, we've had a political bifurcation of the entire world, between a Soviet/Communist model and a capitalist model. The whole theory of noncapitalist development and socialist orientations, as well as the political movement of nonalignment, was predicated on the division of that world. Now you have a collapse of that bifurcation, so sisters and brothers in Europe are confronting race in a new way. What are the alternatives, when you have neofascism, which is part of the parliamentary power and the governing coalition in Italy? What are the alternatives, when you have a crisis of progressive politics in the Caribbean, as social democratic parties are desperately seeking neoliberal solutions in a period of globalized capitalism?

WEST: I think the most important feature of what happened in 1989, with the collapse of the Soviet empire, was that you no longer had in place, on a global scale, a countervailing power to U.S. capital.

What I mean by that is, the American empire itself is primarily concerned both with geographical/geopolitical presence and expansion, as well as the various markets for capital accumulation, primarily taking the form of transnational corporations, but not solely that. With the collapse of the Soviet empire, given all of its inequalities and brutalities, etc., it did nevertheless provide a countervailing force, so that persons in Africa, leaders in Asia—what have you—could pit both against one another in order to try to create some space for themselves. It was very difficult, but it was a world in which they were able to gain access to resources, for example, from the Soviet empire, even as it repressed and regimented its own people. This was not just morally unacceptable, but led to a political backlash in terms of people being open to any social change. That's the situation we face now.

But I think the most important thing for radical democratic politics today is to attempt to create countervailing institutions, associations, vision, and perspectives vis-à-vis the global "commodification" that is occurring under the aegis of, for the most part, transnational corporations. That is a gargantuan task, but a fundamental one. Why? Because if in fact we're unable to create some countervailing forces, we are going to see humanity perishing on a level we've never seen before, and it's already prefigured, less than a mile from here [Harlem]. It's already prefigured. It's just not highlighted, because we live in a nation that puts such little value on black pain. But if the same pain were at work in white working-class communities, you'd either have a full-fledged "Baptist" movement or a full-fledged radical democratic movement.

MARABLE: One of the things that a number of my students have asked about are details concerning your own intellectual, personal, and political evolution. We are all connected, Cornel, with a black intellectual tradition of sisters and brothers who have attempted, over a period of time, to critique the Leviathan you've just described. How would you characterize your own work ideologically and theoretically? Who had an impact upon your own personal and theoretical development?

WEST: That's a tough question. I can get rather narcissistic about these things. I'm not that important to spend that much time talking about my formation.

I'd begin with mom, who's here. (*Applause.*) I'm quite serious about that. You see, as a person of African descent, living in America, my first response to my encounter with this absurd situation is some kind of spiritual source, for starters. So that I began first as a person on a visceral level. What keeps me going has to do with the flow of black love that gave me a sense of myself, as articulated in Coltrane's saxophone solos. . . . What sustains me are those beautiful black voices, whether it be Aretha [Franklin], or even sisters who don't sound as good as Aretha. . . . I have to live everyday. I don't just live in the library with texts. So, early on, I had to have that grounding in this very rich spiritual tradition.

Brother Jim Washington has a book coming out in November called *Conversations with God*, two centuries of prayers that black folk have prayed to deal with their absurd situation. Now we could argue whether religion is the "opiate of the people," etc., etc., and most of it is, yes, but these are how folk are responding to our absurd situation, to keep black love and black joy and black community alive long enough so we can at least believe in ourselves . . .

So once you move toward that sphere, I would certainly argue that Du Bois has meant so much. *The Souls of Black Folk* has meant so much.

MARABLE: Let's explore the connections between faith and social transformation. Is spirituality central to the black intellectual tradition?

WEST: I believe that it is. I believe the first step is to acknowledge that the question is an important one, because we often find black intellectuals who have been so thoroughly duped by a certain truncated secular sensibility that they would deny Coltrane in the name of some intellectual figure, as if he's not a towering intellectual. Black music is one of the great artistic achievements of the twentieth century.

MARABLE: So there is implicitly a political economy in the blues in Leadbelly. By our understanding of what blues means, we may also comprehend the suffering of black farmers and day laborers in the Mississippi delta.

WEST: That's right. That it's not just exotic. Not just a voyeuristic perception of how these "primitive people get turned on." They're trying to make sense of their situation, and the musical tradition has been one of the means by which black creativity and black originality could be articulated, led to struggle at its best.

MARABLE: But, in the context of the political economy of race in the 1980s and 1990s, you would get a "Grand Master Flash and the Furious Five."

WEST: Absolutely right.

MARABLE: But one of the major problems I have with the question of faith, culture, and transformation is the tendency of the oppressed to parochialize our visions of social change. That is, if we contemplate our own situation as one of unmerited suffering, and through our struggle for ourselves, our collective selves, we articulate a vision of humankind, of ourselves as human beings, validating our existence. Yet that validation, all too often, is fragmentary; that is, we struggle against the contradiction of race but do not struggle against the contradiction of homophobia. Or, we don't struggle against the contradiction of gender inequality, or other kinds of social contradictions. So you get voices out of the black struggle that talk about empowerment, that talk about humanity, and yet do not take seriously the fight against sexism. How do we begin to make those kinds of intellectual, moral, and political connections?

WEST: I think ultimately it's a question of moral, political, and ideological maturity. That is to say, all of us are born of circumstances not of our own choosing, therefore find ourselves shaped by a variety of different communities with their own parochialisms. We tend to focus on that which most immediately affects us, and as one lives one's life one can make these connections if one is able to exercise empathetic imagination. That is to say, an imagination that's able to empathize and sympathize with the suffering of others. To expand one's empathetic imagination requires not just courage but maturity, and by maturity all I mean is an acknowledgment of just how complex the world is, and acknowledgment of the fundamental need one has to grow. That's why Malcolm X is such a wonderful example; because Malcolm was somebody who continually challenged himself and grew intellectually and ethically. That takes tremendous courage. Tremendous courage. It calls into question one's own views of the world, based on a particular kind of suffering that was undeniable in his case, and in the case of black folk. It took a tremendous struggle for him to extend his empathetic imagination and recognize, lo and behold, "the suffering that I have been so preoccupied with has certain analogies with the suffering of white working men, with brothers and sisters in Appalachia, and has connections with brown folk and sisters of all colors." That's a very difficult process, and certain bonds of affection will support you when you feel as if the world that you are calling into question can no longer support you. I think, again, the internationalism and the universalism of the best of the radical democratic tradition and the best of the democratic socialist tradition are the means by which certain standards of moral, political, and ideological maturation, or maturity, can take place.

Now this doesn't mean that one simply trashes people who are obsessed with one particular kind of oppression. You simply push them, lovingly, firmly, to see that the world is more complex. Because people often say, "Wait a minute. You're trying to push me to make a connection to another form of oppression, such that it's going to downplay the oppression I began with." And they're right, that has often happened: "Oh, don't be so concerned about the black thing, the black suffering. Don't you know there are people over here who are suffering too? Yeah, but that doesn't help me. You see? 'Can't we talk about this?' Well, I'm suspicious talking about both of them, because you want to displace mine."

You see, there's a certain kind of suspicion that's built into that kind of language. Therefore, radical democrats like ourselves have to be able to come up with strategies to show people that this black suffering that you've been concerned about, or maybe this black, male suffering that you've been fundamentally concerned about is not going to be erased, downplayed, or ignored if you focus on black female suffering. If we're able to talk about them in such a way, then you can move with what you began with, and also grow and mature—to make these kinds of connections. Why? Because in the end, you're fundamentally concerned about freedom. In the end, if you really want to engage in forms of struggle that are effective, not just morally but also politically, you're going to have to make these connections. Partly because what you're up against is the power of capital, the rule of capital. They've already made the connection; that's why they want to keep us divided. They've made the connection: "Keep all these folk, brown versus black versus yellow, fighting each other. Because we, the oligarchy of our day, the plutocrats of our day, the pigmentocrats of our day, we know if these folk keep fighting, then our power and privilege are secure. And anytime they start organizing, we'll either kill their leaders, or try to buy them off, or incorporate them or absorb them. But if you have enough of a grassroots movement, they're going to bring some power and pressure to bear." (*Applause.*) That's what we're all about. That's what a radical democratic struggle is all about. (*Applause.*)

MARABLE: More than almost any intellectual in this country, you have been identified, over the last decade, with the vision and politics of democratic socialism. Now we're in a period of time where democratic socialist options seem very bleak. Throughout western Europe, the left has been losing electorally. In the United States, the left is weaker than it has ever been in the twentieth century. Do you continue to have faith in the possibility of something that approximates democratic socialism, and, if so, what?

WEST: When we talk about socialism, we're not engaged in some kind of internecine ideological debate about who or what does not have the blueprint for the future. We're talking about all those who have a desire for justice and freedom, under what we are up against, and what folks around the world are up against, in the twenty-first century. That's why I like the countervailing forces, as I said before. But what socialism has always claimed was that there must be some institutional means by which capital has accountability to everyday folk. That's the basic claim, and it's a radically democratic claim. Because, if that's the case, then they're more likely not going to choose to be poor or have inadequate health care or decrepit education, etc. . . .

I must say, living in the moment which I do, on the surface, it looks bleak. No doubt about that. You don't' have to read the front page of the *New York Times* to realize how bleak things are. But the *New York Times* gives you the image and the symptoms, they never give you the cause of the problem. The image and the symptoms really make you fell powerless and enforce stereotypes. All these black folks here think of themselves as victims, unable to engage in action or resistance. That's typical mainstream media coverage of black folk. Black folk are "problem people" who have problems they themselves are unable to come to terms with. On the surface it looks bleak, but this is the way both the issue of vision and the issue of hope and the issue of spirituality come in. Because no one chooses to be a freedom fighter, based solely on the fact that victory's around the corner. (*Applause.*)

22

Race in American Life:
A Conversation with John Hope Franklin

On Monday evening, November 9, 1998, Dr. John Hope Franklin, noted historian of the African American experience, engaged in a conversation with Manning Marable, sponsored by the Institute for Research in African-American Studies at Columbia University. Dr. Franklin had just completed a turbulent year as head of President William Jefferson Clinton's National Initiative on Race. Dr. Franklin discussed his personal history and development as a young black man growing up under segregation, his craft as a historian and scholar, and his views on the politics of race today. The following remarks are selected excerpts from the actual exchange, only slightly revised.

JOHN HOPE FRANKLIN: You don't know how good this makes me feel to be back in touch with real live students and have the opportunity to exchange ideas, points of view, thoughts, and so forth, with you. I've lived a fairly long time—not as long as some people, but longer than most people—and I am continuing to learn. I have had experiences in the past six months that have taught me things that I never thought I would learn. I have also learned that human nature is slow to change, if indeed it ever changes. I'd think that the questions that are going to be propounded by Manning Marable will give me the opportunity to say many of the things that I would say if he were not questioning me. So let me just say one or two brief things that perhaps he will not be concerned about.

One of them is that I was born in a village eighty-three years ago with no running water, no electricity, no plumbing of any kind (not indoors, anyway), and with the bleakest, most difficult days and nights: wondering what to do, how to do [it], and if there was anything to do. That was my life until I was ten years old, when it was suggested that a certain candidate for the Supreme Court did not have running water until he was seven years old. And now that he's an associate justice, I think that if you don't get running water until you're ten years old, you might be a candidate for the chief justiceship.

But for those of you who don't know what it is to live under those circumstances: no parks, no libraries. One of our great recreations was to clean the chimneys of the lamps that we would use in the dark. Another was to get the Sears Roebuck catalogue with my sister. She would pick out things on her side and I would pick things out on mine, wondering if you're gonna have anything during Christmas or for any other holiday. The thing that I think sustained us the most was—you might not believe this—our family, our parents, were educated people. My mother was a graduate of Roger Williams University. My father went to Roger Williams, Morehouse College (then called Atlanta Baptist College). Their presence, their outlook, their point of view sustained us.

My mother used to tell me she didn't want me to do very much, but she wanted me to do the best I could. And she would be satisfied with nothing less than the best. She used to add to that "the angels couldn't do any better than the best; be satisfied with nothing less than your best." And as for my father, he read all the time, day and night. Until I went to college, I never saw my father a night where he wasn't reading or writing. I thought that that was what you were supposed to do at night. I'm still having problems with television because I have to write, because that's what my Daddy did. One of the greatest pleasures of my life was to take some of his writings, [as] I did three years ago with my son, and edit the autobiography that he wrote in his late years. That was a kind of realization, even after his death, of the great aspirations that he had all his life. Those two people have been a kind of model for me, rigorous and uncompromising.

[During] my life as a kid, the Chicago Civic Opera Company came to Tulsa, Oklahoma each year after they completed their winter and spring tour in the city of Chicago. They would come there for about ten days and I went to the opera—but not with my parents. They wouldn't be caught in any place that was segregated. They were very liberal. They said, "If you want to go and demean yourself, disgrace yourself . . ."

I said in a documentary that that is when I learned to love *La Bohème*, *Traviata*, *Madame Butterfly*. Then I reproached myself—as I continue to reproach myself—that I learned under those conditions. I said I shouldn't have gone. I am just suggesting some of the things that have had an impact on me one way or the other. Until this very day, I regret having learned opera under those circumstances.

What I'm trying to suggest is that my parents had higher ideals, and much higher standards and much greater honor and much greater self-respect. I aspired to be like them because they were really something. I haven't reached there, but, with the help of society, at least I don't go to Jim Crow places. I don't think that's to my credit. It's to [the] credit of the society in which we live. And I'm going to stop, Manning, and maybe we can just talk about the things you want to talk about.

MANNING MARABLE: Your initial comments are a good segue to talk about how you grew up in Oklahoma and attended Fisk University in the Jim Crow era. We had an earlier conversation this evening and you talked about our mutual love of Fisk University. When I taught there, what I loved about it was the history of the place. In the chapel, where I'm sure you've spoken many times, you stand behind the podium and you can recall Du Bois's famous challenge in 1924 against Fayette McKenzie in his effort to turn Fisk away from higher education. A decade later, Du Bois delivered a famous speech at that same podium, addressing the future of the Negro college.

FRANKLIN: I heard him deliver that speech.

MARABLE: I wonder if you could talk about growing up in the Jim Crow South in the 1930s, attending college, growing up in Oklahoma. I knew about the Tulsa race riots in 1921 and that was a background for how you grew up.

FRANKLIN: I was born in the village of Rentersville, where I was, by the way, a few weeks ago. It's just a pittance of a place. I don't think the population is even one hundred now. My father, who moved there in 1911, could not make a decent living for his family there. He decided to leave and he went to Tulsa in 1920. He left us there [in Rentersville]. My mother's school was not out, and we were in school. As soon as school was out, we [would move to] Tulsa, where he had already made wonderful connections. He was thriving as a youngish lawyer and got a house for us and furnished it.

All of a sudden we could hear nothing. We couldn't hear from him and we didn't know what had happened. Then we got the *Muskogee* [newspaper] and we learned there was a race riot in Tulsa. There was no telephone, radio, television—no way to communicate those seventy-odd miles, except if you were lucky to get a newspaper. This newspaper described the riot, and we didn't know if my father was living or dead. They said dozens—scores of people—had been killed. The homes of black Tulsans had been looted and then bombed. This was the first use of the bomb after World War I on civilians in this country. They just bombed us out. We finally got a message from my father saying he was still alive and unhurt, but absolutely without any resources—not even a change of clothing, because he had been interned in the convention hall with hundreds of other blacks. To make a long story short, we couldn't move that summer because there was nowhere to move, nowhere for anyone to move. We had to endure four more years in Rentersville. We did not move until 1925.

Then I went to middle school and then high school in Tulsa and graduated from the high school—the Booker T. Washington High School—in 1931. I (fast forward) was there last year to be inducted into the Booker T. Washington Hall of Fame. It is now the finest and most sought-after high school in the city. It is not even on the borderline; it's over in the black ghetto. But white people in Tulsa would kill to get their kids in. David Boren, the former senator, was telling me—when I was in his house a few months ago, in Oakland and Norman, Oklahoma, where he is now president of the University of Oklahoma—he says it's the best high school in the state.

I had my first real experience with segregation, with racial humiliation, in Tulsa. Going through a small town south of Rentersville, where we did our shopping, the railroad train had stopped because we had flagged it down. We got on the coach in front of us and sat down, and then we found out it was a white coach. We were told by a white conductor that we could not sit there. My mother said, "We cannot move while the train is moving. My children might get hurt." And he said, "Well, I'll stop the train." Instead of letting us move to another coach, he put us off in the woods.

That was one incident that gave my mother the opportunity to tell us what this was all about. I was crying, and she said, "Don't cry. There's nothing to cry about. Man put us off and that's all right. What you need to remember is that there was no one on the train better than you. Only because there is some crazy law that says you must not sit with these other people, that's why you were put off. But remember, you don't have the time or the energy or the emotion to waste crying about some terrible people like this." She says, "You must remember one thing: that you are good enough to ride anywhere with anybody. You take that through life." On that day I stopped fretting and worrying about all this foolishness that we've seen. I have to put my energies somewhere else and try and solve some of the problems which I confront, which all of us confront.

There were many other instances in Oklahoma. But I thought that now, since I was leaving Oklahoma, I was leaving that behind me. I was going to Tennessee. I was going to a university, and perhaps I would be sheltered from that. To the extent that I could, I did shelter myself from that, to be very frank. But I did have to go downtown now and then in Nashville, Tennessee.

I went down when I was a freshman. It was the first week or so when I was in Nashville. When we got ready to get on the streetcar to come back out to Fisk from downtown Nashville, I found myself with one piece of money, and that was a $20 bill. I think that was the only $20 bill I ever had in college. I walked to the window of the transfer station, and as I put my money in the window, I apologized for having a large bill. I said, "Sorry, this is all that I have. However you want to change—if you want to give me dollar bills or anything" And he said, "Listen. No nigger tells me how to make change." I'm sixteen. I don't know what's going on. He says, "You can't tell me how to make change," and then he proceeded to give me back my change in nickels and dimes. I had just a wadful. I don't know whether it was $20 or not: $18, $19.75. I don't know, but it was a searing experience. I said, What in the world was going on? I can count how many times I went back to downtown Nashville after that over the next four years. I just couldn't stand it. I couldn't bear it.

Many years later I was doing research in the state department archives in history in Montgomery, Alabama. The then-archivist [was] Ms. Marie Bankhead Owens, the sister of John Bankhead and the senator Bankhead and the aunt of Talulah Bankhead. I went in to see her to get permission to look at the Governor Winthrop papers that were still under seal in connection with the research I was doing. I went into her office, and she did not invite me to sit down, and I did not sit down. I told her what I wanted, and she said, "Sure. You can have whatever you want." She said, "How are they treating you?" And I said, "They're treating me very well, thank you very much. I was able to get all the materials I want, and this is the one thing they told me I'll have to get permission from you." And she said, "Well, I'm delighted to give you permission."

And then she said, "They tell me there's a Harvard nigger here. Have you seen him?" And her secretary was in the next room—I learned all this etiquette: the doors don't close between a white woman and a black man, you see, and her secretary could hear everything she was saying to me—and she said, "That's him, Ms. Owens. That's him." And she said, "You a Harvard nigger?" And I said, "I went to Harvard, yeah." And she said, "You don't act like a Harvard nigger." I didn't know how one was supposed to act.

She knew. She said, "You got right nice manners." And she said, "Sit down." (At last I can get off my feet.) She said, "You got right nice manners." And she said, "Where were you born and raised?" And she said, "That won't do it." And then she said, "Where did you go to college?" And I said, "Nashville, Tennessee." And she said, "That's it, good ol' Confederate state."

And I thought about that man in the ticket booth: that's where I learned my manners? She came to all those conclusions just by my standing up and not sitting down until she asked me, just being gracious to her as I only knew how to be. Then she wanted to keep me all afternoon to talk to me and I was in a hurry to get back and work on those papers and get out of there. I then became great and good friends with her. I don't know how she would feel now that my own Ph.D. student is head of the archives, but I hope that she would like it. Wherever she is, maybe she found out. I don't know.

MARABLE: One of those things that is most interesting for my generation of black intellectuals and historians is exploring the connection between you and Du Bois. Part of that connection is Fisk University and part of that connection is the craft of history. How and why did you devote your life to history and the pursuit of African American history, at a time when very few scholars took that step? Second, what was your actual relationship with Dr. Du Bois?

FRANKLIN: Du Bois was an icon all during my childhood and my young manhood and at home and later at Fisk. I am named for W. E. B. Du Bois's best friend, John Hope, who taught my mother and father at Roger Williams College. It was my father who had followed John Hope to Atlanta Baptist College when my mother had graduated and gone back to west Tennessee to teach. There was always W. E. B. Du Bois before me because I had been named for John Hope. So when Du Bois came to Tulsa, Oklahoma, in February 1926, my mother and father were so excited that Du Bois was coming to town that they took me to see him. I don't remember much about that visit. I was eleven years old. I was trying to hear him, but one of the things that distracted me was that he had on a full dress suit and I had never seen a full dress suit before—white tie and tails—and I wondered why all this getup. Later I learned that he was wearing his decoration, two great decorations he had received from Haiti and Liberia. And you only wore those when you wore full dress clothes. So there he was. If I didn't remember what he said, I do remember that outfit, and I said, This man is worth watching anyway.

I saw him many times after that. You mentioned that he visited Fisk. He not only came to Fisk and turned it around in 1924 when he spoke there and literally was the cause of a revolution and the running away of the white president, Fayette McKenzie, but he came back often. He was there in 1933, when he delivered this remarkable speech on the role and function of the American Negro college. And then he came back more than once when I was there. I never got close to him during that period of time

MARABLE: Did anybody get close to him?
FRANKLIN: I think not many people. I was never even introduced to him. I didn't get a chance to even meet him. My father and mother did not know him when he came to Tulsa. They just admired him because he was who he was. It was not really until I was in graduate school at Harvard that I saw him again. He came to speak, not at Harvard. He wouldn't speak at Harvard in those days. Professor Schlesinger, my seminar adviser and the father of the present Arthur Schlesinger Jr., suggested to us that we ought to go. He told us about his great admiration for Dr. Du Bois, so we all went down to hear him and, once more, I didn't get a chance to say anything to him. It was not until I had completed all my graduate work and was working on my dissertation in North Carolina that I saw him close up for the first time.

I was having my meal at a small hotel in Raleigh. You must remember this was 1939 and there is no place in North Carolina or in Virginia that you could even go to the toilet. So you had to discipline yourself from Washington to Atlanta. And there's no place to eat except [a] hotel in Richmond and the Arcade Hotel in Raleigh. And you can sit in this dining room and see everyone. They all pass through there and the word was out: if you wanted to eat, you eat in the Arcade Hotel in Raleigh. That was the last place you could eat without getting out and fending for food in some backwater.

I sat there eating my dinner one evening and I saw across the room: the man. He was driving from New York to Atlanta (or vice versa), and he was teaching at Atlanta University at that time. So I said, This is my chance. I got him all to myself, and I'm gonna make the most of it.

So, pulling myself up and taking all the courage I had (I was all of twenty-three at the time, or something like that), I went over to him. He was eating or reading, and I said, "Dr. Du Bois, my name is John Hope Franklin." I wanted that "John Hope, John Hope"—I was named for his best friend. He didn't even act like I was in the room. He was reading and eating.

That's one down, I got two to go. I said, "I am a graduate of Fisk University, class of 1935." That's the most clannish crowd of Fisk graduates. I know, I can name most of them. Charles Wesley's class and other classes, we just know them all. We were familiar with them. I knew he was the class of 1888. Everybody, all Fisk people, knew that. Not a word, not a word.

Then finally I said to him (this is all I got left), "I am a graduate of Harvard University in the field of history and I am now working on my doctoral dissertation." Without even looking up to see what I was or who I was or how I was, he said, "How do you do?"

Later when I got to know Du Bois quite well, I reminded him of that, and I asked him, "Why did you do that?" He said, "Well, you know I am very shy." And he also said, "You know I am also always very preoccupied." And that was all. That was his explanation. It was a very good lesson for me. I didn't tell him this: I said that night, when he wouldn't even look at me, wouldn't even speak to me, I said, "If I write ten less books, I will never treat a graduate student like that." I've tried to keep that promise to myself.

But this had to do nothing with my deep respect for him, my esteem for the man and the mind. He remained the icon. No bad manners of his could get around the fact that he was one of the great minds of our time. I greatly admired and respected him then, as I do now, and I think that that was generally true.

You see, we didn't have multitudes of people to look up to, but people like Du Bois and, later, [E. Franklin] Frazier and, later, [Alain] Locke and Oliver Cromwell Cox and [Carter G.] Woodson—just a few others. These were our icons. These were the people we held in the highest esteem. When one of them came to Fisk's campus you couldn't get near the place a half-hour before they were scheduled to speak. It was just jam-packed because they meant so much to all of us. We continue to hold these people in the highest esteem. They were the great intellectuals. They were the ones telling us how to go, what to do, how to husband our time and how to organize for the future and how to remain courageous and strong in the face of the most unmitigated insults and degradation. It took a lot to withstand that type of experience. They helped us do it and so we thought a great deal of them.

MARABLE: *From Slavery to Freedom* has been a kind of core text in the canon of African American thought for half a century. How did you become committed to the life of the mind of the historian of the black experience? And how did you write—why did you write—*From Slavery to Freedom*?

FRANKLIN: Let me say my commitment at the outset was not to African American history but to history. I had a mentor at Fisk, a white man by the name of Theodore Currier. He was the chair of the department of history. He was a young man, just twelve years older than I was when I entered Fisk, and just a remarkable teacher. First of all, I went to Fisk to be a lawyer. I just couldn't wait to get back to practice law with my father. You see, I recognized the fact that he was a good lawyer. (Here I was at sixteen making a judgment.) But he was not a good businessman, because we were always poor. What he needed was a partner who was not only versed in the law but who was tough and who could get those bills and get that money and pay for that mortgage, especially when we lost our house my first year at Fisk. I was just determined.

But it was this professor at Fisk who came into our course in contemporary civilization and he gave a couple of lectures, and I said, "That was pretty good." And I said, "I better take a course with him." That was my own doing. I took a course and I forgot I was going to study law. I was so fascinated by the study of history. It was the study of history per se.

When I went to Cambridge—Harvard University—and I was going to study history, I was going to study British history. I got to Harvard and I found that if you studied Turkish history, you went to Turkey. If you studied British history, you went to Britain. And how was I ever gonna get to Britain? It was much more out of the question in 1936–1937 than going to the moon was. Anyway, where in the world is England? It's over there somewhere. Although I was terribly into British history, I said I better just let it alone.

Then I got interested in the beginnings of Christian Socialism. And then I learned that [another scholar] had finished his work and was publishing a book in that field. I said, "Well, that's not for me either. I can't make a mark there."

Then I remembered a paper I did on the free Negro in the antebellum South, just a general term paper. I remembered that and said, "Maybe there's something there." That's how I got interested in anything with respect to African Americans and history. [As] I pushed towards the end of my residence work at Harvard, I decided I'd like to get into that. So I looked around and then I decided to write my dissertation on free Negroes in North Carolina. That aroused my interest in the African American scene generally. There had not been a great deal at Fisk on the subject. So I didn't have a course in African American history. If you can keep this to yourself, I have never had a course in African American history.

By the time I got into the history of free Negroes in North Carolina, I did begin to spread out and see this was a very engaging field. But I never put my foot altogether in that field because I began to define it differently from what some other people might. You see, I don't think there is any such thing such as American history without African American history. You can't talk about the history of the United States without talking about African Americans. They are a part of it. All this talk about, "Now we'll do African American history." We've done it already, and I insist on that.

One of the things I've tried to do as I have branched out, and I have looked at the whole field, I have dragged along United States history with me. Sometimes I write about white people primarily, as in *Militant South* or as in *Southern Odyssey*. On the question of *The Militant South*, when it came out [there was] all this hustle and bustle undercover (which I've now discovered in the manuscripts at the Huntington Library) of "Franklin! What's Franklin doing writing about us?" I think I can write about them because they are us and we are they. I mean, we all are one in the effort to make this country strong, great, whatever. So I saw there were these big gaps and this lack of understanding and knowledge of one part of the history of this country and that was the part we call African American history. So I began to focus on that and make honest the entire field of American history. That's what I've tried to do in all of these efforts over the years.

I wish I could say I woke up one morning and had a great vision of writing the whole history of my people. That sounds good, except that's not the way it happened. I got a letter from Alfred Knopf, the senior college editor, saying, "We'd like to publish a history of Negroes" (as they said at that time) "and we understand you are the person to do it." And they had done a lot of asking around. They had written Schlesinger at Harvard and some of them nominated me. And so they came after me, and I said, "No thank you. I'm busy."

I was working on *The Militant South* at the time. I told him what I was doing, hoping they'd say, "Well, that's fine, we'd like to publish that." They didn't say a thing like that. They came back with the argument that while "this is a great subject you have, and it will be good at anytime, but the thing we need now is a history of Negroes in the United States. And we wish you'd reconsider."

Then he came down. I was living and teaching at the North Carolina College for Negroes in Durham and he came down there and talked me into it. He literally talked me into it. He offered me an advance in royalties—$500—and I was just swept off my feet. It was at that point that I really thought I was an author. I had arrived, you see: I got an advance on royalties. I accepted his offer and then I went off to write.

I began in the fall of 1945, just sort of looking around, and I found there was no model. I knew the [Carter G.] Woodson book, and, while it was a valiant effort, it was not my kind of book. By that time, I knew Mr. Woodson, too. I had gone to the Association for the Study of Negro Life and History for the first time in 1936 and met him there and admired him greatly for what he was doing—a remarkable man, tremendously devoted to this cause.

But there was no model. Then I was just stumbling around, just reading the shelves, and I found some other things. There is a very important segment of history, literature, folklore, anthropology, that dates from about 1875 to 1915 or 1920—books that were written by blacks in defense of themselves. It was almost sad. These people were writing books about the "Negro beast" and this sort of thing, and they were trying to answer them—black intellectuals. Crogman down in Atlanta and then even Booker T. Washington took a hand in writing the story of the Negro. Either he wrote or it is rumored that someone wrote it for him. It's rumored that Robert Andrew Park . . .

MARABLE: Robert Park did write that.

FRANKLIN: But there were not any models. But then I ran into a book that was written earlier in this period in 1882 by a man named George Washington Williams. It was two volumes, it had footnotes, appendices, bibliographical notes—in 1882!—and I was curious about him. He almost threw me off track because I got more interested in him than I got in this subject. But I put him back on the back burner, and next time I was in Washington I said to Dr. Woodson, "What's with this character George Washington Williams?" "Well, he's a very interesting man and he died before I was old enough to know anything about him," and, he said, "I think he deserves a great deal of attention." And I said, "He certainly does, I think." And he said, "Why don't you write a paper on him and read it at the next meeting of the association?" Which I did. I read it, and it's the first published piece on George Washington Williams. Later I was to turn my attention entirely to him.

But for the moment I was working on a book that would be called *From Slavery to Freedom*. I finished it and published it in less than two years in 1947. And it celebrated its fiftieth birthday last year. I went along for the ride. It does have a life of its own. It's now in its seventh edition and we're working on the eighth edition. I will not review it because it would take a fair amount of time and, second, I would be more critical than it deserves in its venerable age.

MARABLE: I'm sure the audience would like you to talk about your role as chair of the president's advisory board, the President's Initiative on Race. How did President Clinton first approach you on this issue?
FRANKLIN: I first met the president in 1992. He was running for president at the time and I was in Durham in North Carolina and he was coming to Durham. He was governor of Arkansas at the time. One of his advance people called me on the phone and said, "Governor Clinton would like to see you and would like to meet you. Can you be in town tomorrow and can you meet him?" I said, "Well, I don't know. I'll work him into my schedule." So I did and I met him the next day. It was a very interesting experience. At the same time, I met Al Gore, who was traveling with him, and both of their families. They were in this big bus. I met Hillary and Tipper the same day, and their children.

Well, he talked not about politics at all. We talked about history and I said, Well, this man is very well read, remarkably well read. And he and

Al Gore were talking about the origins of man, where civilization began; they wanted to talk about the argument for its having begun in Africa and so forth. We went on like this for forty-five minutes, like there was not a campaign going on. Finally someone said, "We are three hours late. We got to go to Wilmington." So we wrapped that up and they went on.

The next time I had an opportunity to get involved with the administration on race was when Al Gore asked me if I would manage some sessions he wanted to have on race at the vice president's residence in Washington. He said, "I want to have it, but you're the one who knows it. And I want to give you the opportunity to lead us on." He and Tipper had three dinners, at the end of which we had about a two-and-a-half-hour discussion on race. They had different people there each night. He told me at one point how interested the president was in this whole matter.

Shortly after that I won the Charles Frankel Award, which was presented at the White House for my work in the humanities, and the president and I had another opportunity to talk together about this. I sent him some books and he wrote me back profusely thanking me for them. It was clear he had read them. Then he presented, to my great astonishment, the Presidential Medal of Freedom in 1995, and once more we had a long talk. In presenting me to the audience in the East Room, he said things about me that I had no idea he knew about: my struggles and some of the efforts I had made to do something about this race problem. He called me on that day a "prisoner of American racism." And so I knew those things about him.

He did not call me. He asked Bob Nash to call me, the head of White House personnel called me, and said, "Look, the president wants you to do this. Will you do this?" And I said, "I don't know whether I will or not." I said, "I can't say yes or no, now. I have to think about it." And he said, "That's fair enough."

And so I thought about it a while. I had practical matters: first, is my health good enough to stand all this carrying on? So I went to my doctor and I talked to him about it. Then I went to my cardiologist and I talked to my cardiologist. I would have talked to, if I knew then what I know now, I would have found me a psychiatrist. But back then I didn't have one.

Then I talked to my son, because it was a family matter. And then I talked to a few friends confidentially, and I decided that this was a remarkable opportunity. Being a historian, I knew what had happened in this field beforehand. I knew, for example, that no president of the United

States had ever—without pressure on him immediately as a result of riots or something like that—had said, "Let's look at this thing and see what we can do" under relatively peaceful times, without a breathtaking, hair-raising emergency. I said, This is somewhat encouraging. The man isn't playing. He isn't playing about this, so maybe it's worth taking on.

But I knew that there would be opposition from all kinds of quarters. There'd be political opposition from knee-jerk politicians who wouldn't want him to have credit for anything; they would be opposed to it. Then there were people who felt that we had already done enough, you know: "What in the world do you need? You got the civil rights act, you got the Voting Rights Act. Now you want something else? What else do you want?"

The president apparently felt there was something else. I thought that was worth examining, since I felt that he would be on the side of wanting something else, you see. So I decided that I would take it on, knowing full well that it was going to be a terrible physical strain, emotionally and intellectually, perhaps. Everybody is gonna pick at you and pick on you. I did the best I could in trying to bury myself in the struggle of the next fifteen months, and it was a remarkable experience. I would be glad to share it with you, any part of it that you want me to share.

MARABLE: There have been a series of criticisms and controversies surrounding the President's Initiative on Race and I wondered if you could respond to four brief points.

The first criticism about the board was that its composition was flawed, because it should have included ideological conservatives such as Shelby Steele and Abigail Thernstrom, or even Dinesh D'Souza, people who oppose affirmative action.

Second, there was no representation of American Indians on the advisory board and there was criticism that Native American issues were not adequately integrated into the conceptual framework or definitions of the tasks of the board.

The third criticism [is] that the White House intervened in a heavy-handed manner. There are two sources that one could cite on the board itself. [First is] Thomas Keane, a Republican former governor of New Jersey and a member of the advisory board, who stated for the *New York Times* in September: "There is timidity on this question of race. As the year rolled on, people became, not the board but the people in the administration, became concerned. We were not encouraged to be bold. My recommendations were much bolder than anything contained in this report."

The fourth concern is the Monica Lewinsky scandal. The Monica Lewinsky scandal diverted the administration's attention and the president's attention from the vital work of the board. The example people give is how, during that fifteen-month period, the president's focus, which was wholehearted in June and July of 1997, shifted dramatically. At the first formal session of the National Conversation on Race, the president was in attendance. The first several meetings, several members of the Cabinet participated. But the last six months, no cabinet administrator was there, even when they were talking about issues that impacted that particular department. These were some of the major criticisms and I wondered if you could respond.

FRANKLIN: You walk me through them again as we go along. The one about the composition of the board [and] the critics who make that statement—I am sure they have many examples of presidents of the United States who will say, "Now I am going to appoint Franklin, who is for me, and I'm gonna appoint Abigail Thernstrom, who is opposed to me." Have you ever head of a president composing a commission, a board of people, who are opposed to his position? I haven't. I never heard of that. And, if he had appointed D'Souza, he then could not have appointed John Hope Franklin. It's as simple as that.

But this notion that when a president of the United States gets ready to appoint the Federal Trade Commission or whoever or whatever, that he's gonna appoint people who are in favor of him and people who are opposed to him, I don't know that's the way the political animal works. And so why would you expect the president to appoint to a board dealing with a problem that is so controversial, so highly explosive as race—and appoint a member of the Klan and a member of the NAACP? You know, like: That's a good spread. I don't know of any example.

Of course there are some commissions which are created bipartisan and in a bipartisan fashion. The law says you have so many Republicans and so many Democrats and so forth. That's understandable, because then you have to look around and find a decent Republican or a decent Democrat. I don't see that that as a valid criticism.

Now with respect to the Native Americans . . .

MARABLE: With the whole controversy that happened in Denver . . .

FRANKLIN: I think it was rather unfortunate the president did not appoint a Native American. He would have had a problem appointing a Native American because, don't forget, there are over five hundred tribes. He's not gonna satisfy the Choctaw if he had appointed someone from the Chickasaws or whatever. But I still would have hoped that he had appointed a Native American, and then we could have fought that out about what kind of Native American and whether this was a satisfactory thing. For, after all, they were here. It's theirs. We ran over them. We've done everything conceivable to degrade and dehumanize them.

So I was for it [the appointment]. But I didn't make the appointment and I have had no explanation on it. What we tried to do as a board was to make all kinds of amends. One was to appoint as senior consultants to the board two Native Americans, then to make every effort to give them a voice. We met with Indian leaders all over this country. We didn't meet with any other group as officially. We didn't meet with African Americans as a group. We didn't meet with Korean Americans or Hispanic Americans. We met with Native Americans more than once, not only in Denver, but in Phoenix and in San Jose. And then there were other meetings that were not regular board meetings where we met with them. So we did everything possible. We seriously considered holding a board meeting on a reservation. I think that was shot down by them themselves in the way they treated us in Denver.

We had met in Denver. I rushed to Denver, did not register at the hotel, went immediately to the area where there was a meeting with forty or fifty Indian leaders, tribal leaders, and met with them for two hours. It was a very cordial meeting. I rushed from there to register in the hotel to get a bite to eat before a public meeting at 7 o'clock, and Federico Peña and I were the program that night. The subject of the session was stereotypes. He was going to talk about his experiences being stereotyped in this country by non-Hispanics and how he was treated as a result.

Well, we got the impression, even while he was speaking, that there was some unrest, because he's a favorite son and all that, but they were mumbling and grumbling. He got through this and then I was to speak and they said no, "Oh, no, no." And I was not permitted to open my mouth. The American Indian Movement, I understand, a particular group of very extreme radical activist types, simply said, "You can't speak. We don't want to hear a thing you got to say." And, of course, that's all they had to do. I'm a peace-loving man, not combative at all. I didn't try to speak.

I thought it was unfortunate that this happened—and no one had more sympathy for the Indian cause than I. But I thought it was unfortunate that other people, especially white people, could see the two most degraded groups in this country fighting each other; the two farthest down were combating while someone runs off with the spoils. So I thought this was very unfortunate but there was nothing I could do about that at all. And we have a very strong recommendation in our report to the president about this question and about the need to do something in all kinds of areas, especially in economic and education and whatnot. We strongly recommended that to the president and hope he will do something. We made recommendations before our final report.

MARABLE: The third issue is about Tom Keane and the concerns that the actual proposals themselves were too timid and not vigorous enough.
FRANKLIN: Well, Tom Keane, let me say first—I don't mean anything, I'm not trying to get back at him—Tom Keane was the only member of the president's advisory board that did not attend many meetings.
MARABLE: He's been the most vocal critic.
FRANKLIN: Yes, he's been the most vocal critic. Now if we were under any pressure from the White House, I failed to feel it myself. He did go to the White House once when Abigail Thernstrom . . . when that crowd went to the White House. I was invited. I chose not to go. I go to the White House enough and I knew their line. And I didn't have time to go. They were having their day, and Tom Keane [was] the only member of the advisory board who went that day. Now, if he felt a lot of pressure, I did not. And I don't know other members of the board who felt a lot of pressure. We spoke openly, we met the president a number of times. I met him more than some of the other members of the board, and I always told him what I thought.

One day we were in the Oval Office and one of his assistants said to him, "Mr. President, your advisory board is really picking up steam. They're really gonna be active now." This is when we had been in existence for six months. I said, "Mr. President, I object to this line, to this interpretation of our activity." And I said, "We hit the ground running as much as we could." I said, "After all, you wouldn't expect any group to be doing the first month of its existence what its doing the sixth month of its existence." I said, "We were doing all right that first month." And he said, "I couldn't agree with you more." And so he left this person sort of hanging out there to dry.

Now with respect to the great, great recommendations that Tom Keane made that we didn't have, I don't know what they are. He was there when we voted on our recommendation. I think he was there. He wasn't there all that much. But I think he was there that day, and, frankly, he didn't say, "This is too timid, we got to go there and shake the the people up." I don't remember him saying anything like that.

So I am not going to entertain that as a valid criticism. I wish that he had been at more of the meetings and I wish that he had shared with us some of the strong feeling he had. Maybe we would have been a better board.

MARABLE: What about the Monica Lewinsky scandal?
FRANKLIN: I don't know, let me say, first of all, we were an advisory board. We were a board advising the president. We were not a commission like the Kerner Commission. We were not an agency like the Committee on Civil Rights that advised President Truman. And we certainly did not have the power that Archbishop Tutu had in South Africa. What we did do, I think, was to look at the problems which were before us. We sought to deal with them in a manner most expeditiously and most effectively as we could. Now I didn't expect the president to attend every meeting. After all, there are a few more things in the world for him to do beside ride herd over seven people and tell them to get on the stick and get busy. He came to a meeting and he might have stayed away because of the press.

The press misrepresented the board and its position in the most remarkable and unforgivable manner. Let me give you an example. The president and the vice president came to a meeting in September, September 30th, I believe it was, and we got to talking. We were all just discussing matters and we were talking about education and what we were going to try and do about education. The president made some comment about . . . he said, "Over there in Fairfax, Virginia, I understand there's a school where kids from a whole hundred language groups are there in the one school and they get along, and they are moving on, and they are studying." And he said, "This is remarkable. This is the sort of thing we ought to be interested in doing."

Well, the next day the paper said: "President Straightens Out the Board"; "President Commands the Board to Look into the Fairfax County Schools." And this is true. This is true. That was the kind of interpretation put on it. A woman from the Associated Press called me and said, "They tell me you're about out now." She says, "What are you gonna do when this is over?" and "You won't be there this time next month, will you?" And I said, "What are you talking about?" And she says, "The president is through with this board." You see what I'm talking about?

I don't know if the president had any idea of firing us or going to get anybody else. Every time I wrote—and what this young lady didn't know is that I wrote to the president every month, made a report to him, told him what we were doing—he would write me back, "Thank you very much" and throw in a comment on what we were doing. A lot of this isn't shown anywhere. He could march down there as he did at the Mayflower Hotel and sit in, and sit by me and the vice president there on the other side, and show the world that he is with the board. But that isn't getting the board anywhere. We had work to do, you know, if we were in Phoenix, or San Jose, or in somewhere else. You think he has time? I don't know that he has time to come and meet with us all the time. I read the minutes of the Kerner Commission and I don't think he met with them at all. Nor did Truman meet with his board at all. Now they expect, every time we meet, they expect the president of the United States to jump on a plane and jump somewhere and be with us and deliberate with us. I don't believe that is the way a presidentially appointed commission functions anyway.

Now with respect to the other members of the administration, I can't call the roll, but I am sure that Janet Reno has been at a meeting of ours less than six months ago. Rick Riley was at our meetings so frequently that I wondered whether the Department of Education was doing all right. And I was glad. I said to him one time, "Rick, you came to see whether Judy [Winston]'s doing her job." She was the undersecretary of education and general counsel, and she was our executive editor. She took me from the Department of Education. And I said, "You're just coming to all these meetings to be certain that Judy is all right."

I don't know that there was any great falling off. Of course, there was this burst of enthusiasm where one cabinet member after another came. Donna Shalala came and [Andrew] Cuomo came and the secretary of education, and so forth. And they got their word in and talked to us, but I didn't expect them to attend every board meeting—why should they attend every board meeting? And there were other people there. There were all kinds of people from the federal government and all that. When we got to talk about housing, we needed certain housing specialists and they came, they came. When we were talking about crime and the administration of justice, we had people from the Department of Justice. Janet Reno was there for that, and other people. And that wasn't six months ago. I don't know where this comes from.

MARABLE: You've gone through this experience with the initiative, you've studied the life and the historical experience of the African American people. What we've had to confront in this country fundamentally is a system of racial inequality. Can racism be dismantled in this country, based on your experience? How optimistic are you that we can one day triumph over racism?

FRANKLIN: I am cautiously optimistic. But if I were not optimistic, I would jump out the window or something, because I couldn't stand it. I believe in the redemption of man, the rehabilitation of man. I believe that it is entirely possible to overcome the awful, awful difficulties we've had in this country. The institution of racism was carefully constructed by man, and that which he built I think can be dismantled. I think it will take a long time and I am willing to fight the long haul. The historian is not of the opinion that this will happen in his lifetime. And we need more historians among us, a more historical-minded people among us. I saw people would come up to me at the end of six months and say, "Well, how's it coming? You still working on this? I thought it ought to be over, it ought to be finished by now."

If you lived in 1940 and you've lived in 1998, you could see that it's not the same. This country is not the same. It is not the same as it was a decade ago, minus some awful things. You see when the man was killed in Jasper, Texas, and dragged all over and that awful, brutal, inhuman thing, and some people suggested we ought to go and have a board meeting in Jasper. If we're gonna have a board meeting every time somebody is killed or demonized or dehumanized or whatever, we not only would meet all over the country, we would be meeting every day.

So let's put things in perspective. What we try to do is get fewer Jasper, Texas incidents. And they are fewer than they were in the beginning of this century anyway. You look at the lynching statistics in 1900 and look at them in 1998 and they aren't the same. They aren't the same. They're fewer. I am not boasting on it. Every scratch that anyone gets as a result of inhuman and indecent treatment, it breaks my heart—don't get me wrong. But there just aren't as many as there were one hundred years ago, and I don't think there will be as many one hundred years from now. But the job—ours—is to make certain that we do everything we can to eliminate it, to put it behind us, to create a society of absolute equality, absolute fairness, absolute justice. If we all do that, it will be a better world.

Contributors

Dr. Molefi Kete Asante is professor, Department of African American Studies, Temple University, and executive director, the Afrocentric Institute. Professor Asante is the author of forty-two books, among the most recent *Scream of Blood: Desettlerism in Southern Africa* and the *African American Atlas*. He received his Ph.D. at the age of twenty-six from UCLA and was appointed a full professor at the age of thirty at State University of New York at Buffalo.

Dr. Asante is the creator of the first doctoral program in African American studies, the author of more than two hundred articles, the founder of the Afrocentric philosophical movement, the Afrocentric Institute, the Cheikh Anta Diop Conference, and the Association for Nubian Kemetic Heritage.

Sought after as a keynote speaker by many national organizations, Dr. Asante was born in Valdosta, Georgia, August 14, 1942, and educated in Tennessee, Texas, and California. He led SNCC at UCLA in the 1960s, directed the Center for Afro-American Studies at UCLA, and trained journalists in Zimbabwe after the liberation war in the 1980s. He is a poet, dramatist, painter, and gardener.

Lee D. Baker is associate professor of Anthropology and African American Studies at Columbia University and is author of *From Savage to Negro: Anthropology and the Construction of Race, 1896–1954* and numerous articles on the history of anthropology. Baker received his Ph.D. in anthropology at Temple University where he worked closely with the students and faculty in Temple's Department of African American Studies.

A longtime board member of the National Council for Black Studies, he studied with one of the pioneers of the field, William A. Little, as an undergraduate at Portland State. Baker is currently working on a book entitled *The Racial Politics of Culture: Anthropology and the Negro Problem, 1895–1948*.

Amiri Baraka is one of the most prolific and influential African American intellectuals in the twentieth century. He is currently professor emeritus from the State University of New York, Stony Brook, where he served for twenty years. In March 1998 he was appointed "Artist in Residence" at New York University. For the past fifteen years he has been codirector, with Amina Baraka, of Kimako's Blues People, a multimedia arts space dedicated to forwarding revolutionary art. Baraka's forthcoming publications include *Digging: The Afro-American Soul of American Classical Music, Unity and Struggle: Political Essays, RAZOR: Essays on Revolutionary Art for Cultural Revolution*, and *The People of Newark vs. Papa Doc Donald Tucker*.

Melba Joyce Boyd is the author of five books of poetry, *Letters to Che, The Inventory of Black Roses, Thirteen Frozen Flamingoes, Song for Maya*, and *Cat Eyes and Dead Wood*. She is also the author of a biocritical study, *Discarded Legacy: Politics and Poetics in the Life of Frances E. W. Harper, 1825–1911*. Boyd has made a documentary film, *The Black Unicorn: Dudley Randall and Broadside Press*, the publication of which in a written version as *Dudley Randall, Wrestling with the Muse* is forthcoming.

Boyd's poetry, essays, and reviews have appeared in books and periodicals in the United States and Germany, where she was a senior Fulbright lecturer at the University of Bremen, 1983–1984. She received her Doctor of Arts in English from the University of Michigan-Ann Arbor in 1979. She was an assistant editor at Broadside Press (1972–1977) and has held professional positions at the University of Iowa, Ohio State University, and the University of Michigan-Flint, where she was director of the African American Studies Program. She is currently chair of the Department of Africana Studies at Wayne State University in Detroit.

Johnnella E. Butler is professor of American Studies and adjunct professor of English and Women's Studies at the University of Washington, Seattle. Most recently, she served as editor of *Color-Line to Borderlands: The*

Matrix of Ethnic Studies in U.S. Higher Education (Seattle: University of Washington Press, 2000), a work first intended as a monograph report to the Ford Foundation but that evolved into a volume contributed to by fourteen leading scholars in American Indian studies, African American studies, Asian American studies, Chicano/a and Latino/a studies, and women's studies. A pioneer in the field of curriculum transformation, she is currently working on a comparative study of ethnic literatures.

Johanna Fernandez is a Ph.D. candidate in American history at Columbia University. Her dissertation explores the emergence of radicalism in the late sixties through the history of the Young Lords Party in New York. As a research fellow at the Institute for Research in African-American Studies, she is collaborating with Manning Marable and Leith Mullings on a reader of black radicalism in the U.S. from 1968 to the present.

Bill Fletcher Jr. is assistant to the president of the AFL-CIO. He oversees the Departments of Education, Civil and Human Rights, Field Mobilization, Safety and Health, the Working Women's Department, and the George Meany Center for Labor Studies and its National Labor College. Previously, Bill served as AFL-CIO education director for three years. Prior to coming to the AFL-CIO, Bill served as assistant to the president, East and South, for the Service Employees International Union. Also during his service at SEIU, Bill directed the Public Sector Division, Field Services, and Education.

Bill's union staff experience also included serving as the organizational secretary/administrative director for the National Postal Mail Handlers' Union. Prior to the Mail Handlers' Union, Bill was an organizer for District 65-United Auto Workers in Boston, Massachusetts.

Bill got his start in the labor movement as a rank-and-file member of the Industrial Union of Marine and Shipbuilding Workers of America. Combining labor and community work, he was also involved in ongoing efforts to desegregate the Boston building trades. He is a graduate of Harvard University and has authored numerous articles published in a variety of newspapers and magazines. He is also the coauthor of the pictorial booklet *The Indispensable Ally: Black Workers and the Formation of the Congress of Industrial Organizations, 1934–1941.*

While in Boston, Bill served as an adjunct faculty member at the University of Massachusetts-Boston, where he was connected with the Labor Studies Program.

John Hope Franklin is James P. Duke Professor of History Emeritus and seven-year professor of legal history at Duke University's Law School. An Oklahoma native and graduate of Fisk University, he received his M.A. and Ph.D. degrees in history from Harvard University. Perhaps most widely known for his *From Slavery to Freedom: A History of African-Americans*, Professor Franklin is author of such works as *The Emancipation Proclamation, The Militant South, Reconstruction After the Civil War*, editor of *My Life and an Era: The Autobiography of Buck Colbert-Franklin*, and has recently published his *Runaway Slaves: Rebels on the Plantation*.

Dr. Franklin is the recipient of the Presidential Medal of Freedom, the Legal Defense Fund's Equal Justice Award, and, in 1997, was appointed by President Clinton as chairman of the Advisory Board for One America in the Twenty-first Century: The President's Initiative on Race. Professor Franklin is currently writing his autobiography, *The Vintage Years,* a culmination of his life-long efforts to examine the African American experience.

Dr. Mindy Thompson Fullilove is an associate professor of clinical psychiatry and public health at Columbia University and a research psychiatrist at New York State Psychiatric Institute. Since 1986 she has studied problems of HIV/AIDS in minority communities in the United States. In addition to numerous scientific papers, Dr. Fullilove is author of *The House of Joshua: Meditations on Family and Place,* in the University of Nebraska Press's Texts and Contexts series edited by Professor Sander Gilman.

Henry Louis Gates Jr. is the author of several works of literary criticism, including *Figures in Black: Words, Signs, and the "Racial" Self, The Signifying Monkey: A Theory of Afro-American Literary Criticism* (1989 winner of the American Book Award), and *Loose Canons: Notes on the Culture Wars*. He has also authored *Colored People: A Memoir,* which traces his childhood experiences in a small West Virginia town in the 1950s and 1960s, *The Future of Race,* coauthored with Cornel West, and *Thirteen Ways of Looking at a Black Man*. Professor Gates has edited several anthologies, including *The Norton Anthology of African American Literature* and *The Oxford-Schomburg Library of Nineteenth-Century Black Women Writers*. In addition, Professor Gates is coeditor of *Transition* magazine. An influential cultural critic, Professor Gates's publications include a 1994 cover story for *Time* magazine on the new black renaissance in art as well as numerous articles for the *New Yorker*. He and Professor Kwame Anthony Appiah are the coeditors of an encyclopedia about the African Diaspora. This work is published by Microsoft as a CD-ROM entitled *Encarta Africana* and as a single-volume print edition from Perseus Books as *Africana: The Encyclopedia of Africa and the African-American Experience*.

Professor Gates earned his M.A. and Ph.D. in English Literature from Clare College at the University of Cambridge. He received his B.A. summa cum laude from Yale University in 1973 in English language and literature. Before joining the faculty of Harvard in 1991, he taught at Yale, Cornell, and Duke Universities. His honors and grants include a MacArthur Foundation "genius grant" (1981), the George Polk Award for Social Commentary (1993), the Chicago Tribune Heartland Award (1994), the Golden Plate Achievement Award (1995), *Time*'s "Twenty-five Most Influential Americans" list (1997), a National Humanities Medal (1998), and election to the American Academy of Arts and Letters (1999.)

Joy James teaches political and feminist theory at the University of Colorado at Boulder. She is the 1999–2000 distinguished visiting professor in the Institute for Research in African-American Studies at Columbia University. James is author of *Resisting State Violence: Radicalism, Gender, and Race in U.S. Culture, Transcending the Talented Tenth: Black Leaders and American Intellectuals, Shadowboxing: Representations of Black Feminist Politics*, as well as editor of *The Angela Y. Davis Reader* and *States of Confinement: Policing, Detention, and Prisons*.

James Jennings is director of the Trotter Institute and professor of Political Science at the University of Massachusetts, Boston. He teaches courses on race, class, and public policy in the Africana Studies Department. Dr. Jennings has published widely on black and Latino political affairs as well as on community and economic development in urban areas. His books include *Understanding the Nature of Poverty in Urban America, The Politics of Black Empowerment*, and *Blacks, Latinos, and Asians: The Status and Prospects for Activism*. He is currently completing a book that focuses on the impact of welfare reform on institutional capacities in black and Latino communities. He is also completing a comprehensive study of the history and involvement of black churches in the civic and political life of Boston, Massachusetts.

Dr. Maulana Karenga is professor and chair of the Department of Black Studies, California State University, Long Beach, and chair of the President's Task Force on Multicultural Education and Campus Diversity, CSULB. An activist-scholar of national and international recognition, Dr. Karenga has played an important role in black political and intellectual culture since the sixties and he has lectured on the life and struggle of African peoples on the major campuses of the United States and in Africa, the People's Republic of China, Cuba, Trinidad, Britain, and Canada. He holds two Ph.D.s, one in political science (USIU) and another in social ethics (USC), as well as an honorary doctorate from the University of Durban, South Africa.

Dr. Karenga is chair of the organization Us and the National Association of Kawaida Organizations. He is the author of numerous scholarly articles and books, including *Introduction to Black Studies,* the most widely used introductory text, *Selections From the Husia: Sacred Wisdom of Ancient Egypt, Kawaida: A Communitarian African Philosophy,* and *Odu Ifa: The Ethical Teachings.* Dr. Karenga is the creator of the Pan-African cultural holiday Kwanzaa and the Nguzo Saba (Seven Principles) and author of the definitive work on the subject, entitled *Kwanzaa, A Celebration of Family, Community, and Culture.*

Kamala Kempadoo is assistant professor in Women's Studies at the University of Colorado-Boulder. Her research and teaching activities focus on the intersectionalities of gender, race, and class in the context of globalization. She is coauthor and editor of *Global Sex Workers: Rights, Resistance, and Redefinition* and *Sun, Sex, and Gold: Tourism and the Sex Trade in the Caribbean.*

Martin Kilson studied at Lincoln University (B.A.) and Harvard University (Ph.D.). He has taught political science at Harvard since 1962 and is now Frank G. Thomson Research Professor. His publications include *Political Change in a West African State, The African Diaspora: Interpretive Essays,* and the two-volume forthcoming *The Making of Black Intellectuals: Studies on the African-American Intelligentsia.*

Brian Meeks is chair of the Department of Government at the University of the West Indies, Mona. His books include *Caribbean Revolutions and Revolutionary Theory: An Assessment of Cuba, Nicaragua, and Grenada* and *Radical Caribbean: From Black Power to Abu Bakr.* He was a commonwealth fellow at Cambridge University (1989–1990) and visiting faculty at Michigan State University (1995–1997). His areas of interest include comparative Caribbean politics and political thought and notions of hegemony in popular culture and the theorizing of revolution. He is currently working on an edited collection of essays, *New Caribbean Thought*, and a new book entitled *Careening on the Edge of the Abyss: Hegemony and Resistance in Jamaica and Beyond*.

Leith Mullings is Presidential Professor of Anthropology at the Graduate School, City University of New York. She is author of *Therapy, Ideology, and Social Change: Mental Healing in Urban Ghana* and *On Our Own Terms: Race, Class, and Gender in the Lives of African American Women*, editor of *Cities of the United States: Studies in Urban Anthropology*, and, with Manning Marable, coeditor of *Let Nobody Turn Us Around: Voices of Resistance, Reform, and Renewal, an African-American Anthology*. She has written numerous articles and is currently completing a book about Harlem. Professor Mullings received her M.A. and Ph.D. from the University of Chicago. Before joining the Faculty at CUNY, she taught at the University of Dar-es-Salaam in Tanzania, Yale University, and Columbia University. For most of her life, Professor Mullings has been active in struggles for social justice.

Barbara Ransby is a historian, writer, and longtime political activist. She received her B.A. from Columbia University in New York and her Ph.D. in history from the University of Michigan, where she was a national Mellon fellow. She is currently completing a biography of civil rights activist and intellectual Ella Jo Baker (1903–1986), which will be published by University of North Carolina Press next year. Barbara Ransby is an assistant professor at the University of Illinois at Chicago in the Departments of African American Studies and History.

Professor Ransby has published numerous articles on her research on Ella Baker, the twentieth-century black freedom movement, and black women's history. Some of those publications include "Black Popular Culture and the Transcendence of Patriarchal Illusions," coauthored with Tracye Matthews, in *Words of Fire: An Anthology of African American Feminist Thought*, "Afrocentrism, Cultural Nationalism, and the Problem with Essentialist Definitions of Race, Gender, and Sexuality" in *Race and Reason*, "Ella Jo Baker: African American Radical and Intellectual," in *The American Radical*, "A Righteous Rage: African American Women in Defense of Ourselves and Black Women's Response to the Hill-Thomas Hearings," in *Reflections on Anita Hill: Race, Gender, and Power in the*

United States, and entries on Ella Baker and Eslanda Goode Robeson in *Black Women in America: An Historical Encyclopedia.*

Nikhil Pal Singh is an assistant professor of history at the University of Washington, Seattle. He is the author of a forthcoming book, *Color and Democracy in the American Century,* and coeditor with Brent Edwards and Penny Von Eschen of a forthcoming anthology, *Re-Thinking Black Marxism.* Professor Singh has published articles in several journals, including *American Quarterly, Radical History Review, Souls: A Critical Journal of Black Politics, Culture, and Society,* and *New Labor Forum.*

Beverly Xaviera Watkins is a Ph.D. candidate in history, Columbia University, and a research fellow, College of Physicians and Surgeons, Division of General Medicine, Columbia University.

Cornel West is a widely recognized intellectual who has changed the way those who study his work view their world. Professor West's philosophy is not an abstract discipline but rather a "polemical weapon that attempts to transform linguistic, social, cultural, and political tradition to increase the scope of individual development and democratic actions." His work—influenced by traditions as diverse as the Baptist Church, American transcendentalism and literature, the Black Panthers, and European philosophy—seeks to revive the best of liberalism, populism, and democratic socialism.

Professor West is the author of over thirteen books including the two-volume *Beyond Eurocentrism and Multiculturalism, Breaking Bread, Race Matters, Keeping Faith, Jews and Blacks: Let the Healing Begin,* coauthored with Michael Lerner, *Restoring Hope: Conversations on the Future of Black America,* and *The War Against Parents: What We Can Do for America's Beleaguered Moms and Dads,* coauthored with Sylvia Ann Hewlett. Besides his numerous publications, Professor West is a well-respected and highly popular lecturer; his speaking style, influenced by his roots in the Baptist Church, provides a blend of drama, knowledge, and inspiration.

Professor West earned his M.A. and Ph.D. from Princeton University and his B.A. magna cum laude from Harvard University. He served as professor of religion and director of the Afro-American Studies Department at Princeton before joining the Harvard faculty in 1994.

About the Editor

Manning Marable is professor of history and political science and the founding director of the Institute for Research in African-American Studies at Columbia University in New York City. Born in 1950, he received his doctorate in American history at the University of Maryland, College Park, in 1976. Professor Marable was the founding director of Colgate University's Africana and Hispanic Studies Program, from 1983 to 1986. He was also chairman of the Department of Black Studies at Ohio State University from 1987 to 1989. Since his appointment at Columbia University in 1993, Professor Marable has initiated two academic journals, *Race and Reason* (1994–1998) and, beginning in January 1999, *Souls: A Critical Journal of Black Politics, Culture, and Society*, published jointly by Columbia University and the Westview Press. He is the author of thirteen books, including *Black Leadership, Beyond Black and White, Race, Reform, and Rebellion: The Second Reconstruction in Black America*, 2d rev. ed., *W. E. B. Du Bois: Black Radical Democrat*, and *Black American Politics*. Anthologies by Professor Marable that are currently in production include, as editor, *Let Nobody Turn Us Around: Voices of Resistance, Reform, and Renewal, an African-American Anthology,* and *No Easy Victories: An Anthology of Black Radicalism from 1968 to the Present,* both with coeditor Leith Mullings.

Index

DATE DUE

MAR 1 2 2010			
NOV 0 8 2001			
NOV 0 5 2001			
NOV 1 4 2001			
AUG 0			
JUL 0 2 2004			
AUG 2 4 2009			

Demco, Inc. 38-293